Legislature by Lot

The Real Utopias Project

Series editor: Erik Olin Wright

The Real Utopias Project embraces a tension between dreams and practice. It is founded on the belief that what is pragmatically possible is not fixed independently of our imaginations, but is itself shaped by our visions. The fulfillment of such a belief involves "real utopias"—utopian ideals grounded in the real potentials for redesigning social institutions.

In its attempt at sustaining and deepening serious discussion of radical alternatives to existing social practices, the Real Utopias Project examines various basic institutions—property rights and the market, secondary associations, the family, the welfare state, among others—and focuses on specific proposals for their fundamental redesign. The books in the series are the result of workshop conferences, at which groups of scholars respond to provocative manuscripts.

Legislature by Lot

Transformative Designs for
Deliberative Governance

John Gastil and Erik Olin Wright

VERSO
London • New York

First published by Verso 2019
The collection © Verso 2019
Contributions © The contributors 2019

The moral rights of the authors have been asserted

1 3 5 7 9 10 8 6 4 2

Verso
UK: 6 Meard Street, London W1F 0EG
US: 20 Jay Street, Suite 1010, Brooklyn, NY 11201
versobooks.com

Verso is the imprint of New Left Books

ISBN-13: 978-1-78873-608-4
ISBN-13: 978-1-78873-612-1 (HBK)
ISBN-13: 978-1-78873-611-4 (US EBK)
ISBN-13: 978-1-78873-609-1 (UK EBK)

British Library Cataloguing in Publication Data
A catalogue record for this book is available from the British Library

Library of Congress Cataloging-in-Publication Data
A catalog record for this book is available from the Library of Congress

Typeset in Sabon LT by Hewer Text UK Ltd, Edinburgh
Printed and bound by CPI Group (UK) Ltd., Croydon, CR0 4YY

Contents

Preface

The papers in this volume are drawn from a September 2017 Real Utopias Project conference on the idea of creating a legislative assembly in which legislators are chosen through a civic lottery. The conference was anchored by a specific proposal we prepared, along with a postscript by Erik Olin Wright. We make the argument for a bicameral legislature in which the legislators in one chamber are selected through elections and in the other are chosen by random selection. Our opening essay reviews the democratic flaws intrinsic in electoral representation, lays out a set of principles that should guide the construction of a sortition chamber, and argues for the virtue of a bicameral system that combines sortition and elections. Participants in the September 2017 conference responded to this proposal, and a selection of those appear in this special issue.

The first set of response essays looks at our proposal in the contemporary context. Yves Sintomer begins with "From Deliberative to Radical Democracy: Sortition and Politics in the Twenty-First Century." He presents a broad historical overview of the role of sortition ideas in democratic theory. James S. Fishkin draws on extensive experience using deliberative minipublics, as well as some lessons from ancient Athens, to explore what could be the optimal use of sortition in a legislative system. In "Random Assemblies for Lawmaking: Prospects and Limits," he argues against a long-term full-function sortition legislature in favor of a more targeted use of sortition assemblies.

Teams of coauthors provide the other three essays in this first section. Tom Arnold, David M. Farrell, and Jane Suiter offer their perspective based on one of the best real-world analogies to our proposal in "Lessons from a Hybrid Sortition Chamber: The 2012–14 Irish Constitutional Convention." Pierre-Étienne Vandamme and his coauthors present an empirical exploration of attitudes toward sortition in Belgium, including a sample of political officials. In "Intercameral Relations in a Bicameral Elected and Sortition Legislature," they provide a context for discussing the possible public support for sortition proposals. Andrea Felicetti and Donatella della Porta then consider how sortition would operate in relation to movements in "Joining Forces: The Sortition Chamber from a Social-Movement Perspective."

The next set of essays focuses more squarely on problems— and opportunities—presented by sortition in relation to core democratic principles. In "Should Democracy Work Through Elections or Sortition?," Tom Malleson lays out a general score-card for evaluating the democratic quality of different legislative systems, then makes a point-by-point comparison of electoral assemblies and sortition assemblies. Jane Mansbridge offers a novel perspective on sortition's connection between legislators and citizens in "Accountability in the Constituent-Representative Relationship." Lyn Carson stresses the procedural features neces-sary for effective governance in "How to Ensure Deliberation Within a Sortition Chamber." Dimitri Courant suggests that sorti-tion's distinctive qualities have nonobvious democratic virtues in "Sortition and Democratic Principles: A Comparative Analysis." Finally, Arash Abizadeh extends Gastil and Wright's argument for a bicameral approach through his chapter, "In Defense of Imperfection: An Election-Sortition Compromise."

The final collection of essays considers alternative approaches to incorporating sortition in a democratic system. Deven Burks and Raphaël Kies begin with a note of caution in "A Gradualist Path Toward Sortition." David Owen and Graham Smith advance this argument further in "Sortition, Rotation, and Mandate: Conditions for Political Equality and Deliberative Reasoning." They are sympathetic to the goals of sortition but skeptical about the viability of a full-function sortition legisla-ture. Brett Hennig questions the necessity of pairing sortition with an elected chamber in "Who Needs Elections? Accountability, Equality, and Legitimacy Under Sortition." Finally, in "Why Hybrid Bicameralism Is Not Right for Sortition," Terrill Bouricius argues strongly against retaining an electoral chamber and against the feasibility of a full-function sortition legislature. His favored alternative uses a series of more special-purpose sortition lawmaking bodies.

We close the volume by offering reflections on sortition informed by all of the response essays and the September 2017 conference that gave rise to this volume. In "Sortition's Scope, Contextual Variations, and Transitions," we acknowledge difficulties in our original proposal, but we stress the need for a sortition chamber with a broad remit. We acknowledge the difficulty of designing a system apart from a specific sociopolitical context, and we recognize the variety of paths that sortition could take. Before long, small and large bodies may begin to experiment more vigorously with this ancient method of democracy. We hope this set of essays helps clear the path for this transition.

I. THE ARGUMENT

Legislature by Lot: Envisioning Sortition Within a Bicameral System

John Gastil and Erik Olin Wright

Democracy embodies a tension between utopian aspirations and practical realities. The utopian ideal holds that ordinary people should be empowered to govern themselves. Democracy means rule by the people, not by elites, and if this were fully realized, the people would themselves actually rule. In practice, even the most robust democracies delegate most rulemaking to professional politicians, who are elected by the people or by bureaucratic officials employed by the state. Ordinary citizens may choose their rulers and hold them accountable, but the people do not themselves rule.

In the United States and most other mature democracies in recent decades, many people believe this gap between ideals and reality has been widening. In the worst cases, elections have become a symbolic sideshow hiding the real exercise of power by elites operating behind the scenes. Even in the best democracies, the gap remains. There has never been a golden age in any actual democracy that approximated the democratic ideal.

Can this gap be narrowed? Is it possible to more fully realize democratic ideals, despite the constraints of large and complex contemporary societies? One strategy is to try perfecting the mechanisms by which political elites are elected and held accountable by ordinary citizens. There are many good proposals to accomplish this, such as insulating electoral campaigns from the influence of private wealth, changing the rules of the game for electoral representation, or enhancing the ability of citizens to deliberate meaningfully on policies and candidates.[1] These kinds of reforms, if implemented in a serious manner, would certainly improve the democratic quality of elections, but they would still leave intact the fundamental feature of electoral democracy in which ordinary citizens are ruled by political elites. The question, then, is whether there are ways to reduce the gap between democratic ideals and realities other than improving electoral mechanisms. Are there alternative foundations for democratic institutions that might better realize democratic ideals?

In this opening chapter, we propose a different kind of strategy for deepening democracy. Before going into the details, we can summarize our idea as having four basic elements.

- The legislature would have two chambers, one consisting of elected representatives and the other a "sortition assembly" of randomly selected citizens.
- The two chambers would have equal powers, each being able to initiate legislation and vote on legislation passed by the other chamber.
- The members of the sortition chamber would be well compensated to make participation attractive to those randomly selected for service.
- Sortition appointments would be for a number of years, with a new cohort selected each year as the most senior cohort finishes its term. Those selected would receive extensive training and professional support staff.

The idea of choosing representatives by lot harkens back to the method ancient Athenians used to choose legislators, jurors, and municipal officers. Athenians believed that this method could retain power in the hands of the public.[2] In the modern world, the idea has gained traction and recently received an endorsement from former UN secretary general Kofi Annan, who called for democracies to "reintroduce the ancient Greek practice of selecting parliaments by lot instead of election." In his view, such a system "would prevent the formation of self-serving and self-perpetuating political classes disconnected from their electorates."[3]

We begin our argument in section 1 by reviewing some of the familiar pathologies of electoral democracy. In section 2, we show how a randomly selected citizen assembly might deepen democracy. We lay out the principles for evaluating the design of a sortition legislature in section 3. This is followed by sketching the broad contours of the institutional design itself in section 4, then justifying a complementary electoral chamber in section 5. We conclude by discussing how a sortition legislature might come into being and offering an addendum that makes an anti-capitalist case for this institution.

The Pathologies of Legislative Elections

Two broad categories of problems within conventional legislative elections are especially important: those directly associated with the electoral process and those associated with the behavior of elected legislatures.

Electoral Failures

In every phase of the electoral cycle, problems persist that sortition could eliminate or substantially mitigate. The Electoral Integrity Project has documented the deficiencies in electoral systems across the globe, and some of these failures plague even the most highly rated electoral systems.[4] Endemic problems include campaign finance, adverse candidate selection biases, and problematic media coverage.

Campaigns require huge sums of money, which typically come from concentrations of wealth. How such money influences electoral outcomes depends on a system's laws, but private money always finds a way because so much is at stake. Even the best public financing schemes designed to thwart such influence come at a price, such as reinforcing major parties to the exclusion of others.[5] What does campaign finance buy? Some of the money goes to mobilization campaigns, which serve to increase voter turnout but may have little secondary benefit. The bulk of the spending, however, pays for campaign advertisements, from online posts and banners to direct mail to radio, cable, and broadcast commercials. To augment their paid media, candidates play up to broadcast and social media by vilifying opponents and grandstanding on behalf of themselves, their parties, or their preferred cause. Precious little of this discourse contributes to genuine public deliberation, whereby voters might learn more than the partisan leanings of the candidates on offer.[6]

Elections, and particularly national ones, too often attract the wrong kind of candidate. Many sincere, capable, and well-intentioned individuals seek and win public office. Once elected, however, these individuals find themselves surrounded by a greater number of peers who exhibit an excess of ambition, ego, and stubbornness—the traits best suited to winning partisan elections.[7] This reality, along with the practical obstacles posed by electoral competition, dissuade many civic and community leaders from seeking office in the first place.[8]

Even when electoral contests pit a talented and virtuous candidate against a scoundrel, that contrast may not become apparent to voters, owing to a dearth of high-quality media coverage. The Electoral Integrity Project gave more than a third of all electoral systems a failing grade on media coverage, but even higher-rated systems have problems. Governing parties often enjoy an unfair advantage, sometimes owing to their ownership or direct influence over major media providers. Particular political parties and organizations are denied coverage or disparaged, due to ideological biases in the media system. When the media do aim to provide more balanced coverage, sometimes that imperative engenders a reluctance to call out poor arguments or outright falsehoods.

Legislative Behavior

These electoral challenges generate behavioral problems within legislatures. Too often, elected legislatures have erred, by commission or omission, at times carelessly but often willfully. The most visible of these failings become textbook cases of corruption or lobbyist influence. Laws have been passed to provide dubious tax breaks, to legalize monopolies, and more. Legislatures mete out the bulk of such favors beneath the radar of the media, even when policy watchdogs bark wildly.[9]

One factor contributing to legislative failure is that the ideological commitments required for effective party membership limit the candidates' creativity in generating novel solutions. As political scientist Murray Edelman observed in *The Symbolic Uses of Politics*, victorious candidates take office having already decided on the appropriate solutions. They spend many of their years in office choosing which problems require their preselected remedies.[10] Even when all parties recognize a problem's optimal solution, one party's leadership may decide to block legislation because it can't afford to grant the other a political victory.[11]

Ongoing partisan activity often amounts to a tremendous waste of human and financial resources, which are spent not on articulating principled policy and values but instead on posturing, strategizing, fundraising, and advertising. In a deliberative democracy, on the other hand, the floor of a legislative chamber could serve as the most visible stage for public argument, whereby legislators and citizens alike might reconsider their views on weighty issues.

Given the absence of such deliberation, it is no surprise that legislators cannot ensure the public legitimacy of the chambers they occupy. In the United States, every metric of trust in government, and Congress in particular, is at or near an all-time low.[12] But trust in government is by no means a uniquely American problem. In the vast majority of OECD nations, most citizens

7

distrust their national government, and trust scores have fallen from 2007 to 2016 for two-thirds of OECD countries. In European OECD countries, trust in political parties has hovered near 20 percent during a similar period.[13]

Sortition as a Democratic Alternative

Our proposed institutional design aims to address the problems of elections and conventional legislative behavior, but we do not argue that sortition needs to replace electoral or direct democratic systems altogether. Rather, it should stand as an equal among more familiar democratic institutions.

Table 1. A comparison of elections, sortition, and direct participation as democratic alternatives.

	Locus of decision-making	Expression of equality	Extent of direct public involvement	Government decisions made by ordinary citizens
Electoral representation	Elected council, parliament, etc.	Each ballot has equal weight	All registered voters	None
Citizen sortition	Sortition assembly, juries, etc.	Equal opportunity for selection	Limited to those chosen	All
Direct participation	Participatory budgeting, town meetings, etc.	Equal direct authority	Anyone interested in being involved	All

Table 1 juxtaposes these alternatives to make their relative virtues clearer. Electing representatives to councils, legislatures, and parliaments gives every registered voter equal say through the ballot, but lay citizens exercise authority only during elections. Direct participation, through such things as town meetings or participatory budgeting, gives citizens direct and equal authority throughout the decision-making process, but these processes have been limited by scale and scope of authority.[14] By contrast, a sortition assembly would express equality through each citizen's chance of selection while still exercising citizen authority directly on matters of government.

Each of these has a place in an ideal democratic system. Whenever feasible, a direct participatory process might prove effective at tackling a wide range of local public problems. At larger social scales, however, a trade-off emerges. Elections embody the ideal of government *by* the people (the full electorate), whereas sortition advances the goal of government *of* the people (the sortition assembly). Pairing those together, as we suggest, helps ensure a good measure of both in legislative bodies.

The question of which method best governs *for* the people— that is, in the public's interest—is an empirical question ultimately settled only through experience. We will say more about this in our proposal for a sortition assembly, but our critique of electoral processes suggests three reasons why sortition might produce better outcomes. First, elected bodies favor the ideological and class interests that gave the governing parties a financial advantage in elections. Money plays no role in selecting sortition assembly members. Second, reelection pressures and party discipline constrain deliberation in elected bodies, but a sortition legislature is more likely to study problems with open minds and discover creative solutions that transcend conventional electoral divides.[15] Third, the demographic diversity in a sortition assembly further increases the prospects for robust deliberation by ensuring a greater diversity of experiences and perspectives than appear even in those legislative bodies that impose demographic quotas on their memberships. Direct contact with diverse participants can lead to recognition of marginalized voices, as has been observed in previous large-scale deliberative processes using lay citizens.[16]

In sum, sortition has a straightforward rationale as a democratic process of self-government. To advance the idea of a sortition assembly, however, we have to make clearer the principles on which one should be built. Once we've done that, we will spell out in more detail our specific vision for the design of such a body.

Principles for Evaluating the Design of a Sortition Legislature

Serious questions must be addressed in designing a sortition legislature, and we wish to lay out two sets of related evaluative principles before undertaking such a design. We view these as the principles that should guide any legislative reform or over-haul. We phrase these in the broadest possible language to ensure that we convey them as general principles, which might be satisfied in any number of ways—including ones that lie outside our own vision of a sortition legislature.

The principles we use to build our proposal address different levels of concern. The first set of principles—inclusion, control, and equality—aim to ensure that the legislature embodies fundamental democratic values. The second set focuses on the deliberative quality of a legislature, including the education and resources required by the legislators, the necessary conduit connecting the public to its representatives, and the need for an accountability mechanism.

Democratic Principles

Political theorist Robert Dahl offers a definition of democracy that emphasizes five principles a democratic system must embody: inclusion, control of the agenda, effective participation, voting equality, and enlightened understanding. Dahl stresses that no existing system can fully meet these five criteria, but they serve as a sound basis for judging ostensibly democratic institutions, such as the sortition legislature we propose.[17]

Inclusion

The first principle is inclusion, which requires that a democracy make every effort to include all the persons within a political unit, save those who are transient (such as nonresidents and tourists) or incapable of representing their own interests (such as children and the most severely mentally ill). For our legislative design, this means that the body's membership should be as representative of the citizenry as possible. Representational legitimacy hinges on meeting this criterion.[18]

The logic of random sampling has much in common with the inclusion principle. Survey researchers worry over response rates, landlines versus cell phones, and other recruitment challenges. As the Pew Research Center insists, each person with a telephone of any kind should "have roughly the same chance of being called." Census workers face a similar but greater challenge. They aim to find and take note of every person residing in a country, regardless of whether that person has a phone or even a home address.

We leave open the question of what population data provides the standard against which one can best judge inclusion. A sortition legislature's realization of the inclusion principle could be judged against a census of the adult population, survey data collected by nonpartisan polling firms, or official voter lists in those countries with inclusive registration systems. Whichever serves as the sampling frame, the principle of inclusion calls for equality in the likelihood of selection.

A second concern, however, arises once an initial random sample is collected. The inclusion principle further requires that every person so selected has an *equally viable opportunity* to serve in the sortition legislature. In jury service, for example, the summons from the courthouse comes with a legal protection for those who might worry that serving on a jury could put their job at risk. The jury selection process may not go far enough, however, in that long-term service—such as on a murder trial or an ongoing grand jury—could be financially ruinous for someone whose income supports a family. Thus, a serious effort must be made to realize the inclusion principle by making the sortition service opportunity a real one for people from diverse life circumstances.

Control of the Agenda

Dahl also requires that a fully democratic system have control of the policy agenda. A system lacking this power is one in which citizens or public officials might make important choices, but the questions they address are beyond their control. In the abstract, this principle is a straightforward requirement that a political unit not be subject to agenda constraints imposed by a "foreign" power. In practice, democratic systems operate with multiple levels and institutions, such that a given body might have legitimate constraints. Thus, a provincial legislature works within limits imposed by a national constitution and federal laws. Furthermore, larger economic forces inevitably impose constraints on the agendas of democratic systems.

A sortition legislature will have limits analogous to those for existing legislative assemblies. The agenda principle, though, argues for the broadest possible scope for its deliberation. It should be authorized to exercise its influence on the same range of issues as other bodies at comparable levels of government. For practical reasons, one might initiate a sortition legislature with a more limited mandate, but the training wheels should come off the bicycle as soon as the body is ready to explore the wider policy world.

Effective Participation and Voting Equality

Our third principle joins the next two of Dahl's criteria, which require that each member of a democratic system have an "adequate and equal opportunity" to express policy preferences and vote at the decisive stage of decision making. In a legislative context, these go hand in hand.

The members of a sortition legislature may divide themselves into committees, set up rules regulating floor speech, and otherwise organize their work, but none of those policies should result in unequal opportunities for legislators to speak and vote. If the body differentiates assignments and authorities, such as the power to bring a bill to the floor for debate, it must do so in a way that avoids concentrating power over time in a subset of the legislature.

Dahl stresses the *adequacy*, as well as the equality, of opportunity to avoid another hazard that citizen bodies often face. Deliberative polls, for example, often bring together hundreds of people to discuss a series of issues in small meetings and large plenary sessions.[19] Even with numerous breakout sessions, the agenda is so crowded and the issues so complex that a single person has little chance to do more than tell anecdotes, ask some questions, and get answers from a panel of experts. Toss in a few spirited conversations during breaks, and it adds up to a moving experience of frank political talk for those fortunate enough to serve.[20] The sum of such interactions is not, however, adequate for the task of making decisions in a legislative assembly.

The implication for a sortition legislature is that special care must be given not merely to equalizing participation and voting but also to preparing the legislators for the complexity of the task placed before them. This concern flows directly into the next set of principles we consider, which aim to ensure the legislative body's deliberative capacity.

Deliberative Principles

Dahl has a fifth requirement that takes his definition of democracy beyond many conventional conceptions of the term. He insists that a political system can fulfill its democratic promise only if it achieves "enlightened understanding." In Dahl's words, "Citizens ought to have adequate and equal opportunities for *discovering and validating* ... the choice on the matter to be decided that would best serve the citizen's interests."[21] Of course, as with the other principles, the full realization of this principle is attainable only by degrees. Nevertheless, the aspiration toward it encourages careful attention to the quality of deliberation.

Education and Resources

Every form of citizen deliberation has built into it an educational component, along with staff and resources that make it possible for citizens to do their jobs. Juries have an orientation, a commissioner, a bailiff, and unseen support staff at their disposal. Even the judge serves the jury by doing a tremendous amount of pretrial work to make the proceedings run smoothly. Recent jury reforms in the United States, such as allowing jurors to take notes or ask questions (through the judge), have been implemented by courts to make more manageable the demanding task that they give to their juries.

Professional legislatures have even more elaborate systems of education, staffing, and professional assistance. To take the US Congress as an example, the members receive an extensive orientation to their job after being elected. Members then have access to a Congressional Research Service, a Congressional Budget Office, personal and caucus staff, and everything from web designers to tour guides to custodial staff to make their institution run properly. The Budget Office alone has an annual appropriation approaching fifty million dollars.[22] A properly designed sortition legislature can draw on resources such as these, but it will require a more fundamental training process for members unfamiliar with government's basic operation.

Deliberative Public Input

Legislatures already have numerous vehicles for soliciting public input. To write to one's MP or congressperson is almost a cliché of public engagement, though such letters are usually counted more conscientiously than they are read. Periodic town meetings and open committee hearings both afford opportunities for lay citizens to speak, but these events often devolve into performative rituals. To have two minutes at a microphone with no response is hardly an adequate opportunity.

The deliberative input principle does not require dispensing with traditional forms of speech, but it calls for the creation of a surer conduit for gathering, recording, and responding to reflective public input to inform the legislature's deliberation. Were this an elected body accountable to campaign contributors and party leaders, such input might carry little weight, but a sortition legislature comes into being without a fixed agenda. Its members may prove more receptive to public input, particularly if the voices it hears come from the same kind of deliberation now asked of the citizen legislators.

Fortunately, there already exist numerous models for gathering public input through various means. Some of these gather small samples of citizens, using the same sortition model. Citizens' juries, consensus conferences, and planning cells have all proven their ability to produce sensible judgments.[23] In the case of a sortition legislature, though, the imperative is to devise a process that more readily draws in the wider public. After all, the sortition legislature itself provides a deliberative microcosm of the full citizenry. Experiments in crowdsourcing legislation, adaptations of face-to-face issues forums to the digital environment, and other online technologies could be harnessed to facilitate such communication.[24] In spite of the public's reputation for cynicism, research suggests that citizens relish opportunities to participate in these kinds of forums, if the events connect back to a public official with the authority to act on their input.[25]

Oversight and Accountability

The final principle in this set aims to address a problem common in all legislative bodies, be they elected, appointed, or selected at random. The design for a sortition legislature must put in place some mechanism for internal oversight to hold its members accountable, at least to one another.

This is one instance where removing elections takes away a vital function—the means of removing from office during reelection (or by recall) an official who violated the public's trust. As an unelected body, the sortition legislature will require a mechanism for overseeing its operations and taking stock of its members' behavior. Legislators who willfully violate the spirit of the body, for instance, may need to be censured, or even removed from office. Just as in elected legislatures, citizens in a sortition legislature are vulnerable to bribes when important legislation is being considered, and some mechanism of accountability needs to be in place to deal with this.

One way of seeing the importance of such an accountability mechanism is noting the inefficacy of ethics committees in existing legislatures. Such bodies typically have little reach, owing to mutual distrust of oversight by leaders in the major parties. Alternatively, they become vehicles for partisan attacks that rely on an inconsistent application of ethical rules across different parties. Nonetheless, the mere existence of such committees underscores the need for some analogue—and hopefully a superior one—in our plan for legislative reform.

Proposal for a Sortition Legislature

Just as there exist a variety of parliamentary and legislative designs, so are there numerous ways one could configure a sortition legislature following our principles. There is good reason to be wary of discussions for new institutions that come with highly specified blueprints, since problems with fine-grained details will always need to be worked out in practice. Nevertheless, we will present the basic contours of a design in sufficient detail to clarify the problems that a sortition legislature must address. Our specific solutions to these problems should be taken as illustrations of possibilities rather than as claims about the optimal design. In what follows, we describe our design in terms of its random selection method, training and staff support, procedural rules, accountability mechanisms, and direct public engagement.

Selecting a Sortition Method

The defining feature of a sortition legislature is the method of selecting its participants. Three factors go into our selection method: identifying a target population and then drawing a sample; specifying qualifications and disqualifications for service; and creating incentives to those invited to become legislators.

Sampling from a Target Population
In principle, the sortition sample should be drawn from the population of adult citizens old enough to sit in an elected assembly. In practice, the operational definition of this target population will vary by nation. In countries where all citizens have identity cards, direct sampling will be possible. In a

country like the United States where there is no administratively accessible comprehensive list of citizens, we believe voter registration lists would be appropriate only once current state-level impediments to registration are eliminated.[26] Ideally, as part of the reform package that created a sortition legislature, universal and automatic voter registration would also be instituted.

When it comes time to draw a sample, one possibility would be to have a truly random sample. This could be appropriate in some circumstances, but we believe the legitimacy of the sortition assembly would be enhanced by a sample stratified along demographic lines. Appropriate criteria for drawing a stratified sample would be a politically contested matter, but candidate criteria could include gender, age, socioeconomic status, and geography (for example, the districts for the complementary electoral body), as well as race, ethnicity, and indigeneity.

Ideally, the selection criteria for a stratified sample should be few and simple. Because of the relatively small size of even a large assembly, there are practical constraints on the number of categories in terms of which the sample design for an assembly can be meaningfully stratified. We are wary of including explicit criteria for stratifying the sample that could have the side effect of reinforcing divisions that limit the deliberative capacity of the assembly.

That said, when historic hostilities continue to divide ethnic, racial, national, or religious groups, proportional representation along these lines may be necessary to secure representational legitimacy. We have particular sympathy for giving special consideration to aboriginal or native peoples. "Minipublics"— bodies of randomly selected citizens tasked with studying public policy questions—have made special allowances for such populations to give them a voice in deliberation. In New Zealand, there are seven reserved seats in elected parliament to ensure Māori representation, and if that country convened a sortition assembly, indigeneity would seem an appropriate criterion for sample stratification. In such cases, the sampling method should ensure the inclusion of legislators from these, or other, historically marginalized populations.[27]

Beyond this, we provide no further a priori guidance to optimizing sample frames. As with many institutional design problems, the optimal solution to the trade-offs between the ideal of faithful demographic representation and practical exigencies can be worked out only through a political process. That said, the sample frame and selection algorithm should be as transparent as possible, such that an ordinary citizen can comprehend them.

Qualifications and Disqualifications

As was the case for the sample frame for demographic representativeness, there are many possible criteria for disqualifying individuals from service in a sortition assembly. Some of these would be uncontroversial and likely to be adopted in any context. For example, little controversy would be likely to result from disqualifying persons currently serving prison sentences. Excluding those currently on probation or parole after conviction for a felony would also likely seem reasonable to most people.

Other potential exclusions might raise objections. Should ex-felons who have served their time be eligible for the sortition body, or should some categories of ex-felons, say murderers or rapists, be permanently barred from selection? Should the sortition body exclude candidates based on tests of minimal cognitive competence or diagnoses of serious mental illness? Or should those previously elected to an equal or higher level of government be excluded?

These are difficult issues. Experimentation with sortition should clarify which exclusions are needed, but the burden of proof must be on those who want to establish such criteria. No data exist yet that show how a modern sortition legislature would suffer from including among its ranks those who lack literacy, deliberative skills, and political experience. To the contrary, countless public processes, including the modern jury system, attest to the collective competence of even small bodies of citizens that include novices.[28] An illiterate member of parliament, for example, might require special assistance, just as a diplomat requires a translator, but this is a difference of degree.

After all, even veteran legislators rely on professional staff to navigate the details of proposed legislation.

Service Incentives and Term of Office

Our vision of a sortition legislature draws people out of every walk of life for a period of time, then returns them to their prior vocations, or whatever new life course they may choose after having what will for many be a life-changing experience in government.[29] People will vary tremendously, however, in their life circumstances at the moment when the invitation arrives in the mail. The right set of incentives must be in place so that none would suffer an undue burden should they choose to serve.

Legal protections against employer retaliation would be a bare minimum, but such laws cannot resolve the dilemma faced by small-business owners who risk financial ruin if they step away for even a month, let alone two years. One strategy would be to set incentive levels (such as for salary, benefits, travel allowances, and the like) equivalent to the complementary elected chamber. As a starting point, what is good enough for elected legislators should be sufficient for the members of the sortition body. There will be high-income earners who choose not to forego their exceptional incomes in exchange for such a salary. For example, if the annual sortition legislature salary in Britain is set at twice the median pretax income, the top 13 percent of earners would take a pay cut by serving.[30] That pay rate might strike the right balance, but the body's legitimacy might suffer if it could not attract at least some members from each economic stratum.[31]

The term of office could also prove an incentive or disincentive, depending on how it is viewed by the prospective legislator. There are many possible formulas, and they could vary by the level of the political system where the assembly resides. The terms for a local sortition assembly could be different than for a provincial/state or national assembly.

One design would have citizens serve a two-year term, with an option to serve a second term. This flexibility makes the term of appointment short enough for a person to return quickly to work, family, or other opportunities and commitments that call them back home. It also permits a more substantial term of service for those who would want the opportunity only if they could serve long enough to make a more substantial impact. Terms of legislators would be overlapping, ensuring that there would always be a mix of experienced and novice citizen legislators in the assembly. Those who choose to stay might gain additional motivation from renewing their commitment to serve in the legislature.

An alternative design would have citizens serve a five-year term, with roughly one-fifth of the members replaced each year. This allows for experience to accumulate over the length of service. Members could resign at any time, but an explicit expectation could encourage at least two years for every member. The size of each cohort of new legislators would vary depending on how many legislators end their service in a given year.

Impediments to Participation

There are many other issues that would need to be resolved in fine-tuning the incentives and terms of office for sortition legislators. For example, an important issue that might interfere with a person accepting a legislative invitation is the timing of the service. It might be desirable to permit—or even encourage—deferral of one's service to a later session. This would add some complexity to the selection process, especially when filling quotas in a stratified sample design. It could, however, add the flexibility necessary to accommodate the complexities of personal circumstances. A person with a newborn, or one in the midst of a degree program, for example, might opt to participate two or three years after the initial invitation.

Even with deferral, life disruption poses a special challenge for a sortition assembly compared to an elected chamber, because the new members of elected chambers all *planned* to join that body, at least from the day they filed papers to run for office. To take but one example, primary caregivers would have responsibilities that could make a full-time legislative job challenging or unwelcome, despite the generous financial compensation it offered. There is no need to belabor the specifics of how to anticipate such cases, other than to acknowledge that a sortition assembly faces this problem to a far greater degree than do one-off minipublics, which form and disband after asking only a few days or weekends of their members.

We eschew such short-duration designs, because only an ongoing assembly will have the time required to manage the complexity of multi-issue policy trade-offs and to craft larger-scale solutions to problems beyond the scope of a conventional minipublic. For the same reason, we prefer a single sortition assembly that takes on a full range of issues, rather than issue-specific legislatures, such as those described in Alexander Guerrero's "lottocracy" proposal.[32]

Training and Staff Support

If incentives are set right, a large proportion of those selected for the sortition legislature should agree to serve. The timing of that decision point, however, is less obvious than it is for a person who wins an election after enduring the crucible of an election. Elected legislators move quickly, and without hesitation, from candidate to public official, but someone who agrees to serve may come to have doubts as the date of their appointment approaches. For this reason, we have in mind a particular sequence of orientation and training, which we will now describe, along with questions of committee assignments and staff support.

Legislative Orientation and Training
We envision an initial introduction to the sortition legislature reaching all prospective members even before they decide whether to serve. The British Columbia Citizens' Assembly used a process like this to give invitees a clearer idea of how assembly service would present both unique opportunities and special responsibilities.[33] For the sortition legislature, this approach could prove useful as an opt-out mechanism for those who come to feel overwhelmed, but it might also retain prospective members if it allays their fears or doubts. Simply meeting with

those who have served previously could reassure hesitant citizens of their capacity to execute their assigned duties.

There may still be a problem of some people agreeing to serve simply because of the generous legislative salary, rather than out of any desire to participate in good faith. One strategy for inducing such people to withdraw is to give the selectees the "Zappos offer."[34] The online retailer of the same name holds paid training sessions that end by putting before each trainee a check amounting to a three-month severance package. Roughly one in seven trainees opt out at that point by taking the offer, which Zappos views as a strong indicator that the person was not going to prove a dedicated employee. For the sortition legislature, this weeds out those who view the job as an easy paycheck. The three-month salary offer (for no further effort whatsoever) should pull those persons out of the pool, just in time for an alternate (who is also given the option to accept or decline the offer) to join the legislature before its most intensive trainings begin.

Even with this filtering process built into our orientation, critics may harbor doubts about the readiness of the average citizen to take on legislative duties. There will be considerable variance in such capability among those who choose to serve. Electoral systems, however, produce officials who also have substantial knowledge deficits, exacerbated by ideological commitments that include rigid (and often grossly incorrect) convictions about government, society, and the natural world.

To remedy this problem for newly elected officials, numerous academic and nongovernmental organizations offer closed-door training sessions. For the US Congress, the Aspen Institute has brought hundreds of people to its Congressional Program, funded by philanthropic organizations. Attendees discuss domestic and international policy problems with invited experts (with no staff, lobbyists, or media present).[35] Harvard's Kennedy School of Government also offers a Bipartisan Program for Newly Elected Members of Congress. In addition to policy discussions, it includes workshops that delve into the practical questions of how to work effectively with colleagues in Congress and how to interface with the media and the other branches of government.[36] Programs offered by entities such as the National Institute for Civil Discourse focus more squarely on the importance of working through political differences, and the institute has reported success with its state legislative trainings.[37]

Such programs will be of great service to the sortition legislature, but we propose two important deviations from the preceding examples. First, such orientations should be treated as paid mandatory training. Making attendance mandatory provides one more opportunity for an uncommitted selectee to decline the offer to participate. In addition, it provides for a more even footing, in terms of professional knowledge, for all new members. Attending these sessions together also will help new legislators bond over a common experience, prior to feeling the pressures of lawmaking.

Second, we believe many of these training sessions should be opened up to public viewing, such as through livestreaming of key sessions. Closing off trainings protects newly elected officials from partisan scrutiny, but the selectees in a sortition system owe no party or lobby for their selection. Opening some of the trainings also will give lay citizens a better sense of what it would be like to be selected. It might even showcase the open-minded inquiry and learning taking place among their randomly selected peers.

Committee Assignment and Specialization

At some point during the orientation period, committee assignments will be made for the new selectees, who will be joining a body already populated by veteran legislators. The status quo assignment process rewards seniority and party loyalty, but the sortition legislature could place more weight on interest, experience, and ability. New members would have already learned about the full breadth of potential assignments during their training, which serves the function of a job fair. Current committee members who remain in the assembly could retain their most preferred committee assignments, then enter into a lottery with the rest of the selectees, each of whom would have ranked their preferences like students signing up for courses.

Once the new committee seats were filled, another round of training would bring together continuing and new legislators to go over the specific responsibilities of each assignment. At this point, professional staff would be paired with the new legislators, based on staff capabilities and interests. Legislators would later have the authority to release staff for reassignment (or termination) if they could not work together effectively, but it would avoid a hiring phase that could prove a distraction, or worse (should it introduce nepotism).

Staff, Services, and Legislative Capacity

At this juncture, a concern arises about the ability of professional staff to shape legislators' agendas and policy preferences. Experienced staff already have influence over elected legislators. The concern of many public policy scholars is not the hidden power of committee staff but rather the difficulty staff have getting and holding legislators' attention. Trust between staff and elected officials can develop over time, but biased hiring practices and unpredictable electoral turnover can make this challenging.[38]

The National Conference of State Legislatures views effective staff as part of a larger category of resources and services that develop legislative capacity. As the political scientist Alan Rosenthal defines the term, capacity is "the wherewithal for the legislature to do its job." It is, he explains, the sum of "time in session and in the interim period, the size of the professional staff, [and] the adequacy of facilities and technology."[39] The disposition and capabilities of the legislators also influence capacity, but in the US, professional state legislatures—such as those in Pennsylvania and California—do not necessarily generate more capacity than ones where lay citizens predominate, as in New Hampshire or Montana.

In terms of legislative capacity, members of a sortition legislature may have a significant advantage over their colleagues in the elected chamber. One of the hidden costs of elections is the toll they take on the schedule, energy, and morale of legislators. In countries without public financing, this problem is acute: members of the US Congress, for example, spend at least a third of their typical day fundraising. The fundraising is often for their own reelections, but the "permanent campaign" requires raising money for one's party, regardless of the safety of one's own district.[40] Putting that lost time back into the daily schedule of sortition legislators, they should have a greater opportunity to develop their expertise and policy viewpoints, working both with and independent of their staff.

Avoiding Technocratic Capture

Whatever its advantages, the sortition assembly will face one common problem to a greater degree than professional legislatures. All such bodies risk technocrats seizing control of the policy agenda if their members become too dependent on professional policy advisers. The case of the European Union is instructive, however, in that the body has managed to balance technical expertise with external political pressures that can hold experts accountable.[41] Put another way, advocacy coalitions that form naturally in policy disputes organize technical information in relation to their different political agendas.[42] This in turn will help lay citizen legislators make sense of expert information, rather than relying on those same experts for their political interpretations. This offers one more justification for keeping the sortition assembly tethered to a parallel elected chamber, which shares bureaucratic information resources that serve both chambers.

Deliberative Procedures and Norms

The norms and rules that govern a deliberative body come in so many useful varieties that we can't specify a single set best suited to the sortition legislature. Instead, we offer guidelines to follow in setting up such rules. In addition, we consider the formation of caucuses and the management of committee and floor debate.

Oversight Commission

A sortition legislature would need an oversight commission to periodically review the process for random selection, manage staff hiring and firing, and oversee new member orientation and training. The commission could also review and amend the rules for committee processes (such as holding hearings and bringing bills to a vote), floor debates (turn taking, amendments, closure, and the like), and the status of caucuses.

There are many alternate designs for such a commission. One possibility is for the commission to include a mix of current and former sortition legislators, with additional members from the complementary elected chamber and some appointed by the executive branch (e.g., via a prime minister or governor). The legislators on the commission would be chosen by their peers, with former officials having been elected in their final year of service. We see no irony in using an electoral process here because peer selection within small deliberative bodies bears little resemblance to the large-scale elections we critiqued earlier. To simplify this process and diversify commission membership, however, random selection could be used to create a short list of candidates from which sortition legislators might choose their representatives.[43]

The commission could play a stronger role if it oversaw legislative procedures and moderated the assembly's deliberation, directly or through professional facilitators. Modern forms of citizen deliberation typically have used trained forum moderators, who often work in teams to help citizens move through their agenda, manage speaking time, and ensure respectful discourse. This goes far beyond the uncontroversial role of a passive parliamentarian, but the difficulty of sustaining meaningful debate in legislatures suggests the need for experimentation along these lines.[44]

Privacy and Publicity

Open meeting and "sunshine" laws have pushed for ever-greater openness in elected bodies. It is less clear that a presumption of openness would always serve the purposes of a sortition legislature. Even for conventional legislatures, democratic theorists have noted the importance of granting legislative bodies a measure of privacy so that members might negotiate with opponents to craft politically feasible policies in the public interest.[45]

In the case of sortition chambers, there are additional considerations. Elected politicians, by the very nature of their careers, are used to public speaking and generally crave public exposure. Because of the likely distribution of dispositions, many ordinary citizens selected for a sortition chamber are likely to be less comfortable with oratory; for them, the presence of public media during legislative discussion could prove intimidating.

Though the sortition chamber does not have conventional campaign and partisan pressures, negotiating agreements in the midst of heated ideological conflict can be seen as a sign of moral failing.[46] If meetings in the sortition legislature occur only in the presence of cameras and microphones (from both news media and informal social media), brokering a compromise in which concessions are made in the interest of the common good becomes exceedingly difficult. Sortition legislators have no fear of losing elections, but even these members might wince at the backlash from segments of the public whose support they value. Thus, private space for honest and reflective deliberation has a purpose in both elective and sortition assemblies.

Consider the example of minipublics, such as the previously discussed British Columbia Citizens' Assembly. Plenary discussions among its members were open to public view, as the citizen body began to refine its questions and ideas for British Columbia's electoral laws. During that phase of its process, however, the assembly frequently broke into subgroups in smaller rooms, which were not as open to public view. Once its members reached tentative conclusions, they held hearings across the province to test and refine their judgments before reaching a final decision.[47]

Most minipublics benefit from a period of private—or semi-private—discussion analogous to the time jurors spend in their aptly named "deliberation room." These are times when citizen participants can express candidly their fears, uncertainties, and controversial attitudes. Whatever insights emerge from such discussion must ultimately become part of the minipublic's explicit rationale for its choices, but the initial expression and reformulation of such arguments might require relative privacy.[48]

More controversially, we recommend affording sortition legislators privacy in their votes akin to that enjoyed by most juries. When it comes time to cast final votes, we believe members should use secret ballots. The votes of individual legislators should be recorded securely, such that a member's vote cannot be known by colleagues or by the general public. A member might publicize how she intends to vote, then make claims about how she voted, but the official voting record can neither confirm nor disprove such assertions.

The reasons for this are very much in line with the justification of the secret ballot for citizens in ordinary political elections. Of particular importance is the possibility of corruption if the votes of individual sortition legislators were made public. This would enable vote buying through various mechanisms, since interested parties would have proof of how a legislator voted. Even if this were formally illegal, there are invariably ways around legal prohibitions (such as giving jobs to relatives). A secret ballot makes this more difficult.

A visible vote would also increase the possibility of undue pressure and retaliation for legislators who vote against the wishes of segments of the public. Members may choose to make their votes known, and reap the benefits or suffer the consequences, but they will not have the obligation to do so.

Caucuses and Connections

Though sortition legislators are not chosen as members of political parties, a place for traditional caucusing should remain part of the legislative process. Even though the sortition legislature eschews parties and elections in its formal structure, it should not pretend that its legislators will each conceive of the same general will at the conclusion of their deliberations. It should be possible for reasoned and honest debate to yield both consensus and principled disagreement.[49]

As an alternative to traditional party caucuses, however, members could organize themselves into a larger number of more cohesive groups of like-minded legislators who share common values and priorities. Some democratic theorists stress that these spaces create valuable opportunities for "enclave deliberation," during which legislators would sharpen their understandings of issues from a particular perspective.[50]

Whatever the caucus structure, there need to be direct connections between the sortition legislature and its electoral counterpart. When both chambers pass different versions of the same legislation, for example, there will need to be a reconciliation process. Joint hearings and regular informal exchanges would create much-needed opportunities for cross-pollination. The potential for the sortition body to influence the elected body outweighs the risk of partisan contagion, in our estimation, because partisan messages and pressures transmit regardless of such meetings. Bringing the bodies together periodically increases the odds that the elected chamber can work effectively with its upstart cousin—and perhaps even learn the virtues of its distinct deliberative processes and norms.

Limited Accountability Mechanisms

One understandable anxiety about sortition assembly members concerns their accountability to the electorate, which has no say in their selection or retention. That anxiety reflects the reality of this chamber, which we believe should *not* have grafted onto it an electoral accountability mechanism (such as recall). Such a lever would undo the very point of sortition—to bring together citizens freed from political pressures and asked to govern to the best of their abilities.

That said, prudence requires there be some means of removing assembly members whose behavior undermines the assembly's legitimacy or its ability to govern efficiently. Consider a member who has come to demonstrate profoundly diminished mental capacity, delights in aimless outbursts, or refuses to participate in deliberation.[51] Dismissal should come rarely, but there should be some means for the legislative system to dismiss such a legislator from continued service.

There are many specific procedures that could be used to deal with this problem, depending on the terms of service in the assembly and other considerations. One possibility is for this to be a function of the oversight commission, which could review complaints from members of the legislature (if they reached some reasonable threshold). It could then make a recommendation to the full chamber, which would then have to vote on expulsion. A dismissal vote would require a large supermajority.

Direct Public Engagement

The final feature of our proposal serves multiple purposes simultaneously. A deliberative governmental institution should not only have a robust internal decision-making process but also an interface with the wider public. Though it lacks regular elections, the sortition legislature should include a more direct and ongoing form of public engagement. This connection with the public could not only make the legislature publicly accountable but also improve the quality of that same public's judgment.

Consider the resources that the legislature could devote not to public relations but to genuine public outreach. Traditionally, legislative support serves three roles—informational (such as the Congressional Budget Office), policy and procedural (such as committee staff), and political (such as campaign staff). With no elections, the third staff role could change to facilitating public consultation.

This public consultation could be as simple as coordinating with nongovernmental organizations. In the United States, organizations connected to the National Coalition for Dialogue and Deliberation and the National Civic League already sponsor innumerable opportunities for public engagement. The sortition assembly could interact with these organizations in diverse ways. Or consider the various forms of participatory budgeting that have spread from South America. These processes could be tethered to the sortition legislature to influence some of their budgetary priorities, at every level of government.[52] Beyond fiscal questions, the People's Lobby recently piloted in Utah aims to organize public deliberation into a cohesive policy agenda, which the public then advocates directly to government.[53] The British Columbia Citizens' Assembly has also provided a model, now used in the UK and elsewhere, to craft legislative proposals, which could come to the sortition legislature for review.[54]

A civic educational component could also become part of the legislature's regular functioning. Imagine how different a high school's Model Congress program might feel when students realize that once they turn eighteen, they will have the same likelihood of sitting in the sortition legislature as anyone else. Curricula could be developed that also introduce the aforementioned civic engagement mechanisms with the legislature, any number of which could become regularized institutions. Changing the public's role through these means could fundamentally change the way citizens relate to government. It could help citizens appreciate the complexity of governing and reduce their appetite for more autocratic approaches, thereby boosting the legitimacy of the government itself.[55]

The Complementary Electoral Chamber

Regardless of the specific details of how a sortition chamber should be organized, we believe an elected chamber should serve as its complement. This may disappoint those who wish to do away with elections altogether, but we argue that an optimal bicameral legislative system would work best with a combination of electoral and sortition mechanisms.

A Justification for Retaining an Electoral Chamber

We have already reviewed the legion limitations of elections. We now offer three main reasons for the coexistence of electoral and sortition chambers.

First, in the absence of elections, political parties would atrophy even more than they have. At their best, political parties can play an important role in formulating political programs, educating the public about policy alternatives, formulating broad visions for social change, and mobilizing people for politically relevant collective action. While the adversarial impulse of parties can create failures in practical problem-solving, the absence of organized adversarial politics can narrow the space for thinking about alternatives.

When Jane Mansbridge titled her classic work *Beyond Adversary Democracy*, she meant to encourage proposals that tempered the adversarial impulse, but her writings since have just as often cautioned deliberative democratic theorists not to lose sight of the virtues of partisan conflict.[56] At their best, parties articulate policy agendas that tap into discontent from distinct constituent groups spread unevenly across the political spectrum. The greatest legislative accomplishments often have emerged not from a national consensus but in the midst of a pitched battle between competing parties.

A robust party system is especially important for popular social forces. In capitalist societies divided by class inequalities of wealth and power, political parties offer the popular classes a potential way of collectively organizing to advocate for their interests. Historically, political parties and unions were the only organizations capable of mobilizing sustained collective action on behalf of the working class and other economically subordinated groups. Though recent decades have witnessed considerable deterioration in the coherence and vitality of political parties in many countries, the absence of competitive elections would make party revitalization all but impossible. Without parties, it would be much more difficult for successful social mobilizations to emerge in response to substantive policy conflicts.

Second, given the nature of power and inequality in contemporary societies, there are conflicts of interest that cannot be resolved simply through disinterested deliberation. Thus, bargaining and compromise will remain an important part of politics.

A randomly selected legislature would have some members able to represent specific interests in a bargaining process, but that chamber is not designed for that purpose. Bargaining needs highly articulated expressions of interests with authorized representatives who can forge compromises. An elected chamber with political parties is better suited for that task.

Third, elections create the possibility for political careers and the development of skillful politicians as political leaders. People can enter politics at the local level, running in elections for city councils and other local offices. They gain experience, then run for offices at higher levels. As we discussed earlier, electoral rules and finance systems too often subvert this process. It is certainly the case in the United States today that a person with money or celebrity can obtain a high office with no experience whatsoever. Nevertheless, if all elected legislatures and councils were replaced by sortition, a crucial way of discovering and cultivating political leadership would be lost.

For these reasons, we believe that the optimal design for representative democracy combines a sortition citizen assembly with an elected chamber. If the latter is designed to minimize the pathologies of electoral processes and encourage coherent political parties, then a bicameral legislative process could be driven by a creative tension between deliberative problem-solving in the sortition body and adversarial negotiation in the elected chamber.

Optimal Electoral Rules

The rules that best complement a sortition body might differ from the rules appropriate for a purely electoral system. For instance, nonpartisan elections would not be well suited to this role, since they would undercut the interparty bargaining function of the elected chamber. In addition, since the sortition body ensures regular turnover in its membership, the electoral body might avoid strict term limits and place more emphasis on sustaining its institutional memory.

It is beyond the scope of this book to specify the ideal complementary electoral process, but we have suggestions. We favor systems that avoid the flaws inherent in first-past-the-post systems (also known as "winner-take-all") that use single-member districts. A variety of alternatives exist, including instant-runoff voting, cumulative voting, optional preferential, and single transferable vote. All of these variations are designed to extract maximum preference information from voters to choose representatives.[57]

An ideal electoral chamber will provide voters the most tangible sense of direct representation by political parties and officials who share their particular views. This parallels the sortition process's emphasis on representative legitimacy, but it stresses the role of organized parties and electoral competition. For this reason, we recommend a system that uses large, multi-member districts that elect legislators with legislative power in proportion to their level of public support. Voters in a given district would consider candidates from different political parties, then rank their preferences. Candidates whose proportion of first-choice ballots falls below a threshold (say, 20 percent) would be dropped; the ballots for dropped candidates would then move to their second choices, and so on, until each remaining candidate crossed the threshold. All of those candidates would be elected. Then, when voting on a bill in the legislature, a representative would cast a number of votes equivalent to the number of ballots received in the election (for example, a candidate who receives three hundred thousand votes in the election would become a legislator whose yea or nay carries a weight of three hundred thousand votes).[58] This might seem unwieldy since every legislator would cast a different number of votes in the legislature, but software can make the vote-counting a seamless process.

In this system, every vote counts to a greater degree than in other voting systems. The weighting of legislators' power neutralizes the impact of gerrymandering and district boundaries more generally. The system also strengthens representatives' direct ties to their constituencies, since legislators act as a kind of proxy voter for their supporters. At the same time, this system sustains the relevance of parties and collective mobilization central to elections.

Reciprocal Influence

At various points, we have stressed the value of retaining the elected chamber alongside the sortition assembly. Many of those benefits fall under the broader category of "reciprocal relationship." When justifying sortition, we acknowledged that the elected body gives every citizen an equal voice in the voting booth, but no direct voice thereafter. That full franchise serves as a counterweight to sortition, which gives each citizen an equal chance to serve but exercises its real citizen power downstream, in the randomly selected assembly.

More indirect connections include how the two bodies might influence one another once constituted side by side. The elected body provides a stream of politically motivated policy analyses that citizens in the sortition chamber can observe and selectively adopt. More important than that, the sortition body forces its elected counterpart to consider whether prospective bills will pass muster in a relatively deliberative assembly. Since the citizens' sortition assembly can block party-generated policy, the elected chamber has to craft policy that not only meets its political objectives but also has a good prospect of withstanding citizen scrutiny.

Where to Begin?

We have made the case for the desirability and viability of a sortition legislature as an institutional design that advances democratic ideals, but is this proposal achievable? In one way or another, new institutions always involve the transformation of existing ones; they never emerge fully grown in an institution-free context. Some preexisting institutional structures can make it much easier and others harder to introduce particular kinds of changes. Three institutional settings seem relatively favorable for the possibility of introducing a sortition chamber.

The simplest setting is one in which a sortition body is a replacement for appointed upper houses in Westminster parliamentary systems. This change would bring broader powers and a dramatically more representative membership to bodies that range in size from 105 members (Senate of Canada) to more than 800 (British House of Lords). Such a situation could gain an immediate legitimacy boost by appropriating the real estate and resources of a dubiously democratic body. Thus, it is no coincidence that proposals for sortition legislatures have appeared in the UK, Canada, and other nations that find themselves in this circumstance.[59]

Another suitable institutional setting is one in which sortition could replace the lower house in a large bicameral legislature within a modest-sized state or province. Examples in the United States include New Hampshire's 400-member lower house and the 203-member Pennsylvania General Assembly, whereas the largest lower houses in Australia carry roughly 90 members (New South Wales, Queensland, and Victoria). In each case, the legislature is large enough to ensure a diverse random sample, with a smaller elected body providing a complementary legislative chamber. These changes would require constitutional amendments, but doing so in a state, province, or territory might prove more feasible in the near term than making such an attempt for an entire nation.

A third context potentially favorable to introducing sortition is a government that itself is relatively new, or newly forming. Such a legislature could complement an existing one that is either unicameral or only weakly bicameral—meaning that one chamber dominates the other. The European Union, as currently configured, has a popularly elected European Parliament with over 750 members, which is complemented by a Council of Ministers made up of just two dozen national representatives. In contrast to these two bodies, a sortition chamber with 250 members would provide a popular counterpoint. Nations just beginning to develop democratic systems might be open to *beginning* with a sortition chamber in their legislature, or even during their process of constitutional design. Nepal, for example, chose to elect the 601 members of its Legislature Parliament, which serves as the legislature until it completes its task of passing a new constitution. A sortition body could have served as a useful complement to the parliament, or it could be written into the constitution as a permanent part of that nation's bicameral system.

Regardless of which nation or state first adopts sortition, the method should come into place through a democratic process. It could come about through a political party that chooses to self-destruct the body it governs (or seeks to govern). After all, the British Columbia Citizens' Assembly arose from a party advocating fundamental structural reform, then delivering the mechanism it had promised. Participatory budgeting in Brazil also emerged from a political party's empowerment platform, as have related popular reforms in Kerala, India, and elsewhere.[60] It could also be that sortition might come about through popular referendum in a country such as Switzerland that has a tradition of direct democratic governance.[61] Or it might first appear at the subnational level in a state like Colorado, where amending the constitution requires only a simple majority vote in a statewide election.

Sortition could also emerge more gradually as part of an electoral body. One idea floated in Iceland, for example, would permit voters in ordinary parliamentary elections to choose "a random citizen" instead of a party.[62] Under that nation's rules of proportional representation, whatever proportion of the electorate chose that option would then make up the same proportion of the parliament, with individual members selected through a sortition process. Such a concept might find fertile soil in Iceland, which used lay citizens in its National Forum during its 2010 constitutional overhaul.[63]

More modestly, the idea of a sortition legislature might gain stature gradually through lower-stakes institutions that build on the successes of experiments like citizens' assemblies, deliberative polls, and citizens' initiative reviews. Each of these minipublics draws random samples for bodies that form and then disband in the space of a few days, weeks, or months. Indigenous nations that have not found externally imposed electoral systems suitable to their needs might try hybrids that stand between such minipublics and full-fledged sortition.[64] Sortition processes might be tried within large worker collectives or nongovernmental organizations that seek to reinvigorate their memberships by giving them a more direct stake in decision-making. Online versions of such bodies might hold particular appeal for youth-led entities, which have a membership native to digital environments.[65]

The modern idea of self-government has an enduring appeal, and people have been reluctant to let go of institutions that afford them greater direct control. If the sortition legislature delivers even half of what we envision, it will not only clear the low bar set by elected chambers, but it will also demonstrate the citizenry's true capacity for self-government.

2

Postscript: The Anticapitalist Argument for Sortition

Erik Olin Wright

In the preceding chapter, John Gastil and I made a case for sortition that addresses mainstream political concerns with the institutions of democratic governance. Our argument fits well within both progressive and conservative political ideologies, in that it aims to reinforce the liberal democratic regimes in which those dueling philosophies operate.

The case for sortition can also be made in terms of its relationship to more radical social, political, and economic transformation. Thus, I offer this postscript to make the case for sortition from a Marxist perspective. Many readers may harbor misconceptions about the modern Marxist theory of the state and democracy, so I will review this theory briefly before explaining how sortition could become part of an anticapitalist political strategy.

A Marxist Theory of the State

Marxist theory describes the operation of capitalism as a specific kind of economic system organized through a particular structure of class relations. Marxism describes the social processes through which capitalism develops, is sustained, and could eventually be transcended. At the center of each of these processes lies "the state," a term that encompasses formal government institutions, laws and regulations, and less tangible social processes of governance within a society.

Development

Wherever capitalism exists, the state has played a critical role in initially consolidating the conditions for capitalist property relations and capital accumulation, and subsequently surmounting periodic obstacles to continued capitalist development. This was never a smooth, harmonious process of the state simply doing what was best for capitalism. Rather, state actions were contested by both elites and popular social forces, and sometimes the actions of the state contributed to disruptions of capitalist development and even to catastrophic system failures. Fostering capitalism often requires dramatic—and contentious—changes in the fundamental structure of the state itself. Examples include the Meiji Restoration in Japan and the various episodes of revolutionary destruction of premodern state structures in Europe and elsewhere. Other times, more modest reforms of state institutions are necessary for effectively resolving crises, such as when the Great Depression spurred the New Deal in the United States.

Sustaining Capitalism

The state plays a pivotal role in maintaining (or "reproducing") capitalism, particularly its class relations. Theoretical debates within (and over) Marxist approaches to the state focus on this "function" of the state, with some arguing that the very *form* of the state helps reproduce capitalist class relations.[1] Marxist state theorists have generally argued that the specific form of democracy in the capitalist state—pejoratively called "bourgeois democracy," or more descriptively, simply "capitalist democracy"—is designed to protect capitalism.[2] In particular, Marxist theorists argue that electing political officials through competitive elections stabilizes capitalism by containing and deflecting class struggles.[3] The democratic deficiencies of elections cataloged in the opening chapter of this volume nevertheless play a positive role in reproducing capitalist class relations. Private campaign finance, for example, reduces the likelihood of anticapitalist parties prevailing in elections.

Transcending Capitalism

Perhaps the most politically contentious debate within Marxist theory concerns the role electoral institutions can play in transcending capitalism. The destination "beyond" capitalism traditionally has been called "socialism," but regardless of the label, the substantive aim is an economic structure with a relatively egalitarian distribution of income and a democratic distribution of power.[4] Revolutionaries argue that electoral politics might aid political mobilization and consciousness raising and thus strengthen anticapitalist political parties, but robust socialist policies cannot occur within a capitalist democratic state. In this view, transforming class relations requires a rupture and transformation of the state itself through political revolution.

Reformists, in contrast, argue that even the rigged political system in a capitalist democracy can be used to transform capitalism. Campaigning for anticapitalist public policies can gradually tame the economy to counteract the most harmful aspects of capitalism. The challenge for reformists is using the machinery of the capitalist state to weaken the reproduction of capitalism and secure anticapitalist initiatives.

There is a third position in debates within the Marxist tradition over the problem of transcending capitalism. This third approach, which is neither strictly revolutionary nor reformist, advocates what has been referred to as "nonreformist reforms."[5] Here the idea is to struggle for reforms in the institutions of the state that have three kinds of simultaneous effects: they solve some pressing problem in the system as it exists; they enlarge, rather that close down, the space for future transformations; and they enhance the capacity of popular social forces to fill that space. The central argument is that the capitalist state is an internally contradictory configuration of principles and mechanisms, and thus it is possible, under appropriate historical conditions, to achieve such nonreformist reforms of the capitalist state itself. Simple reformists don't worry about the second and third conditions; revolutionaries deny their possibility.

Sortition's Radical Potential

The question, then, is whether a sortition legislature would be receptive to laws challenging the dominance of capitalism. Relative to a conventional electoral body, would a sortition process be more likely to support or oppose popular mobilizations with egalitarian objectives, such as income and wealth redistribution? Would a sortition legislature be more likely to expand state provision of public goods and services and more control over the power of finance capital?

Answers to these questions depend on the political, economic, and cultural context of sortition reforms. That said, a more deeply democratic state structure should make it more likely to raise issues of social justice. Ordinary citizens wielding legislative power—with the opportunity to access sound information and deliberate together—will be more open to reform and more skeptical about self-serving arguments for inequality preferred by rich and powerful elites. Citizen legislators should also prove more interested in finding policy solutions that push in egalitarian directions. Thus a sortition legislature should prove more capable than an elected one at reforming capitalism, as well as potentially pursuing a trajectory that moves beyond capitalism.

If this prediction is correct, however, this reduces the likelihood that a capitalist state would permit the creation of a sortition assembly. For the same reason that wealthy elites have supported political reforms that undermine electoral democracy, especially in the United States, they are likely to oppose reforming the representational mechanisms of the capitalist democracy, lest it become more receptive to egalitarian policies. The implication, however, is not that sortition is impossible, but that it will require significant political mobilization and struggle if it is to be instituted in a way that truly deepens the democratic quality of the state.

II. CONTEMPORARY CONTEXT

3

From Deliberative to Radical Democracy: Sortition and Politics in the Twenty-First Century

Yves Sintomer

John Gastil and Erik Olin Wright present legislature by lot as a real utopia, which would further a long democratic tradition coming from Athens and revitalized by contemporary minipublics at the end of the twentieth century. A number of convincing arguments tend to demonstrate that this is a promising way of democratizing the political system. However, some questions should be raised. What kind of democracy is at stake—deliberative democracy, as most of the proponents of minipublics advocate? Radical democracy, as induced by the frequent reference to Athens? A mix between both—or even something quite different? What is the specific value of sortition? Although defending a mixed constitution and a complex vision of democracy,[1] Aristotle famously wrote, "It is considered democratic that offices should be filled by lot, and oligarchic that they should be elective."[2] Jacques Rancière goes in the same direction when he writes, "The scandal of democracy, and of the drawing of lots which is its essence, is to reveal [...] that the government of societies cannot but rest in the last resort on its own contingency."[3] The political scientist Bernard Manin, in his seminal book on representative government, seems to share the same idea.[4] I advocate for a much more complex narrative. The idea that sortition in politics has sustained a transhistorical democratic logic is more a myth than a historical fact, as political sortition has been used in quite different functions in history.[5]

I will defend four claims, two historical and two normative ones. The first historical claim, which will be central in my argument, is that when analyzing the experiments that have taken place in the last decades, two waves have to be differentiated, based on partly different concrete devices, embodying different social dynamics and pointing toward different kinds of democracy. To a large extent, the rationale of political sortition has changed from the first wave to the second one. The second historical claim is that the rationale of the first wave of democratic innovations based on randomly selected minipublics largely differs from the dynamic of political sortition in Athens, as it embodies a logic of deliberative democracy rather than a logic of self-government and radical democracy. Conversely, the second wave is more differentiated and more compatible with a neo-Athenian perspective, and empowered sortition processes that have emerged during the second wave better capture the spirit of radical Athenian democratic traditions than do consultative minipublics. My third claim is normative: these empowered sortition processes are promising for a real democratization of democracy. My last claim is that any proposal of a legislature by lot has to rely on this lesson when trying to defend a normatively convincing and politically realistic perspective.

In what follows, I will take a critical approach, which studies real democratic experiments (historical and present) to better understand the normative and political claims that come from society, rather than trying to assert pure philosophical principles. I will first describe the initial wave of experiments— composed by deliberative pools, citizen juries, and consensus conferences—that have used sortition in politics at the end of the twentieth century. These experiments have been mostly top-down consultative minipublics. They have complemented representative democracy with deliberative democracy, and the latter has been differentiated from, or opposed to, radical democracy and social movements. These devices have been akin to what Europeans call "protected designations of origin" (PDO): carefully designed, closely monitored, and often patented by their inventors. I will briefly oppose this logic of deliberative democracy based upon randomly selected minipublics to the logic of radical democracy and self-rule that characterized Athens.

In the second part, I will present the second wave of experiments. It has been much more plural than the first one. From citizen assemblies to the Oregon Citizens' Initiative Review, from the Students' Association of Lausanne University to a left-wing political party in Mexico, and from the use of sortition between 2011 and 2016 by Occupy-like social movements such as the Syntagma Square in Greece, the anti-austerity 15-M in Spain, and the Nuit Debout in France to French president Emmanuel Macron's political movement (En Marche), the devices have been hybridized and inventive, offering spaces for creative imagination to both practitioners and theoreticians. Most of them have been directly linked to some real decision-making and may therefore be analyzed as empowered processes. They have been coupled to representative government but also to direct democracy and to grassroots democracy. They often have articulated deliberative democracy with radical democracy.

In the third and conclusive part, drawing the conclusions of my analysis of the two waves of sortition experiments, I will develop my normative claims and explain why legislature by lot can be a crucial dimension for a radical democratization of democracy.

The First Wave of Modern Political Sortition: Deliberative Minipublics

Over the last two decades, tools that bring selection by lot back into politics, such as citizen juries, consensus conferences, and deliberative polls, have spread to other countries and resulted in many new experiences. Thousands of citizen juries have been held around the world.[6] Between 150 and several hundred consensus conferences have been held, nearly half of them in Denmark.[7] Dozens of deliberative polls have been conducted in the United States and around the world.[8]

Citizen Juries, Deliberative Polls, and Consensus Conferences

These trends can be understood only in relation to the social upheavals of the 1960s and 1970s and a broader push for democratic change. The ideas of participatory democracy or self-management began to inspire activists, finding an echo in the academic world. These themes built on old arguments about the elitist character of representative democracy and sounded the charge against the existing political system. However, random selection came to public attention only gradually. Its advocates were concerned with giving institutional expression to the critique of representative democracy but took a distance from radical left-wing tendencies that were modeled on the workers' councils of 1905–20. Sortition appealed to ordinary citizens, and its attraction increased as the fascination for vanguards began to wane. The title of one of the first volumes to defend the idea of broadly using selection by lot in politics, *After the Revolution?*, is thus quite revealing.[9]

The idea of selecting a small group of citizens to deliberate within a regulated procedural framework also ran counter to some of the grassroots-democracy ideologies of the 1970s, which saw the general assembly as the highest embodiment of democracy. In this sense, deliberative polls, citizen juries, and consensus conferences are all part and parcel of a "deliberative turn" in participatory practices, as greater attention is being paid to the quality of debates and to the institutional tools that allow people to have their say on a balanced and egalitarian basis.

The idea of random selection in politics reemerged separately in Germany, where Peter Dienel argued in 1969 for "planning cells" (*Planungszellen*), the first ones being tested out in the winter of 1972–3, and in the United States, where Ned Crosby created a similar structure in 1971 that he called the "citizens' jury."[10] In 1988, James Fishkin invented "deliberative polling" and in 1994 experimented with it for the first time in Britain. All three of these men were political or social scientists, and because they had no initial support from a movement, party, or institution, all three endeavored to found an institution that would disseminate, or indeed, commercialize the concept. All three moved quickly to patent it, even if Ned Crosby continued to work from a more activist perspective. Independently of these experiments, the *Teknologiradet* (Danish Board of Technology) decided in 1987 to open up consensus conferences to "lay" citizens, after a period during which they had been used in medical circles in the United States. Only in the late 1990s did political and academic figures begin to consider the consensus conference, the citizen jury, and deliberative polling as largely convergent procedures, and the first moves were made to produce both conceptual and empirical hybrids.

Meanwhile, whereas the earliest conceptual justifications of random selection in politics had been closely tied to an experimental urge, a more theoretical process of reflection began to gather steam. From the 1990s on, three fast-developing currents independently helped to give theoretical nobility to these procedures, at first indirectly and then in more direct ways. One of these currents has based itself on the work of John Rawls and Jürgen Habermas to theorize the practice of deliberative democracy in politics.[11] The work and action of James Fishkin has been important to link deliberative democracy (whose main authors initially did not speak about random selection) and sortition.[12] The other trend of literature, central for consensus conferences, has concentrated on the vast realm of "technical democracy," drawing theoretically on the social history of the sciences.[13] On a less massive scale, a few books and articles that defend or indirectly legitimize the reintroduction of random selection in politics helped to further awaken interest in the subject, especially in English-speaking and French-speaking countries.[14]

Eight Common Features

Beyond their differences, eight features characterize these devices of the "first wave":

1. They constitute minipublics—that is, randomly selected representative samples, or at least a "fair cross-section of the community."[15] Most often, they are composed through some kind of stratified random selection in order to increase their representativeness.

2. Most of these experiments are top-down. Those who organize them are public authorities, or in some cases foundations, in collaboration with social scientists. They are not linked to social movements. They can even be opposed to grassroots democracy.

3. These devices have been what Europeans call "protected designations of origin" (PDO): carefully designed, closely monitored, and often patented by their inventors. They function well and are highly interesting for a scientific analysis of the ordinary deliberation between lay citizens. The dark side of the protected designations of origin is that the political imagination of actors remains limited and the diffusion hindered.

4. Most of these devices have been one-shot events. The number of institutions that have organized such minipublics several times is quite reduced compared to those that have organized them once or twice. The main exception is the *Teknologiradet* (Danish Board of Technology) and its citizen conferences. But

even in this case, the minipublic has not become part of the "constitution."

5. Random sortition is linked to a high-quality deliberation. The minipublic is a place where a high-quality deliberation can take place, with carefully balanced briefing materials, with intensive discussions in small groups and in general assembly, with facilitators helping an equal and inclusive discussion, and with the chance to question competing experts and politicians.

6. Most of these devices are only consultative. They give a recommendation to public authorities or provide them a counterfactual enlightened public opinion. They complement representative democracy. The aim is not to make decisions, but to improve the decision-making process with a device that enables a sophisticated deliberation among lay citizens. The minipublics allow us to know "what the public would think, had it a better opportunity to consider the questions at issue."[16]

7. The minipublics are not embedded in everyday social and political relations. Citizens have no link with each other. Nor are they organized or mobilized. They discuss in an artificial institution.

8. These devices are concrete embodiments of deliberative democracy. In most books of political theory, deliberative democracy is differentiated or even opposed to participatory democracy.

The Contrast with Athens: Representative Sample Versus Self-Government of the People

The supporters of citizen juries, deliberative polls, and consensus conferences generally consider that civic participation in politics is crucial for the good health of our political system. Even if we bracket the obvious and important differences in the social, political, economic, and institutional contexts of modern democracies on the one hand, and those of ancient Athens on the other, is it enough to diagnose a partial resurgence of the ideal of Athenian radical democracy?

The close link between sortition and democracy in Athens is well known. Athens had a mixed system of aristocratic and democratic elements, and sortition was crucial for the second dimension. Each citizen could stand for selection by lot. This operated in four major types of institutions. First, it served for the yearly constitution of the *boule*, the main council of Athenian democracy. Second, most of the magistracies were filled by random selection.[17] Third, a sort of supreme court called the *nomothetai* was selected by lot in the fourth century. Finally, all the judges were selected by lot. Citizenship entailed the unalienable right to participate in the assembly and to become a juror, and selection by lot became a routine activity.[18] The *kleroterion*, the allotment "machine" most likely mentioned by Aristophanes as early as 393 BC,[19] made the procedure quicker and more straightforward, while simultaneously protecting it from any attempts at manipulation.

In Athens, however, the link between random sortition and deliberation was complex. On the one hand, the Greeks theorized a form of public debate that would involve all citizens. Nevertheless, the concrete dynamic of deliberation was differentiated according to the institutions. In the people's assembly, an essentially contradictory debate unfolded, wherein orators attempted to convince the audience: a practice conceptualized by Aristotle as rhetoric.[20] Nonetheless, the public could actively express their feelings by speaking loudly. The practices of the *boule* were doubtless more interactive, whereas one-on-one political discussions took place in the various public spaces of the agora. In the courts, by contrast, juries were required to form their opinions by listening to the various parties but without deliberating, as all discussion among jury members was prohibited.

The coupling of rotation of the functions of power with selection by lot became a highly rational procedure that was particularly effective in warding off the professionalization of political activity and the monopolization of power by experts in a realm cut off from the citizenry. Of course, the Athenian city-state excluded women and slaves from political life and used its strength to subjugate allied cities. Within those and other important limitations, however, the Athenian way of life revolved around political activity, and citizens participated on a highly egalitarian basis in comparison with other systems known to history. Nearly 70 percent of citizens aged over thirty were *bouletai* at least once during their lifetimes,[21] and a still higher proportion were called upon to be jurors. These institutions functioned as schools of democracy in a society with a developed civic culture where face-to-face contact made mutual checking easy to achieve. Within the relatively narrow circle of citizens, power was largely exercised *by* the people.

A crucial difference opposes Athens's use of sortition and contemporary practices: the representative sample.[22] In Athens, sortition and the rapid rotation of offices enabled citizens to govern and be governed in turn. This is why, in classical political thought, random selection has been associated with democracy and elections with aristocracy. Compared to present representative democracy, Athens embodied an example of radical democracy. The contemporary use of random selection is quite different. The real likelihood of being selected for a citizen jury, a deliberative pool, or a consensus conference is very low. The idea is to use sortition to select a microcosm of the citizenry, a group that has the same features and the same diversity as the citizenry, but on a smaller scale. A group of hundreds of randomly selected citizens tends to be statistically a representative sample of the citizenry as a whole. A smaller group of twelve to twenty-five persons cannot be truly representative, but this "fair cross-section of the community" incorporates some of the people's diversity. Both types of panels embody a specific kind of descriptive representation.

The notion of representative sample is familiar to twenty-first-century readers thanks to decades of its intensive use in statistics and opinion polls. This is why it seems "quite rational to see lotteries as a means to the end of descriptive representation."[23] However, the representative sample is a late nineteenth-century invention. It was first introduced in politics with the opinion polls in the 1930s; it became an instrument for selecting trial juries only at the end of the 1960s[24] and the political minipublics in the 1970s. There could be no relation between random selection and descriptive representation in Athens, as the idea that random selection statistically leads to a cross section of the population was not scientifically available at the time. Chance had not yet been scientifically "tamed."[25] Descriptive representation was important during the age of the French and North American revolutions. Mirabeau argued that the assembly should be "for the nation what a scaled-down map is for its physical area; whether in part or in full, the copy should always have the same proportions as the original."[26] But because it was impossible to rely on the notion of a representative sample, promoters of descriptive representation ignored sortition and put forward other technical solutions. Mirabeau suggested the separate representation of different social groups through what we today could call corporatist methods. The anti-Federalists proposed small constituencies.[27]

Bernard Manin was the first to wonder why selection by lot disappeared from the political scene along with the modern revolutions.[28] He gave a two-part answer. On the one hand, the founding fathers of the modern republics wanted an elective aristocracy rather than a democracy, and so it was logical that they should reject random selection. On the other hand, the theory of consent, deeply rooted in modern conceptions of natural law, had gained so much ground that it seemed difficult to legitimize any political authority not formally approved by the state's citizens. These two arguments are important, but they do not tell the whole story. In particular, they fail to explain why radical minorities did not demand the use of selection by lot in politics, even though they campaigned for descriptive representation.

To understand these developments, one has to point to a number of other factors. We have to abandon the realm of "pure" political ideas and look at the way in which they take material shape through governance techniques and various tools and mechanisms. The lack of a statistical concept of representative sampling at the time of the French and American Revolutions, when probability and statistics were already well established but not melted together, was a crucial reason why legislation by lot seemed doomed in modern democracies—as well as why those who upheld a descriptive conception of representation inevitably had to select other tools to advance their ideals. The sheer demographic and territorial size of modern republics seemed to forbid any serious consideration of political lotteries, since it could not allow all citizens to govern and be governed in turn.

Conversely, the present comeback of random selection is also related to representative sampling. Random selection as it is practiced in politics today is inseparably bound up with that concept. In modern democracy, the deliberation of a fair cross-section of the people is not the same as the people's self-government. It gives anybody the same chance to be selected, but because this chance is very small, it does not allow all citizens to hold public office in turn. It leads instead to a mini-public, a counterfactual opinion that is representative of what the larger public opinion *could think*. John Adams wrote that the microcosmic representation he was arguing for "should think, feel, reason, and act" like the people. For contemporary deliberative democrats, the statistical similarity between "descriptive" representatives and the people is only a starting point. The minipublic has to deliberate, and during this process, it changes its mind. It begins to think somehow differently, and this is precisely the added value of deliberation.[29]

The Second Wave: Liberating Democratic Imagination

The inventors of the first wave of deliberative minipublics had hoped that these techniques would soon or eventually come into general use, but up to now they have had no standardized application on a large scale. This, according to Hans-Liudger Dienel, the leading expert on citizen juries in Germany, is partly due to the fact of the promoters' concern to preserve the "purity" and seriousness of procedures: "I wonder whether the protagonists of deliberative democracy, with their societal approach, with their academic and ideological culture, might be a major obstacle for mass application of citizens juries and other direct deliberative instruments. Do they, do we, really want to leave the niche and join new coalitions to see mass application of deliberative democratic tools?"[30]

Another reason was the position of those who wanted to promote participatory democracy in politics and in the academy. They were more interested in other mechanisms and processes, such as Latin American participatory budgeting, which were bound up with the social mobilization of subaltern classes or challenges to the existing order. Although advocates of participatory democracy have been attentive to the deliberative quality of new participatory procedures, they have thought of them mainly as instruments in the service of social change; they initially ignored or had a rather skeptical attitude toward mechanisms based on random selection, since by their very nature they give little scope for citizen mobilization and are mainly introduced top-down.[31]

This situation has changed with a second wave of experiments relying on political sortition. This second wave has not replaced the first one: some of the experiments of the former began very early, and the three "classical" devices of the latter are still experimented. In addition, the second wave has taken advantage of the achievements and lessons of the first one: the techniques for organizing a good deliberation among lay citizens; the demonstration that these lay citizens can enter reasonable deliberation when organized in such conditions; the values of impartiality, epistemic diversity, and democracy attached to political sortition; the increasing public legitimacy of this particular kind of democratic innovation; and so forth. Last but not least, some of the promoters of the first wave have also been very active in the second one. However, the second wave has much broadened the panorama. The numbers have increased and the types of experiments have diversified. Four main streams can be differentiated.

Randomly Selected Minipublics and Direct Democracy

The first direction of innovation tends to couple deliberative democracy, embodied by minipublics selected by lot, and direct democracy. Citizen assemblies are the most well-known examples of this trend. The first experiment was the British Columbia Citizens' Assembly (2004), followed by the Ontario experiment the year after. British Columbia became a source of inspiration for other regions. In November 2009, Iceland was profoundly shaken by the financial crisis. Huge social movements imposed new elections and a new deal between business and unions. A citizens' assembly of 950 randomly selected individuals and a few hundred qualified persons was created. The assembly was tasked with identifying the most important points for constitutional reform. Iceland repeated the process with a new assembly, this time entirely selected by lot, before using universal suffrage to elect a kind of jury from among the population, composed of twenty-five ordinary citizens responsible for elaborating a new fundamental law based on the material produced by the previous assembly. This process has led to a dead end due to the opposition of the new ruling parties.

Another experiment, in Ireland, has been more successful. Following an initiative launched by an NGO movement, a citizens' assembly of 100 individuals met in June 2011. Calling itself the Citizen Parliament, the group sought to make suggestions for constitutional reform. It was met with significant response in the media. After the 2011 election, the new government accepted the idea supported by the majority of the different parties and organized a constitutional convention, sixty-seven of whose one hundred members were ordinary citizens randomly selected from the electoral register. The others were politicians, in order to avoid the negative pushback from political parties that had made the adoption of the proposals coming from the citizens' assemblies in British Columbia and Ontario more difficult. From the work of the convention emerged the proposal to legalize same-sex marriage, which was ultimately validated by a referendum in May 2015. One of the most ambitious attempts to combine deliberative and direct democracy was thus ultimately a great success.[32] The process was repeated in 2017 and 2018 with new issues and a constituent committee entirely selected by lot, leading to a constitutional amendment legalizing abortion approved by 66 percent of voters in May 2018. Other examples have been organized bottom-up, the most well known being the G1000 in Belgium.[33]

In Oregon, one of the most interesting experiments with citizen juries has been conducted, called the Citizens' Initiative Review. Following a grassroots movement calling for deliberative democracy to be reconciled with the existing forms of direct democracy,[34] and benefiting from the expertise of Ned Crosby, the inventor of citizen juries, members of government from both sides of the aisle decided to institutionalize the use of randomly selected citizen panels. The Citizens' Initiative Review was officially adopted in 2011. Its principle is the following: once a collection of signatures meets with success but before voting takes place, a panel of citizen voters is organized to debate and evaluate the ballot measure in question. The panel's decision is then shared with citizens, as well as the informational material distributed (opinions from both an initiative's supporters and opponents).

With this kind of procedure, deliberative democracy does not short-circuit direct democracy but rather increases its rational component. Moreover, it should be noted that at the end of deliberations, the panels are forced to elaborate a majority position, rather than find consensus. The proposals submitted to the citizen panel and the popular vote have addressed mandatory minimum sentencing, legalizing medical marijuana dispensaries, corporate tax reform, and more. The evaluations that the procedure has received have been largely positive: overall, the quality of its deliberations has been touted,[35] and the impact of the review panel's opinions on voting outcomes has been non-negligible.[36]

Randomly Selected Minipublics and
Participatory Democracy

A second trend of innovations make use of randomly selected minipublics within larger participatory dynamics. Randomly selected minipublics have been combined with participatory budgeting. The citizen juries of Berlin, organized between 2001 and 2003, were one of the most interesting examples, where Peter Dienel's planning cells have been hybridized in an interesting way (Peter Dienel himself was not satisfied with this innovation). In each of the capital's seventeen districts federally targeted for urban renewal, a sum of five hundred thousand euros was made freely available to a group of inhabitants for the support of local projects. They were composed half of people selected by lot from the list of residents, and half of citizens organized or active in their local area. They were given decision-making powers, and the local authority endeavored to follow their advice to the limits of its jurisdiction and the legislation then in force.[37] The random method has also been used in the participatory budgets of other German and Spanish cities and in Pont-de-Claix, France, during the period of 2001–8.[38] Since 2005, and with moderate success, the Chinese borough of Zeguo has even mixed the participatory budgeting taking place in the city of Wenling (an eastern Chinese city with a population of over one million inhabitants) with a version of the deliberative polls.[39] Later, a quota was established to allow for the overrepresentation of entrepreneurs, so that this social class, important for local economic development, could wield more influence than its demographic weight would otherwise allow.

Randomly Selected Permanent Councils
Within Institutions and Associations

Democratic imagination has been so prolific that it is in fact impossible to describe all of the different forms taken by the contemporary political use of random selection. Nonetheless, some important examples of a third trend-making use of random selection in order to establish permanent councils within institutions or associations should be mentioned.

Following a cooperation with James Fishkin's Center for Deliberative Democracy at Stanford University, Mongolia passed a law in 2017 that makes it compulsory to organize a deliberative poll before any constitutional amendment. On April 2017, the Mongolian Parliament did just that when it brought together 669 randomly selected citizens from across the country to Ulaanbaatar for the first-ever national deliberative poll on the future of the Mongolian constitution. Although negatively affected by a number of procedural defects,[40] this initiative could launch a new era of institutionalization at the national level for one of the most well-known minipublics.

A more bottom-up and original initiative took place in Switzerland. The Federation of Student Associations of the University of Lausanne, which enjoys institutional recognition and plays a significant role in the university's operations, is organized around a statutory assembly composed half of representatives from student school associations and half of representatives supposed to speak on behalf of the federation as a whole. Until 2011, the latter were elected. Lists were drafted by the youth chapters of the various political parties on campus, and their debates were not aligned with those of the student school associations representatives, who were more likely to discuss the everyday problems of students than issues of partisan politics. In 2012, it was therefore decided that federation representatives would be randomly selected. Several variations were tried out, but the general principle remained that a lottery would be organized among students who voluntarily presented themselves. The first evaluations to emerge show that discussions within the federation have become more peaceful and more constructive, but the presence of less politically informed students simultaneously strengthens the influence of the bureau, composed of more politicized volunteers who henceforth have no true political counterweight within the federation.[41]

On a broader scale, in 1969 the French military welcomed the

Conseil Supérieur de la Fonction Militaire, whose delegates are randomly selected following quotas that correspond to the various military corps. The council was design to create a consultative body that allowed soldiers to express their requests while avoiding any kind of politicization or union activity, both of which are legally prohibited in France within the armed forces. Since then, the designation procedure has been modified numerous times. In 2015, it was based on a combination of random selection from a group of volunteers (first step), followed by an election within this group (second step). The Conseil Supérieur de la Fonction Militaire is viewed as highly legitimate within the French armed forces and is a powerful interlocutor for the minister—much more powerful than its police equivalent, elected from trade union lists. In this case, random selection has helped to forge a representative body, to level the playing field between representatives of different ranks, and to encourage discussions oriented toward the general well-being of soldiers. As the representatives do not enjoy any sort of individual legitimacy or power by virtue of being randomly selected, they tend to encourage a form of collective "legitimacy of humility" based on their impartiality and the quality of their deliberations.[42]

A number of other examples exist worldwide. In France, for example, since the middle of the 2010s, randomly selected citizens' councils are compulsory in the most disadvantaged neighborhoods, and Paris's youth council is also selected by lot. Both citizens' councils and Paris's youth council are advisory, but they are included in the law or at least official rules and are not mere one-shot events depending on the goodwill of the majority. However, in the absence of grassroots social movements that would push in favor of empowered minipublics and verify whether they are well organized (and whether their recommendations produce real changes in public policies), the impact of such institutionalized randomly selected bodies may still be reduced.

Random Selection in Party Politics

A last trend makes use of sortition in order to select new kinds of representatives, instead of a minipublic. A series of experiments have used random selection in order to select party candidates in the frame of competitive party elections. A first experiment, inspired by the procedure of the deliberative poll, took place in 2006 in Marousi, a medium-sized town in the suburbs of Athens. One hundred thirty-one randomly chosen local citizens voted for who should be the mayoral candidate of PASOK, a Greek social-ist party.[43] At the beginning of 2010, the local Metz chapter of the French Greens randomly selected its candidates for local and legislative elections.[44]

It is ultimately in Mexico that the most ambitious form of random selection has been used to choose candidates for an election. The procedure was intensely discussed for several years in academic circles but also in politics. It was then proposed by the Movimiento Regeneración Nacional (MORENA), the party of the former left-wing presidential candidate Manuel López Obrador and one of the opposition's main political organiza-tions.[45] MORENA decided to select two-thirds of its candidates for the legislative election on June 7, 2015, by using a combina-tion of election and lottery (the other third was reserved for external candidates who were not members of the party). In each electoral district, party supporters met in assemblies to elect ten individuals (five men and five women) from which the candidates were in turn selected using a giant lottery system. This experiment has already had a significant impact through-out Latin America's second-largest country, allowing outsiders who would never have been selected to become candidates and, in a number of cases, members of the new parliament. In July, 2018, Obrador was elected president, while MORENA, using the same system, won a majority of seats in both the parliament and the Senate.

This mix of sortition and elections recalls how a lot of elec-toral processes took place during the Middle Age and early modern period in Italian and other European communes and at the beginning of the nineteenth century in Mexico. Conversely, there is no historical precedent for another innovation that introduced random selection in order to select members of party assemblies or central committees. In Spain, regional sections of the left-wing parties Izquierda Unida and Podemos have also introduced sortition within their internal procedures. In Andalusia, Izquierda Unida has randomly selected 15 percent of the delegates of its 2017 assembly. In Valencia and Murcia, Podemos has randomly selected 17.5 percent of the members of its standing committee, and the procedure should be extended to Baleares and Aragon. In France, 25 percent of the central committee of République en Marche ("Republic get started"), the new French president Macron's political organization, were randomly selected among members in 2017. The radical left-wing political movement La France Insoumise also used sortition in order to select among the members the twelve hundred delegates to its 2017 national convention, while smaller parties randomly selected their legislative candidates or the members of their standing committees.

Selection by Lot as a Tool for Radical Democracy?

What are the main differences between the first and the second wave of experiments? A very serious challenge of randomly selected minipublics concerns the tension between their deliberation and the wider public sphere.[46] By definition, deliberative minipublics aim to reach a counterfactual opinion of what public opinion could be—they are better informed and enjoy a reasonably satisfactory setting in which to be formulated—that may well differ from wider popular opinion. Deliberation and participation may be presented as opposite models of democracy.[47] This must not be the case, but some trade-offs are inevitable.[48] A majority of deliberative minipublics of the first wave did not have much impact on the wider public sphere, and in the worst-case scenario, the democratic deliberation of a small circle of randomly selected citizens could replace a deliberative democracy including all citizens.[49] In such circumstances, deliberative minipublics could be implicated in a kind of elitism, at the antipodes of radical Athenian democracy. This deliberative elitism would argue that the implication of lay citizens in politics could only ever take place within the managed arena of minipublics, other forms of participation being suspected of contributing emotional and nonreasonable elements. The first wave of experiments was also top-down and consultative (and most often, they were only for one-shot experiments). This limited strongly their potential impact on social change. They have been successful in demonstrating the possibility of a reasonable deliberation among lay citizens— but they have not been efficacious in substantially changing the real lives of citizens. Given that their existence has stemmed solely from the willingness of public authorities, it was unlikely that they could really be subversive with regard to power structures and massive injustice.[50] Reasonable discussions in modest committees are not enough to impose positive change in a world where the structural resistance of dominant interests is enormous.

Had minipublics not entered the second wave, their legitimacy would have remained weak. We needed these bodies to become more than "just talk." This happened with the second wave, which has opened the door to more dynamical experiments. Because they have been characterized by hybridizations, the political imagination of practitioners has been liberated. Often, concrete experiments have not been pure examples of deliberative democracy, and deliberation has not been perfect, but a lot of them have been empowered. This is a major difference with the first wave. In addition, random selection has also been advocated within social movements such as 15-M in Spain, Syntagma Square in Greece, and Nuit Debout in France. There are now real grassroots movements that reclaim "real democracy now" and include in this perspective the reintroduction of random selection in politics and even legislature by lot. For many of activists who advocate the coming back of random selection in politics, such as Étienne Chouard in France or David

Van Reybrouck in Belgium, the legitimacy of this device has to do with some radical democratic quality it is supposed to have. In some cases, as in Mongolia, the sortition device has been institutionalized, and rulers now *have* to organize randomly selected minipublics. This could lead to major breakthroughs: in 2006, Ségolène Royal—who was to become the French Socialist Party candidate for the 2007 presidential elections—envisaged "popular scrutiny" of political leaders and a requirement that these should "regularly give an account of themselves to citizen juries selected by lot."[51] She lost the elections but had planned to revise the constitution and introduce sortition in case of success. Also important is the fact that sortition is no more a mere supplement to representative democracy. A number of experiments have coupled deliberative with direct or participatory democracy. It is also striking that random selection has been introduced within party politics in order to make it less elitist but has at the same time been proposed as a new path to democratization in authoritarian contexts: the well-known Chinese intellectual Wang Shaoguang, one of the most prominent figure of the "New Left," has advocated legislature by lot instead of Western-like elections in order to make China more democratic and its political system more representative.[52]

According to many of the supporters of these deliberative instruments, the return of sortition in politics, after centuries of eclipse, implies that some of the ideals of ancient democracies are coming back. James Fishkin, who invented the deliberative poll, describes it as a "neo-Athenian solution" and even argues that "the key infirmities in modern democracy can find a constructive response in modern refinements and improvements in the two essential components of the ancient Athenian solution—random sampling and deliberation."[53] I have argued that random sampling was a modern invention, unknown at the time of Pericles, and that the first wave of minipublics could seem at odds with radical democracy. However, relying on the second wave, and especially those cases of empowered experiments, it now seems possible to reclaim the radical democratic imaginary that was coupled with sortition in the Athenian democracy. Table 3 summarizes the main features of political sortition in Athens and in the two waves of contemporary experiments.

From Minipublics to Legislature by Lot

In Switzerland, starting in 2015, a group of activists called Génération Nomination has been preparing a citizen initiative that would propose to replace the lower chamber with a sortition chamber. Although it will probably not succeed, it shows that legislature by lot is not only a proposal from theoreticians. This was also manifest in France with Nuit Debout, when legislature by lot was considered as a natural and self-evident dimension of democracy. The invention of the welfare state in the nineteenth and twentieth centuries was the outcome of quite different actors: the revolutionary labor movement and statesmen such as the German chancellor Bismarck, churches who wanted more solidarity, and businessmen who wanted to sell their products to their workers. The return of random selection in politics could follow a similar path.

As grassroots NGOs and social movements make their voices heard, the perspective of transforming the political system and society becomes more credible, as organized citizens embedded in their social world are necessary to impose real democratic changes. They could encounter theoreticians interested in democratic theory, entrepreneurs or scientists disgusted with corruption and short-term political games, and politicians in search of a new profile. The ancients thought of mixed government as coupling the virtues of democracy, aristocracy, and monarchy. A sortition chamber could become part of a new kind of mixed government that would couple deliberative democracy with direct, participatory, and representative democracy. When linked to social, economic, and ecological changes, this new mix could be understood as part of a radical democratic turn. (For a summary, see table 3.)

Table 3. Comparing political sortition in Athens and in the two waves of contemporary experiments.

	Athens	First wave of experiments	Second wave of experiments
Main logic of the device	Everyone takes turns to govern and be governed	Counterfactual deliberative public opinion	Various: counter-factual delibera-tive public opin-ion, selection of political repre-sentatives, of juries with decision-making power, etc.
Model of democracy	Radical democracy	Deliberative democracy complementary to representative democracy	Deliberative democracy combined with representative, direct, participa-tory democracy
Institutions	Council, tribunal, magistrates	Minipublics	Minipublics, representatives
Where the initia-tive comes from	Not applicable	Top-down	Top-down and bottom-up
Relation to first inventors	Not applicable	Patented by the inventors	Hybridized by the practitioners
Institutional-ization	Full institutionaliza-tion	Quite limited or no institutionali-zation, the use of sortition depends on the arbitrari-ness of the public authority	Various. Complete institutionaliza-tion and compul-sory use of sorti-tion possible
Repetition in time	Permanent institutions	One-shot	Various. Repetition possible
Link to decision-making process	Binding	Consultative	Various: consulta-tive, binding, in between
Link to deliberation	Variable	Consubstantial	Consubstantial in minipublics, no link for the selec-tion of representatives
Link to the notion of repre-sentative sample	Inexistent	Consubstantial	Mostly consubstantial
Link to the ordi-nary social/politi-cal life	Consubstantial	Disembedded	Various

However, as contemporary schemes based on random selection rely on representative samples and not upon the self-rule of citizens, legislature by lot should have specific features that differ from Athenian democracy. Gordon Gibson, the creator of British Columbia's Citizens' Assembly and former councilor of the prime minister, justified the experiment in the following manner:

> We are ... adding new elements to both representative and direct democracy. These new elements differ in detail but all share one thing in common. They add to the mix a new set of representatives, different from those we elect ... The idea of deliberative democracy is essentially to import the public interest, as represented by random panels, as a muscular third force. The traditional representatives we elect are chosen by majority consensus, for an extended period, as professionals, with unlimited jurisdiction to act in our name. The new kinds we are talking about are chosen at random, for a short period, as lay citizens for specified and limited purposes.[54]

When widely used for a sortition chamber, in party politics and in social movements, sortition could be even more significant by coupling strong participatory elements to the deliberative ones. It should contribute to the pluralization of the forms of democratic legitimacy.[55] Focusing on a sortition chamber and drawing the lessons of the two waves of experiments, I will conclude by highlighting some of its key features.

Randomly selected bodies should be institutionalized: their organization cannot be left to the arbitrariness of rulers. These bodies should be empowered and have a real decision-making power—a counterfactual and merely consultative enlightened public opinion alone will not be able to really change the lives of citizens. There will not be one perfect model that could apply everywhere: democratic innovations are always hybridized and highly influenced by the context and path dependencies.

Legislature by lot empowers a random selection of the people and not the all citizenry; its concrete institutional design should take this crucial feature into account. First of all, experience shows that randomly selected minipublics work much better when they have to focus on a specific issue rather than on general topics. This is why a sortition chamber should take the form proposed by David Owen and Graham Smith in their chapter within this volume, "Sortition, Rotation, and Mandate." As the Athenian popular courts, the sortition chamber should be a popular body of six thousand citizens, and pools of members will be frequently randomly selected for participation in minipublics working on concrete issues. The six-thousand-citizen body would itself be rotated on a regular basis of one to a few years.

What would be the topics at stake? History shows that selection by lot has had a clear advantage over other forms of selection, including elections, when the imperative of impartiality is high (either because a conflict of interest is probable, such as in the case of an elected chamber reforming the electoral law, or because of massive trade-offs and complex modeling of dynamic systems, such as those involved in long-term environmental policies). In modern democracies, elected officials, experts, and organized interests have a strong tendency to defend particular interests. Conversely, legislature by lot will tend to recruit nonpartisan people without career interests to defend, encouraged by the deliberative procedural rules to reach a judgment tending toward the public interest. In addition, when both representative and direct democratic processes have difficulties representing the values at stake, legislature by lot is a good alternative. This is the case when it comes to dealing with the preservation of the ecosphere and living conditions for future generations. This is why a sortition chamber should have three main tasks: defining the rules of the political game; proposing solutions to highly controversial issues, such as lesbian and gay marriage or abortion in Ireland; and legislating for the long term.[56] In order to increase the legitimacy of its most important decisions, it is probable that they should be validated by referendums at large: the coupling of a sortition chamber and direct democracy that has been experimented with several times seems promising.

What would be the legitimacy of the sortition chamber? In addition to its impartiality, its democratic nature will be crucial. As Lyn Carson and Brian Martin put it, "The assumption behind random selection in politics is that just about anyone who wishes to be involved in decision-making is capable of making a useful contribution, and that the fairest way to ensure that everyone has such an opportunity is to give them an equal chance to be involved."[57] The deliberative quality of randomly selected minipublics focusing on specific issues is high and usually much better than that of elected chambers. Deliberation by lay citizens conducted in good conditions leads to reasonable results.

A representative sample or a fair cross-section of the people has epistemological advantages over representative government and committees of wise men: good deliberation must include diverse points of view, so that the range of arguments considered will be broader and discussion will be more inclusive.[58] Randomly selected minipublics have the advantage of being socially—and therefore epistemologically—richer than committees of experts or of political leaders but also than publics where participants come purely from volunteers or from already organized civil society. This input is important in a world of increasing complexity.

Last but not least, a specific kind of accountability will be developed in the sortition chamber. It is often claimed that the advantage of election compared to sortition is that elected politicians are accountable to their constituencies, when randomly selected citizens are not. In fact, this is far from evident, and not only because the real accountability of politicians is questionable. Sociological observation of contemporary minipublics clearly shows that citizens who have been randomly selected feel themselves to be strongly accountable. First, to the public authority that initiates the process. Second, to each other: a distinctive feature of the minipublics is that those who are perceived as speaking for particular interests rather than for the common good are quickly marginalized; either they rectify their behavior, which happens in most cases, or their voice does not count anymore. Third, citizens who take part in a minipublic feel accountable to the wider public that they represent. When dealing with the future of the ecosphere, a sortition chamber could bring a clear benefit compared to an elected one: when the latter feels accountable to its electors (and in some cases to the donors who finance the elections), the former would more easily be accountable to future generations, a group that does not exist yet.

It would be naive to think that politics will just continue as usual, with minor changes compared to the previous century. Given the size of the recent financial crisis, the increasingly dire impasse produced by the current production model, and the massive disrepute into which institutional politics has fallen, preserving the status quo is neither realistic nor adequate. Recent experiments show that legislature by lot could be part of a radical democratic renewal and a key element to make such a change sustainable in the long run.

4

Random Assemblies for Lawmaking: Prospects and Limits[1]

James S. Fishkin

After more than two decades of successful experimentation with deliberating microcosms or minipublics, it is natural to raise the question, how might they be institutionalized in the lawmaking process?[2] One key focus is the possibility of some sort of second chamber or legislative body. From the standpoint of deliberative democracy, a second chamber could provide an additional venue for deliberation about legislative proposals. This function might occur before or after the operation of the first chamber. The second chamber might have limited authority to delay a proposal for reconsideration, as in the British House of Lords, or it might be a coequal part of the legislative branch, such as the US Senate, with slightly different responsibilities in certain issue domains. Would it be useful to select the members of a second chamber by lot (random sampling) of the citizenry?

I will organize these reflections as follows:

1. I will argue for a deliberative body of randomly selected citizens as a supplement to our lawmaking process. This deliberative body might connect with the legislative process among elected representatives, or it might connect with an alternative

lawmaking process such as direct democracy. In either case, it could have an institutional role in the lawmaking process.

2. I will offer skeptical considerations. There are issues to be confronted about the challenges facing citizen deliberation, particularly for a second (or third) chamber that would meet on a continuing basis and look much like a legislature.

3. I will argue that instead of a full-fledged legislature selected by lot, there are advantages to deliberative convenings for a short period on the model of a deliberative poll. These convenings might better serve the desired functions for a second chamber, particularly if their role were institutionalized. I believe the short convenings would best respond to the objections in number 2 above while also delivering a deliberative input into lawmaking.

4. I will draw inspiration from institutions in ancient Athens, particularly in the fourth century BC, to suggest appropriate institutional designs. Some of these designs will precede the key lawmaking process, and some of them will follow it. I will refer to the former as *pre-filter* designs and the latter as *post-filter* designs. In either case, the deliberative body does not do the actual lawmaking, but rather it filters the agenda (in the pre-filter cases), or it provides final approval (in the post-filter cases).

5. I will sketch three scenarios, two of them pre-filter and one post-filter. These three scenarios do not begin to exhaust the range of institutional designs, but they illustrate what might be done.

Four Forms of Democracy: Finding a Place for Deliberative Lawmaking

There are many notions of democracy, but in my view they boil down to a few competing democratic principles and how they combine to form what we will call *four forms of democracy*, four conceptions of democratic practice. In actual institutional designs, none of these forms of democracy are self-sufficient. They coexist and connect with other institutions, usually exemplifying other forms of democratic practice (as well as other modes of decision-making, such as judicial decisions or administrative processes). But we will focus here on explicitly democratic elements and on how these four forms of democracy can work alone or in combination to provide a satisfactory picture of rule by the people. A focus on competitive democracy and its limits clarifies the question of how it might be supplemented—and what forms of democracy can be engaged to respond to its limitations.

There are so many kinds of democracy; how can we get a handle on their variety?³ It is useful to think of some core component principles—political equality, (mass) participation, deliberation, and avoiding tyranny of the majority (which I call non-tyranny). Three of these principles are internal to the design of democratic institutions, and one (non-tyranny) is about the effects of democratic decision, effects that have long worried critics of democracy. If we consider these four principles essential components of a democratic theory, then the variations in commitment to them provide a kind of rudimentary grammar that allows us to specify the range of alternative normative theories of democratic practice. In other words, we can get a handle on different forms of democracy according to whether or not they accept or reject these component principles. Table 4 shows that four prominent forms of democracy (described below) each commit to two of the principles just mentioned (indicated by a "+"), yet each remains agnostic to the other principles (as shown with a "?").

Table 4. A comparison of the democratic principles foregrounded by four forms of democracy.

	Form of democracy			
	Competitive	Elite	Participatory	Deliberative
Political equality	+	?	?	+
Participation	?	?	+	?
Deliberation	?	+	?	+
Non-tyranny	+	+	?	?

Note: "+" indicates commitment to a democratic principle, whereas "?" indicates a more agnostic stance.

By *political equality* I mean, roughly, the equal consideration of one's views as these would be counted in an index of voting power. Does the design of a decision process give each person a theoretically equal chance of being the decisive voter? Or, to take an obvious example, do voters in Rhode Island have far more voting power than voters in New York in selecting members of the Senate? By *participation* I mean actions by voters or ordinary citizens intended to influence politics or policy or to influence the dialogue about them. By *deliberation* I mean, roughly, the weighing of reasons under good conditions in shared discussion about what should be done. The good conditions specify access to reasonably good information and to balanced discussion with others who are willing to participate conscientiously. This summary is a simplification but should do for now. By *non-tyranny* I mean the avoidance of a policy that would impose severe deprivations when an alternative policy could have been chosen that would not have imposed severe deprivations on anyone.[4] Obviously there are many interesting complexities about the definition of severe deprivations, but the basic idea is that a democratic decision should not impose very severe losses on some when an alternative policy would not have imposed such losses on anyone. The idea is to rule out only some of the most egregious policy choices and leave the rest for democratic decision.

There are sixteen possible positions defined by acceptance or rejection of these four principles, but the useful models of democracy reduce to just four.[5] Variations that aspire to more than the four are either unworkable or merely utopian. Those that aspire to less include elements of one of these but are less ambitious than necessary. The rejection of all four would be an empty form of nondemocracy.

The four positions have all been influential. In some cases, I modify a familiar position to make it more defensible, in order to get the strongest version of each position. By *competitive democracy* I mean the notion of democracy embodying electoral competition in a context of constitutional guarantees for individual rights. Most influentially, this approach was championed by Joseph Schumpeter and more recently by Richard Posner and others.[6] This approach to democracy is in fact the one that is most widely accepted around the world.

In this view, democracy is not about collective will formation but just a "competitive struggle for the people's vote," to use Schumpeter's famous phrase. Legal guarantees, particularly constitutional ones, are designed to protect against tyranny of the majority. Within that constraint, the key desideratum is competitive elections. In Schumpeter's view, it is a mythology left over from ill-defined "classical theories" of democracy to expect the will of the people to be meaningful. Electoral competition—*without* any constraints on whether candidates or parties can mislead or bamboozle the voters to win—is what matters, in this view.

Of course, any developed view of competitive democracy would require a specification of the people whose views are to be considered equally. Robert Dahl rightly criticized Schumpeter for leaving this unspecified.[7] Modern democratic norms embrace the franchise for the full adult citizen population with only minor exceptions.[8]

Schumpeter argues that we should not expect a "genuine" public will, but rather "a manufactured will": "The will of the people is the product and not the motive power of the political process." Further, "the ways in which issues and the popular will are being manufactured is exactly analogous to the ways of commercial advertising." In fact, he believes that competing parties and interest groups have "infinitely more scope" on public issues than in commercial competition to manufacture the opinions they hope to satisfy.[9] Competitive democracy, at least on Schumpeterian terms, sees little likelihood and little need for deliberation by the people.

However, the model of competitive democracy, particularly when the role of constitutional protections for individual rights is foregrounded, provides some guarantees against tyranny of the majority. That is why our chart carries a + not only for political equality in elections but also for non-tyranny, at least as an aspiration.[10]

Turning to the second column in the chart, by *elite deliberation* I mean the notion of indirect filtration championed by

Madison in his design for the US Constitution. The constitutional convention, the ratifying conventions, and the US Senate were all supposed to be small elite bodies that would consider the competing arguments. They would "refine and enlarge the public views by passing them through the medium of a chosen body of citizens," as Madison said in Federalist 10 when discussing the role of representatives. Madison held that the public views of such a deliberative body "might better serve justice and the public good than would the views of the people themselves if convened for the purpose." This position, like the last one, avoids embracing mass participation as a value. The passions or interests that might motivate factions are best left unaroused. The founders, after all, had lived through Shays' Rebellion and had an image of unfiltered mass opinion as dangerous. If only the Athenians had had a Senate, they might not have killed Socrates.[11]

If modern legislatures functioned like Madison's vision of the Senate, there would be far less of a case for new institutions to bring citizen deliberation into lawmaking. The representatives would deliberate on behalf of the people. There would not be a deliberative deficit at the legislative level to respond to. But the emergence of political parties, direct election of the Senate, and party discipline in legislatures, not only in the US but around the world, has greatly limited the opportunities for deliberation by representatives. They are constrained to follow the party whips, and only in acts of political courage or when there are explicitly open or free votes of conscience do they get to follow their deliberative preferences rather than the party line. Hence I mention elite deliberation as a theoretical alternative but one unlikely to be realized much in practice by elected representatives. Who would currently call the US Senate "the world's greatest deliberative body"? It is an idea much invoked in theory but rarely followed in practice.

By *participatory democracy* I mean an emphasis on mass participation combined with equal counting. While many proponents of participatory democracy would also like deliberation, the essential components of the position require participation, perhaps prized partly for its educative function (as Carole Patemen argued[12]) and equality in considering the views offered or expressed in that participation (even if that expression is by secret ballot). Advocates of participatory democracy might also advocate voter handbooks, as did the Progressives, or perhaps new technology for voter information,[13] but the foremost priority is that people should participate, whether or not they become informed or discuss the issues.[14]

A fourth position, which I call *deliberative democracy*, attempts to combine deliberation by the people themselves with an equal consideration of the views that result. One method for implementing this twofold aspiration is the deliberative microcosm chosen by lot, a model whose essential idea goes back to ancient Athens for institutions such as the Council of Five Hundred, the *nomothetai* (legislative commissions), the *graphe paranomon*, and the citizens' jury. Modern instances of something like this idea include the citizens' assemblies in British Columbia and Ontario and the deliberative poll. A second possible method for implementing deliberative democracy by the people themselves would involve some scaled-up institution of mass deliberation. Bruce Ackerman and I have discussed such designs in *Deliberation Day*.[15]

These four forms of democracy highlight the limited possibilities currently available for deliberative lawmaking. Competitive democracy does not incentivize deliberation. Candidates do not wish to win the argument on the merits as much as they wish to win the election. If they can do so by distorting or manipulating the argument successfully, many of them are likely to do so. Representatives elected through such processes are looking ahead to the next election while in office. They have only occasional opportunities to deliberate on the merits because of party discipline. Participatory democracy, at least at the scale of ballot propositions, is no more deliberative than party competition-based mass politics. And the fourth model, deliberative democracy by the people themselves, lacks an institutional home for any connection to lawmaking. The lack of deliberation in our current institutions of competitive, representative, and participatory democracy provides an opening for arguments that might institutionalize deliberation by the people themselves in a lawmaking process.

Legislature By Lot: Some Skeptical Considerations

Yet there are reasons for skepticism that the lack of deliberation in our current forms of democracy can be remedied by a full-scale legislature chosen by lot. I present three challenges.

Technical Expertise

The modern legislative process involves numerous technical questions. It is highly complex. Legislators who are unprepared are left in the hands of staff and lobbyists. The whole history of term limits has demonstrated that instead of creating effective waves of citizen legislators, it has created waves of legislators who are more dependent on staff and more vulnerable to lobbying.[16] Random selection would greatly exacerbate these problems if it were to constitute a full-function, full-time legislature.

On the other hand, our experience with deliberative polling amply demonstrates the competence of random samples in an organized setting to weigh trade-offs and make reasoned choices to set priorities among competing, value-laden options. Other minipublics also report considerable success at stimulating citizen deliberation for this kind of task. This function should be incorporated into new lawmaking designs. But the full operation of a legislature requires engagement with many technical questions, far more complex than weighing such trade-offs and setting priorities. I will refer to the function amply demonstrated in deliberative polls as *priority setting*. Priority setting is at the heart of determining support or opposition to a piece of legislation. But it is only one component in the functions required to create new legislation from scratch.

It might be argued that the Citizens' Assembly in British Columbia produced a ballot proposition in appropriate, modern legal language as a result of extensive deliberation. But this process of producing a single piece of legislation from scratch took a whole year of deliberation.[17] A fully functional modern legislature would be expected to produce and deliberate about many pieces of legislation in a comparable period.

Corruption

With a full-function, full-time legislature, the period of vulnerability to corruption is greatly extended as compared to our experience with minipublics convened for a weekend. In a deliberative poll, there is a highly structured set of activities for the weekend, and the names and identities of the deliberators are generally not made available. But over a multiyear period of legislation, all the deliberators would become public figures. If the decisions were consequential ones, with great interests at stake, there is a serious risk that efforts to bribe or promise later employment to members of the sample would distort the deliberations. We have never actually encountered this problem in any of the deliberative polls, now held in twenty-seven countries. But only a subset of the deliberative polls have been part of government decision processes. And the identities of most or all the participants have not been publicly available beforehand. As the decisions of the random sample become more consequential and the public identities of the deliberators become more available, and as the duration of their time in office increases to a year or two, the challenge of protecting the process from corruption increases dramatically.

Maintaining the Conditions for Deliberation

Deliberating microcosms such as the deliberative poll, which convene a sample for the weekend, are carefully organized to enable citizen deliberators to weigh competing arguments, have access to competing experts, engage in mutually respectful and moderated small-group discussions, and carefully work through an agenda of choices, ensuring that the pros and cons of each choice have gotten a hearing. The process produces relatively equal discussion, promotes reasoned choices, and avoids distortions, such as domination by the more advantaged or polarization in Cass Sunstein's sense of increasing extremity. There is considerable evidence that the participants arrive at their conclusions based on the merits of the argument rather than on some distorting pattern of small-group psychology.[18]

If the roles and behaviors of randomly selected full-time legislators were anything like the ones we are familiar with for legislators in modern society, then there would be a host of behaviors outside any such deliberative structure. There would be many individual meetings, caucuses, and meetings with lobbyists, staff, constituents, and so forth. Individual representatives might deliberate or they might not. But we have no institutional design to reliably predict that they would. The deliberation-enabling structure that we know works for a weekend's task of priority setting with ordinary citizens would not be maintained for the much broader range of activities we can expect in a legislature. Without a structure, we have no way of knowing how much they would deliberate on the merits rather than simply bargain or build coalitions. Of course, there is a deliberative element in such activities. But it is not deliberation that answers to the key hypothetical, which would be the point of inserting deliberation into the legislative process.

The key hypothetical is, what would the people think under good conditions for contemplating the issue in question? That is a disarmingly simple idea, but it requires both external validity in the representativeness of the sample in attitudes and demographics and internal validity for the causal inference that some version of "good conditions" is producing the resulting opinions or considered judgments about what is to be done. That representation of what deliberative opinion on a topic is, or would be, can provide an input to legislative priority setting. The aggregation of all the individual deliberative opinions on a given issue can be taken as a recommendation for the appropriate direction for collective self-rule. Many individual side bargains and coalition activities, all part of normal legislation, would not amount to any kind of coherent answer to this simple but basic hypo-thetical question.

I would not claim that the precise deliberative poll design is the only way of providing an answer to this key hypothetical ques-tion. I am sure that as technology and innovation advance, there will be many credible ways of doing so. But my point is that the key hypothetical is what needs to be inserted into the policy process and indeed the lawmaking process for the deliberations of the people to contribute to collective self-rule. Sometimes, as in an Ackermanian constitutional moment, the hypothetical might be the same as what actually emerges from national public engage-ment. But such situations are admittedly rare. For lawmaking amid normal politics, it would be immensely useful if there were a deliberative input showing the considered judgments of the public about what needs to be done. That input can have an effect on an advisory basis or just as a media project sponsored by civil society. But here we are considering a further step, one that has been taken on occasion for deliberative polls (for example, in Texas, Japan, Macau, Greece, and Mongolia) of incorporating the poll as an official input into government decision.[19] All of these cases involve short-term convenings of a sample from the relevant population. None of them involve a full-function, full-time legislature.

These skeptical arguments are not necessarily dispositive. One might argue, for example, that the Council of Five Hundred, an Athenian institution I invoke in the next section, was *not* a brief convening and functioned well with great responsibili-ties.[20] It met for a full year. However, it was nothing like a full-function, full-time legislature. Its only role in the legislative process was agenda setting. And it had many other administra-tive functions and alternated responsibilities among groups of fifty on a rotating basis. It also drew on a citizenry that was constantly rotating in and out of public responsibilities, provid-ing considerable preparation. So it seems a slim basis for prece-dent that a modern random sample of the citizenry as we know it could function equally well as a full-function, full-time legis-lature. But here we are pushing historical analogies too far. Perhaps an appropriate modern analogue could be developed and tested at some point. In the meantime, the Athenian case offers ample inspiration for reflecting on democratic possibilities. Let us turn to its design now in more detail.

Athenian Reflections

Hence our focus is on how the more limited task of deliberative priority setting might be institutionalized in a legislative process. Consider the Athenian system as it developed in fourth-century Athens. It suggests various roles that randomly selected deliberators could serve in an actual lawmaking process. While the scale and context are utterly different from modern nation-states, some of the insights suggested by their rich institutional innovations may well be applicable.

The "first democracy" in ancient Athens is often pictured primarily in terms of the assembly where the people made authoritative decisions.[21] In sight of the Acropolis, about six thousand citizens could fit in an area called the Pnyx, discuss proposed laws, and vote on them by show of hands in the assembly. However, the citizenry of Athens ranged between thirty thousand and sixty thousand males during the periods of democracy. Women, slaves, and *metics* (legal resident aliens such as Aristotle) could not vote. Hence most of the population—indeed, most of the eligible citizenry—could not vote at any given meeting of the assembly. Nevertheless, this first democracy set an example for direct rule that has reverberated through the ages.

However, after the disasters of the Peloponnesian War with Sparta, the Athenians briefly lost their democracy. When they managed to reinstate it (in 401–2 BC), they devised a number of reforms that emphasized what we call deliberative democracy. Some of these institutions claimed earlier vintage, but they were put together in a systematic way with the reforms. It is the redesigned Athenian democracy of the fourth century that we want to examine to get a glimpse of deliberative democracy institutionalized.

Mogens Herman Hansen sees a clear motive for the redesign: "The tendency of the reforms is clear: the Athenians wanted to obviate a return to the political crises and military catastrophes of the Peloponnesian War."[22] The orators could goad the assembly into hasty or unwise actions, including disastrous wars. The Athenians had learned that "a skillful demagogue could win the citizens to his project irrespective of whether it was really in their interest."[23]

In the new system, a decree passed by the assembly could not become a law unless it was approved by the *nomothetai*, a randomly selected sample of five hundred or more citizens who would deliberate for a day, hearing the arguments for and against the proposal. Only if the proposal got majority support by this body could it become a law. A. R. W. Harrison suggests that they had "deliberately invented a perfectly democratic brake to slow down the machine." It was designed to maintain "the restored order against the possible ill effects of snap votes in the ekklesia" (the assembly).[24] "A perfectly democratic brake" suggests that instead of restricting their democracy, they had introduced another kind of democratic institution, one that was also democratic but in a different way.

The system now had deliberating microcosms chosen by lot before the assembly, during the assembly, and after the assembly. Before the assembly, only proposals approved by the randomly selected Council of Five Hundred could be considered in the assembly. During the assembly, orators had to be mindful that they were subject to a special court, the *graphe paranomon*, which could prosecute an illegal or unwise proposal made in the assembly. The purview of this special court, which also had five hundred or more randomly selected members, was broad (and sometimes misused).[25] But the intention was clearly to provide incentives against irresponsible demagogues turning the assembly to their will. After the assembly, there was now a clear distinction between mere decrees, which the assembly could pass, and laws, which had to be approved by the *nomothetai*.[26] This provided a multistage process hemmed in before, during, and after the meetings of the assembly, so that the direct democracy was fused with deliberative institutions representing all the people through random sampling.

As George Grote, the noted historian of ancient Greece from Victorian times, concluded, "There can be no doubt that the Nomothetae afforded much greater security than the public assembly for a proper decision." The revised system "hedged about the making, annulling, or amending of nomoi (laws) with an elaborate process in which the nomothetai played an important role."[27]

The reforms were designed to "hedge about" the assembly with deliberative groups chosen randomly who could ensure more responsible decisions. The samples were not precisely what modern experts would call random samples, but they seem to have been regarded as such.[28] People had to put themselves on the list from which the random sample would be drawn. But the sense of public duty was widespread among those privileged enough to be male citizens, presumably motivating participation. Participation in all aspects of Athenian self-governance was extraordinary.[29] And the sampling process was taken seriously. In earlier times, the method was to draw beans from a container.[30] The Athenians perfected the process with an allotment machine, the *kleroterion*, which yielded random samples of those who put themselves on the list. The sampling was conducted in public ceremonies. Some argue that random sampling was an embodiment of equality. Some argue that it was a guarantee against corruption and a method of dispute resolution. Both rationales are relevant for our purposes.

There were no property qualifications for serving in the assembly or in the courts and the various randomly selected institutions. There was, however, an age requirement of at least thirty years for the Council of Five Hundred and the *nomothetai*. Some have thought this was an effort to get more sober judgment in these institutions. Still, on balance the whole process was remarkably democratic— within the limitations of who was considered a citizen.

In viewing the system as a whole, there was also another key point: rotation. There were so many opportunities to be selected randomly and so many meetings of the assembly that people could take turns "to rule and be ruled," as Aristotle noted in the *Politics*.[31] Hansen calculates that "something like every third citizen served at least once as a member of the Council" and three quarters of all members had to serve as the rotating head of government for a day. "Simple calculation leads to this astounding result: Every fourth adult male Athenian citizen could say, 'I have been twenty-four hours President of Athens.'"[32]

Fourth-century Athens did not rely entirely on deliberative democracy any more than fifth-century Athens before it had relied entirely on direct democracy. The reformed design was clearly a mixed system still with a very prominent element of direct democracy. But this system gives the first sustained picture of deliberation playing a key role in popular control of the laws. The people deliberated, they had impact, they made choices. The Athenian system has often been dismissed, like the democracy of the modern town meeting, as something only suitable for the small scale. But that limit is most clearly posed by the assembly. There are only so many thousand people who can gather together in a face-to-face meeting. But the deliberative elements of Athenian democracy do not face the same limitation. The random samples that deliberated could, in theory, scale to much larger populations. We now know from modern statistics that one does not need a larger sample to accurately represent a larger population. The statistical precision with which a random sample can represent a population varies primarily with the size of the sample, not the size of the population. Hence these deliberating microcosms can be applied with credibility to much larger populations than the Athenian demos. The rotation aspect is also in principle replicable, but it would take a design offering numerous opportunities at various levels of government. One might imagine local, state, and national deliberations occurring frequently as inputs to government for various kinds of issues. But that takes us beyond our topic here.

Modern Adaptations: Three Scenarios

Consider three patterns: the deliberating microcosm preceding legislative decision, the microcosm following legislative decision, or the microcosm preceding participatory democracy (via ballot propositions) to set an agenda. We can picture these three as:

Deliberating microcosm ⟶ Representative democracy
Representative democracy ⟶ Deliberating microcosm
Deliberating microcosm ⟶ Participatory democracy (ballot propositions)

Pre-Filter: Mongolia

It is worth examining a modern instance of the pre-filter to fix ideas. It is institutionalized now in Mongolia, a competitive democracy with a private property market system. It is a democratic system with both the advantages and the ills now all too common in other competitive democracies (hyperpolarization between the parties, issues of corruption, a dialogue often distorted by social media, and so forth).

In February 2017, Mongolia passed legislation requiring "deliberative polling" *before* a constitutional amendment could be considered by the legislature. To prepare for its first implementation, a cross-party committee in the legislature advised by two other committees that had conducted public consultations and done research on the need for amendments came up with a bipartisan agenda of possible proposals affecting the legislature, the role of the president, the powers of the prime minister, and the issue of protecting the civil service and the judiciary from politics. These topics yielded eighteen specific proposals, some supported by members from one of the two major parties, some supported by members from the other. On April 28–30, 2017, a national random sample was convened in the government palace in the capital city of Ulaanbaatar. The National Statistical Office, the same government agency that conducts the census, recruited an excellent stratified random sample: 1,568 households were randomly selected with participants randomly selected within the households; 96 percent of the people selected completed the initial interview; half of those interviewed were randomly selected to be invited; and out of the 785 who were invited, 669 came and completed the two full days of deliberation. All expenses were paid by the government, but no honorariums were offered. Our analyses show that the sample was highly representative of the citizenry, both in attitudes and demographics.

The Deliberative Poll included eighteen questions about specific aspects of the proposals. Responses to ten of those eighteen questions changed significantly between the pre-deliberation survey and the final survey taken afterward. It is worth discussing both the significant changes and the proposals that rated most highly at the end, regardless of change. The highest rated proposals withstood all the criticisms and still came out at the top of the list.

Support for two of the most ambitious proposals dropped dramatically with deliberation. The proposal for a second chamber based on the model of the 1990 constitution, a proposal with strong support in some opinion polls, dropped dramatically. "Creating a Parliament with two chambers: a people's representative body (People's Great Khural) and legislative body (State Baga Khural)" went from 63 percent to 32 percent, a drop of 31 points. With deliberation, the public became more skeptical that "a second chamber would provide effective oversight of the lower house of Parliament." Agreement with this idea dropped from 72 percent to 41 percent. More specifically, there was increased agreement with the criticism that "both chambers would be controlled by the same political parties, thereby not providing proper oversight." Those agreeing with this proposition rose from 43 percent to 59 percent. Lastly, there was a significant increase from 53 percent to 58 percent in those who agreed that "adding a second chamber would create too many politicians."

A second major drop in support occurred with the proposal for an indirectly (rather than directly) elected president for only a single six-year term. There were two components to this proposal, the change in the term and the indirect election. Support for "Electing the President for a single six-year term, without reelection" dropped from 61.5 percent to 41 percent with deliberation. Support for "Electing the president for a single six-year term by an expanded plenary session of the Parliament that includes Parliament members and the Citizen's Representative Councils of aimags and the capital city" started at 40 percent and ended at 34 percent (not a significant drop, but showing a low level of support after deliberation). There was a significant drop in support for one of the arguments in favor of indirect election: "If the President is indirectly elected by the Parliament and the Citizens Representative Councils, then he/she will be someone acceptable to all sides and above political fray." Agreement with this conclusion dropped from 61.5 percent to 41 percent. On the other hand, there was strong agreement before and after with one of the key arguments in favor of direct rather than indirect election: "If the President is directly elected s/he can better speak for the interests of all people" (85 percent before, 80 percent afterward, no significant change).

By contrast, the deliberators supported an amendment that would increase the power of the prime minister: "Granting the Prime Minister the authority to appoint and dismiss the members of his/her Cabinet." This proposal increased significantly from 62 percent to 73 percent. Deliberators agreed that "If the Prime Minister cannot even appoint the members of his/her own Cabinet then s/he lacks the authority to get anything done." Seventy-two percent agreed before and 67 percent agreed afterward (not a significant drop).

After all the arguments for and against, it is worth noting that nine of the top ten proposals were directed at protecting the civil service and judiciary from political interference or corruption. These were clearly the public's highest priorities after deliberation. The concerns from the ruling party that the president needed to be indirectly elected and from many members of the main opposition party that there was a need for a second chamber were rated much lower.

The results of the deliberative poll served as an effective filter on the proposals that the parliament can take seriously in formulating its amendment. The deliberative poll did not generate proposals from scratch. Rather, it filtered the proposals put forward by the competing parties and allowed the public's deliberations to judge which ones deserved to go forward. Before the law on deliberative polling, the parliament would have had the power to pass an amendment by two-thirds or the power to put an amendment proposal to referendum. At the moment, the majority party has more than a two-thirds majority. Now the deliberations of the people in microcosm serve as an effective filter on what they will consider.[33] This experience so far argues for the viability of the pre-filter legislative model for a limited purview of issues, such as constitutional change.

Post-Filter: Return of the Nomothetai?

Let's return to the Athenian examples. We can imagine modern applications of the *nomothetai* idea in the context of the current debate about second chambers selected by lot.[34] Just as the ancient *nomothetai*, selected by lot, had the role of providing a "perfectly democratic brake" on the decisions in the assembly, a modern minipublic selected by lot could provide a brake on decisions in the parliament or lower house of a modern nation-state. I am not thinking of a fully developed second chamber by lot. Rather, imagine a role parallel to that of the *nomothetai*, convened briefly to pass judgment on a specific proposed law with the case for and against the proposal deliberated for a weekend on something like the deliberative poll model. But which laws? It would not seem practical to convene a new minipublic for every law.

Imagine the challenge if such an institution were inserted into the last stage of decision for a new law in a modern constitutional democracy with competing parties. Suppose there was a requirement that the final decision go to the minipublic for any law that does not pass by two-thirds in the parliament. If there is merely a majority but not a supermajority, then the people, convened in microcosm, have the final say. But if there is a supermajority in the parliament, then there is no triggering of the requirement to convene the people. This design would arguably create real incentives for even highly polarized parties to work together. It would also provide a barrier to turbocharged bare majorities that wish to ram though a proposal without any regard to the other side or sides. Placing the deliberations of the people in this position in a deliberative system might provide strong incentives for overcoming polarization among the elites, and it would motivate elite deliberation across the aisle in the parliament. We can picture it thus:

Parliament (if 2/3 support) ⟶ *passage of legislation*
   Parliament (if majority
support but less than 2/3) ⟶ *minipublic for final decision*

Perhaps for efficiency, the minipublic could be convened when there are multiple bills to be considered. The identities of the random sample should not be announced beforehand to protect against bribery or lobbying of ordinary citizens.

Such a design might incentivize the parties to work together, limiting the current extreme polarization characteristic among representatives in so many other countries. It would also perform as a "brake" on unwise proposals, allowing the people, as in ancient Athens, to stop proposals in the final stage. A positive vote is required, allowing the people in effect a veto on objectionable new laws.

Once again, the idea is brief convenings under specified conditions, not a standing body. A standing body would trigger the concerns mentioned earlier about corruption, lack of structure, and the need for broad-based expertise. Note that by imagining the *nomothetai* role served by a deliberative poll design, we add the element of small-group discussion. The ancient legislative commissions of five hundred or more heard the arguments in an amphitheater. Modern investigations demonstrate that much of the deliberative opinion change comes from the discussion.[35]

Pre-Filter: Deliberative Agenda Setting for Ballot Propositions

In 2011, a statewide deliberative poll in California was convened to consider governmental reforms in the initiative system, the structure of the legislature, taxation and budgeting, and other

issues. A highly representative statewide sample of 412 deliberators gathered for a long weekend in Torrance, California, and
produced results on proposals in all these areas. Some of the
initiative reform proposals fed into the deliberations of an initiative reform effort and have become law after having been adopted
by the legislature.[36] But the underlying motivation for the project
was to pilot a bigger idea. That pilot was only partly successful.
The idea was that a deliberating microcosm of the public could
be periodically convened to propose public-interest initiatives
that could go on the ballot. In fact, a proposition loosely connected
with the deliberations, Proposition 31, did go on the ballot. But it
included additional provisions—supported by well-meaning
public-interest organizations—that attracted opposition, and
Proposition 31 was defeated. We showed that there would have
been stronger and perhaps successful support for the elements in
the proposition that corresponded to the results from the deliberative poll. This experience suggests a possible institution that
could be adapted for lawmaking by the people.

Consider the California deliberative poll (What's Next
California, or WNC) as a pilot for an institution that could
empower the public to help set the agenda for the initiative.
How would it work? Several problems have to be solved. It has
to be nonpartisan and scientifically credible yet also connected
enough to the political fray that the selected proposals have
actual proponents to advocate them to the electorate at election
time. It needs to live up to the same sorts of criteria that we have
used to evaluate WNC and other deliberative polls. It needs to
be representative of voters in both attitudes and demographics.
It needs to be large enough in scale that its claims to representativeness and its results are meaningful statistically. If there are
briefing materials or sources of information for the deliberations, they need to be balanced, and deliberators must be given
an appropriate opportunity to interact and seek further information. And lastly, the proposal or proposals selected in the
deliberative process have to be followed up with something on
the ballot appropriately connected to the deliberations and
advocated at election time. Voters around the state should have

an opportunity to consider the same reasoning that led the microcosm to support the proposal.

To fix ideas, imagine this scenario. A random sample of voters, about the size of WNC, is convened every two years to consider possible proposals to go on the ballot. Where do these proposals come from? Groups that wish to be proponents of initiatives develop proposals and satisfy a low threshold of signatures, low enough that civic groups could satisfy them with reasonable effort but without necessitating paid signature gathering. The reason for the (low, rather than onerous) signature threshold is that there has to be some way of distinguishing serious from frivolous proposals. If a proposal is selected by the microcosm, it then qualifies without the burden of the full signature collection. Saving the expense of most of the signature collection is an incentive for groups to submit their proposals to this process. A second incentive is that they can identify their proposal as endorsed by a representative and informed microcosm of the people. Once voters become familiar with the process, such an endorsement could be very valuable. We know that a prime question voters ask about any initiative is, who supports it and why?[37] Endorsements are a key heuristic or informational shortcut influencing support or opposition to ballot propositions.[38] In this case, the answer is that a proposal got on the ballot partly because a random sample of the people thought it was a good idea after they thought about it in depth. As that idea catches on, so that less of the history needs explaining, it is likely to become more effective and valuable as a property of referendum campaigns, increasing the incentives for groups that could act as proponents to seek the thoughtful and representative endorsement of the people.

We can imagine that the entire process would be supervised by a nonpartisan commission or advisory group. Several key functions would need to be fulfilled. The briefing materials for and against each proposal would need to be scrutinized for balance and accuracy. Perhaps proponents could provide the case in favor and potential opponents the case against, but all have to pass scrutiny from a balanced advisory committee appointed by the commission to have final say on the briefing materials. When there are contested facts, the competing versions are included in a balanced format. Perhaps proponents and opponents would each have a right to reply. If there are no opponents, then some could be appointed to serve that role for this preparatory stage. At the deliberations, there would be a list of experts who could respond to questions in the plenary sessions, and these again would be scrutinized by the advisory committee. These are all functions that have been accomplished in past deliberative polls, even on highly controversial issues.

How could the design ensure a connection between the people's deliberations and what goes on the ballot? The people would deliberate in choosing between developed proposals. We might imagine a small window for the proponents to improve their proposals in light of the deliberations with the opportunity for a follow-up confirming vote from the microcosm if the proposal changed. There are two aims at this stage—identify the preferred proposals and get the best version of them in light of the deliberations. Obviously, there are many variations and details, but this scenario sketches an approach that builds directly on the What's Next California pilot.

We can imagine such a process as an alternative route to the ballot, not the sole route. The idea would be to provide a supply of at least some public-interest propositions that the people would find meaningful. If such a design proved successful, it could be expanded. Perhaps it might begin with the selection of one proposal each cycle. Then the number could be increased, and perhaps more than one microcosm could be convened if the number of proposals became large. Given the extraordinary expenditures on campaigning for proposals once on the ballot, it seems appropriate to imagine relatively modest expenditures for the crucial agenda-setting process. Like Oregon's Citizens' Initiative Review process, it might even begin with foundation funding and only then move to government funding after a track record of successful implementation.

What's Next California showed that it is practical to convene a microcosm of the state's voters to consider propositions in a balanced and thoughtful way. The microcosm satisfied our expectations: it was representative in attitudes and demographics, it gained knowledge, it evaluated a number of proposals, and it produced many significant changes on the basis of identifiable reasons. Some of its conclusions even fed into the legislative and the initiative process. It showed that a deliberating microcosm could provide a possible institutional design for setting the agenda for initiatives.

The initiative process is supposed to be the people's process. But the agenda-setting function has been captured by those who can afford it. Why not recapture it for the people, using this ancient device? The key would be institutionalization and follow-up, not only to put the people's choice before the entire electorate but also to make the reasoning available as a basis for choice. That would add a truly deliberative element to mass direct democracy and fulfill many of the initial aspirations of the initiative to empower the people to engage in thoughtful self–government.

Conclusion

In all three scenarios a deliberative-poll-like process offers a brief convening for the limited role of priority setting—for possible constitutional amendments, for final approval of legislation, or for agenda setting for ballot measures. These roles and entry points for deliberation hardly exhaust the possibilities. But already, they illustrate the many possibilities for officially incorporating the conclusions of a deliberating microcosm in the lawmaking process.

I am not advocating the position that every deliberative input should be conducted via deliberative polling. As noted earlier, I am sure that with the development of technology and innovative experimentation, we will find even better models. However, the deliberative poll satisfies some basic design features that I believe should be satisfied if we are to have confidence in the key hypothetical inference: *This is what the people would think about the issue under good conditions for thinking about it.*

Below is a list of considerations. Other decision processes can also be constructed to satisfy them.

1. There should be credible random sampling with attention to both attitudinal and demographic representativeness. If the microcosm is unrepresentative in either respect, then that could easily distort the deliberations, as some views or interests will not be represented. Hence it is all the more important that initial data be collected to ensure that it is possible to evaluate the representativeness of the sample.[39]

2. The size of the sample of deliberators needs to be large enough so that statistically meaningful analyses can be conducted not only of their representativeness but also of any opinion changes. Hence the need for data collection at the individual level both before and after deliberation.

3. The agenda and basis for deliberation need to be balanced and transparent. An advisory group is very useful as a source of public assurance. The deliberative poll usually has initial arguments in favor and against each and every proposal listed in tabular form for easy reference. But there are many techniques to ensure both the balance and accuracy of the arguments and information in the deliberations as well as many different techniques for how the information can be presented.

4. Any informational background materials need to be accessible to ordinary citizens, whether the materials are in written or video form.

5. Access to competing experts to answer questions can be immensely useful. This aspect was employed in the British Columbia Citizens' Assembly as well as in the deliberative poll. In any ongoing deliberation, new questions will arise. They cannot all be anticipated. Having balanced experts facilitates engagement with the competing sides of an argument.

6. Moderated small-group discussions facilitate relatively equal participation. In our view, moderators should be trained never to offer opinions or provide information but rather only to facilitate civil discussion.

7. Collection of qualitative as well as quantitative data to

provide information on the reasons that weigh with the sample in coming to its conclusions is critical. Transcripts of small-group discussion can be analyzed systematically. Other techniques could be used, such as formulation of agreed statements after the individual-level data is collected.

8. Also necessary are analyses of the small groups to ensure that they are not subject to systematic patterns of distortion, such as small-group polarization or domination by the more advantaged. Such distortions would cast doubt on whether it is "the force of the better argument" that is determining the conclusions, rather than social coercion within the groups.

These are only some of the key components that have served deliberative polling in its claim to provide good conditions for a random sample to deliberate. Perhaps one or another can be dropped or modified after study in further controlled experiments. Or perhaps simulations in virtual reality (or some other new technology) can provide an entirely different method for a population to deliberate—to weigh the competing arguments and come to considered judgments. The future is more inventive than we can imagine. But we know already that the aim of deliberating with random samples is practical for convenings long enough to perform certain essential political functions in a lawmaking process. I urge the continuation of such experimentation and dialogue.

In my view, some of the key functions of a second chamber could be successfully performed by randomly selected microcosms in brief convenings. Perhaps my list of challenges to full-time, full-function legislatures by random selection can eventually be overcome with the right design and experimentation. But that is an unsettled question. In the meantime, we have ample basis for credibly advocating the insertion of random assemblies in brief convenings to accomplish priority setting in a lawmaking process.

5

Lessons from a Hybrid Sortition Chamber: The 2012–14 Irish Constitutional Convention

Tom Arnold, David M. Farrell, and Jane Suiter[1]

Ireland's 1937 constitution is one of the most enduring in Europe. It is also one of the very few constitutions to have been changed through a process that began with a mixed sortition chamber.[2] This chapter discusses the operation, outputs, and outcomes of the 2012–14 Irish Constitutional Convention, a unique minipublic that seated randomly selected citizens alongside public officials.[3] This process resulted in a referendum to guarantee marriage equality in Ireland, thus making it the first country to do so through a public vote.

In this chapter, we focus on the uniqueness of the Irish Constitutional Convention. By combining a sortition element (the random selection of members from the general public) and a representative element (the proportionate allocation of places to members of parliament), the Irish case provides a test case of the potential of deliberation in mixed sortition bodies. Mixing two very different sets of members risked inequalities of voice—with the politicians dominating the proceedings—and suboptimal outcomes.

To recount the experience of the convention, we first outline how random selection came to be adopted as a legitimate method for debating constitutional reform in Ireland. After detailing the origins and design of the convention, we describe its deliberative process, which followed key principles aimed to achieve equality among the convention's members, but especially between the citizen and public representative members. We then review the convention's outcomes, including its realization of procedural equality. We conclude by discussing the ongoing efforts to incorporate sortition into Irish governmental and constitutional decision-making.

The Origins of the Irish Constitutional Convention

Ireland was one of the European countries most affected by the Great Recession. Its banking sector imploded and required an EU/IMF financial bailout in November 2010. There was a general sense that many of the major institutions of Irish life—the political parties, the Catholic Church, the banking system, the civil service—had failed the Irish people and that a process of renewal was required.[4] Indeed, the crisis prompted a reassessment of relations between the government and citizens, with questions over the existing political system's overall fitness.[5] For many observers, the crisis showed that Ireland's political and economic establishment had failed. This led to calls for political reform and reform of the 1937 constitution, which critics found increasingly wanting.

This provided an interesting dichotomy: In Ireland the sole route to constitutional change is via referendum and a binding majoritarian vote of the people (with no minimum turnout threshold). The word of the people is binding, yet the people have no role in determining the subject of referendums—or even their wording. There is no citizen initiative in Ireland. Instead, placing policy questions on the ballot is the purview of the executive.[6] There were some civil society activists and academics (two of the current authors included) who argued that constitutional reform should take a deliberative approach, using sortition to directly involve citizens. This could give the process democratic legitimacy and potentially reconfigure future democratic practices.[7]

It was in this context that all of the major Irish political parties published substantial sections on political reform in their manifestos before the 2011 election.[8] In particular, the two parties that went on to form the government set out specific proposals for a citizen-oriented constitutional review process. The Labour Party proposed a constitutional convention to draw up a new constitution for the Ireland of the twenty-first century. The party stated that it was "time for a fundamental review of our Constitution, by the people to whom it belongs." Labour proposed that one third of the convention's members would be drawn from the parliament, one third would be members of civil society organizations (or have relevant legal or academic expertise), and one third would be ordinary citizens chosen by lot. This body's mandate would be to review the constitution and draft a reformed one within a year. The larger Fine Gael party's proposal was for a citizens' assembly "along the lines of those used in the Netherlands, to make recommendations on electoral reform." This was to be a sortition assembly composed of up to one hundred members chosen from the public to reflect the demographic makeup of the country.[9]

In negotiations between these two parties to form a coalition government, they reached a compromise. The Programme for Government proposed establishing a constitutional convention to implement "a process to ensure our Constitution meets the challenges of the 21st century, by addressing a number of specific urgent issues."[10] The convention would be given a brief to report within twelve months on seven specific matters: review of the Dáil (parliament) electoral system; reducing the presidential term to five years (from its current seven); provision for marriage equality; amending the clause on women in the home;[11] measures to encourage greater participation of women in politics and public life; removing blasphemy from the constitution; possible reduction of the voting age. Also welcome were any "other relevant constitutional amendments that may be recommended by the Convention."[12]

In other respects, the program was vague, notably on the composition and operation of the convention and the extent to which it would use sortition. Further details came in February 2012 when the Department of the Taoiseach (prime minister) produced a memorandum for government that proposed an agenda for the convention, its composition, reporting lines, and a timetable for its work.[13] The memorandum confirmed the commitments in the Programme for Government, but with additional details and clarifications.

On the agenda, the memorandum clarified that the proposed voting-age reduction would be from eighteen years to seventeen. One additional topic not included in the Programme for Government was added: "Giving citizens the right to vote at Irish embassies in presidential elections." The memorandum also proposed that the convention should consist of sixty-six citizens, thirty-three politicians, and an independent chair. The citizens would be chosen by sortition to be representative of the population as a whole. The politicians would reflect relative party strength in parliament. The memorandum specified that the chair would be someone with "very high levels of public acceptability, known fair-mindedness, effective chairmanship skills, and knowledge of the Constitution and the law with an ability to arrive at workable solutions, while ensuring as far as possible that all participants get a fair hearing."

The decision that lay citizens chosen by lot would make up two-thirds of the convention was an important innovation. Nothing like this had been tried before in Ireland. Irish policy makers were influenced by the citizens' assemblies on electoral reform in the Canadian provinces of British Columbia (2004) and Ontario (2007) and the 2006 Dutch citizens' forum (Burgerforum),[14] as well as by the 2011 We the Citizens process, a deliberative experiment run by two of the authors of this chapter.[15] In all these cases, citizen members were selected at random and deliberation was the modus operandi. The convention would differ from all these, however, by including members of parliament in the deliberative body.[16]

A number of interest groups had sought seats at the convention, but the government took the line that lay citizens should be the members of the convention. Nongovernmental organizations and advocacy groups would be invited to present their views on the different topics. Sinn Féin, a political party that advocates for a united Ireland, had suggested that citizens from Northern Ireland be involved in the convention. The government proposed instead that each of the political parties in Northern Ireland would be asked to nominate one person from the Northern Ireland Assembly for a seat at the convention.

The proposals in the memorandum provided the basis for consultation between the government and other political parties during the first half of 2012. This in turn led to the formal resolution on the establishment of the convention presented to the Irish parliament in July 2012.[17] The resolution reflected the content of the memorandum for government, but it provided additional detail. The convention composition was confirmed, along with a list of ninety-nine substitutes selected on the same criteria as the convention members. The convention was also required to have "appropriate regard to the Good Friday Agreement and the St. Andrews Agreement."[18] Beyond that, the convention would "agree [to] its own rules of procedure for the effective conduct of its business in as economical manner as possible."

Introducing the resolution in the Dáil, Taoiseach Enda Kenny provided important insights into the government's approach toward the convention. He stated that the convention should be founded on the principles of being innovative, independent, and influential. Innovation was reflected in the composition of the convention, with a majority of citizens. "For the first time," Kenny said, "both the legislators who bring forward proposals for constitutional reform and the citizens who decide on the merits or otherwise of those proposals will jointly and publicly consider whether constitutional reform is necessary or desirable."[19] The independence principle meant that the convention would be independent of government, would be established by resolution of both houses of parliament, and would report to them. The influence principle could be achieved only if the convention's recommendations "are responded to in an appropriate and timely manner." This was the basis of a government commitment to give a response, through parliament, to each recommendation from the convention within four months. Where the government accepted a recommendation for a referendum, it would include a time frame for such a vote.

Following the formal establishment of the convention, the government put in place a number of administrative arrangements. A secretariat was appointed, headed by a senior civil servant who had extensive experience with parliamentary committees and working with parliamentarians. The secretariat hired a polling company to assist in the selection of the sixty-six representative citizens in a process of stratified random selection, requiring the sample to fill proportionate quotas (based on the electoral register) for gender, age, social class, and geography. In practice, about one in forty of the citizens approached ultimately agreed to become convention members.

Four political parties from the Northern Ireland Assembly agreed to participate in the convention: Sinn Féin, the Social Democratic and Labour Party, Alliance Party, and the Green Party. The two main unionist parties—the Democratic Unionist Party and the Ulster Unionist Party—refused the invitation.[20] This meant that the political representation in the convention consisted of twenty-nine parliamentarians from the republic, reflecting party strength in parliament, and four members of the Northern Ireland Assembly. The formal announcement of the appointment of Tom Arnold as chair was made to the Dáil in October, and the first meeting of the convention was set for Dublin Castle in December 2012.

In the lead-up to the opening meeting, skepticism about the convention was expressed in political, academic, and media circles. Some critics judged the convention's agenda as too narrow. Others questioned whether the proposed model of deliberative democracy, involving randomly selected citizens and politicians, would work. In addition, there were questions over whether the government would take the exercise seriously, notwithstanding the commitment to provide a response to each recommendation within four months and set a time frame for those recommendations that should go to referendum.[21]

Institutionalizing Equality in the Convention Process

Opening the first working meeting of the convention on January 26, the chair proposed that the convention should work on the basis of a series of operational principles, of which the key one was equality, namely that all members should be given equal voice in the deliberations of the convention. This goal was of overriding importance given the mixed membership: there were initial concerns that the politician members with their greater expertise in public affairs and public speaking than most of the citizen members might dominate proceedings.

The other principles that the chair enunciated—openness, fairness, efficiency, and collegiality—while significant in their own right, were in large part designed to support the main goal of equality. *Openness* referred to the need to operate with complete transparency, with all plenary sessions being broadcast live on the convention's website. Submissions on each topic would be solicited from the public and interest groups and all submissions would be published on the website. The convention would also be *fair* in the sense that the full spectrum of views would be heard on every issue, and the briefing material for convention members should be impartial and of the highest quality. This was especially important as the convention would deal with sensitive topics such as marriage equality and blasphemy, on which there would be deeply held and divided views within Irish society. It was important too that the convention would operate *efficiently*: well-run meetings would be necessary, as they would take place from a Saturday up until lunchtime on

Sunday. This was a short time for deliberation and decisions on complex issues and thus required effective use of meeting time. Finally, there was the principle of *collegiality*, which was required to ensure that the one hundred convention members would operate in a spirit of friendship and common purpose.

In proposing these operational principles, the chair had not drawn on any existing blueprint. Rather, he had formulated the principles based on reading the literature of other examples of deliberative democracy,[22] and making a judgment on what was appropriate for Irish circumstances and political culture. The deliberative approach was also reinforced by the facilitators, who asked members to follow the world café rules of respectful and inclusive participation. The convention's deliberative procedure included mixing open plenary sessions with private round-table discussions; arranging members in mixed (politicians and citizens) groups at tables of eight; and using trained facilitators to ensure that all members had an opportunity to speak, discussions stayed on topic, and members were respectful of each other's opinions.

In general, each weekend-long session had the following components: presentations by experts who had prepared the briefing papers for convention members; presentations by advocacy groups representing a range of perspectives on the topic under discussion; roundtable discussions, guided by suggested questions; presentations of the content and conclusions of these roundtable discussions back to plenary sessions; framing of a ballot paper on which to vote; securing agreement from the convention on this ballot paper; voting on the ballot paper; and reporting the outcome to the convention.

A number of practical issues arose while trying to follow this meeting format. The academic and legal team played an important role in identifying and securing top-quality experts to prepare briefing papers for convention members. Papers were required to be short (typically four to five pages in length), written in simple and clear English, and free of any advocacy. The papers were circulated one week in advance of the meeting. Then the experts needed to be available on Saturday morning to make a presentation and answer questions at plenary sessions and during roundtable discussions.

Selection of the advocacy groups requested to present to the convention was done by the chair and secretariat in consultation with a steering group that included citizen and politician members. This required an exercise in judgment, guided by the operational principles the convention had adopted, as there were invariably more groups who wanted to present than there was time available to hear them. Public submissions, academic "expert" presentations, and stakeholder panels informed the convention's deliberations. In the case of invited speakers, care was taken to ensure a wide range of opinions, perspectives, experiences, and political views. A close eye was kept to the gender mix of presenters and panelists. The convention also monitored the gender balance at the roundtables. Members' feedback was sought each weekend to ensure the process was reflective and responsive to members' needs.

Each roundtable discussion included groups of seven or eight members. These tables were arranged in advance by the head of the secretariat, who ensured that there was an appropriate mix of politicians and citizens and that no cliques emerged. A trained facilitator and notetaker sat at each table. The task of the facilitator was to moderate the discussion and to ensure that everyone was involved. The notetaker captured the range of discussion and any conclusions reached. The notetakers subsequently reported to the academic and legal team, who presented a summary of the discussion back to plenary (typically using a slide presentation). This was regarded as the most efficient use of time, obviating the need for individual tables to report back, and allowing further discussion at plenary.[23]

Work on framing a ballot paper on which to vote normally commenced on Saturday evening, involving the chair, secretariat, and academic and legal team. The ballot paper was finalized on Sunday morning and presented to a plenary session for approval. Both framing the paper and securing approval for it were frequently challenging, but they were always done within the allocated time.

Examining Convention Outputs

In the next section we assess the extent to which the convention abided by its operational principles—and particularly its key principle of equality. Before getting to this, we first summarize the main outputs of the convention.

The agenda of eight topics set out in the resolution establishing the convention were covered in seven meetings during 2013. The convention then obtained agreement from the government for a two-month extension to its twelve-month time frame, giving it time to examine two additional topics—Dáil reform and economic, social, and cultural rights.[24]

In total, the convention operated for fourteen months, meeting on average about once a month (with the exception of the summer period). The ten topics it discussed resulted in almost forty recommendations, which appear in table 5.1. Over half of these would not require constitutional reform to implement (for instance, recommendations to establish an electoral commission).

Table 5.1. The outcomes of the Irish Constitutional Convention.

Topic	ICC output	Government reaction	Action?
Reduction of presidential term	Three recommendations	Government accepted two; rejected one	Referendum on presidential age defeated May 2015
Reduce voting age	One recommendation	Government accepted this	Referendum promised for 2019
Role of women in home/public life	Two recommendations	Ministerial task force to investigate further	Referendum on women in the home held in October 2018
Increasing women's participation in politics	Three recommendations	Ministerial task force to investigate further	No further updates; appears to have disappeared from the political agenda
Marriage equality	Two recommendations	Government agreed to referendum and to supporting legislation	Referendum passed (May 2015) and legislation passed

Electoral system	Ten recommendations	Government promised to establish an electoral commission and to task it with addressing four of the other recommendations; remaining five recommendations rejected	Parliamentary Committee on the Environment published a report (January 2016) supporting electoral commission establishment; its establishment is still an "active" promise of the government
Votes for emigrants / N. Ireland residents in presidential elections	One recommendation	To be investigated further	Referendum promised for 2019
Blasphemy	Two recommendations	Government has agreed to principle of referendum, but no date set	Referendum promised for October 2018
Dáil reform	Thirteen recommendations	Government accepted three, rejected two, and gave ambiguous responses to the rest	There was a major overhaul of Dáil procedures that implemented the bulk of the ICC's recommendations.
Economic, social, and cultural rights	Two recommendations	To be investigated further	Appears to have disappeared from the political agenda

Note: For more details, see Farrell et al. (2017).

The convention's recommendations were nonbinding: it was an advisory rather than a declaratory body. On its establishment, the government committed to responding to its reports in a timely fashion by way of parliamentary debate. Eighteen of the convention's recommendations would require constitutional reform, and of these just two were taken forward to a vote of the people in May 2015 (on marriage equality and the age of presidential candidates). The remainder, together with the bulk of the recommendations that wouldn't require referendum, have faced a longer path to implementation, as reflected in the final column of table 5.1.

Undoubtedly, the most significant constitutional output of the convention was a recommendation to hold a referendum on marriage equality—a cause the Irish LGBTQ community had championed for years. The smaller coalition partner, the Labour Party, had promised a referendum on this issue in its election manifesto in 2011. However, the more senior partner, Fine Gael, had a more lukewarm position on the matter—one reason why it was referred to the constitutional convention in the first place.

When the convention's July 2013 report recommended that the constitution be amended to introduce marriage equality, it marked the first time in Irish history that a referendum was called as a result of public deliberation. It was also one of the first times in the world that a deliberative process based on sortition resulted in a constitutional referendum. More than that, the vote succeeded:[25] in May 2015, the referendum passed with support from 62 percent of Irish voters.

On the same day as the marriage equality referendum, voters were asked if they wanted to reduce the minimum age for presidential candidates from thirty-five to twenty-one years of age. This referendum, which also emanated from a proposal at the constitutional convention, was sidelined due to focus on the marriage equality referendum. It attracted virtually no coverage, and it was evident on Election Day that most voters were unaware of this second referendum.[26] The proposal barely won the support of one-quarter of the electorate (26.9 percent), marking the worst outcome of any Irish referendum.[27]

Equality of Voice in a Hybrid Sortition Chamber

In examining how the convention operated, we can refer to the five operational principles established by the chair at its first meeting. As discussed above, each of these was in large part centered on the fundamental guiding principle of equality. In this section we start with an analysis of how each of the principles were operationalized in practice. This is followed by a more detailed assessment of the extent to which the convention was successful in meeting the overriding goal of equality.

Operationalizing the Convention's Five Principles

The principle of *openness* was expressed in practice through the development of a convention website and the livestreaming of the convention's plenary sessions. In effect, the focus of this principle was on equality of access for those outside the process. The website contained all the submissions made to the convention. A total of 1,536 submissions were made on the eight topics on the original convention agenda, while an additional 800 submissions were made on the two additional topics agreed on following public consultation. The livestreaming of the convention's plenary sessions had a significant number of viewers, both in Ireland and abroad.

The *fairness* principle was designed in large part to ensure that all members had equal opportunity to become informed on the matters being discussed. This is shown in terms of the documentation presented to convention members and the selection of experts and advocacy groups to present to the convention. The advisory and legal team played a key role in identifying academics who were the leaders in their fields and were noted for their independence and not being identified with a partisan position on the different topics. Adhering to these criteria meant excluding a significant number of people whose public position of a particular topic was known and who were effectively advocates for a particular position. Experts commissioned to produce papers were given guidelines by the academic and legal team on the expected length, format, and balance of the papers.

Advocacy groups were normally included in the program on Saturday in the late morning or after lunch, following the presentation of papers by the chosen experts and a first set of roundtable discussions. There were inevitably more advocacy groups who wished to present to the convention than there was time available; thus, choices had to be made by the secretariat in consultation with the steering group as to which groups were to present. This was done with the aim of ensuring that a spectrum of views on the particular topic was presented to the convention. Guidance was given to the advocacy groups chosen as to the time they had available and the mode of operation of the convention.

The need to properly consider complex topics and arrive at recommendations in the space of one and a half days put a particular importance on the operational principle of *efficiency*. At the most basic level, this required strict timekeeping—namely, starting and finishing all the different component parts of the weekend on time. Infrastructure was put in place to ensure that the convention ran efficiently, including an effective secretariat, the advisory and legal team, facilitators and notetakers, a communications team, and a website with the associated support. It was a distinct advantage that the head of the secretariat knew most of the parliamentarians and carried authority. It was also critically important that the chair and the head of the secretariat developed a warm personal relationship and effective working arrangement.

The budget allocated to the convention was modest—€300,000 in 2013—so the secretariat was required to show ingenuity in securing services at competitive prices. This was backed up by a considerable spirit of voluntarism and pro bono contribution: the convention members were giving freely of their time albeit with their traveling and accommodation expenses being covered. Thus, none of the experts who prepared papers or otherwise contributed were paid.

The *collegiality* principle was of profound importance to the success of the convention. This was about helping to create a positive atmosphere within the group, seeking to avoid any domination of voice by any members, and ensuring a spirit of respect between members and toward the process. The design of the weekend had a role to play in assisting the development of collegiality. Many of the members from parts of the country outside Dublin arrived at the hotel on the Friday evening: a reception provided the basis for people to get to know each other at the beginning and renew friendships as the convention developed. The Saturday program was intense, albeit with coffee breaks and lunch, and concluded on time at 5:30 p.m. An informal dinner was held on Saturday evening. The dinner, along with whatever continuation there was in the bar afterward, was an important part of building relationships between convention members, whether citizen or politician.

The availability of convention members on the Friday evening was also used, for certain of the sessions, to provide them with a more detailed briefing on the topics they would consider over the weekend. This was particularly important for a number of the citizen members who were not well informed about topics such as electoral reform and Dáil reform.

While the value of establishing collegiality among the convention members could be regarded as a positive, it could also bring the risk that over time the members might settle into a routine of uncritically adopting recommendations. To guard against this, the head of the secretariat arranged the membership of the tables at each meeting. This ensured that there was an appropriate mix of politicians and citizens at each table, and it aimed to ensure that no cliques emerged with different arrangements each week.

Finally, the primary principle of *equality* had applied in advance of the establishment of the convention through the process of selection of members. There had been a concern that politicians might dominate citizens in the proceedings, given their greater expertise in public affairs and public speaking. As it turned out, this was not a problem. The citizen members, after a slow start in some cases, proved more than capable of holding their own in the discussions. The chair also had the responsibility of ensuring that a balance was struck during the plenary sessions between politicians and citizens and that no particular voice or voices were allowed to dominate. The fact that facilitators were present at the roundtable discussions, with instructions to ensure engagement of all the people in the group, assisted in this regard. Indeed, the facilitators also ensured equality of voice between the participants in order to ensure that those who had more formal education—or more assertiveness—did not dominate.

Assessing the Equality Principle

We know from many deliberative forums that simply including people in a process, though essential, does not guarantee equality of voice.[28] As political scientists Christopher Karpowitz and Chad Raphael note, ensuring "inclusion in practice is often far more complex than merely opening the doors of the forum to all comers or even than inviting a simple random sample of the public at large."[29] In this instance of a mixed sortition chamber, there was good reason for concern that the professional politicians, used as they are to public speaking and debate, could dominate the discussions.

The issue of politician dominance over a deliberative process featured in a recent British experiment. The 2015 Democracy Matters Citizens' Assembly research project was a joint venture involving academics and practitioners who sought to test the potential for a constitutional minipublic in the British context. Informed by the Canadian and Irish experiences, the research team designed two city-based minipublic experiments, one involving only citizen members (the Canadian model) and the other a mix of citizen and politician members (the Irish hybrid model). Their evidence from surveying the members is that citizen members in the latter group were more inclined to feel that some members dominated the discussions: when probed it was clear that for the most part it was politician members who were seen to be domineering. The report's authors conclude, "At least in the short term, inclusion of politicians decreases the quality of deliberation (including the amount of perceived domination)."[30]

As we shall see, however, the Irish case produces quite different findings. In a series of semistructured interviews with nine of the citizen members that were carried out in the final days of the convention, the question was posed whether the politicians dominated the roundtable discussions.[31] For the most part, the citizen members held the view that the politician members did not seek to dominate. As one citizen member (male) put it quite bluntly, "[The politician members] never tried to take over the table. They'd say what they had to say, and then they'd shut up." Another concurs: "At the roundtables, I thought everyone was pretty much equal most of the time."

There were some exceptions to this general view. A few of the interviewees referred to individual politician members occasionally being more dominant, particularly when technical issues were being discussed (such as electoral or parliamentary reform—both issues that politicians could be expected to have strong views on). Furthermore, some interviewees noted the "subtle ways" that politicians sought to exercise influence, such as giving guidance to the notetaker on the summary of a discussion. But these appeared to be minority instances of politicians trying to dominate the roundtable deliberations. For the most part, the views of the citizen members about the role of the politician members were very positive. In addition, they did not feel that they were dominated by other citizens, whether older or better educated or for any other reason.

We have survey evidence to support this. For eight of the meetings of the convention (which each occurred over a weekend), we surveyed the members at the start of each meeting (on the Saturday morning) and toward the end (late on the Sunday morning). These surveys attracted a response rate of 57 percent to 75 percent, the bulk of the response rates being in the mid- to high sixties. In the second weekend survey in seven of the eight weekends, we asked the members whether they agreed or disagreed with the statement that "Some participants tended to dominate the discussion."

Table 5.2. Responses to the question of whether some members dominated discussions.

	Strongly agree	Agree	Neither agree nor disagree	Disagree	Strongly disagree	Sample size
Citizens	5%	9%	16%	14%	57%	310
Politicians	3%	6%	26%	14%	51%	93
Total	4%	8%	18%	14%	56%	403

Source: Weekly surveys of convention members.

Breaking down the 403 responses between the citizens and politicians, a marginally larger number of citizens (14 percent versus 9 percent) believed that some participants tended to dominate (see table 5.2). However, a marginally larger number of citizens also disagreed that some participants dominated the discussion. Overall, however, these numbers and the differences are too small to expect that they might have an appreciable impact overall. In a regression analysis (not reported here) that includes the week number and other demographic characteristics of the participants (age and sex), we find that the difference between politicians and citizens is not statistically significant.

And what of the politician members? It is not inconceivable that the (successful) strategy of the convention organizers to ensure equality of voice might have resulted in some frustration on the part of the politician members, who could have good reason to complain that *their* voices were not being heard sufficiently. However, based on their public utterances, it is clear that the views of the politician members of the convention were largely positive. As one independent member of the Dáil, Catherine Murphy, observed,

> An important and astonishing message which has emanated from the convention is that when 100 people are put in a room together in the expectation that they will engage in a quality debate, they can be trusted to do just that. Such individuals do not have to be members of political parties or formal groups in order to take part in debates of that nature. It is amazing how people can follow a debate or a conversation and reach their own conclusions. It is a privilege to be a member of the convention which, I hope, will be given a much wider remit in the future.[32]

Many of the parliamentarians admitted to having been skeptics at the start of the process. As Seán Ó Fearghaíl, then the chief whip of the main opposition party, Fianna Fáil, observed in another Dáil debate,

Many of us had some doubts at the start of the convention as to whether it would be possible to maintain the level of public interest and the level of participation by members of the public and politicians in the process. However, the manner in which it has been organised and the parity of esteem which is obvious for members of the public and political representatives has ensured that, to date, the convention has been a great success.[33]

Another deputy—John Lyons of Labour—remarked on the growing camaraderie that grew among the citizen and politician members over time:

Thinking back to our first meeting in Dublin Castle, there was a bit of an "us and them" scenario, with "us and them" being citizens and politicians. I can remember one particular citizen standing up and asking attendees not to let the politicians do all the talking. I thought, "Oh God, here we go, this is going to be a disaster of nine months if this is the attitude." But the ice was broken in Dublin Castle that day. Anyone who is a regular attendee of the convention at the weekends has seen that friendships have developed at each and every table across all parties, sexes and ages.[34]

This overall positive attitude—and particularly the willingness to admit to having been skeptical at the outset—was reflected in face-to-face interviews carried out with a number of the politician members in late June to early July 2014.[35] The general view was that the convention worked "as a process." The parliamentarians liked how the meetings went, and how everyone was engaged. A particularly appealing aspect was the informal method of operation. As one opposition Teachta Dála put it, it was "casual clothes in your head." In short, there was plenty of positive reaction to the process.

Conclusion

Ireland's national experiment with sortition has proven a success in at least three respects. In the first instance, the government implemented a large portion of the convention's recommendations, albeit slowly in a number of cases (see table 5.1). Most prominent among these were the successful referendum on marriage equality in 2015, along with the major overhaul of parliamentary procedures in the Dáil implemented in 2016.[36]

Second, the convention was successful in meeting its primary organizational principle of equality. Despite its hybrid nature—in mixing sortition with conventional representation, the evidence presented in this chapter shows that both citizens and politicians were satisfied that the process was fair, respectful, and lacking in domination by one side over the other.

A final measure of the success is the fact that a subsequent Irish government decided to establish a second sortition chamber, on this occasion a pure one consisting solely of citizen members. The Programme for Partnership Government (of the current government, elected in early 2016), agreed between Fine Gael and some independents, plus the tacit support of the largest opposition party (Fianna Fáil), included a commitment to a citizens' assembly seated entirely by sortition. This new body, which sat from late 2016 through to the spring of 2018, made recommendations to the Dáil on five further constitutional and political reforms: abortion, climate change, aging, fixed-term parliaments, and the manner in which referenda are held. Of these, the recommendations on abortion have had the most political impact to date, resulting in a government promise to hold a referendum, which was fulfilled in 2018.

The Irish experience demonstrates the virtue of sortition in providing space for reflective, respectful deliberation. Both the 2012–14 Constitutional Convention and the 2016–18 Citizens' Assembly, however, are discrete experiments in deliberation. There is no clamour in Ireland to institutionalize this into a permanent structure, along the lines of the sortition chamber advocated by Gastil and Wright. That said, there is every likelihood that Ireland will use other sortition chambers in the future. In that sense, at least, they are likely to become part of the ecology of democratic institutions.[37]

6

Intercameral Relations in a Bicameral Elected and Sortition Legislature

Pierre-Étienne Vandamme, Vincent Jacquet, Christoph Niessen, John Pitseys, and Min Reuchamps

John Gastil and Erik Olin Wright propose a hybrid bicameralism, with one chamber composed of elected politicians and the other of ordinary citizens chosen by sortition. Though they envision interactions between the two chambers as a "creative tension," the question of intercameral relations deserves more careful attention. We argue that the chambers would not only have different virtues but also different legitimacies, which might become particularly conflictual if each chamber has the power to veto the proposals of the other, as Gastil and Wright recommend. If the elected chamber proves less popular than the sortition one, the legitimacy of elections might come into question. In turn, elected representatives might try to discredit the sortition representatives as, for example, lacking experience or accountability.

To imagine these intercameral relations, picture a triangular relationship among the two chambers and the public. To understand how those relationships might develop, we wanted to get a preliminary measure of the *public* support for each mode of selection. In addition, we sought to grasp current *political* support for sortition among elected officials. We investigated these questions in Belgium, where the idea of sortition has received particular attention in recent years. We conducted a survey among a representative sample of the Belgian population and Belgian members of parliament (MPs) to assess their views of sortition, if it were used for political representation.

As we explain in detail later, the results show that a pure sortition chamber will be difficult to achieve politically, due to limited public support and even lower support among politicians. Our findings also suggest that, once installed, a sortition chamber might continue to face resistance and opposition from the political class. Hence, to test the viability of Gastil and Wright's sortition chamber proposal, we must imagine intercameral relations and their effects on the perceived legitimacy of the two chambers.[1] Beyond our survey findings, we also offer theoretical reflections on the respective legitimacies of elections and sortition—and on their potential antagonisms. This leads us then to consider the effects of different possible distributions of power between the chambers as a crucial determinant of their interactions.

Conflicting legitimacies are not a problem per se. For instance, in existing democratic systems, the relations between legislative, executive, and judiciary powers involve constant tension between their respective rationales. Nonetheless, it cannot be taken for granted that the coexistence of an elected and a sortition chamber would strengthen, rather than weaken, the overall balance of legitimacy in a democratic system. Sortition could challenge the very basis of electoral legitimacy, so intercameral interactions must be considered carefully.

We begin by explaining why Belgium is the right site for investigating these issues; then we present the results of our survey. In the second section, we explore the complementary virtues and competing legitimacies of elections and sortition in theoretical terms. We then draw on our data regarding legitimacy perceptions—and on more general observations about bicameral interactions in contemporary democracies—to consider different potential distributions of power between the two chambers and their potential political consequences. We will review four institutional scenarios: 1) an elected and a sortition chamber having identical powers; 2) the elected one being subordinated; 3) the sortition one being subordinated; and 4) a single mixed chamber, which combines elected and sortition representatives. We weigh the pros and cons of these four options in light of both our data and our theoretical considerations.

Public and Political Perception of Sortition in the Belgian Context

Belgium provided an ideal setting for our surveys because the political debate on sortition in that country has received considerable public attention.[2] In addition to proposals made by scholars and activists, several politicians recently advocated the use of random selection to draw citizens into political decision-making. Some have proposed, more specifically, using sortition to select members of the Senate (that is, the Belgian upper house). Hence, debates have addressed the competence and legitimacy of randomly selected representatives, as well as the best institutional design for including lay citizens in the legislative process. Some argue for a parliamentary committee chosen by sortition, others for a mixed Senate combining election and sortition, and others prefer a full sortition Senate.

If the public debate about a sortition chamber is now vivid in Belgium, it does not mean that the proposal has a popular majority. Most Belgian political parties have refused to take an official position on the idea, and current proposals lack serious legislative follow-up. Nonetheless, versions of the idea keep reappearing in media and political debates.[3]

To get a more precise estimate of political and public support for a sortition chamber, or other variations on that idea, we surveyed members of the regional and national parliaments in Belgium, along with a representative sample of Belgian citizens. For MPs, data was collected via online and paper questionnaires from June to August 2017, with a response rate of 26 percent ($N = 124$). (Appendix figure 6.A2 shows sample demographics.) The survey company iVox collected a representative online sample of citizens ($N = 966$).

Our survey examined whether, in light of the contemporary mistrust of the political class, respondents would show more confidence in a sortition chamber than an elected one. We also measured public and political support for the general idea of a sortition chamber, as well as for the idea of a chamber that mixed randomly selected citizens and elected politicians—a method close to the model of the Irish Constitutional Convention.[4] Finally, because of our interest in power distribution between chambers, we asked who should make the final decision when the two chambers disagree.

The main results of our survey appear in figure 6.1, which includes the exact question wording for both politicians and citizens. (Appendix figures 6.A1 through 6.A6 display these results in more detail.) As for MPs, the data shows a highly critical posture toward the use of sortition for the appointment to parliament: 77 percent disagree with installing a sortition chamber.[5] Nearly two-thirds of politicians (65 percent) also oppose a mixed chamber. When considering the scenario of a disagreement between elected and sortition chambers, 89 percent want the elected chamber to make the final decision, with 75 percent having that view if the second chamber is mixed. Finally, only 5 percent place more confidence in sortition than in an elected chamber, with 17 percent remaining neutral. (That is the highest neutrality score among our five questions.)

For the representative sample of citizens that we surveyed, the picture is quite different, though we do find majority support for neither sortition nor a mixed chamber. Many respondents remained neutral, with a high of 40 percent unsure whether to make elected or sortition members the final authority. This suggests considerable room for movement in public opinion, if the debate on sortition intensifies. When citizens do take a position, we find a much closer split between those who favor or oppose these propositions. More citizens oppose than support the sortition chamber (40 percent versus 29 percent), but a plurality (47 percent) favor a mixed chamber, with only one-quarter of respondents opposing it.

Figure 6.1. Distribution of survey responses for politicians (n=24) and citizens (n=966).

Preface: "On the national level, one sometimes discusses that legislative chambers could be composed by random selection..."

□ Fully agreeing ▢ Rather agreeing ▨ Neutral ▨ Rather disagreeing ■ Fully disagreeing

Question 1: ...Do you think that the institution of a legislative chamber that is composed of randomly selected citizens would be a good thing?

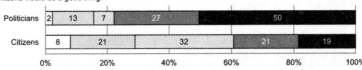

Question 2: ...Do you think that the institution of a mixed legislative chamber that is composed of both elected and randomly selected citizens would be a good thing?

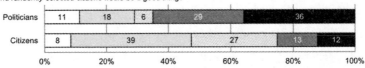

Question 3: ...The Parliament is composed of two legislative chambers. If one chamber which is solely composed of randomly selected citizens is instituted, it has to have the final say in case of disagreement with the elected chamber.

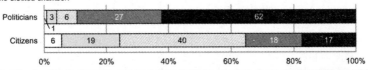

Question 4: ...The Parliament is composed of two legislative chambers. If one chamber which is partially composed of randomly selected citizens is instituted, it has to have the final say in case of disagreement with the elected chamber.

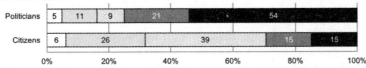

Question 5: ...A legislative chamber composed of randomly selected citizens inspires more confidence than an elected chamber.

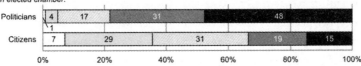

To check whether support for sortition or mixed chambers varied by respondents' partisan identity or demographic characteristics, we conducted chi-square tests of independence. Table 6.1 shows several statistically significant differences. (More detail appears in appendix figures 6.A2–6.) The most striking result was that of the fourteen Green MPs surveyed, all but two supported establishing a mixed chamber. As for gender, for samples of both politicians and citizens, women were less critical than men toward sortition and more supportive toward a mixed chamber. In the public sample, 74 percent of younger respondents (thirty-four and under) supported a mixed chamber, compared to less than two-thirds (63 percent) of their older counterparts (thirty-five and over). Finally, citizens with the highest levels of formal education and income were least supportive of sortition or a mixed chamber—by margins of 10 to 30 percent—relative to respondents with the lowest income and education levels. (For detailed breakdowns, see appendix figures 6.A5–6.)

Table 6.1: Chi-square coefficients of the support for a sortition (Q1) and mixed (Q2) chamber.

Tested variable	df	Politicians		Citizens	
		Sortition chamber χ^2	Mixed chamber χ^2	Sortition chamber χ^2	Mixed chamber χ^2
Party affiliation	4	1.05	32.03 **	-	-
Gender	1	5.28 **	5.86 **	1.88	5.67 **
Age	2	0.09	0.35	1.87	7.03 **
Education	2	-	-	28.55 **	4.81 *
Income	2	-	-	18.61 **	8.58 **

** $p < 0.05$, * $p < 0.1$

These results come at a moment in history when neither a sortition nor mixed chamber exists, and there has been no robust debate of such proposals. Nonetheless, the data offer insight into the near-term prospects of these ideas in the Belgian context—or perhaps in any similar country when these ideas first begin to percolate.

First, MPs strongly oppose the idea of a full sortition chamber, whereas citizens remain ambivalent. By comparison, a mixed chamber appears more achievable. A plurality of citizens favor it, and fewer MPs oppose it. Whether a mixed chamber could serve as a stepping stone toward full sortition is a question our survey cannot address.

Second, politicians' strong opposition to the introduction of sortition confirms that the proposal is not yet on the legislative agenda—Greens being an interesting exception. We were not surprised that the proposal is resisted by those who have a vested interest in the status quo. In other words, our results can be interpreted as a confirmation that elites see sortition as an existential threat.

Third, there is openness to a sortition body composed of lay citizens. Although there is no clear indication that citizens would be willing to trust a sortition chamber more than an elected one (nor that they trust the latter more), they tend to show more trust in sortition than MPs do. What is more, elections possibly benefit from a psychologically documented status quo bias or path dependency. Whereas sortition, still often perceived as bizarre by people unaware of its historical precedent, could gain popularity if it were to become common practice.

Not only do these results provide some information regarding the achievability of a sortition chamber, but they will also feed into our theoretical analysis of intercameral relations. Before moving to that, we try to shed more light in the following section on the reasons that might explain political resistance to sortition even though it has virtues complementary to elections.

Complementary Virtues and Competing Legitimacies

We agree with Gastil and Wright that sortition and elections have complementary virtues, but our reasoning differs from theirs. By increasing social and cognitive diversity, sortition helps reducing the risks of biased decisions. By freeing representatives from party allegiances and electoral precommitments, it creates conditions for high-quality deliberation. Relative to sortition, however, elections offer a more inclusive space for public participation, leave more room for contestation, include a dimension of choice in the selection of representatives, and provide an (admittedly deficient, yet institutionalized) accountability mechanism.[6]

There are thus good reasons for trying to combine these respective virtues and for resisting the temptation to abolish the elected chamber as other contributions to this volume suggest.[7] Yet nothing guarantees that this combination of elections and sortition will be easy, nor that it will have beneficial effects. The creation of a sortition chamber might further decrease the perceived legitimacy of elected representatives. The unequal public interactions between charismatic elected and unexperienced randomly selected citizens might discredit the latter. Tension between two chambers with veto power might result in political deadlock, to the benefit of those unjustly favored by the status quo. Taken together, these dynamics could undermine public trust in the entire legislative system.

One cannot expect peaceful interaction between the two chambers because elections and sortition embody competing and mutually undermining conceptions of representation. Electoral politics is conceived as a matter of meritocratic competition. A good politician ideally demonstrates political commitment, conviction, persuasive skill, and strategic acumen. The electoral process should bring to power the best representatives, or at least the ones voters want most from the available options. In sortition, everyone is seen as endowed with a capacity for political judgment and able to take active part in collective decision-making.[8] Given these conflicting models, tensions arise immediately because sortition challenges the elitist electoral model and the distinctive legitimacy of elected politicians.

The use of sortition also might increase public hostility toward political parties. Modern party politics has many deficiencies, but parties also play positive roles in articulating a multiplicity of societal demands in coherent political programs. Parties organize political majorities and public opposition.[9] Yet parties' legitimacy is closely tied to electoral legitimacy and the conception of representation as competition, which is probably why our survey showed Belgian MPs so strongly opposed to the creation of a sortition chamber.

The important point is that parties and elected representatives will have incentives for trying to delegitimize the sortition chamber.[10] If the latter becomes more popular, the incentives could change, as the elected class might become afraid that attacking sortition would undermine its own popularity.[11] Yet, in the period of transition toward a widely accepted use of sortition in political representation, it is very important to address this issue of conflicting legitimacies. Failure to do so risks jeopardizing the potential benefits of pairing elections with sortition, and it could delegitimatize completely the very idea of sortition. Thus, we turn to the question of how to reshape existing political institutions such that this conflict becomes an asset, rather than a risk, for democratic legitimacy.

Intercameral Relations

Besides perceived legitimacy, the crucial factor to either increase or decrease the potential intercameral competition will be the distribution of power between the two chambers. Political scientists traditionally draw a distinction between *strong* and *weak* bicameralism.[12] The main difference between these is not the selection process but the veto power of the second chamber. Either it is an *absolute* veto (a legislative proposal has to be ratified by both chambers) or a *suspensive* veto (the second chamber can at most *delay* the legislative process).[13] In the former case, the second chamber performs functions of checks and balances, such as promoting stability, reducing the power of the majority and of the agenda setter, and making corruption more costly. When operating with only a suspensive veto, a body's function is mostly deliberative, as it works to improve the quality of proposed legislation through amendments or anticipation of the other chamber's reaction.[14]

It is an absolute veto power that Gastil and Wright envision for their proposed sortition chamber. Though it is interesting to imagine how the veto power by itself would affect intercameral relations, another part of the picture consists in considering methods for overcoming disagreements between chambers. As we focus on Gastil and Wright's proposal, we shall limit ourselves in this paper to the examination of the power distribution between the chambers. After having considered the potential effects of an equal distribution of power, we consider the three other alternatives mentioned earlier: a consultative elected chamber, a consultative sortition chamber, and a (single) mixed chamber.

Equal Power: Fight for Public Trust or Mutual Delegitimation?

The main attraction of giving equal power to both chambers comes from the fact that it empowers the sortition body, elevating it to the same standing as its elected counterpart. One might be tempted to see this arrangement as most likely to reap the full benefits of both election and sortition. If both types of representation enjoyed a similar degree of public trust (as in our survey), this might seem like the perfect compromise.

We have our doubts, however. Our main worry relates to a more general criticism of strong bicameralism. If a bill has to pass two chambers to become law, with each having an absolute veto, it becomes more difficult to overcome the status quo, compared to unicameral or weak bicameral systems.[15] By itself, this consideration could induce realist utopians to not give veto power to a sortition chamber, or to remove the veto power of the elected one. If capitalism is to be overcome, as Gastil and Wright suggest in their postscript, the status quo does not need unnecessary protections. Equal veto powers for both bodies could also induce constitutional rigidity and thereby create intergenerational injustices.[16]

Two particular aspects of the dual veto are likely to worsen this status quo bias. First, the preferences of both chambers could diverge significantly. We expect important disagreements between the two chambers because both are likely to become autonomous epistemic communities with their own procedures, functioning, and internal power relationships. What is more, one advantage of representation by lot is supposed to be its capacity to yield a strong deliberative dynamic that is likely to increase the opinion gap with the (less deliberative) elected chamber. Again, the net result is making it harder to overturn the status quo.

Second, the conflictual coexistence of the two chambers would not be mitigated by the presence of political parties in both bodies. When sortition and elected representation coexist, the coagulant function of cross-chamber party platforms is reduced. One cannot expect a sortition chamber to organize itself on partisan affiliations in the same way an elected chamber does. Nor can one expect a sortition chamber to follow the political directions of the government the same way an elected chamber usually does in a parliamentary system. Across the conflicting chambers, legislative votes become more uncertain, the number of negotiating rounds increases, and the entire legislative process slows down further.[17] Paradoxically, the increased policy stability (or deadlock) that would result from such a dynamic could lead to even higher social and political conflict.[18]

Citizens in countries like the US might be so accustomed to political deadlock that such threats do not worry them.[19] Nevertheless, the equal power solution presents the greatest risk for the competing legitimacies that we referenced earlier: each chamber might be tempted to contest the very nature and source of legitimacy of the other. For example, the elected chamber could point out the intrinsic incompetence and lack of accountability of the sortition chamber, while the sortition chamber could critique the intrinsic elitism and partisanship of the elected one.

This dynamic could produce widely varying results, some of which could benefit the political system. Conflict between the bodies could spark a more vivid debate between the chambers on policy issues. It could foster a virtuous fight for public trust, if each chamber tries to be the "best" representative of the public. The divergence between the chambers could also result in a larger autonomy of the representative bodies vis-à-vis the executive branch, in a parliamentary system; the sortition chamber would be less subordinated to the government, and the elected chamber could use the negotiations between the chambers as a leverage for acquiring more autonomy.

These optimistic scenarios may come to pass, but equally plausible is a race to the bottom, in which each chamber discredits the other until the public becomes disgusted with both. Structural deadlock could lead an increasing part of the population to think that hybrid bicameralism highlights the complementary *vices* of sortition and election more than their virtues. This system could lead people to call for a more efficient political body, led by a powerful executive, even if that meant a less *democratic* government. Given the frequency of irony in political history, such unintended consequences are certainly possible.

A Consultative Role for the Elected Chamber?

If one is worried about the conservative effects of strong bicameralism (or about the risks of de-legitimation of the sortition chamber by the political class), one alternative institutional design subordinates the elected to the sortition chamber. In light of the political resistance to sortition expressed in our survey, this might be the least achievable option, politically. Let us nonetheless consider its theoretical desirability.

If the intended benefits of elections are real, and if the complete replacement of elections would entail a loss for which sortition cannot entirely compensate, this option requires careful design. Sortition must increase the legitimacy of the political system as a whole, not dig the grave of elections.

If the sortition chamber was conceived as (or became) the main chamber, with a mainly consultative role for the elected one, prima facie, this empowers sortition without strong bicameralism's drawbacks. What is more, a consultative role does not amount to powerlessness: the subordinated chamber (which may keep a constituent role and a power of initiative) usually exercises influence through its suspensive veto power.[20] The power to delay decisions gives the subordinate chamber leverage when its counterpart is impatient to pass the legislation, sometimes due to the unreliability of its majority.[21]

Even so, the social and political status of elections would be affected by setting up a subordinate role. First, if the imbalance of perceived legitimacy between election and sortition increases over time (as people become more acquainted with sortition), the public might encourage the sortition chamber to ignore the elected one. Second, elections provide a moment where political stakes are staged and discussed in the media. Political oppositions and interests are made visible. Representatives are tested and must give account of their actions. Would these functions endure if citizens had the impression that elections matter even less than before? If voter turnout declined, the legitimacy gap between the chambers could grow even wider.

In parliamentary systems, the elected chamber could retain the power to nominate the prime minister. The stakes of legislative elections would thus remain substantial—especially considering the shift of power, in most democracies, from the legislative to the executive branch.[22] This would lead to an unprecedented configuration of the relations between the executive and the legislative branch, with one chamber having the power to nominate (and influence) and the other the power to decide. Yet there would also be a high potential for deadlock because governments would have no guarantee of support by the main (sortition) chamber. Under such an arrangement, political parties would face strong incentives to recruit members of the sortition chamber for the government to gain stability and for the opposition to gain strength.

In presidential systems, to the contrary, legislative elections would lose much of their appeal. The political stage would be mainly occupied by two actors—an elected president and the sortition chamber. At first glance, such equilibrium could preserve the main benefits of elections. On closer inspection, however, elections could be reduced to a presidential plebiscitary ritual. In this configuration, there would be a risk of a further shift of power from the legislative branch toward the executive if the former is dominated by the sortition chamber.

A Consultative Role for the Sortition Chamber?

Another institutional alternative gives a consultative role to the sortition chamber. In this scenario, the sortition chamber could enjoy powers of initiative, second reading, and amendment, but the elected chamber would always have the final say. Based on our survey results, this might be the arrangement most acceptable to the political class. If the function of sortition is primarily to empower lay citizens or mitigate an imbalance of power in favor of elites, a subordinate role could appear unsatisfactory. If, however, the sortition chamber is envisioned as a deliberative input in the legislative system, a consultative role might be the best possible fit.

Since power resurfaces whenever the stakes are high,[23] a subordinate role might be most suitable for a sortition body, which would then have less risk of corruption by external interests. In the elected chamber, the structures of traditional political parties can provide a firewall between the representatives and external pressures, be they legal (lobbies) or illegal (bribery). Lacking such protection, a fully empowered sortition body would be more susceptible to corrosive external influence.

If we admit that impartiality and deliberative quality are intrinsically or instrumentally valuable, a subordinate sortition chamber might best realize these virtues. By having only a suspensive (and not absolute) veto power, the incentive to produce reasoned recommendations after high-quality deliberations would be increased.[24]

What is more, a consultative sortition chamber could have substantial influence on the workings of the elected chamber. We have already mentioned how second chambers gain leverage when the elected one fears any further delays. In the particular case of hybrid bicameralism, however, the popularity of the second (sortition) chamber might increase its influence even more. If a sortition chamber were to garner considerable popular support, elected representatives would have a strong incentive to seek its consent—to take into account its suggestions for legislative amendments and to take up its legislative proposals. Knowing that citizens may reward or punish representatives for failing to follow the recommendations of the consultative sortition chamber, the elected majority might be ill advised to neglect its input. Ironically, electoral accountability could thus play in favor of sortition. Yet this will depend on the public identification with the sortition chamber, its media coverage, and the effectiveness of electoral accountability, which is often denounced as poor—not the least by partisans of sortition.

Even if the deliberative effect of a consultative sortition chamber were real, there are risks in this design. The subordinated role might decrease the public's willingness to serve in the sortition chamber.[25] If people fail to see the real power of a consultative chamber, it might create public anger toward an elite that only pretended to give citizens genuine political power. As with the previous arrangements, such drawbacks must be weighed against potential advantages.

What about a Mixed Chamber?

The last institutional option features a chamber composed of both elected and sortition representatives, as was used by the Irish Constitutional Convention. In the Belgian context, several politicians have advocated replacing the current Senate with such a mixed chamber, with the first chamber remaining as it is. This option received the least critical reception by MPs in our survey, and it received the highest public support. A variant of such a scheme would avoid bicameralism's status quo bias by creating a unicameral—but "bi-representative" —chamber.[26]

A mixed chamber can mitigate the public battle between professional politicians and lay citizens. If both groups have incentives to work together in subcommittees, they could learn from each other. The public could observe them cooperating closely, exchanging views, and trying to understand each other's concerns. In light of the contemporary distrust of politics and politicians, this could restore public legitimacy to the legislative process.

Another benefit of a mixed chamber might be that elected politicians who have collaborated with lay citizens would be more willing to defend the recommendations of the mixed chamber in their parties (in government or in the elected chamber if there is one). This, again, would reduce the battle between elected and sortition representatives.

Again, there are risks. Most of all, sortition might lose its intended benefits if mixed with elected representation. Under a unicameral arrangement, this risk would be greatest. The sortition representatives would arrive free from party attachments, but parties would have a strong incentive to form alliances with these unaligned lay representatives. For parties, it could become more appealing to invest time and money in recruiting sortition representatives already chosen than in canvassing the general public to attract more voters. If an additional elected seat requires winning fifty thousand more votes, why not seduce and enroll an independent sortition MP instead? In this scenario, we could imagine a case where a small yet opportunistic party gathers a plurality of (mostly sortition) MPs while earning only a small fraction of the popular vote.

Preventing such political recruitment is hard to imagine, given that parties and sortition MPs would interact on a daily basis and join forces to make majority decisions. Even a rule forbidding political careers after a sortition mandate would not solve the problem entirely. Coalition building is a natural outcome of political battles. If sortition representatives want to weigh on legislative decisions in such a scenario, they will be better off joining existing coalitions—or forming new ones. They might retain more independence than elected representatives, which would attenuate the drawbacks of party discipline, but this outcome would not reap the full fruits of pure sortition.

We believe things might go differently in a bicameral framework scenario, though only where the mixed chamber is subordinate to the elected one. The stakes being lower, party competition might be weaker; hence, the temptation to recruit the sortition MPs into parties might be lower.

Either way, the mixed chamber faces another hazard—the intellectual domination that sortition MPs might suffer when seated among professional politicians. One does not even need to assume hostile intentions on the part of elected representatives. The fact is that there will probably be an asymmetry of experience and self-confidence, which might turn out to be detrimental to sortition representatives. If some participants' voices are perceived as more legitimate, or more articulate, deliberation could suffer.[27] Empirical evidence on this subject is equivocal,[28] but to secure high-quality deliberation, such domination must be prevented.

Conclusion

Elections and sortition have complementary virtues that provide promising ground for being combined in a bicameral legislature. At the same time, competing legitimacies need to be considered when thinking about the intercameral distribution of power. Representative surveys of the Belgian population revealed an ambivalent reception of the sortition chamber idea, with many citizens still undecided on the question. Our survey of MPs, however, showed strong resistance to sortition.

Those results go along with our theoretical consideration of sortition and election as having not only *different* legitimacies, but also *competing*—and potentially *conflicting*—ones. The reintroduction of sortition into modern representative systems will be difficult to achieve, but sortition will likely face continued resistance once installed.

For that reason, it is important to try to anticipate the results of potentially conflictual intercameral relations under hybrid bicameralism. A crucial factor affecting intercameral relations will be the distribution of power between the chambers, which Gastil and Wright envision as roughly equal in their proposal.

Path dependency can explain their choice for such a strong bicameralism, but it is not enough to *justify* it. When opening the debate on the introduction of a legislature by lot, one must also open the debate on this distribution of power. We did so by thinking through four scenarios.

First, we considered an equal power solution. Though it appears as the natural combination of the respective virtues of elections and sortition, this institutional design has the effect of protecting the status quo, and it could push the two chambers to mutual delegitimation.

Second, we explored the possibility of subordinating the elected chamber to the sortition one. Such an option appeared more plausible in a presidential system than in a parliamentary one, but either way, it risks political recruitment of sortition representatives, reduced electoral legitimacy, and greater transfer of power from the legislative to the executive branch.

Third, we discussed the scenario of a sortition chamber being subordinated to the elected, while playing a deliberative role. Doing so would probably attenuate, but not annihilate, sortition's political impact. The ruling majority might be ill advised to neglect the input of the sortition chamber because this would delay its legislative projects and could even jeopardize its future electoral success. Yet a subordinate role for the sortition chamber might also have demotivating effects and engender public frustration.

Finally, we explored the idea of a mixed chamber composed of sortition and elected MPs. The joint work of these two types of representatives could create a positive logic of mutual learning and cooperation. But we also stressed the risks of political recruitment and intellectual domination of the politicians on the lay citizens.

Every one of these power distributions has advantages and drawbacks with important consequences for the political system. If a government decided to undertake such a radical reform, the choice between these different options should be made in consideration of the institutional context and of the societal changes that the reform would seek to achieve.

Appendix

Five questions, corresponding to those in figure 6.1, were asked with exactly the same wording in our two surveys. Respondents were provided no additional explanations or context for these questions. Table 6.2 shows the response rates for the MP survey, and figure 6.A1 shows the precise choices of politicians and citizens regarding a sortition and a mixed chamber. Figures 6.A2–6 show the detailed response distributions across partisan and sociodemographic dimensions used for the chi-square tests. Support for a proposal was operationalized as the sum of those "fully agreeing" and "rather agreeing," with the same done for opposition. Respondents with a neutral position were not taken into account for the chi-square tests.

Table 6.2. Response rates for survey among regional and federal members of parliament.

	Sample	Population	Response rate
Total	124	473	26%
Men	79	283	28%
Women	45	190	24%
Dutch speakers	56	234	24%
French speakers	56	214	26%
German speakers	12	25	48%
Christian Democrats	29	85	34%
Greens	14	40	35%
Liberals	28	106	26%
Socialists	30	115	26%
Nationalists	13	87	15%
Other	10	40	25%

Fig. 6.A1. Detailed choice of politicians and citizens regarding a sortition and a mixed chamber.

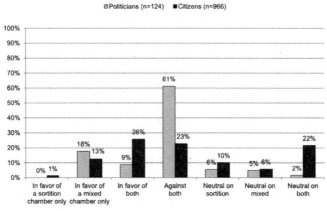

Fig. 6.A2. MPs' support for a sortition and a mixed chamber by party affiliation.

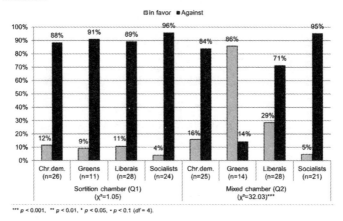

*** $p < 0.001$, ** $p < 0.01$, * $p < 0.05$, • $p < 0.1$ ($df = 4$).

Fig. 6.A3. Support for a sortition and a mixed chamber by gender.

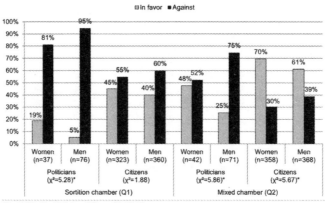

*** $p < 0.001$, ** $p < 0.01$, * $p < 0.05$, • $p < 0.1$ ($df = 1$).

Fig. 6.A4. Support for a sortition and a mixed chamber by age.

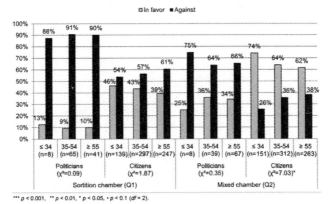

*** p < 0.001, ** p < 0.01, * p < 0.05, • p < 0.1 (df = 2).

Fig. 6.A5. Citizens' support for a sortition and a mixed chamber by education.

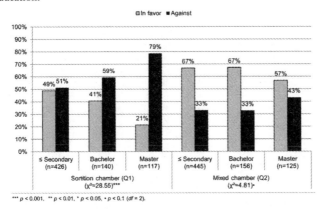

*** p < 0.001, ** p < 0.01, * p < 0.05, • p < 0.1 (df = 2).

Fig. 6.A6. Citizens' support for a sortition and a mixed chamber by income.

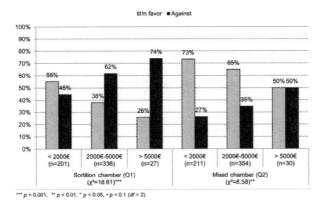

*** p < 0.001, ** p < 0.01, * p < 0.05, • p < 0.1 (df = 2).

7

Joining Forces: The Sortition Chamber from a Social-Movement Perspective

Andrea Felicetti and Donatella della Porta

Minipublics and social movements might provide valuable resources in deepening democracy and addressing the legitimacy crisis of advanced capitalist societies. On the one hand, an ever-growing variety of deliberative assemblies is inspired from ideals of democratic deliberation: they provide carefully designed spaces where randomly selected citizens can meet, reason together, and decide upon political problems. On the other hand, social movements are widely acknowledged as an integral part of democratic societies. Their ability to articulate dissent, organize protest, and build political and social alternatives is central to a vibrant democracy.[1]

Although the growing body of scholarship on minipublics and social movements greatly contributes to debates on democracy, these studies tend to consider the two phenomena independently from each other and give little attention to how minipublics and social movements interact. As we claim in this chapter, the fact that both minipublics and social movements aim to democratize our political systems offers potentials but does not guarantee a positive relationship between them. Rigorous thinking is needed to develop such synergies.[2]

In this chapter, we adopt a social-movement perspective to envision ways to promote a positive relationship between minipublics and grassroots actors. In doing so, we hope to shed critical insight on a specific idea—Gastil and Wright's proposal for a sortition chamber, as presented in the lead chapter of this volume. Though the sortition chamber promises to inject participatory and deliberative politics into the core of democratic systems, its chances of success might be increased by reflecting on the role of social movements in such processes. The experience of social movements' interactions with minipublics, which also rest of principles of sortition, will help clarify this problem.

Our work is therefore guided by two overarching questions. First, how have minipublics in the past interfaced or conflicted with movements and movement organizations? Second, how might a sortition assembly be designed to positively interact with social movements within a larger deliberative democratic system?

Briefly, we will argue that tensions between minipublics and movements are bound to emerge, but a positive relationship can be promoted if minipublics are properly introduced and designed. Sortition chamber advocates should work with movement activists to develop institutions that meet the democratic ambition of the public and support other democratization efforts. To successfully develop the sortition chamber idea, advocates should adopt a demand-driven approach. This means building a bottom-up campaign in collaboration with activist enclaves, in which activists develop a realistic expectation of providing consequential input. This approach will help to grant the support of movement activists to the sortition chamber idea in three fundamental respects: in introducing the sortition chamber proposal in political life, in implementing this project, and in making sure that this deliberative body has an impact on the political system.[3]

We begin our argument by presenting key theoretical considerations on the relationship between movements and sortition assemblies. We then give concrete examples of interactions between social movements and minipublics to illustrate how they might contradict or complement each other. Having shown how the quality of interactions changes in different contexts, we discuss how the relationship between movements and minipublics is evolving. To conclude, we present recommendations on how a sortition chamber could create a synergy with social movements' struggles for democracy.

A Complex yet Neglected Relationship

Deliberative democratic scholarship has examined both minipublics and social movements but for different reasons. Minipublics have long been considered the main sites to pursue deliberative and democratic engagement, whereas social movements were pushed to the margins of deliberative scholarship because of their allegedly poor deliberative credentials, only to regain status thanks to critical deliberative democrats and social-movement scholars. The reemergence of a systemic approach to deliberation has stressed the need for deliberative institutions, such as minipublics, to positively interact with other democratic actors and entities, including social movements.[4]

Although examination of practical experiences is fundamental to understanding the relationship between minipublics and social movements, we begin with some key theoretical points. We do so because Gastil and Wright's sortition chamber proposal takes for granted popular support for this idea. This presumption overlooks the fact that sortition's democratic potential depends also on the broader democratic context in which it is embedded, not just its relationship with formal political institutions.

Sortition advocates and social movement activists might share similar conceptions of democracy. Yet tensions between the pursuit of empowered democratic deliberation on the one hand and movements' struggles in affirming their countervailing power on the other are bound to surface at times.[5] The key problem is this: minipublics, in contrast to social movements, put citizens' deliberation, not activism, at the center of the political stage. A minipublic aims to find a (good) answer to a political problem. In doing so, activists' points of view, when successfully included at all, become just one among many starting points for citizens' deliberative efforts.[6]

Tensions also arise from the fact that not all political conflicts can be reduced to—and find resolution within the boundaries of—deliberative interaction. When movement activists perceive deliberation as unsuitable for ideological or strategic reasons, they might undermine public forums. For instance, in a pluralized world with major power imbalances, some activists might see the search for rational consensus as a dangerous fantasy. Furthermore, in some cases, processes other than deliberation might be more conducive to outcomes that are more in line with preferences of social-movement actors.

Overall, activists have the option to participate in, ignore, or protest against minipublics.[7] A sortition chamber aiming at a positive interaction should take as many measures as possible to encourage movement actors to engage with it, because there is much to lose in pitting minipublics and movements against one another.[8]

A growing number of movement activists sympathetic with deliberative democratic ideals may welcome the addition of an authentically deliberative, inclusive, and effective chamber for citizen participation. As shown in Sintomer's contribution to this volume, a growing range of movements and partisan actors are, in fact, increasingly interested in the sortition legislature idea.

Movements also have instrumental reasons to consider deliberation a resource. Because Gastil and Wright's sortition chamber proposal sees this option as working alongside an elected body with a proxy-voting weighted PR system, social movements would retain a space for expressing movements' partisanship. They might still mobilize to support particular candidates and parties and strongly influence them in the electoral chamber. At the same time, they might also promote their views in a thoroughly deliberative body such as the sortition chamber. The logics of deliberation promise to empower actors endowed with better arguments (but limited resources) over those with poorer arguments (but greater means to promote them).[9] Nevertheless, movements will not win all battles fought on the deliberative field. For instance, citizens will not always arrive at the most radical conclusions that some activists reach after engaging in praxis more open to fringe ideas.[10]

From the point of view of the promoters of a sortition chamber, preliminary consideration is necessary to appreciate fully the importance of movements. Social movements articulate a critical voice and express dissent on a wide array of issues exactly because of their marked partisan views and their familiarity with an array of democratic practices. Movements' contributions to society-wide deliberation are not generated by relying on deliberative means only. Rather, they also use different political strategies, including boycott, strikes, marches, internet activism, and various forms of disruption.[11] These varieties of participation are not only often legitimate from a democratic standpoint but also manifest the idea of democracy as a space for self-organized participation of citizens. It is fundamental, therefore, to make sure that a sortition chamber is conceived not as a substitute for these forms of dissent but as an addition to them.[12]

Social movements' involvement in the process might benefit the sortition chamber in several distinct ways. First, movements articulate critical social perspectives that enrich public deliberation if there are processes in place to properly channel them. Second, movements can produce collective identities and provide a special kind of adult civic education, without which citizens chosen by lot could act on the basis of a selfish and fragmented definition of their own material interests and could more easily be captured by institutional privileges.[13] A sortition chamber is fundamentally different when it draws from a society with vibrant social movements or from an atomized social world.[14] Finally, activists can be strategic partners for sortition chamber advocates by helping to set the stage for innovation and strengthen its legitimacy in the implementation phase. In the next two sections, we provide negative and then positive empirical illustrations of how the relationship with movement actors affects how minipublics are introduced and executed, as well as their capacity to influence the democratic system.

Learning from Missteps: Some Basic Lessons

The first empirical illustrations in this section are drawn from John Parkinson's study of deliberative forums in health and disability politics in the United Kingdom. Parkinson's investigation is especially interesting to us because it sheds light on what happens when the complex relationship between deliberative processes and public sphere actors is not taken into account properly.[15] The second illustration comes from the Australian Citizens' Assembly on Climate Change (CACC), a deliberative forum proposal that was never implemented also because of widespread opposition from social movements. Described by deliberative scholar Lyn Carson as an exemplary case of "how not to introduce deliberative democracy," the CACC's tale is worth considering lest the sortition chamber idea face a similar fate.[16]

National Health System Deliberations in the United Kingdom

John Parkinson's study of National Health System (NHS) deliberations is a pioneering research of how minipublics interact with broader deliberative systems. Parkinson investigated four case studies: two citizen juries, one deliberative poll, and one ad hoc multistage deliberative process. The first citizen jury was held in Belfast in 1998. Commissioned jointly by the organization responsible for planning and delivery of health services in the region and by its patients' watchdog body, it aimed to respond to a white paper setting out the UK government's agenda for the NHS. The second citizen jury was held in Leicester in 2000. It was organized by the local health authority, whose choice to reconfigure three local hospitals had spurred a storm of protest the previous year. The third case was a fully televised deliberative poll commissioned in 1998 by the NHS itself, on the occasion of its fiftieth anniversary. The event, like other deliberative polls, aimed at generating public debate about the NHS based on recommendations developed by citizens after deliberation. The last case was a multistage process in 2000 to develop a white paper on NHS institutional and regulatory reforms for the next ten years.

To begin with, Belfast's citizen jury was "a case of micro deliberation largely in isolation from more macro processes."[17] That is, the citizen jury was unable to link up with core health and disability agencies in Scotland and Westminster. It was also unable to interest civil-society organizations and the public at large, given the lack of popular demand for this event in the introductory phase. Similarly, the NHS deliberative poll also fell short of its ambition to generate widespread public debate. While the extent to which televised broadcasting was successful is disputed, the event almost completely lacked connection with civil-society actors and did not resonate with the public or policy makers.[18]

The basic problem with the Leicester citizen jury related, instead, to its being conceived largely as an effort to convince the public of the righteousness of the heavily contested choices of decision makers. Since its inception, it was met with great popular resistance; it was perceived as an illegitimate and insufficient initiative. Disability activists complained about a deliberative process that was "unable to give disabled people's concerns due weight because of the narrow agendas and motivations of those who set up a deliberative forum."[19] Furthermore, in terms of outcomes, the citizen jury made recommendations that authorities were not ready to implement.

The last case was the iterative deliberative process to write the NHS white paper. In Parkinson's view, this was the only one that gave "emphasis on putting public and patient involvement at the heart"; hence, it was the only one that played a "useful macro-deliberative function."[20]

The above cases show that the relationship between different actors and forms of participation in a deliberative democratic system deserves greater attention. In three out of four cases under examination, the relationship between minipublics and civil-society actors was set on a negative footing. In particular, it seems either ignored (Belfast citizen jury), bypassed by an optimistic reliance on traditional media (NHS deliberative poll), or experienced as a problem altogether (Leicester citizen jury). Before looking at ways to favor synergies between minipublics and movements, we briefly discuss another negative experience, this time involving a national-level minipublic.

The Australian Citizens' Assembly on Climate Change

The CACC proposal was first introduced by Julia Gillard, then Labour prime minister of Australia, during a heated federal electoral campaign. Climate change had been an issue of bitter controversy between the government and the Conservative opposition party. A long dispute over the opportunity to implement an emission trading scheme had led to an adversarial and polarized confrontation over climate change. When the CACC proposal was advanced by the Australian prime minister, it met a widespread negative response, which led its proponent to silently drop the idea. In their careful reconstruction, Bosswell et al. argue that the CACC represented a "stark example [of] elite resistance to democratic innovation."[21]

This account captures the sentiments displayed by many actors. Nonetheless, attention should also be paid to the fact that progressive actors in the Australian Greens Party, as well as leftist activists, attacked the proposal as a delaying tactic— an ill-concealed attempt by the Labour Party to avoid serious political action on climate change.[22] Discussing the merits of these accusations and the extent they might find support in the public at large is beyond the scope of this paper. Nevertheless, the harsh condemnation of the CACC proposal reaffirms the importance of how such ideas get introduced. Parachuting a democratic innovation down to the public, at the direction of an elite political actor, is hazardous at any time, let alone in the midst of an escalating power struggle. In such a context, deliberative innovations are likely to be interpreted as a targeted political strategy, rather than a broader democratic reform. This can jeopardize the possibility of a genuine bottom-up campaign for democratic innovation.

In addition, the CACC lacked the credibility necessary to win the support of social movements. During the Copenhagen Climate Change Conference, Australian environmentalists had first seen the Australian government signing up to a modest commitment to reduce Australian emissions by 5 percent by 2020. Furthermore, they saw the Labour Party withdrawing their proposal for a carbon-emission trading scheme amid divisions within the government and across the country. In the face of such a record, activists' support for a deliberative strategy to address climate change was understandably hard to muster. Involving deliberation-friendly political elites might be necessary to advance the prospect of the sortition chamber, yet it might be insufficient. The possibility of realizing this project and exploiting its democratic potential also lies in the ability to work constructively with social movements.

Success Stories and Their Insights

We will explore the potential for a positive relationship between movements and minipublics starting with a series of deliberative polls on energy issues held in Texas and Louisiana between 1996 and 1998. We then discuss the Oregon Citizens' Initiative Review (CIR), a small body of randomly selected citizens in charge of examining ballot measures and writing a succinct report featured in the voters' pamphlet during statewide initiative elections. Finally, we consider the Belgian G1000, a case of public deliberation directly emanating from a grassroots movement.

Deliberative Polls on Energy

Unlike the deliberative poll we discussed in the previous section, here we show how a different instance of this device proved remarkably consequential and interacted positively with movements. In occasion of the Texas deliberative polls on energy, the randomly selected participants were given information about cost and benefit and trade-offs between environmental protection and cheap energy to enable them to reason together about future energy policy. The subsequent reflections of these citizens provided decision-makers with the opinion of a representative sample of the population after deliberation. After talking through the issue, participants' opinions showed major shifts toward greener energy, with a willingness to accept higher electricity costs. This result fed into a broader statewide political reform agenda, which transformed Texas from a laggard to a leader in renewable energy in the United States.[23]

The above achievement can be attributed partly to the synergy between social-movement activities and the deliberative poll in seeking better forms of engagement on energy issues. By looking at the genealogy of Texas deliberative polls, we see how movements can prepare the groundwork for effective public deliberation and for the reception of its conclusions.[24]

In light of structural developments in the Texas economy, in the 1990s, environmentalist movements, NGOs, consumer groups, and renewable-energy firms formed a coalition of actors supporting policy change and insisting on the need to revise the procedures through which energy choices were made. Environmentalists did not ask for deliberative polls, as such, but they sought meaningful ways to consult the public on energy.[25]

Eventually, the Texas legislature empowered the Public Utility Commission to figure out how engagement should occur. The commission, which supervised the electric utility companies (then monopolies), made clear that companies would be expected to follow the results.[26] In light of this provision, electric utility companies found conventional methods unsatisfying. According to Fishkin, opinion polls were problematic because utility companies "knew that the public did not have information, or even opinions about the issue worth consulting"; with focus groups, instead, the problem was that companies "knew that they could never demonstrate to regulators that such small groups were representative"; and finally, town meetings "would be dominated by lobbyists and organized interests." Therefore, companies adopted deliberative polling, a method developed a decade earlier for surveying informed public opinion.[27]

This case offers insight also with respect to the execution of public deliberation. In particular, care should be taken to maintain the credibility of the project and to give activists an important role—if not in the deliberation itself, then in the wider process. In this sense, deliberative polling organizers took three important measures to address some standard criticisms of deliberative experiments that make activists skeptics: ineffectiveness, disenfranchisement of partisan actors, and manipulability of deliberation.

Organizers made sure that "the relevant official decision makers were embedded in a process that mandated strong consideration of the poll results."[28] This gave credibility to the process and created a reasonable expectation that deliberation would be consequential. Second, organizers insisted that deliberative polls be open to the public and transparent. This makes possible procedural fairness assessments by the public in general and for attentive observers, such as movement activists.

Furthermore, organizers called for an advisory committee of stakeholders to supervise the organization of the experiment (such as agenda, briefing material, and questionnaire). The committee included "consumer groups, environmental groups, advocates of alternative energy and more conventional energy sources, and representatives of the large customers."[29] From a movement standpoint, this last measure is especially relevant since it enables them, or for that matter any relevant actor, to actually contribute to the event from within. Though not necessarily unique to this case study, these design features help establishing a positive relationship between minipublics and movements.

Oregon Citizens' Initiative Review

Originally established by the Oregon legislature in 2009, the CIR has been considered by other state legislatures, counties, and cities as a means to produce a more informed electorate for votes on state initiatives.[30] The CIR offers interesting insights on the intimate connection between grassroots and deliberative politics and on the possibility to successfully overcoming tensions between the two.

To begin with, social-movement activists played an important role in initiating this form of public deliberation. As Gastil and Knoblock's in-depth study of CIR shows, the anti-WTO mobilization in Seattle provided fertile ground in which the CIR idea could be developed. In particular, activist circles in Washington State offered a network for the CIR idea to circulate and a source of people committed to a project to be eventually implemented in the neighboring state of Oregon.[31] In other words, these circles effectively functioned as what Mansbridge calls "deliberative enclaves."[32]

The CIR also offers insight on how the tensions that are bound to emerge between activists and deliberation advocates can be soothed. In line with deliberative democratic ideas, the CIR does not grant any special role to activists in the deliberative body. However, it does allow activists to advocate for their views while the citizen panel reviews ballot measures. Including activists' views—among those of other relevant actors—helps give space to all relevant voices. A public deliberation that silenced the voices of civic-society organizations mobilizing for or against a given issue would be gravely flawed.

This was exactly the risk faced by one CIR assembly when a nonprofit progressive coalition decided to boycott the deliberative process. In particular, the group unexpectedly refused to advocate before the CIR assembly in favor of a measure for which they were campaigning. They then tried to discredit the deliberative assembly in a local newspaper by labeling it as inconsequential—not worthy of their attention. CIR organizers had to quickly find new advocates and defend themselves from accusations in order to avoid a significant undermining of the process.[33]

The response of CIR organizers to this emergency provides a positive illustration of how to address the incidents that inevitably arise during the execution of public deliberation. In the first place, in the variegated world of grassroots politics and despite the boycott, organizers were still able to find valid activists willing to argue in favor of the measure under examination. In addition, the tension between the CIR and the advocacy group was disclosed to deliberators, who had learned of it through the local press. Although deliberators investigated the matter during deliberation, they remained focused upon discussing the content of the measure under examination. Indeed, they ended up favoring the measure, in spite of its proponent's boycott.

Meanwhile, organizers were able to counter accusations thanks to the CIR's reputation. As we saw previously, grassroots actors, and the public in general, might unyieldingly oppose even the very idea of public deliberation when promoted by partisan political actors. At the same time, they might well continue supporting a democratic innovation and a group of innovators that have cultivated credibility and trustworthiness even when a substantial problem occurs. Indeed, after this episode, the divergence between the boycotting advocacy group and the CIR process subsided and collaboration was reestablished.[34]

Belgium G1000

Held in Belgium between 2011 and 2012, the G1000 was national-level experiment that aimed at engaging a wide audience in political discourse and generating bottom-up policy suggestions. The experiment was born and developed within the context of a wave of grassroots mobilizations that emerged in 2010. Protests were stirred by a parliamentarian crisis during which, for more than five hundred days, political parties were unable to install a government, and popular trust in government fell dramatically.[35]

The extent of embeddedness of the G1000 in grassroots politics is unique. To begin with, ideas underpinning the G1000 project resonate widely with those of social movements critical of contemporary democracies.[36] For instance, the idea of a crisis of democracy—manifested in a growing gap between citizens and politics, in political agendas that seem more responsive to elites' rather than popular demands, in a passive citizenry—was at the basis of this citizen-led initiative. Further, the G1000 was intended to be "a grassroots initiative by and for citizens" that was "run entirely voluntarily" and rooted in civil society. The effort was crowdfunded entirely through the support of more than three thousand donors.[37]

The wave of grassroots mobilizations from which the G1000 emerged was a reaction to Belgium's political impasse, but also to the related tension between the Flemish and Walloon communities. During the crisis, in a "climate where regionalist sentiments and discourse skyrocketed and any compromise was explicitly labelled treacherous, Belgium witnessed the rise of a number of protest movements," which included the Shame protest march, the Not in My Name initiative, and the Fries revolution. Against this backdrop, in the words of Caluwaerts and Reuchamps, the G1000 stood out as "the only systematic initiative that truly succeeded in putting dialogue between the communities center stage on the political agenda."[38] Street protest having generated no substantive effect, grassroots actors adopted an ambitious deliberative experiment to try to mend, from the bottom up, a political situation brought to a stalemate by actors at the top of the political system.

A second important aspect concerns the implementation of this experiment and its remarkable ability to meet deliberative standards. Despite limited resources and a lack of institutional support, the G1000 allowed for actual deliberative engagement to occur across a fairly wide sector of the Belgian population. The process was articulated in three stages: public consultation, large-scale citizen summit, and in-depth citizen panel. Agenda setting was not predetermined by organizers, but open to public input. Online public consultation—the first stage of the process—allowed for anyone to suggest themes and issues for discussion at the G1000 summit.

That summit in Brussels—the second phase of the experiment—was modeled after the town hall meeting idea, with participants selected through sortition and targeted recruitment. In the last phase, thirty-two people among summit participants were randomly selected for a more in-depth deliberation and asked to provide final propositions. Despite the experiment's significant limitations from a deliberative standpoint, G1000 activists managed to conceive and implement a large-scale deliberative process, relying on public rather than institutional means.[39]

As for the impact of the G1000, it arguably had valuable effects in line with its promises. Its lack of any substantial impact on policy making is hardly surprising, as other deliberative assemblies that were closely coupled with institutions and committed to influencing policy had also failed to do so. Importantly, the G1000 never raised the expectation that it would impact policy making. Rather, the experiment was explicitly aimed at delivering a different and important outcome—revitalizing public debate and addressing deep division within the national political community. In this respect, it fared significantly well. Ideas and methods of the G1000 "stirred public opinion" and set in motion a public debate "about the quality and organization of democracy," the meaning of contemporary citizenship, and "how politics should be shaped in order to meet the demands from the citizens."[40] Furthermore, the G1000, which attracted substantial coverage in the media, contributed to the fact that today in Belgium, according to Caluwaerts et al., "most political parties now advocate some form of participatory and deliberative democracy."[41] Finally, the G1000 inspired similar events in Flanders and Wallonia and abroad, for example in

Spain, the Netherlands, and the United Kingdom.[42] Minipublics endowed with institutional support or resources from powerful foundations can only rarely boast such achievements.

The Evolving Settings of Minipublics, Movements' Interaction

Having demonstrated the changes in the relationship between public deliberation and movements in different contexts, we will now briefly discuss developments in the way sortition assemblies have been related to movements. Based on the above illustrations, we distinguish three settings: minipublics catering to movements and the public; experiments executed in interaction with movements; and minipublics fully developed in-house by civil-society actors.

The first type of engagement seems typical of more traditional deliberative experiments. It is illustrated by the Texas deliberative polls and the NHS deliberations. This approach, whereby minipublics are devised by a small circle of actors largely removed from the rest of the system, configures a passive, limited involvement of social-movement activists. If deliberative processes are properly designed, this approach might be adopted to deal with a moderately contentious issue in which relevant actors seem interested in trying the option of a deliberative process to come to a solution (such as Texas deliberative polls). This approach might be ineffective for involving actors uninterested in minipublics (such as the NHS deliberative poll and the Glasgow citizen jury), or it might backfire altogether when minipublics are imposed upon civic-society actors who are already highly mobilized in contention (such as the Leicester citizen jury and the ACCP).

Though it embeds elements of the passive involvement approach, the Oregon CIR also features some aspects of the more interactive approach. In particular, activists' environments offered a space for developing the CIR idea, and activists contributed to each CIR's deliberative process. The ability to attain effective deliberation and to bolster the democratic potential of minipublics will crucially depend on the establishment of working and trusting relationships with movements. As the CIR shows, these are necessary to buffer the tensions that are bound to occur when activists and deliberation advocates work closely. The interactive approach might represent an ideal development for political institutions aiming to engage with deliberation. Nonetheless, weak institutional commitment to deliberative democracy and low public trust might jeopardize institutional ability to pursue this approach. Against this backdrop, civil-society actors might be more interested in deliberating at a distance from the state than within it.

The G1000 is a case of public-based deliberation, whereby minipublics are devised by, executed within, and meant for the public. It bears witness to the ability of movement activists and civil-society actors to autonomously engage in deliberation. Even if nondeliberative politics has not lost its centrality to movement politics, movement actors seem increasingly capable of and interested in deliberation. Because sortition chambers aim at entering the legislative process, they cannot be developed at a distance from institutions. Yet, the bottom-up deliberation model reminds us that deliberation is not a sole prerogative of the state and that activists can actively contribute to give shape to critical publics as well as deliberative platforms.

Conclusion: Rooting the Sortition Chamber in Democratic Ground

The ability of minipublics to establish a successful relationship with movements varies greatly. On the one hand, three of the UK deliberations studied by Parkinson as well as Australia's Citizen Assembly on Climate Change served as illustrations of conflictual relationships. On the other, the deliberative poll on energy in Texas, the Oregon Citizen's Initiative, and the Belgian G1000 attested to the possibility of a more positive interaction.

All of the four negative cases share three important and related features. First, they are introduced largely as top-down projects; second, in their development they are largely disconnected from the deliberative system; and third, they fail to attain substantial outcomes. Regrettably, the deliberative literature is replete with experiments catering to communities that did not ask for deliberative innovations. Minipublics tend to stem from the initiatives of policy makers, experts, and practitioners, rather than from popular demand for deliberation. Actors outside the restricted circles of supporters of the deliberative experiment might well have no significant access, voice, ownership, or interest in the development of these projects.[43] This creates poor conditions for connecting the minipublic with the wider deliberative system, jeopardizing the potential to elicit public-sphere debate or to impact policy making. While insufficient to steer the interest of unengaged publics, octroyed deliberation often elicits suspicion among mobilized actors. This dynamic harms movements and deliberative advocates alike because it prevents grassroots actors from distinguishing between those experiments that are intentionally top-down and window dressings and those that, instead, represent genuine efforts toward participatory empowerment, deserving of greater consideration. Deliberative and democratic as they might be, deliberative innovation projects need broad support to affirm themselves in the political system.[44]

The three positive cases offer insight on how to create a better context for minipublics based on synergy with movements. The deliberative polls on energy, the Oregon Citizen's Initiative Review, and the G1000 illustrate how movements might provide an important platform to initiate public deliberation and a strategic partner to sustain it and bolster its effectiveness.

The creation of a strong basis upon which to build public deliberation is particularly important to the sortition chamber idea, since this will be the first and hopefully the next stage of its realization. To begin with, the deliberative polls on energy were built upon a political demand by movements for meaningful and consequential involvement of the public. This circumstance seems particularly felicitous when compared to efforts to introduce deliberation in which there is no public demand for more deliberative engagement or where political confrontation has long been unraveling. The CIR case, instead, shows how politically active grassroots communities might be incubators for specific deliberative innovations. Support from high-level political actors is necessary to bring to life a deliberative forum. Nonetheless, the CIR illustrates how nesting an idea in activist enclaves provides a preliminary step, whose importance should not be underestimated. Baiocchi and Ganuza show how a powerful democratic idea such as participatory budgeting might lose its critical bite when it shifts from "a tool of emancipation" into yet another template for participation, a "technical solution."[45] Radical soil is good ground for critical ideas to grow strong. In the case of the G1000, the extent of embeddedness of public deliberation within grassroots politics is unprecedented. The public's ability to engage in mass deliberation in reaction to a paralyzed and divided political system is remarkable. This kind of public might well be a more receptive and dynamic partner than are the actors at the top of the democratic system. As Vandamme et al.'s chapter in this volume shows, the public's view on democratic innovations is deeply shaped by the way in which public deliberation is introduced. Insensitivity to the preferences of the public comes at a price for democratic innovation.

Once a minipublic has been introduced appropriately in its own context, design issues can help it to work effectively. In particular, activists' continued support for a sortition chamber will also depend on the quality of the proposal, particularly on the measures taken to grant its credibility. In this sense, the Texas deliberative polls give us a good sense of essential moves to be taken to tackle the traditional weaknesses of minipublics. First and foremost, activists should be given a substantial role in the deliberative process. Built-in mechanisms should ensure that movements (and other partisan actors) can contribute to shaping the agenda of the deliberation and advocate for their positions. Moreover, movement activists should not only be observers of the deliberative process, helplessly disenfranchised by it. They should have a say in how the process unfolds and challenge procedural decisions they deem unfair. This inclusion of an advisory committee or another body favors this effort toward inclusive governance.[46] This is necessary to grant grass-roots actors ownership and guard against attempts to manipulate the process over the way a deliberative process unfolds. Ensuring that engagement in public deliberation is perceived as being consequential is also highly important. This elicits a reasonable expectation that participating in the process is worthwhile and that deliberation might represent a way to pursue the goals of the movement.

The Oregon CIR offers insight on crises between organizers of minipublics and activists in the execution of a deliberative forum. The main point here is that tensions are unavoidable when a deliberative forum interacts with movements over time. As seen, the deep causes of these conflicts lie in ideological commitments and strategic imperatives that might put some movements at odds with public deliberation in some cases. However, crisis is not and should not be seen as the natural state of the relationship between deliberation and social movements. The CIR shows that credibility and trustworthiness are key assets for a healthy relationship with movements. As seen, projects and innovators that are not credible to the public might founder in the face of mere suspicion about the motives of proponents.[47] Credible actors, instead, might not just weather a momentary stall but take advantage of it to reaffirm their genuine commitment to democracy and their proven record of high-quality deliberative engagement.

Finally, the G1000 attests not only to the ability of the public to conduct public deliberation on a large scale, but also to its capacity to stir substantial public debate on conflictual issues, to spread talk of deliberative reforms at the state level, and to serve as a model for democracy activists. It thus shows that embeddedness in public deliberation is essential to democratic innovations. Nonetheless, the fact that mass public deliberation is organized at a distance from the state speaks volumes to the widening gulf between political institutions and the public. Against this backdrop, a sortition chamber should be designed in a way that allows not only for effective interface with other democratic institutions, but also for a strong link with the public. If the sortition chamber aims, as it does, at bringing citizens into the legislative process, then insights by grassroots critical actors should be treasured as the building blocks of a democratic innovation that is capable of meeting the democratic ambitions of the public.

A demand-driven approach and a bottom-up campaign nested in activist circles are necessary to grounding the sortition chamber idea in the public sphere. This increases the potential for this innovation to work as a connector between the public sphere and public institutions and to be the carrier of critical perspectives, effectively questioning the actions of political representatives and promoting new developments. That is, a sortition chamber grounded in the public sphere would play the transmission and accountability functions that, according to Dryzek, are vital in a democratic system.[48] These arrangements would also allow for movements to work as "inducers of connectivity": actors that can promote a deliberative system "in which the parts do not ignore each other or operate independently," stitching together different parts of the system and increasing the exchanges between discursive arenas.[49] As the ability to keep legislative chambers accountable through electoral mechanisms is increasingly questioned and their responsiveness to elites' interests clashes with their mandate to represent popular constituencies, a sortition chamber with strong ties in the public sphere would represent a valuable, democratic addition to the political system.

III. DEMOCRATIC PRINCIPLES

8

Should Democracy Work Through Elections or Sortition?

Tom Malleson

The current state of representative democracy in many countries is deeply troubling. For many progressives, reforming the national legislature has meant establishing proportional representation and strict campaign-finance regulation. The former serves to increase the representativeness of the electoral system, and the latter tries to limit the distorting effects of money on politics.

Yet in recent years, a number of bolder proposals have emerged, whose advocates argue that the defects of representative democracy would be better cured by establishing a legislature by lot. As with Gastil and Wright's lead chapter in this volume, such proposals would have us select members of the legislature at random from the population at large. Some have argued for a bicameral system involving an elected chamber alongside a sortition chamber.[1] Others have argued more radically, and often more polemically, for the exclusive use of sortition, with the abolition of elections altogether.[2]

On hearing such suggestions, most contemporary democrats will be skeptical of the idea of a legislature by lot, as they share the conventional view that democracy fundamentally *means* elections. Yet it is instructive to recall that for more than two thousand years, from Pericles to Montesquieu, democracy was associated with lot, whereas elections were thought to go hand-in-hand with oligarchy. It is only in the last couple of hundred years that our culture has become certain that democracy means elections.[3] One of my central goals in this paper is to help us unlearn this relatively recent certainty.

The question for progressives, and really for everyone who believes in democracy, is this: Are democratic ideals better served by elections or sortition? Is the ideal national legislature elected, chosen by lot, or some combination thereof?

To properly answer this question, I hope to provide a careful, balanced, and systematic comparison of the strengths and weaknesses of each alternative. In particular, I will emphasize the tensions and trade-offs that may exist when designing institutions to satisfy a variety of democratic values.

There is too little comparative work in the contemporary literature. Of course, almost all of the discussion of sortition involves at least some commentary on its supposed advantages vis-à-vis electoral democracy, but there are very few attempts to systematically compare the two.[4] Moreover, much of the work on sortition that involves a contrast with elections suffers from a deep methodological flaw of comparing the *contemporary empirical reality* of the US electoral system, warts and all, with a *future ideal* of sortition.[5]

Thus, to understand the pros and cons of elections and sortition, I will contrast an imaginary, well-functioning, realistic, and imperfect electoral body (with proportional representation and strong campaign-finance regulation) with an imaginary, well-functioning, realistic, and imperfect sortition body (with a membership drawn from the population randomly, who undertake carefully moderated learning, deliberation, and public consultations).[6] In doing so, I will distinguish between features of these rival systems that are *contingent* (that is, those that good institutional design might mitigate) versus aspects that are *inherent* (that is, those that flow from the very logic of the system itself).[7]

I begin by outlining the key values that democrats want their systems to possess. These values will be the measuring sticks for the comparison that follows. On the basis of these values, we compare a purely elected legislature with a purely sortition legislature, with the assumption that each has the full decision-making powers normally possessed by national legislatures. This big-picture analysis will allow us to get a clearer view of the strengths and weaknesses of the respective systems, the trade-offs, and the open questions that still exist.

In what follows, I compare elections and sortition on the basis of their ability to fulfill the following key democratic values:

1. *Political equality*—meaning that each adult has roughly similar access to influence over government policy. In order to assess this, we examine the issues of a) the descriptive representation of the population in the legislature and b) the reduction of the influence of money, and the power of the rich, on politics.
2. *Popular control*—meaning that the legislature is responsive and accountable to the people.
3. *Deliberative and impartial*—meaning that government decisions are based on good deliberation, and so they are reasonable, open-minded, thoughtful, and aimed at the common good, or at least a fair compromise.
4. *Competency*—meaning that decision-makers are able to come to well-informed decisions.

Political Equality

In considering political equality, I look first at descriptive representation and then at the influence of unevenly distributed wealth on the political system. Both are relevant to the question of sortition, but in very different ways.[8]

Descriptive Representation

Across the world, electoral systems tend to produce low levels of descriptive representation, with wealthy middle-aged males being overrepresented. This descriptive unrepresentativeness appears to be an inherent feature of electoral democracy. Empirically, we see it even in places like Sweden, with well-functioning proportional representation systems. In the Swedish Riksdag, the young (ages eighteen to forty) make up only 10 percent of MPs, yet 44 percent of the electorate; blue-collar workers make up 9 percent of MPs and 41 percent of the electorate; and the low-educated make up 12 percent of MPs and 44 percent of the electorate. Moreover, while there has been progress over the years in getting more women into parliament, other groups have seen no progress at all. Over the last fifty years, the number of working-class members of parliament has actually decreased.[9]

The very logic of election leads to unrepresentativeness because those who have the time, money, connections, and profile required to run successful campaigns are likely to be, on average, wealthy, educated, and from dominant social positions. This is the Janus-faced nature of elections that Manin points to: the democratic aspect that everyone can choose, coexists with the undemocratic aspect that it is elites who invariably tend to be chosen.[10]

By contrast, sortition would be much more descriptively representative. A random sample (presuming it is large enough) or a stratified sample would produce what John Adams memorably referred to as an assembly that is "in miniature an exact portrait of the people at large."[11]

To see how dramatic a change this would be, consider what would happen if the US Senate were to change overnight from an elected to a sortition house. The number of males would go from 79 percent down to 49 percent, while the number of females would go up from 21 percent to 51 percent; the number of whites would go down from 90 percent to 77 percent, and the number of blacks and Hispanics would go up from 3 percent and 4 percent to 13 percent and 18 percent, respectively. Sortition members would be significantly younger (the average senator is sixty-two years old), and less educated (76 percent of senators have more than a bachelor's degree). Finally, the Senate would cease being a club for millionaires; the median senator is worth $3,100,000, and the chamber consists mainly of lawyers, professional politicians, and business people. These would be replaced by wage workers, caregivers, unemployed youth, retired seniors, and others—with a median net worth of $45,000.[12] This government of caregivers and workers has, at least rhetorically, been a long-standing goal of socialist activists and parties, but it is one that has never come close to being realized through elections.[13]

If an electoral body would be less descriptively representative than a sortition body, does this matter? The evidence shows that, compared to white politicians, racial minorities are more supportive of legislation that is important to such minorities.[14] Compared to male legislators, female politicians are more likely to support feminist public policy.[15] Working-class politicians are more likely to support progressive economic legislation than are their upper-class counterparts.[16] In sum, those groups underrepresented in electoral bodies are likely to have their interests better represented by a randomly selected body. With regard to political equality, this is a major point in favor of sortition.

Political Equality and the Influence of Money

The distortions caused by uneven distributions of wealth hamstring ostensibly democratic systems. A well-functioning electoral system will have stringent regulations around money in politics, such as contribution limits, campaign-spending rules, public financing, disclosure requirements, and restrictions on certain types of third-party campaigning. Reforms like these can mitigate the influence of money but never eliminate it. Though outright corruption or bribery will grab occasional headlines, the real problem stems from the very DNA of elections themselves. An absolute precondition of getting elected is for politicians to become well known. Yet all else equal, those with more money will inevitably fare better at communicating their message and mobilizing their base than their rivals. Therefore, it seems likely that electoral democracy, regardless of the campaign-finance rules, will always be somewhat biased toward the rich.

What about a sortition chamber, which has—as Gastil and Wright suggest—full legislative power, and membership tenure lasting several years? Advocates of sortition often take for granted that such a system would result in far less corruption or policy distortions favoring wealthy interests.[17] Indeed, choosing political representatives by random selection could immediately break up the networks of power, influence, lobbying, and patronage surrounding elections.[18] This fact, however, in no way guarantees that sortition representatives will *continue* to be insulated from financial influence over time.[19]

Unfortunately, we have no clear analogies or empirical evidence to guide us here. Though Gastil and Wright point to minipublics as precedent, there is, in fact, a vast difference between the citizens' assemblies convened in British Columbia and Ontario and a full-bore sortition chamber. I call this the *scale-transformation* problem: whereas the citizens' assemblies had the power only to suggest a proposal to be voted on by the electorate, a sortition chamber would have full legislative authority to levy taxes, criminalize dissent, democratize workplaces, or even declare wars (albeit alongside an elected chamber in Gastil and Wright's proposal). Such powers mean that wealthy individuals and powerful corporations would have enormous incentives to influence how sortition members vote. In the US today, for example, there are roughly twenty lobbyists per congressperson.[20] Another major difference is the long tenure. Whereas the citizens' assemblies met for less than thirty days in total over the course of a year, sortition members would be in power for much longer—up to five years in Gastil and Wright's proposal. The danger here is that the longer the period in which one is in power, the more susceptible to corruption one becomes.

Imagine that through selection by lot, a number of people get selected whom we might call Cynical Self-Seekers. They participate purely for personal financial advancement and seek bribes or more indirect rewards, such as offers of future employment. With neither an interest in politics nor a concern for the common good, what prevents them from putting their votes up for sale?

On the one hand, I believe this danger is greater than most commentators have assumed. The temptations will be great. Moreover, sortition members would not have the standard restraints of accountability to constituents or to a political party, which can discipline individual members who threaten its collective reputation.

On the other hand, good institutional design could address these dangers. Protective measures could include a significant initial training period, which stresses norms of public service, honesty, and transparency; requiring members to take an oath to serve the public interest; allowing members to recommend the removal of other members who demonstrably lack integrity and commitment (for example, by not showing up to meetings or participating in the deliberation, or being drunk, disruptive, or disrespectful); increasing the size of a sortition chamber to, say, one thousand people to dilute the utility of bribing any one individual; requiring members to disclose their personal finances during their term in office and for five years following; banning members from accepting any public office for five years following their term; and having strong penalties, including jail terms, for both the briber and the bribed. If all of these measures were in place, I suspect that most Cynical Self-Seekers would decline to serve, given the difficulties of gaming the system and the severity of the risks involved.

Overall, the main difference between the systems is that elected politicians are systemically biased toward money because they must campaign for election or reelection, whereas sortition members are free from such pressures. Though money will have indirect influence on any system of government, the sortition body again fares better in this second dimension of political equality.

Popular Control

In many ways, the heart of democracy is the ideal of popular control and accountability. When a political system's scale is so large that the people cannot directly govern themselves, democracy requires representatives to act on the public's behalf. For this to work properly, accountability is essential. So let us now consider the strengths and weaknesses of elections and sortition in this regard.

For an electoral system, the major limit to accountability stems from the independence that elected politicians have from their constituents when making decisions. One problem is that elected politicians have little to no incentive to respond to constituents from other parties. Moreover, a vote for a candidate—or even for a party—is a blunt instrument to signal one's complex policy preferences. Party discipline, which candidates owe to the party that then steers their votes once in office, further limits a candidate's responsiveness to constituents. Finally, most policy making involves both opacity and complexity,[21] which makes it difficult for constituents to grasp the consequences of representatives' votes on their behalf.

Nonetheless, a well-functioning electoral system still provides a certain degree of blunt accountability.[22] Whereas party discipline does restrain individual representatives, it also allows for accountability in a collective sense by transforming platform promises into policy. Political parties can also tackle complexity and opacity by foregrounding their broadest contrasts with opposing parties. At their best, parties give constituents real choices in terms of broad values and policy priorities. Elections then give voters the chance to hold parties accountable for delivering, or failing to deliver, on those promises. Indeed, anyone doubting the significance of such choices is insensitive to the consequences of electing, say, Donald Trump as opposed to Hillary Clinton.

What about sortition? Since members are not elected, there are no direct mechanisms of accountability in the usual sense. However, Philip Pettit has argued that sortition does provide a kind of popular control, which he refers to as "indicative."[23] To borrow Pettit's example, if I want to have some accountability over, say, a new university committee that has been convened to investigate how to make philosophy more appealing to female students, one way to do this is to have the committee members run for election. But another way is to establish a system (such as sortition or stratification) that ensures that some of the members are "like me" in that they share my values and principles and are likely to make the same decisions I would make if I were on the committee. If such people really are similar enough to me, then Pettit is right that ensuring their presence really does give me some influence and control over what happens. The argument is similar for a sortition body: if the descriptive representation works well so that some of the members are "like me" in their values, then there is indeed a kind of popular control here. Granted, I do not have any direct control over the decision-makers, but if I can ensure that the process includes people "like me," then I do gain some indirect control over the decisions made.

The difference between election and sortition is that while both provide popular influence over representatives at the initial time of selection, as time goes by there is no way for regular people to continue to exert real influence over sortition members. Citizens can try to participate at a public consultation, but only a small number of members will be able to listen to a very small proportion of the citizenry, and even those citizens who do get the chance to participate have no power to make members listen; sortition members are always free to ignore them without consequence. The difference with elections, of course, is that they give representatives continual incentives to be sensitive and responsive to the desires of their constituents.

Another problem with sortition in this regard is that in such a system regular citizens do not get to participate in the formal political system at all. A vote once every few years is not a lot of political participation; but it is meaningful. Under sortition, there is a sense in which the people would be disenfranchised from the political process. What is particularly worrying here is the lack of clear, formal channels for citizens to transform their dissent into political power, and the frustration this might generate. If citizens cannot collectively mobilize through elections to get what they want in a legal, nonviolent way, the incentive to look to extraconstitutional means becomes that much greater.

Another issue relevant to the idea of accountability is whether the deliberations and the final vote should be public or held in secret. There is a difficult trade-off here: secrecy may improve the quality of deliberation, as it makes it easier for members to give up old positions and change their minds; secrecy of final votes may also help with the problem of corruption, since prospective bribers would be unable to verify how any representative voted; and secrecy can also protect the decision-makers from the embarrassment of being shamed or ridiculed (a real prospect in the age of social media). On the other hand, the more that decisions are made in secret, the less accountable the decision-making process.

There is no easy answer here, and I would not pretend to have total confidence in the solution, but my considered judgment is, contra Gastil and Wright, that while occasional deliberations may be confidential, final legislative votes should probably be public. This is because the central weakness of sortition is its lack of accountability, and so we should not exacerbate the problem further. It seems hard to believe that the general public could accept having major decisions made in secret. That would mean having a legislature where not only can we not throw the scoundrels out, but we also cannot even know which scoundrels are making the decisions that are impacting us. That strikes me as a step too far. Allowing sortition members to stay barricaded behind the walls of secrecy does protect them from ridicule, but it also removes them too far from the push and pull of the public sphere. In a democratic society, accountability requires transparency: the right to know precisely who is making decisions, to look them in the eyes and demand the reasons for their actions. An important aspect of accountability is lost if we cannot expose actual human decision-makers to public scrutiny and contestation, and to put pressure on them to take account of what the people think.

If the decision-makers are known, then members of the public can try to exert the pressures of public discourse. The public can try to persuade, convince, shame, encourage, support, and morally exhort sortition members (though threats, malicious slander, and hate speech should be illegal). Decision-makers will know and feel that their final votes are being watched.[24] If, on the contrary, the decision-makers are unknown, then activists cannot communicate with them, cannot write letters, cannot invite sortition members to participate in public debates, cannot send representatives of social movements to reason with them, cannot hold protests or vigils outside their office, and so on. In this way an important avenue of accountability is lost.

This would mean that sortition members have to account to the public and media for their votes. That would certainly be an intimidating thing for regular people to do. But note that the pressures on them are somewhat different than for elected politicians. Before a vote takes place, it would be completely acceptable for a sortition member to avoid media questions by simply saying, "I don't yet have a firm opinion; we are still learning and deliberating." That is legitimate in a way that it would not be for elected politicians, who are always supposed to have a confident answer to every question. This fact would significantly ease potential embarrassment. After the vote, however, sortition members should have to face the music and explain to the public why they voted the way they did.

In sum, elections offer blunt accountability—perhaps more via parties than individual candidates. Sortition gives the public a kind of control over the selection process, but it lacks the disciplining function provided by elections. Making sortition members' final votes public would somewhat help with accountability, though it also risks opening up members to ridicule and censure. All in all, elections do better on this score.

Deliberation and Impartiality

Ideally, a democratic body should make decisions through high-quality deliberation. The people's representatives should be honest, thoughtful, open-minded, impartial, and public-spirited—asking not "what is best for *my group*?" but "what is best for *all of us*?" A chamber populated by such persons would establish consensus where possible and fair compromises when appropriate, and it would always let the force of the better argument prevail.

How well do elections serve this end? One problem is that the public who does the electing is often extremely uninformed.[25] Beyond this, the inherent logic of electoral competition undermines the possibilities for good deliberation. There are at least four reasons for this. First, the skills and traits most useful in elections are in many ways the opposite of those of good deliberators. Second, electoral competition creates a strong and continual incentive to "score points"—to never give one's opponents "a win," even if doing so would better serve your own constituents' interests. Indeed, few things can deflate one's enthusiasm for democracy more than watching parliamentary discussion, with its incessant mudslinging, booing, clapping, and stomping. Third, electoral competition leads representatives to focus on short-term solutions, for which they can claim credit.[26] Such competition also stunts political learning, since veteran politicians can be punished by party and voters alike for changing their minds.

What about sortition? We cannot simply assume that bringing people together results in good deliberation. Designing the conditions for quality deliberation is a difficult task—part art, part science, as Lyn Carson shows in her contribution to this volume.[27] Using this knowledge, it is plausible to envision a well-functioning (though imperfect) sortition chamber, divided up into the major branches of public policy, where members engage in periods of learning from diverse experts, regular public consultations, and ongoing small-group deliberation. Skillful moderation and facilitation can foster relatively equal member participation and a respectful, caring atmosphere, especially if some discussions happen in closed sessions, free from the pressures to perform that come from publicity.

None of this will happen automatically; it will require a carefully managed infrastructure of resources and support, skillful facilitators, and administrative oversight. Since the administrators and facilitators must play a key role in the sortition body, we must carefully structure this background infrastructure (which we might call the Office of Deliberative Administration).

It will need to be staunchly neutral on all ideological and policy questions and concern itself only with the practical matters of deliberation, such as procuring experts.

How exactly this office should operate remains an open question of utmost importance for future research, since it must not be allowed to influence the sortition chamber (for instance by only selecting experts from one side of an issue) or be captured by partisan interests.[28] One possibility might be to require the office to prepare regular reports of its activities, then appear before a committee of the sortition chamber to justify and explain its actions. The sortition members could have some authority to hire, fire, or reconstitute aspects of the office, since the sortition body itself has a vested interest in maintaining its legitimacy by showing itself to be a rigorously deliberative and nonpartisan space.

Advocates of sortition insist that a legislature by lot would perform significantly better than an elected chamber in terms of deliberation and impartiality. Without party discipline or the need to pander to any constituency, members would be free to listen to each other, learn, change their minds, and be guided by the force of the better (and, I would hope, more caring) argument. Moreover, the descriptive representation of the body means that it would be much more socially varied—encompassing the experiences of not just rich white men, but women, the poor, renters instead of owners, and employees instead of employers. As a result, it would be epistemically richer. Indeed, a wealth of recent experiences with minipublics shows that, under the right conditions, citizens can engage in high-quality deliberation.[29]

Beyond this, there is one serious caveat to the deliberative potential of a legislature by lot, which is whether the long tenure of members would lead to factions or parties emerging, thereby undermining the quality of deliberation. Recalling the scale-transformation problem, minipublics have little to say on this issue, given their short lifespans and limited authority.

In bicameral sortition models, like the one proposed by Gastil and Wright, there are several sources of pressure pushing toward factionalization. Elected politicians will have a strong interest in actively lobbying sortition members to join their party—if not formally, then at least as informal political allies. A long tenure means that sortition members themselves will have an incentive to self-organize into factions and coalitions, to be more effective in getting their preferred legislation passed.

On the other hand, one of the strongest motivations to form parties in the first place—winning elections—would be absent. The sortition chamber would have a deliberative structure of small-group discussions, learning, and facilitated exchange of ideas. These encourage people to not just stick to one position, but to evolve in an open-minded way. Additionally, the members themselves have at least some motivation to not form political parties or obvious coalitions, as their own legitimacy (and hence power) depends on being able to convince the public that they are impartial deliberators. Overall, it seems unlikely that a sortition chamber would become as rigidly factional as electoral chambers, so we can expect sortition's deliberation to be somewhat better. Yet we should take note of the trade-off here: longer tenure leads to more competency (as members become expert in their various policy areas), but it may also increase the likelihood of rigid factions forming and deliberation deteriorating.

In sum, electoral systems rarely create the conditions for good deliberation. A sortition chamber has greater potential to deliberate impartially, with less posturing and factionalism. It is fair to say that advocates of sortition are justified in having some optimism on this score, though the lack of evidence from really existing sortition bodies means that it should be optimism of a cautious sort.

Competency

Every now and then, a politician will get elected who is strikingly incompetent. Donald Trump is a paradigmatic example,[30] but such cases are the exception, not the rule.

Getting elected usually requires a long period—often years— of participating in local politics, working one's way up the party ladder, hosting events and fundraisers, engaging in debates and interviews, persuading other party members to select you as a viable candidate, and then convincing tens of thousands of strangers to trust you. This grueling process usually weeds out incompetent people. Political parties also play an important role in generating policy expertise. It is not necessary (nor would it be possible) for individual politicians to be experts on all the different policy areas; belonging to a party provides politicians with a massive infrastructure of knowledge and shared policy goals. Thus, while we should not exaggerate the competency of elected officials, electoral systems tend to generate competency.

By contrast, this criterion poses a challenge for sortition. Will random members of the public prove capable of understanding and making sound decisions on complex policy problems? Consider two types of people that could be problematic for a sortition chamber, whom I refer to as the Unknowledgeable (such as a high school dropout with a learning disability) and the Ideologue (such as a committed white supremacist or doctrinaire Leninist).

The Ideologue poses a manageable problem, as it would become obvious to other members that such an individual is closed-minded, unwilling to work in a deliberative spirit, or disrespectful. In extreme cases where the Ideologue becomes altogether disruptive, members should be able to recommend their expulsion. In more common instances, the sortition body can work around such a person, or simply ignore them.

The issue of the Unknowledgeable sortition member is more difficult. It seems likely that most would not volunteer to participate in the first place. Those who do might be educated in general knowledge and might be helped to develop their capacity for judgment—but only partially. The sortition chamber faces a trade-off in that it could impose some basic competency requirements (such as basic literacy or a high school diploma) to prevent the worst problems of incompetency, but this would also reduce the descriptive representativeness of its membership.

In addition to the problem of the Unknowledgeable, another deep competency problem flows from the scale-transformation issue. Since a sortition chamber would be so much more complex than a minipublic, such as a citizens' assembly, even its more knowledgeable members may not prove competent—at least by comparison with the average elected official.

Consider some of the details about what an all-purpose sortition chamber would have to do. Every year there would be hundreds of bills to discuss, from very different policy fields, each with its own histories and problems, and each requiring its own expertise. Moreover, bills from one policy area would invariably affect very different areas, which means that amending and voting on such bills will require competency *not only* in one's own policy area but also in all the connected areas. This is likely to be a frequent problem because issues often interact with others, and commonly—indeed *very* commonly—bills will affect others because of budgetary constraints.

Almost every political issue affects the budget because policy solutions compete for the use of limited revenues. This is precisely where a citizens' assembly diverges from a sortition chamber. Citizens' assemblies have, for good reason, generally focused on those rare political issues that do not involve money, such as electoral reform or gay rights. This makes them vastly easier to handle competently because they do not involve weighing fiscal trade-offs with competing issues. But imagine trying to do a citizens' assembly on any normal political issue, like day-care policy, education, or environmental protection. How could lay citizens possibly decide what kind of day-care system to implement if they do not grasp the larger budgetary issues it involves? How could they come to a rational decision about whether it is better to provide expensive publicly provided day-care centers or cheap tax credits to partially support families providing their own private childcare, without knowing the relevant trade-offs? Is it possible to provide universal day care only by slashing welfare rates? Can we raise taxes on the rich, or what if we reduce military spending?

For this reason, I believe it is impracticable for sortition members with knowledge solely of their own areas to come to rational policy decisions. This is why proposals for single-policy sortition bodies are unlikely to work well.[31] Such bodies cannot deliberate meaningfully if they are barred from weighing the ramifications of policy solutions for other issues beyond their agenda.

This problem presents defenders of sortition with a serious design question. How could one envision a sortition body that enables competency? Others will have to take up this challenge, but I want to suggest one possible solution. Imagine if sortition members had a tenure of, say, four years, of which the first two years were training—without any legislative powers. The first year could involve training in budgets, debt, taxation, and distributive justice; exposure to the major fields of public policy and the functioning of government; and learning how to deliberate, with empathy, and with a sense of responsibility to the public good. In the second year, members could be selected by lot into one of the major ten or so fields of public policy (environment, health, military, economy, and so on) in which they would spend the rest of their training period "interning," so as to develop familiarity and competency in the area that they will spend the next two years making decisions.[32]

Also, such a body should be large enough that it can divide itself into departments big enough for diverse deliberation and to remain statistically representative of the population. (As noted earlier, this larger size also limits bribery and corruption.) One possibility would be a one-thousand-person body, divided into ten one-hundred-person departments. Each department would focus on policy in its own area before submitting legislative proposals to the entire body. For proposals to become law, the departments would present the results of their deliberations, as well as their recommendation, before a general vote. It would be the job of the entire sortition legislature to weigh the costs and benefits of each proposal against those of other departments before making a final decision.

In sum, electoral systems tend to produce political competency, due to the weeding out functions of elections and the intellectual support of parties. A full-bore sortition chamber faces difficult issues of unknowledgeable people, as well as the problem of complexity arising from the cross-cutting nature of issues—almost all of which have budgetary implications. In theory, a sortition body might overcome such difficulties through having significant periods of prior training, being large enough to allow specialization, and by retaining final authority in a larger body that can weigh the costs and benefits of various proposals. Nevertheless, humility in the face of uncertainty compels me to score electoral systems as faring better in this regard.

Conclusion

Reflecting back on all four criteria, I have argued that the main strengths of the electoral mechanism are accountability and competency, whereas its weaknesses are generating political inequality (via descriptive unrepresentativeness and a systemic bias toward wealthy interests[33]) and a systemic propulsion toward partisanship that undermines deliberation and impartiality. The virtues and vices of a not-yet-existing sortition chamber are more speculative. Nevertheless, such a body would surely perform better in terms of political equality due to its enhanced descriptive representation and its better insulation against the influence of wealthy interests. In addition, a sortition chamber would likely outperform its electoral counterpart at deliberation and impartiality, while getting lower marks for accountability and competency.

Three important conclusions follow from this. First, elections are not the only game in town. In many underappreciated ways, sortition has much to offer democratic theorists and practitioners.

Second, neither election nor sortition *by itself* can satisfy the full range of democratic values. This implies that an optimal democratic system would need to combine both mechanisms, such as through the bicameral system advocated by Gastil and Wright. An additional reason for doing so is that elections and sortition each offer a crucial type of representation. In an elected chamber, the aim is to have representatives of the *entire population* take into account their *actually existing interests*. In such a chamber, discussion would ideally take the form of bargaining among fixed interests, among MPs who are highly monitored and revocable (playing a role as delegates, with limited independence). In a sortition chamber, by contrast, the aim would be to have a descriptively accurate sample of the population engaged in quality deliberation to learn what *a representative sample would want* in ideal deliberative circumstances (with members who are not delegates and so have substantial independence to change their minds). In other words, combining both mechanisms would allow us to profit from having representatives of our actually existing interests as well as our hypothetical postdeliberative interests—both of which are valuable, and neither of which we would want to do without.

Third, it is likely that a sortition chamber will lead to more progressive policy than an elected chamber. This is because there would be less elite representation in government (that is, fewer bankers and lawyers, more caregivers and workers), as well as less systemic bias toward money.

Our comparative analysis has also sought to identify the trade-offs that would exist in building a sortition body, which all future designers will have to grapple with:

- Should terms be longer or shorter? (Longer terms allows for more competency but also more potential for corruption, as well as more potential for the emergence of factions, which are likely to undermine the quality of deliberation).
- Should deliberation be secret or public? (Secrecy can enhance deliberation, prevent corruption, and protect members from embarrassment, but it risks undermining accountability.)
- Should there be some bar for competency, even if this undermines descriptive representativeness?[34]

In addition to these trade-offs, there are also a number of open questions for future research into sortition:

- Who sets the agenda?
- How can the administrative overseers themselves be overseen?
- What would be an ideal relationship between an elected and a sortition body? (Should there be asymmetries of power between them or different functions or different issues that they focus on?)
- Can a powerful, high-stakes sortition body successfully restrain corruption and maintain quality deliberation?
- Is a full-bore sortition chamber really feasible? (Small-scale experiments, such as at the municipal level, will be vital in helping to assess this question.)

In conclusion, contemporary democrats are wrong to simply assume that democracy requires elections and only elections. Our democratic values cannot be well satisfied by the electoral mechanism alone. Nevertheless, that does not mean that we should leap to the false conclusion that elections are worthless. Neither electoral fundamentalism nor abolitionism is an appropriate response to our complex political situation and clashing democratic values. Sortition has significant democratic potential, and democrats should be open to exploring it. However, the largely untested nature of a national sortition body (and subsequent uncertainty regarding its virtues and vices) leads me to conclude that a piecemeal, small-scale, step-by-step approach to introducing sortition bodies would be wise.

Overall, democrats should be more willing to consider implementing sortition mechanisms than they commonly are. Being a democrat means having a number of values, but one of them is the belief that regular people, in good situations of nonviolence, learning, support, and deliberation, can arrive at quality political decisions. In this sense the radical democrat Ella Baker was right: give the people a light and they will find a way.[35]

9

Accountability in the Constituent-Representative Relationship

Jane Mansbridge

Although the last half century has seen many experiments randomly selecting participants for deliberative bodies that advise duly elected or appointed officials, we have little experience in giving bodies of this sort direct power to legislate rather than just advise. Prudence therefore suggests that any steps in this direction be small, tentative, and easily revocable. Prudence also suggests that before beginning our first experiments we try to think through as best we can what problems might arise so that as we take our first tentative steps forward, we can be particularly alert to the potential problems we identified in advance. One of these is accountability.

Many commentators in this volume have pointed out that representatives chosen by lot (or "sortition") do not have the kinds of accountability to their constituents that representatives chosen by election have, at least in theory and very often in practice. This problem of accountability is an important feature of the larger constituent-representative relationship. I will discuss it primarily within the context of that relationship.

Stepping back, the larger context of this question is our growing need, in a world of increasing interdependence, for state coercion to handle the free-rider problems that almost inevitably accompany such interdependence. (The reader should feel free to substitute "regulation" for my preferred term, "state coercion.") As we collectively try to produce "free-use" goods, such as lower crime rates, efficient financial transactions, and a stable climate, we face the problem that the coercion (regulation) needed to produce these goods must be as legitimate as possible. This is true both because that legitimacy is good in itself (that is, "normative legitimacy," or legitimacy that can be supported with good reasons) and because coercion perceived to be legitimate is more effective than coercion perceived as illegitimate. Yet as our needs for legitimate coercion have increased, our capacity to legitimate that coercion has decreased. Demand for legitimacy is up; supply is down.[1]

As human beings, we have evolved the capacity to govern ourselves in ever-larger entities, currently up to the level of the nation-state but now tentatively extending beyond it. In the last few hundred years, we have come to rely heavily on the mechanism of representative elections to produce state coercion that, when the system works well (as it does, for example, in Denmark), is both perceived as legitimate and has a good claim to legitimacy on normative grounds. But partly because of the nature of incentives and barriers to becoming an electoral candidate and partly because of other details of specific competitive electoral processes, these systems do not always produce an assembly that the citizens of a country feel speaks for them. In these circumstances the regulations the assembly promulgates have correspondingly less legitimacy.

Over the last half century, the degree to which the citizenry thinks that the elected legislature speaks for them has declined in many countries. Over that same half century, the absence of major wars in Europe and the Americas also may have eroded the sense of urgent common purpose that enhances the legitimacy of the citizen-legislator bond. For these and other reasons, the gap between the amount of legitimacy we need to regulate our growing interdependence and the amount of legitimacy we can generate with our current institutions has grown. The attempted solutions to this problem include a growing number of advisory bodies based on lot and even serious consideration of legislative chambers based on lot.

Combining two moves, from an advisory body to an empowered lawmaking one and from a temporary body to a more long-standing one, turns the citizen participants in any deliberative body drawn by lot into formal representatives of the full citizenry. Ideally, what should this constituent-representative relationship be? Equally important, what is it likely to be? In comparison to current electoral representation, what is lost in the constituent-representative relationship, and what is gained? The answers to these questions are not currently clear. Both the normative theory and the practical implications are likely to evolve with experimentation in practice.

Here, I will compare conventional electoral representation to representation by lot only in regard to constituent-representative relationships, ignoring other processes and effects. In these relationships, it seems that the most significant losses might come in the constituents' agency and their capacity to inflict formal sanctions on their representatives, whereas the most significant gains might come in the constituents' greater identification (and possible communication) with their representatives. We should also expect changes in the character of accountability—both in the forms of sanction and in the particular ways representatives give their constituents an account of what they did, what they plan to do, and why.

The Loss of Agency and of Sanction

In a functioning system of electoral representation, citizens exercise power when they cast their votes. The effect on the outcome may be very small and is hardly ever decisive, but in many elections the margin of victory also influences the future. Citizens are often aware of the power in their vote. Activists chant, "We'll remember in November!" Ordinary citizens may feel some pride not only in fulfilling their civic duty or expressing their views at the ballot box, but also in contributing their small bit toward the outcome.

I would argue against interpreting the act of casting a vote in an election as "consent."[2] I do, however, see voting as a regular, repeatable, self-constitutive act of agency—one that helps make an individual into a citizen. The equal weight of each vote also makes a powerful normative statement about the status of the citizen, even when undercut by surrounding inequalities in political power. If a polity's legislature were composed entirely of representatives selected by lot, this small but meaningful power in the vote and the agency experienced in exercising it would be lost.

The constituent's power exists not only in the moment of the vote and immediately afterward, when the constituent's vote helps to change or maintain the composition of the legislature. In addition, the constituent's potential vote in the next election changes the incentives of the representatives in the legislature, because elected officials anticipate the next vote and try to please future voters. If a polity's legislature were composed entirely of representatives selected by lot, that power through anticipation would be lost.

In a legislative system based on electoral representation, the constituent-representative relationship is informed to some degree by this constituent power and by both representatives' and constituents' awareness of that power. Citizens and their representatives have a deeply unequal relationship, because the representative's vote can make or unmake the law, and their expertise in the matters under consideration quickly surpasses that of most constituents. Nonetheless, the constituent's vote and the representative's recognition of the power inherent in that vote give some dignity to the constituent and some hesitation to the representative. Although the effect is far less strong—and perhaps nonexistent—for permanent minorities in a district, for those who are often in the majority, a potential majority, or a potential winning coalition, having a vote emboldens the constituent and commands the representative's attention. For the constituent, the anticipatory power of voting in the next election plays a crucial role in the relationship. As constituents see events unfolding in the legislature with which they disagree, they can nurse their own anticipation of the next election. They do not have to stand by helpless, without recourse. They can organize with allies to depose, or at least fight against, their elected representative in the next election. They are not powerless. With a legislature composed entirely of representatives selected by lot, this equalizing, agentic feature of the constituent-representative relationship would be lost.

For reasons anchored in this loss of constituent power and the healthy relationship between constituents and representatives that it fosters, I would oppose any legislative system based *entirely* on lot. Too much of value to democracy would be lost.

Accountability

A focus on sanction and on power, however, misses a significant part of the constituent-representative relationship. That focus, which I have just described, problematically lies at the core of most discussions of "accountability" today. Just as the use of the word *accountability* in English has increased dramatically since the late 1960s (and the use of *transparency* has increased dramatically since 1980),[3] the meaning of the word accountability has also slowly changed. Today it primarily means the capacity to sanction (and to monitor with potential to sanction). Accordingly, when modern writers decry the loss of "accountability" in a legislature based on lot, they usually mean the loss of the constituents' capacity to threaten the representative in the next election with the sanction of withdrawing their votes. A representative chosen by lot for a fixed term (and replaceable only by lot) is not subject to this threat.

Accountability did not always have this restrictive and punitive meaning. It meant *giving an account*—in French *rendre compte* and in German *Rechenschaft abgeben*. Being account-able meant having to describe, explain, and justify one's actions to those to whom one is responsible. This more deliberative meaning of the word signals a constituent-representative rela-tionship based not on threats of sanction but on mutual attempts at describing, explaining, justifying, and persuading.[4] In this understanding, the representative's responsibility to the other representatives, the public, and constituents may be fulfilled through explaining, perhaps ideally in a process of recursive two-way interaction.

How, then, could the members of a representative body chosen by lot be accountable to one another, to the larger public, and to their "constituents" in this more deliberative sense? This question has never been studied. It may never have been asked. Despite many past and current experiments with deliberative bodies chosen by lot, no one as far as I know has investigated the deliberators' relations of accountability to one another or to members of the public who might be considered "constituents."

Such an investigation would look at three levels: the account-ability of the participants in the deliberative body to one another, their accountability to the public at large, and their accountabil-ity, if any, to specific "constituents" whose opinions, perspec-tives, and interests they represented. On all of these levels, it would help to distinguish a) sanction-based accountability versus deliberative accountability and b) formal versus informal accountability.

Table 9 shows the four forms of accountability created by combining these characteristics. In electoral representation, the accountability of representatives to their constituents falls in all four quadrants of the table. It is both sanction-based and delib-erative, both formal and informal. In representation by lot, the formal sanction-based quadrant is relatively empty. In the other quadrants the appropriate and available forms of accountability vary according to who may rightly hold the representative accountable: the other representatives, the public at large, or specific constituents.

Table 9. Types of accountability in legislatures chosen by lot.

Accountability type	Level of formality	
	Formal	Informal
Sanction-based	Laws against bribery and other forms of wrongdoing.	Representatives monitoring and sanctioning the norms of discourse within their own deliberations. Members of the public exerting informal pressures on the representatives.
Deliberative	Collective written accounts to fellow representatives or the public	Representatives mutually listening, explaining, and justifying perspectives, opinions, and interests to one another. Representatives doing the same with the larger public or specific constituents, face-to-face or through the media.

Accountability to One Another

In representation by lot, the accountability of the representatives to one another will be largely informal and deliberative. Of course they will have some formal and informal sanctions against one another, and presumably their committees will produce some formal explanatory and justificatory documents in the course of accounting for their actions to the body of the whole. But we can expect the representatives in a legislature selected by lot to be accountable to one another primarily through their informal mutual explanations and justifications.

In the many modern experiments in which lay participants drawn by lot deliberate only to register their opinions at the end of the experiment, draw up an advisory statement, or at the most legislate on small and relatively "cool" issues, the participants almost always act toward one another with generosity, goodwill, and respect. As far as I know, their relationships of mutual accountability have never been studied. In every instance that I have attended, viewed on tape, or read about, the participants seemed to act as if they felt accountable to the others in the group; they tried to listen to what the others had to say, treat the others with respect, and back up their own views with as good—and as good-faith—justifications as they could muster. Occasionally, some of those general norms were spelled out formally, but most were informally generated and maintained. These norms seemed to arise primarily through the participants' own sense of the appropriate relations of mutual accountability in the informal private sphere. A smaller part derived and was maintained within the specific deliberative setting through informal sanctions of social approval and disapproval wielded by the participants themselves, or occasionally by the facilitator backed by the participants.

It is impossible to predict what might happen in a developed legislature by lot in the heat of political passion on issues that present irreconcilable material and ideological conflicts. As several commentators in this volume have suggested, the underlying conflicts of interest and opinion, perhaps sharpened or even exaggerated by political parties, might well create far greater conditions of mutual hostility than in usual social interactions. Experimentation might suggest that such high-conflict issues be, through some mechanism such as a vote, tabled and sent to the electoral house. In those cases, informal mechanisms of mutual accountability might not be enough to sustain constructive deliberation. On the other hand, the extreme polarization present in the United States today is in part driven by the relatively equal competitive electoral prospects of the two political parties since 1980, which has produced a dynamic in which each party benefits from preventing the other from acting constructively, thereby undermining the other's reputation.[5] This dynamic would be weakened greatly in a legislature chosen by lot.

In discussions of accountability, both social scientists and the public often ignore the accountability of representatives *to one another*. Theorists of organizations, however, recognize the importance of "peer accountability"—the constellation of formal and informal communicative practices and behavioral rules generated by common confrontation with a problem, common experiences of past productive human interaction, and the combination of formal and informal sanctions against significant deviations from those rules. The accountability of members of the professions to one another, for example, is maintained primarily by ongoing mutual justificatory communication, resting on a core of informal commitments to duty and feelings of solidarity and sustained by a small periphery of formal and informal sanctions.[6] University faculties also work largely through peer accountability, as do EU committees and the best instances of the civil service. Even the ways that in most democracies elected representatives are accountable to one another for decent behavior are maintained largely by informal mechanisms of peer accountability. In assemblies of representatives drawn by lot, such mechanisms of peer accountability must play a major role. Without a robust system of primarily informal and deliberative peer accountability, where the character of interaction is drawn largely from larger norms of good informal deliberation, legislation by lot will fail to deliver much of democratic value.

Accountability to the Public at Large

In the accountability relations of a representative body drawn by lot to the public at large, the most important form of accountability will almost certainly be formal and deliberative. We can expect formal statements from the assembly, giving an account of the reasoning behind their decisions, to be the rule and perhaps required by the legislation setting up the assembly. The statements of the Oregon Citizens' Initiative Review panel, placed on the legal referendum ballot by law along with statements by advocates on both sides, exemplify the kind of formal deliberative accountability that is likely to legitimate (or if done badly, delegitimate) representation by lot. The British Columbia Citizens' Assembly concluded with a long formal report explaining and justifying their decision to advocate the Single Transferable Vote electoral system. The US Supreme Court's explanations and justifications of their decisions also exemplify this formal deliberative accountability.

Formal sanctions will not be entirely absent. Although the electoral sanction will be missing, it is unlikely that the public would ever authorize a legislature by lot to operate without formal legal sanctions for various forms of wrongdoing, including bribery. An appropriate oversight body, with judicial due process, would have to monitor the representatives' actions sufficiently to make such sanctions viable. Transcripts of the representatives' formal interactions, even if kept from the public to allow more frank deliberation, would have to be available not only to the participants themselves, to refresh their memories, but also to any oversight body. Various mechanisms would generate sanction-based accountability for wrongdoing. The most significant formal sanction would be the underlying capacity of the public to dismantle the legislature by lot and return to a purely electoral representative system.

Informal sanctions by the public will also have their place. Indeed, fear of such sanctions could provide a significant disincentive for participation in an assembly drawn by lot. In a small New England town meeting, some citizens do not attend the meeting for fear of being laughed at or criticized. This dynamic would be accentuated by participation in a legislature by lot on a state or national scale. Even with high pay and the strong incentives of duty, many potential participants are likely to decline to serve. The most marginal potential participants would probably be most vulnerable to informal sanctions from the public, thus exacerbating the other inequalities in participation that are likely to emerge.[7]

Informal deliberative accountability can be expected to play a relatively large role in the pattern of accountability relations between representatives selected by lot and the public at large. Spokespeople will emerge; the media will fasten on certain explanations and justifications, and some representatives will take upon themselves the task of describing, explaining, and justifying the decisions of the assembly and the thinking behind those decisions. In the British Columbia Citizens' Assembly process, for example, after the conclusion of the assembly's deliberations, some participants informally tried to explain and justify to the public at large the reasoning behind their assembly's decision to advocate a Single Transferable Vote electoral system to replace the existing Single Member Plurality system.[8] One problem for the representatives in a legislature chosen by lot will be the openness of this informal deliberation to the public's informal sanctions. In the primary form of accountability in this process, the formal statement of explanation, the collective production of the statement to some degree protects each individual in the assembly. But in the informal processes of deliberative accountability, the participants are more individually vulnerable.

Accountability to Constituents

Accountability to "constituents"—if there are any constituents beyond the general public—is the most problematic and least well-considered aspect of the patterns of accountability we might expect or want to institute in a legislature chosen by lot. Unlike the jury, the legislature chosen by lot will not be able to promise its members confidentiality.

In the British Columbia Citizens' Assembly (BCCA), the French High Council of Military Function (Conseil Supérieur de la Fonction Militaire, or CSFM), and the Oregon citizens' Initiative Review, the members of the deliberative decision body drawn by lot were and are all known.[9] The members of the BCCA and CSFM also had specific constituents, the BCCA from the various "ridings" or districts in British Columbia and the CSFM from their branches of the armed forces.

Beyond geographic or other formal constituencies, we would also very probably find "constituencies" for each member developing around common interests and descriptive characteristics. Thus, even if the representatives did not have specific formal constituents, or take any actions to create informal constituencies around specific issues, certain groups of citizens would probably constitute themselves informally as the constituents of specific representatives, coalescing around those representatives' expressed positions, their descriptive features, or even their perceived vulnerabilities to pressure or persuasion. Opponents of the actions of specific representatives would also be likely to coalesce, although we would not call such opponents "constituents."

If the representatives were chosen by lot from geographic

districts, as was the case in the BCCA, it is unclear normatively what forms of formal and informal deliberative accountability the representatives ought to have with those constituents. In the CSFM, each member chosen by lot reports in meetings open to all members of the branch of the military from which he or she was chosen. The lively discussions at these meetings serve as a significant mode of formal deliberative accountability to these constituents. In the BCCA, no such interaction with constituents was formally mandated, but some members took it upon themselves to make speeches and otherwise contact constituents in their ridings to explain the assembly's decisions and try to persuade their listeners to vote for the assembly's recommendation in the upcoming referendum. This mode of deliberative accountability was, however, informal and voluntary; many BCCA members did not engage in this kind of outreach.

Mandating formal deliberative accountability of the sort practiced in the CSFM would probably, in the United States, put considerable strain on the 40 percent of the public who say they fear speaking in public in front of an audience. Those with only high school degrees are almost twice as likely to have those fears as those with college educations.[10] In electoral representation, by contrast, those who run for office are highly skewed toward the rich and well educated. They also self-select—and are selected for—interest in politics and the ability to communicate with constituents, in addition, one would expect, to relatively low fears of speaking in public.

Informal deliberative accountability might, however, be enhanced in representation by lot. In the United States, African American constituents are more likely to contact their elected representatives when those representatives are African American themselves.[11] Constituents across a range of ethnicities and classes may be more likely to contact, communicate with, and identify with representatives who are descriptively closer to them than the current predominantly white, male, rich elected representatives. Representation by lot from geographic districts would be likely to produce greater feelings of identification and therefore contact than representation by lot from the state or nation at large, and the range of descriptive characteristics among representatives drawn by lot from a geographic district would presumably be greater than the range among current elected representatives.

If the assembly had no geographic districts and the participants were simply drawn from the state or nation as a whole, the kinds of "constituencies" described earlier might nevertheless form. Even in elected legislatures, advocacy and descriptive representation play a role in creating surrogate constituencies outside a representative's district. For instance, as an advocate of consumer rights, Massachusetts senator Elizabeth Warren has a constituency in this substantive field outside Massachusetts. The openly gay Massachusetts congressional representative Barney Frank had a national constituency concerned with securing LGBTQ rights. The African American congressional representative Mickey Leland was a surrogate representative for African Americans in "the entire Southwest."[12] The same dynamic would appear in a legislature selected by lot. Interest groups might also constitute themselves the "constituencies" of sympathetic representatives, providing them information and expecting support.

Conclusion

Even in the field of electoral representation, few empirical political scientists or normative theorists have interested themselves in the quality of the constituent-representative relationship.[13] Perhaps for the same reasons, among those studying representation by lot, few have engaged the question of constituent-representative relations in general. Although many have worried about the loss of sanction-based accountability, no one, to my knowledge, has addressed the potential losses or gains in deliberative accountability. I have attempted to begin such an analysis, including both formal and informal sanction-based accountability and formal and informal deliberative accountability. Among the representatives themselves, one would expect primarily informal deliberative accountability to predominate.

In the relations of the representatives with the public at large, one would expect primarily formal deliberative accountability, through written statements of explanation and justification. The relations of the representatives with their constituents, whether geographic or self-selected, are currently an open question, both normatively and in practice. With the power of the vote removed, in all cases the level of formal sanction would be low. The level of informal sanction seems, at the moment, unpredictable.

As institutions embodying representation by lot evolve, processes of trial and error are likely to illuminate both problems and potential solutions in the realm of constituent-representative relations as in all other realms. A problem arises in finding testing grounds where the decisions are important enough to generate the dynamics one might expect in a legislature by lot but unimportant enough not to be catastrophic if unexpected dynamics arose to torpedo the experiment. One testing ground of the potential for legislation by lot might be the self-governing boards of tenants' associations.[14] Another could be high school student governments. In both cases, an association or school could institute an elected government one year and a government chosen by lot another year, allowing comparison of internal dynamics, outcomes, and constituent-representative relations. In a high school, however, the lack of issue seriousness might combine with the playful tendencies of that age group to produce in an assembly drawn by lot results that were entertaining for the participants but not useful as stand-ins for what might take place in a state or national legislature. In conducting such experiments one would ideally want to measure and compare not only the quality of the outcomes but also the degree to which constituents felt adequately represented by the two groups, the quality of constituent-representative communication, and the forms taken by both sanction-based and deliberative accountability.

As thinking about representation by lot advances in tandem with the practice, I believe it would be a mistake to assume that empowered assemblies are automatically either better for the participants or more democratic than advisory ones. We, the people, should choose for ourselves those institutions that, after consideration, we conclude can represent us best in various ways. Historically, most peoples have chosen—either explicitly at a founding moment or more subtly by accretion—systems that mixed different forms of representation. The time is probably ripe for adding more institutions chosen by lot into the mix. As we add those institutions, however, we should pay close attention to their many characteristics, including the currently neglected characteristics of deliberative accountability and constituent-representative relations.

10

How to Ensure Deliberation Within a Sortition Chamber

Lyn Carson

It is timely to be discussing a randomly selected legislature amid declining public trust in representative government and elected leaders. The conversation about theoretical alternatives has been building since the late 1980s and has accelerated in this century.[1] Many of the academic works on this subject have been matched by hundreds of trials of different variations of minipublics in local, regional, state, and national spheres of government.[2]

Gastil and Wright have added to this conversation by advancing a proposal of their own. In this chapter, I argue that their proposed sortition assembly can be successful only if adequate attention is paid to its deliberative process. These process design factors are crucial to sortition's success, but they are not always appreciated, or even well understood, by those who develop and debate legislative reform proposals.

Much is known about *who* made the decisions in ancient Athens, the cradle of democracy, as well as the mechanisms for election and selection.[3] Less is known about *how* they made decisions. Scholars classify the ancient Greeks' decision-making processes as a form of direct democracy, rather than deliberative democracy, although Aristotle is said to have claimed "that the people deliberating together could often produce better decisions than an expert on the subject."[4] Direct democracy is an excellent way to gather public *opinion*, but it is not a robust method to deliver public *judgment*.[5] In this chapter, I focus on the latter.

Gastil and Wright recognize the importance of decision-making methods in their proposal, but they only begin to touch on the subject. If sortition is introduced as a strong deliberative alternative to electing representatives, it needs to have distinct methods for more than its selection process. A sortition chamber should not replicate the adversarial or stalled decision-making processes that pervade modern parliaments—or worse, the type of corruption that occurs routinely among elected representatives everywhere.

A former judge, Tony Fitzgerald, who led a corruption inquiry in an Australian state, has noted that power "provides a rich opportunity for personal and political advantage: cronyism, the sale of access and influence and the misuse of public money."[6] Fitzgerald's "impossible dream" for the restoration of trust in politicians could be describing participants in one-off minipublics:

> Politicians will find it impossible to regain public trust unless they behave like *normal, honourable people*: Treat everyone equally, tell the truth, explain decisions, disclose any direct or indirect benefits for themselves or their allies.[7]

In designing their proposal for a sortition chamber, Gastil and Wright aim to follow five democratic principles: "inclusion; control of the agenda; effective participation; voting equality; and enlightened understanding."[8] Most of the authors in this volume attend to the first four principles, but I aim to describe how a well-crafted deliberative process can move a sortition chamber toward enlightened understanding.

Without deliberation in the assembly itself, the flaws of direct democracy or even representative government can arise. Contemporary elected legislatures fail the deliberative test, and it is near impossible to convert an elected assembly to a deliberative assembly—except perhaps when committees are convened. In fact, this provides a clue as to the way forward.[9] We understand the weakness of a chamber that elects or selects a speaker or chair, as happens now, and having that person arbitrate on the debate across the floor of parliament, using something like *Robert's Rules*.[10] Representatives who stand and make speeches, having caucused beforehand, or listened to lobbyists, or succumbed to bribes, are not well equipped to make decisions even via a secret ballot. Curiously, *Robert's Rules of Order* was subtitled *for Deliberative Assemblies* even though these rules deliver very little genuine deliberation. Debate, at least when unleavened by more deliberative moments, does not lead to the best outcome. It may have been a weakness of ancient Athens. Today, however, we know more about group processes and co-intelligence. We know how effective decision-making *can* be achieved consistently, and formal rules are not the answer.[11]

Deliberation does not just happen, and we are not born with deliberative capacity. It must be learned. It requires practice. Providing orientation and training and encouraging dialogue outside the chamber—between participants—would help to build respect and trust, but only collective, egalitarian deliberation will lead to better decisions. The good news is that we can design a more effective decision-making space that exploits the virtues of debate, dialogue, and deliberation, and this has been shown to work.

At the newDemocracy Foundation, we have accumulated a wealth of experience in relation to public deliberation,[12] as have many others.[13] Here are a few of the lessons we have learned:

- A vote can kill deliberation and is best delayed or avoided altogether.
- We can enhance citizens' capacity to think critically and identify biases.
- When subjected to critical questioning, experts can expand citizens' knowledge and understanding.
- The size of a citizen body will not alter its capacity to learn

and to decide, whether it has 25 or 350 participants. Deliberation, however, must take place in small groups, which then build to a collective decision.

- Even a large citizen body can reach decisions that satisfy all—or nearly all—participants.
- Skillful, independent, nonmanipulative facilitation is essential for the group to find its own way.

In summary, sortition as a selection process can deliver descriptive representation—an essential strategy to build trust in government, and it can give decision-making power back to everyday citizens. Beyond that, however, sortition's companion—its best friend—must be a suite of robust, democratic microprocesses to ensure that the randomly selected body is able to make decisions that satisfy the whole group and the wider community.

I will describe the essential elements of deliberation, based on my decades of experience with minipublics.[14] I begin by discussing the general principle of deliberation, then address important subtopics, including critical thinking, working with experts, facilitation, and making decisions. In the third section, I will address one of the most widely debated questions in the field of deliberative democracy: How might the wider population be part of a deliberative system?[15] Unless a randomly selected legislature extends its reach to the wider population, it risks earning the same low levels of public trust that harm the current legislative system. I then consider other unresolved questions and offer a call for attention to process design for anyone interested in adopting sortition.

An Overview of Group Deliberation

The democratic deficit has led to a drift toward populism and demagoguery. There is a disturbing shift in public attitudes worldwide. In some countries, including Australia, Britain, and the US, the proportion of younger people who think it essential to live in a democracy is now a minority.[16] Perhaps even more disturbing is the rise in the share of citizens who approve of having a strong leader who does not have to bother with parliament or elections.[17] If a "major systemic transformation" is indeed under way, the likely end point will be more power-wielding, antiestablishment leaders *unless* we rethink leadership, decentralize decision-making, and limit—or at least share—government power.

Even the most expert leaders are not necessarily the wisest. Consider that if we know a great deal about something, the following happens: We close our minds to alternative pathways; we share our knowledge with people who support our opinion and this, in turn, limits our thinking; our creativity is constricted because we think we know what's possible; and we dismiss anything that sounds unrealistic.[18]

Everyday citizens, gathered in a legislative assembly, can equal or surpass the decision-making abilities of elected leaders, who are rarely experts. They have to do a lot of learning in office, and they rely heavily on outside experts or staff members. Citizens can do that just as well.

There are few opportunities for everyday citizens to exercise their own leadership qualities in the political realm. At newDemocracy, we have watched thousands of people grow through public deliberations.[19] Citizens not only learn; they also collaborate to develop acceptable, sustainable, and innovative proposals. In a sortition assembly, they will be unconcerned about winning the next election, so they are likely to remain focused on solving problems for their communities.

To do this, however, they will need support. To think *critically* together, they will benefit from having an independent facilitator. As Hélène Landemore explains,

in every randomly selected assembly you would find leadership unexpectedly . . . We over-value the Type A elected representative as the model of a leader . . . I think there are many ways to be a leader that can be achieved by people who are more soft spoken, more quiet, leading from behind . . . We just have to reinvent leadership to fit with this model.[20]

This will not happen simply because people are randomly selected. The diversity of the group is a catalyst, but building deliberative capacity will provide the fuel.

Deliberation foregrounds a very important difference in the way political discussions can occur. Here, the focus is on *public* deliberation, not the *internal* deliberation that we each do during contemplation. To explain the difference between public deliberation in, say, a sortition assembly, and what occurs in current parliamentary assemblies, it's useful to provide contrast.

Typical political discussion is *debate*. The aim is to persuade others, and ultimately the majority, to one's own position. Even at its best, it's a win-lose situation where participants are inclined to maintain their original view. Debate can be angry, adversarial, and swift. It can also be rational and drawn out.

Dialogue can help to cut through some of the weaknesses of *debate*, through a slower civil exchange, sharing understandings by listening well, and building relationships. Dialogue places less emphasis on decision-making and more on a respectful, clarifying exchange of perspectives.[21]

Deliberation involves elements of both dialogue and debate.[22] Debate might occur when there is an invited panel of experts arguing about their various positions, and this can be useful input for deliberation. But deliberation is distinct, even though it still involves a "competition of ideas."[23] This is because public deliberation aims to investigate various options by first hearing from experts, then exploring and establishing common ground, and finally reaching a group decision. The fundamental difference between deliberation and debate is whether the end objective is zero-sum or consensus seeking. In the search for consensus, dialogue is an essential element.[24]

At newDemocracy we know when genuine deliberation has occurred in a minipublic because the proof is in the participant feedback we hear. Departing citizens will speak of challenging but surprisingly respectful conversations, despite individual differences. They remark on the deep exploration of issues, with a shared motivation to solve a problem, and they recognize in themselves an enhanced ability to think critically.[25] When newDemocracy collects anonymous feedback post-deliberation, randomly selected participants almost always say they would do it again, and they want elected officials to make many more of these opportunities to their fellow citizens.[26]

It's not a natural enterprise, this deliberative process. It requires skillful facilitation—just enough to keep the group on track and find its own way when the going gets tough. With larger groups, there will always be times when small-group activity is advantageous to accelerate the process and minimize entrenched viewpoints. Exercises designed to challenge cognitive biases and test expert knowledge are used because the group will be weighing up various contested options. The group members will find themselves busy with a variety of tasks: establishing their own agreed behavioral guidelines, setting criteria for evaluation, gathering information, testing it, brainstorming solutions, prioritizing those possibilities, agreeing on recommendations and accounting for minority opinions when consensus is not found, and collectively writing a report. The work is enjoyable and often arduous, but the group feels a tremendous sense of collective achievement once the mission is accomplished.[27]

When a group deliberates, it *seeks* consensus without requiring its achievement. Indeed, minority reports are always encouraged in minipublics. The aim of a deliberative group is to establish the extent of agreement and what each person can live with. Premature voting can be the death knell of consensus because it closes minds before all is known about a topic. If deliberation leads to a final vote, then a *secret* ballot is essential. This is typically done using keypads, with the collective result projected onto a screen.

Deliberative Process Within a Sortition Assembly

Given modern facilitation methods and information technology, to what extent can large groups, like a sortition chamber, achieve good deliberation? I answer this question by returning to four key features of deliberation introduced in the previous section.

In turn, I discuss critical thinking, selecting and hearing from experts, facilitation, decision rules, and the importance of simultaneity.

Critical Thinking

A common assumption is that a randomly selected group of citizens will fail to understand or evaluate expert evidence because that talent takes a combination of natural ability and years of experience. The corollary is, inevitably, that experts and self-nominated politicians have this ability, but everyday citizens do not. I question that assumption.

It is true that citizens only rarely encounter the practice of critical thinking, or even the term itself, unless they have studied in an institute of higher learning. Even then, such training was likely designed to enhance the critical-thinking capacities of individuals doing solitary thinking and learning to think for themselves. In a public deliberation, by contrast, participants are part of a collective consideration of expert knowledge.

Citizens in the proposed sortition chamber will have to make a transition from "how to think for themselves" to "how to think well with others." This extends the practice of individual "critical thinking" to a "collaborative inquiry," or "critical engagement." It is useful to think of the legislature as having a "collective mind" that is more than the sum of the minds of its individual members. Therefore, the training or practice of critical thinking must be embedded in such a chamber.

Considerable recent research has investigated the prevalence and effects of bias. However, it could be argued that neutrality and objectivity are difficult to achieve and that *an exposure* to bias may be a more realistic path to take when deliberating.[28] For that reason, newDemocracy is currently experimenting with various critical-thinking approaches, especially when interrogating experts.

I first designed these exercises for a trial run by MosaicLab in Hobsons Bay, Victoria, Australia, in 2016. I then modified and used them for the Nuclear Citizens Jury in South Australia later that same year.

At Hobsons Bay, thirty citizens experienced the critical-thinking exercise; in South Australia over three hundred citizens repeated that experience. The latter employed a slightly abbreviated version of the original seven approaches considered essential for the practice of critical thinking—namely, clarity, accuracy, precision, relevance, depth, breadth, and logic. (In South Australia, "precision" was deleted because of the overlap with "accuracy.")

Here's how it worked—and this could be modified for the sortition chamber. Participants in both Hobsons Bay and South Australia were allocated a card displaying a single approach, watched a short film on critical thinking, worked in small groups with people who had the same approach, and together developed potential, specific questions to ask experts. Then, back in the plenary, participants shared what proved to be thoughtful and probing questions.

Participants then engaged in a "speed dialogue" session with multiple experts. In South Australia, the expert speakers were drawn from a Nuclear Stakeholder Reference Group or its nominees. Speakers were instructed to speak for only a few minutes and then allow the participants to fire questions. Participants were in small groups of five to six, and in most cases a range of approaches were represented. Experts rotated through the groups and were interrogated by all participants. Participants were told that the combination of all six approaches needed to be used and satisfied to ensure that critical thinking occurred.

To supplement these sessions in the South Australia Nuclear Citizens Jury, there was a "fact-check" wall that became populated with factual claims available for verification. In a later session, there was an opportunity to alert facilitators to gaps in information or knowledge and how the juror believed this gap could best be addressed (such as via a witness or a written response).

Once back in the plenary, participants again worked with

people who were using the same approach to debrief about the questions that worked well and the facts that still needed to be checked. Later, they shared examples of effective questions (that is, those that extracted clear and accurate information, or those that exposed flaws in reasoning). It was good preparation for the next weekend when more experts, of participants' own choosing, would appear as witnesses.

Participants' spirit of inquiry meant that their minds were available for critical thinking. The combination of explanation and instruction about the use of critical thinking, along with opportunities to identify questionable facts, or missing information, provided excellent preparation for a selection of further speakers.

At newDemocracy, I have also begun testing an alternative approach to critical thinking, which asks participants to acknowledge their unconscious human tendencies, which I'm calling "personal biases," as the first step in a public deliberation. Participants do this exercise during the first session (along with critical-thinking exercises on day one), then employ the critical-thinking approaches on day two. The idea is to promote awareness of participants' own unexamined biases before demonstrating how to interrogate expert knowledge. The seven biases currently being used are anchoring/recency bias, bandwagon effect, blind-spot bias, confirmation bias, information bias, and stereotyping.

Selecting Experts

If a sortition chamber has a group of critical thinkers in its midst, then the subject of expert knowledge is important to examine because that group will need the help of experts to become more fully informed. To be successful, these experts must be not only knowledgeable but also representative of different viewpoints, respected by the legislators, and able to communicate effectively with nonexperts. (This includes having good listening skills and the ability to stay on topic.)

But who should select the experts, and how? For minipublics, it is customary for decision-makers (that is, those convening the event) to select expert speakers—either from within their own networks or from known institutions.

In Australia, it used to be common practice when convening a minipublic to form a steering committee of topic experts who then selected relevant expert witnesses (such as the consensus conference on genetically modified organisms in the food chain in 1999, or the citizens' jury on container deposit legislation in 2000). One problem with this method is that occasionally there would be gaps in the expertise offered. For example, the consensus conference participants requested an ethicist, and this category had not been identified by the steering committee. For the citizens' jury, when the beverage and packaging industry speakers withdrew at the eleventh hour, a library of comprehensive information had to be assembled, and the pro-deposit experts were told to stay away so that balanced information could be provided via that library of information.[29] Thankfully, with a large enough group, citizens will spot gaps in information and will ask for additional experts or written information to fill that gap.

newDemocracy has taken on board the recommendation of a research report it funded, by the Institute for Sustainable Futures, that stakeholders play an important role in identifying experts. Stakeholders are now routinely engaged early in the life of any minipublic overseen by newDemocracy.

Further, newDemocracy acknowledges that citizens themselves have varying degrees of knowledge and are able to contribute their own knowledge to deliberations. Any evidence that is brought into the room by jurors or experts, however, must be scrupulously interrogated. Hence, we have developed the exercises described above that explore cognitive biases and enhance citizens' capacity to interrogate their peers as well as expert speakers.

When bringing on board experts, newDemocracy has noted three hazards. One is that randomly selected citizens may not be the best people to select experts to address a particular topic— they don't yet know what they don't know. Another problem is that their personal networks may not adequately cover the full spectrum of views on an issue, and the group members are therefore likely to consider experts with a more public profile. The third problem is that even if the group makes its best attempt to choose a "balanced" group of experts, the media and the wider public often suspect the selection was rigged in favor of particular options.

There is also a weakness that can emerge from confirmation bias—our tendency to want experts to confirm rather than challenge our existing views. newDemocracy tries to address this problem by raising awareness of this bias as part of the critical-thinking training. Some of the "sensitivities around evidence, evidence-giving, and evidence giver in citizens' juries" that are outlined above have also been addressed in a recent study by Roberts and Lightbody.[30]

Compared with selection by decision-makers, these alternative approaches can produce a better balance of views and avoid public and media suspicion of an unfair selection process. They also give the minipublic members a real voice in selecting the experts they will use.

Hearing from Experts

Choosing experts is one thing. Hearing them is another. Experts may be self-defined or may have obtained relevant credentials. They claim to know or *do* know a great deal about their specific area of expertise. These experts could be scientists, academics, government employees, special-interest groups, community activists, and more. For many of them, the so-called banking model of learning persists: learners are empty vessels into which knowledge can be deposited and later withdrawn.[31] Adults do not learn in this way.[32] Experts assume they need only provide a persuasive presentation or a fact-based lecture and their job is done.

One challenge for experts is their audience, when addressing a minipublic. A randomly selected group will have diverse participants—some knowledgeable, some quite ignorant, and many in between. These citizens will be tremendously curious because they are conscientious about giving due consideration to the challenge at hand. That's their starting point—curiosity.[33] Once their burning questions are answered, they will want to dig deeper and will have many more unanswered questions. A process needs to be created that enables these questions to be tackled. There is no point in inviting an expert to offer a lengthy presentation when participants want specific answers to specific questions.

Facilitation

When newDemocracy brings citizens together in a public space, such as a town-hall meeting, we employ a professional facilitator to play that role. It is commonly assumed that any professional facilitator with experience in focus groups or public meetings can run a deliberative forum effectively. Alas, new-Democracy has witnessed many a process go awry, and we have had to replace an otherwise skilled facilitator with someone who more properly understood public deliberation.

Likewise, more formal public bodies, such as legislative chambers, are commonly chaired (in committees) or arbitrated by a speaker (as in parliaments). Having a randomly selected speaker in a sortition assembly would not overcome the adversarial nature of that body, particularly when the physical space emphasizes opposition.

Skilled, independent facilitation and process design will be essential to creating a deliberative sortition chamber. Fortunately, deliberative minipublics teach us a great deal about how to facilitate citizen groups effectively.

A minipublic is not a parliament that is designed to "give people a hearing." Minipublics aim to share opportunities for voicing ideas and experiences and ask people to broaden themselves to other viewpoints, then work to find common ground. As noted earlier, they are *consensus-exploring* and *consensus-seeking*, though not *consensus-insisting*. Dominant and timid personalities inevitably surface, rigid thinking is exposed, and the range of competencies becomes evident. There might also be issues with language or cultural differences. An experienced facilitator can work with these challenges.

Minipublics are often contested spaces, and facilitators can be pulled into those conflicts. I have witnessed instances where participants in a minipublic have insisted that a facilitator be replaced. Another time, a participant declared the facilitator biased because the decision-making was not going his way, only to have the others in the minipublic demand that the facilitator continue to serve (after the participant took over and tried to lead the group in another direction).

At the same time, an effective facilitator supports a group's critical-thinking process, which can bring important conflicts to the surface. A minipublic's diverse membership is meant to resemble the entire population. Participants are often surprised by their ability to work productively within a diverse group, without having to ignore differences, when they have a facilitator who encourages the surfacing of differences of opinion.[34] It is not always easy or comfortable, but there is increased understanding of other perspectives and a willingness to accommodate them. When successful, the facilitator models a style of engagement that participants then carry over into smaller group discussions, where they have more responsibility for self-facilitation.

In longer deliberations, it is important for facilitators to provide a range of ways for jurors to interact. A facilitator can change the rhythm of discussion and the size of small groups and can get people moving, physically, through their meeting space. The facilitator can allow time for quiet, individual reflection and offer activities that respect the different learning styles of individuals. All this can keep the deliberation lively and help participants do their best critical thinking.

Always top of mind for the facilitator is to enable the group to find its *own* way—not to direct or cajole.[35] This requires great skill. A good facilitator must honor the group's own process decisions and be flexible enough to offer whatever microprocess will prove helpful to the group. Sometimes it is important for a facilitator to share his or her knowledge about process. For example, a facilitator might advise the group that voting will not necessarily be helpful because it's difficult to shift one's viewpoint once voting has occurred. If the information gathering, or expert questioning, or decision-making is not working well, the facilitator (or sometimes participants) will need to encourage the group to try something new that works better.[36] To paraphrase Lao Tzu, leadership is best when the people say "We did it ourselves."[37]

A good process design also pays attention to physical space because deliberation need not occur in one room. Sometimes field trips are necessary.[38] Participants can learn an enormous amount on such excursions, and the facilitator must keep up with this, while recognizing that a site visit or hands-on experience does not call for the same facilitation techniques as a plenary session or group discussion.

More generally, it is not important that a facilitator knows anything about the topic under consideration. Indeed, it is preferable that they do not have expertise to share (or hide) because it is easy to subconsciously lead a group toward a predetermined answer. Shared ignorance can make the facilitator and participants companions on the journey of discovery.

Because of the complexity of this job, cofacilitation often works well. Two or more facilitators can attend to both *task* (getting the job done, staying focused on the group's purpose) and *maintenance* (ensuring each group members is being heard, that the group is working harmoniously). A team including many assistant facilitators can prove necessary for larger groups, which often do much of their work in very small groups. For example, the South Australia Nuclear Fuel Cycle Jury had over three hundred participants, and its two principal facilitators led a team of nearly twenty cofacilitators. This required tremendous clarity of purpose and consistency, particularly with very clear and shared objectives for each session. This team also managed the challenges of reconvening and reorienting back to shared goals and outcomes, after splitting into separate groups. Even in plenary sessions, multiple sets of ears and eyes, and different process designers, are better than one—especially since modifications often have to be made on the run.

Whether as part of a team or working alone, facilitators

manage a delicate balance of distance and personal engagement. To help the group reach an agreement, facilitators must hear what group members are saying to give timely and appropriate feedback, while the group pushes through disagreements and uncertainties on its way to a decision. A facilitator who delights in this experience as much as the participants is a rarity, but it is essential for the group's success. The facilitator must have a genuine curiosity, willingness, and ability to help the group surface differences and disagreements, while exploring them respectfully, to reach an outcome that works for all.

Given the importance of this role for a sortition chamber, the hiring and firing of a facilitator or facilitators should be controlled by the chamber itself. It need not be a permanent position: facilitators can be hired and let go, as needed. Above all else, it should *not* be assumed that the skill set for competent facilitation will reside within the randomly selected group. When appointing a facilitator or assessing the merits of an existing one, the chamber must always look for facilitators who view themselves as the servant of the room, not the star of the show.

Decision Rules

Professional facilitators have a tool kit of microprocesses for exploring common ground or prioritizing—whatever is needed to reach a shared decision. The choice of such microprocess will depend on many variables, such as the complexity of the issue or available time.

As for formal decision-making in a sortition chamber, Gastil and Wright suggested secret voting (once known as the "Australian ballot" because of its nineteenth-century origins in my country). Though I understand the need for formal rules in a legislative body, I believe that voting should be the *last resort* when deliberating because it entrenches positions and is not conducive to exploring consensus. Should voting be required (owing to a failure to reach consensus), then many voting tools are available: the Condorcet method, preferential voting, "preferenda,"[39] ranked-choice voting, multi-option voting, and so on.

To introduce nuance, it will be worthwhile to expand the voting repertoire beyond those methods currently used in parliaments.

Simultaneity

One additional way to delay the vote, and extend deliberation, would be to convene multiple or simultaneous minipublics that would feed into the assembly, or to divide the assembly itself into simultaneous consensus-seeking groups. I will say more about simultaneous deliberation in the next section. For now, I will focus on the use of simultaneous small groups *within* the assembly, drawing once more upon the experience of new-Democracy—albeit its experience in local government.

The newDemocracy model for simultaneous minipublics is an attempt to broaden the deliberation to staff members in local government but is transferable to a parliamentary assembly. Here's what we have done so far, and the lessons we have learned.

In 2012 newDemocracy convened a citizens' jury, called a *citizens' panel*, in Canada Bay (metropolitan Sydney, Australia). The staff person responsible for overseeing that citizens' panel was inspired to try something similar among members of the council's staff. She assumed the role of facilitator and the organizer of the random-selection process. She then replicated the activities of the citizens' panel among a diverse group of staff members; this staff jury included senior office workers, rubbish collectors, road workers, and so on. There was considerable overlap between the recommendations of the two juries.

In 2016, newDemocracy convened a citizens' jury in Eurobodalla (coastal district south of Sydney). Again, a staff jury was convened to run alongside the community citizens' jury. This time, the same professional facilitator was used for both. The staff jury was as diverse as the Canada Bay jury, chosen using random selection. Each day of the staff jury followed a citizens' jury meeting. Again, the two juries' recommendations overlapped.

Professional staff are a good resource for skills, knowledge, and expertise that is helpful when informing a citizens' jury. The staff jury and citizens' jury can be integrated to the extent that they can share background materials and expert speakers. They can report to each other as they build knowledge.

In summary, there are real advantages to convening simultaneous minipublics. These include building trust among staff, building trust between citizens and staff, building trust in government decisions, improving the chances of buy-in when similar recommendations emerge, tapping into the additional knowledge that staff bring, exposing staff to democratic innovations, and improving understanding of all operations across the staff population since they are often unaware of responsibilities beyond their own.

This approach provides a way of integrating bureaucrats with randomly selected groups of citizens, but what about the wider public? The next section considers broadening deliberation beyond the sortition chamber itself.

Deliberation Beyond the Legislature

If a sortition assembly remains as unconnected from the wider population as current legislatures, it will fail. The architecture of government is more than a parliament. Deliberative democrats argue that minipublics should be deeply embedded in government decision-making. Community collaboration should be a natural aspect of the policy cycle and governance in general.[40] In this section, I explore four ways to extend deliberation: an agenda-setting forum, proposal teams, the planning cell model, and an accountability forum.

Agenda-Setting Forums

The G1000 model has been used widely in Europe. This method is best used for idea generation and agenda setting, but it has the potential to be combined with other decision-making methods. This would work well in combination with a citizen legislature, to ensure that the wider population (one thousand citizens each time) provides input at an early stage of decision-making. This can help prioritize issues and identify coalitions of participants willing to move an issue forward.[41]

Proposal Teams

For many years, software designer Brian Sullivan has wrestled with the challenge of deliberating online. His latest design—What Do We Think?—has the potential to involve large numbers in curated conversations, using emails.[42] This software platform would enable citizens beyond the assembly to participate as little or often as they wish, but in a way that requires collaboration and thoughtful deliberation to reach agreement on proposals to forward to legislators. Stakeholders and civil-society organizations who have dedicated their lives to advocate positions warrant involvement in the decision-making process so that their ideas are seriously and fairly considered. With this method, multiple conversations are drawn together—curated transparently—to reach agreement. Participants can see the history of the exchanges and how summaries were created. This overcomes the usual problems associated with calling for public input, which can yield thousands of responses, often duplicated, and sometimes expressions that are ill informed or indifferent to the views of others.

Planning Cells

Professor Peter Dienel designed a workable method in Germany (starting in the 1970s and continuing through today) that could be used to take policy development and evaluation to the wider population.[43] His planning cell method uses multiple groups of twenty-five that can be convened simultaneously in different locations, thereby resulting in a public deliberation of, say, twenty by twenty-five—or five hundred—randomly selected citizens. The benefit of this model is that common ground can be easily discerned. For example, if nineteen out of twenty groups recommend a particular decision, the "outlier" can be examined closely to understand the divergence. This model could be replicated within a sortition chamber, but also extended beyond its walls to draw in fresh public voices. Either way, a design choice has to be made about whether to run the meetings simultaneously (for example, through a digital linkage) or consecutively, as they are more often convened in Germany.

Accountability

Gastil and Wright's sortition chamber proposal includes brief notes about an internal oversight mechanism to require a modicum of accountability for the citizen legislators, at least to each other. A more satisfying proposal would go farther, because declining trust in government stems, in part, from the lack of meaningful government accountability to citizens between elections. A chamber without elections would lose even that.

Legislative assemblies often involve annual summarizing addresses to the assembly or the nation—for example, the State of the Union address by the US president to Congress. In Australia, an example would be the budget speech delivered by the federal treasurer to the House of Representatives. In the UK, "question time" serves as an example. These are declaratory one-way statements, meant as a means of accountability on which the media provides commentary.

What's missing in all of these is an accountability *conversation* that is representative, deliberative, resistant to manipulation, influential, and trusted by the public. This could give constituents the chance to join this questioning and analysis and talk about how policy questions bear on their lives.

An example that could be modified for the sortition chamber emerged during the French presidential election in 2017, when an intriguing promise was made by candidate Emmanuel Macron. Macron spoke of the importance of accountability to citizens. He proposed an annual speech, a "State of the Union" address to the parliamentary assembly, and another given to an assembly of randomly selected citizens. He offered few details, but a sortition assembly could try this.

The process could start with the minipublic model, to enhance participants' critical faculties, subject representatives to genuine inquiry, provide adequate background information, and use random selection to deliver a diverse group that reflects the wider population.

Using the Australian example, imagine a model with citizens in the foreground. Organizers could assemble seventy-six citizens (let's call it "C76"), with twelve randomly selected from each state and two from both mainland territories, as with the current Senate. The selection would be stratified to reflect current demographics according to the latest census data in terms of age, sex, education level, and location (regional, urban, remote). A proportion of these seats could be set aside for indigenous Australians, who have been excluded from political decision-making throughout Australia's post-eighteenth-century history. This could happen each year—a national lottery, well publicized.

Before the C76 meets, the government publicizes its forthcoming gathering and gives every citizen an opportunity to pose questions for consideration. Within small teams, interested people work in curated online deliberations to develop and agree upon questions to submit. These questions become the starting point for the C76's early sessions, during which they discuss how to question the sortition chamber about the decisions it has made, or the policy issues still under consideration. This would provide an excellent combination of participatory and deliberative democracy by incorporating public opinion (from the wider population) that leads to public judgment (by the C76 accountability group).

The representatives from the legislature answer questions posted by the C76 in a plenary session, as well as via a rotating small-group model. They need to provide sufficiently clear and direct answers to the satisfaction of the C76. Opportunities are provided to note any facts that require checking, or any gaps in information. The C76 then deliberates and makes recommendations, loosely categorized as *stop*, *start*, or *continue* (a given policy direction). These recommendations are communicated to the sortition chamber and to the wider public, and the chamber has a period of time in which to draft and make public responsive action plans.

Conclusion

I have offered several suggestions for how to achieve a deliberative process within a sortition chamber, as well as beyond it, by drawing it closer to the wider public. In doing so, I drew on my experience at newDemocracy and as an observer of numerous minipublics and other public events. The proposed sortition chamber, however, raises questions that this limited knowledge base cannot answer.

Most of all, newDemocracy's minipublics are one-off events with the longest spanning several months. What happens when a randomly selected group is convened over a much longer period—years instead of months? How might the group dynamics change? Anticipating such changes will have an impact on the deliberative design—a fascinating challenge for any deliberative designer.

Are randomly selected citizens to become modern-day philosophers, recalling Plato's belief that only philosophers should rule?[44] Being philosophical is consistent with the principles of deliberative democracy, which calls for interrogating evidence and questioning everything, including one's own biases. Might this overcome the "corporate coup" occurring in some Western democracies by replacing power seekers with deep thinkers?[45]

More than anything, the overarching question should be, "What can this assembly contribute to a democracy?"[46] The shift from a self-selected, political-party-dominated assembly will make a significant contribution to democracy, but this will be insufficient. We know that the architecture of government, by its very design, can lead to democratic deficits.[47] Institutional structures must be supported by process design that enables collaboration to surface, and a willingness to partner for the benefit of all.

Gastil and Wright were alert to this, and their suggestions about orientation and training of new representatives will be essential, as will be effective staff support. Gastil and Wright have also recommended an oversight commission. This could be modeled on Australia's successful state-based Independent Commission Against Corruption. Or if we want to persist with wider involvement of citizens, then citizens' parliamentary groups could work well as monitors or overseers.[48]

Above all else, I hope this chapter serves as a call to action. We must avoid seeking *only* a change in representation by simply substituting randomly selected citizens for elected ones and blithely assuming an entirely different outcome. In any such reform, careful process design will be essential. What *happens* in an assembly—how decisions are to be made—is of equal importance to how those representatives are selected. Process design can make or break a sortition assembly. Attention must be paid to methods that enable legislators to come to judgment, not merely how to count their personal opinions through voting. Genuine deliberation will be imperative to restore trust in the workings of government.

11

Sortition and Democratic Principles: A Comparative Analysis

Dimitri Courant

After centuries of absence, sortition is making its return through academic research, practical experiments, and activists' calls for linking participation and deliberation.[1] These invocations of sortition, however, offer divergent accounts of the concept and different justifications.[2] Gastil and Wright's proposal for a "sortition chamber" provides one such example, but sortition can be conceptualized more broadly.[3] When properly analyzed in this larger sense, one can better appreciate how sortition satisfies democratic principles—often in novel ways that go beyond those enumerated in the lead chapter of this volume.

To better understand the implications of sortition, I begin by contrasting it with the other modes of selection democracies use to place people in positions of power, including not only elections but also nomination and certification. I then distinguish varieties of sortition that differ by their mandate, the population from which a random sample is drawn, and the degree to which service is voluntary or compulsory. Depending on the design considerations such as these, sortition can provide a novel means of realizing the democratic aspirations of equality, impartiality, representativeness, and legitimacy.[4]

Modes of Selection

When a good, task, or position are wanted by too many people, or undesired but necessary to the collective, a *selection process* is needed. Aside from in small direct democracies, certain missions—particularly deliberative ones—cannot be carried out by all the citizens and need to be accomplished, instead, by representatives. I identify four modes of selection, any of which can be combined with the others.[5] In doing so, I focus on the disadvantages of the mode of selection other than sortition.

Election

The "triumph of election" as the legitimate way of selecting rulers makes us forget that prior to the American and French revolutions, it was common to hold a contrary view, as expressed by Montesquieu: "The suffrage by lot is the nature of democracy. Suffrage by choice is the nature of aristocracy. Drawing lots ... leaves each citizen a reasonable hope of serving his country."[6] In Athenian democracy, most public offices were appointed randomly, ensuring the equality of each citizen and refusing to elect the "better" (*aristoi*), except for few specific tasks. By contrast, Sparta mainly used election and was considered to be an oligarchy.[7]

Manin shows that despite this knowledge, the American founding fathers and the French revolutionaries disliked democracy. They chose election for selecting representatives to create an elected aristocracy, socially distinct from the people.[8] Later the word *democracy* was used as an advertising tool by politicians to lure electors. Eventually, modern political regimes changed their names to "representative democracies."[9]

Election is a selection procedure that *vertically ascends* from the bottom to the top. A majority or plurality of electors choose every few years to which preselected candidate it will surrender power. In terms of the democratic criteria discussed more fully later in this chapter, elections have four limitations. First, they fail to provide *descriptive representation* (that is, a body of representatives demographically similar to the electorate). Second, they produce only a kind of *personal* legitimacy. Third, they cannot ensure *competent* and *impartial* governance. And finally, elections cannot function among true *equals* because they require voters to distinguish between candidates; choosing one person over another would be difficult—if not impossible—when none are considered superior.

Nomination

Nomination is a common selection method in representative governments. In France, for example, the prime minister is nominated by the president, who is elected through direct universal suffrage. The prime minister then nominates government ministers, and the president has to give his approval. Nowhere are federal government cabinet ministers or agency heads elected.

Nomination has significant problems. The nomination process can be accused of being partial, biased, and arbitrary. Like elections, it fails to provide descriptive representation. A nominee's legitimacy vertically descends from the top of the political hierarchy, which can create hostility among the lay public at that system's base. Finally, since nomination gives an office to a specific person, it produces a very individual type of legitimacy.

Certification

Certification is a mainstream selection process (for universities, civil servants, and so on), but because it is seen as technocratic, it is almost never used to produce political representatives in democratic systems. Exceptions do exist, however. Persons wishing to be nominated to judgeships in the United States, for instance, commonly receive ratings from the American Bar

Association regarding their qualifications, with an "unqualified" score sometimes jeopardizing a nominee.[10] Those who wish to be eligible for random selection onto the California Citizens Redistricting Commission must first meet a set of qualifications set out by the state auditor.[11]

Certification has its own problems. Those certified to serve have not been authorized by the public, nor even necessarily by elected officials. It is grounded in a distinction principle, so certified representatives, by definition, do not resemble the represented. Certification creates a type of legitimacy that is both individual and based on superiority. Even though certification seems to guarantee some equality of opportunity between candidates, producing a form of horizontal legitimacy, this impartiality is often illusory. In reality, certification tests are defined and conducted by superiors who may not themselves be accountable to anyone for the certification process. If the decision-makers atop the hierarchy do not directly choose their favored candidates, they create a test where those same candidates are more likely to succeed. Therefore, the legitimacy remains vertical.

Sortition

Sortition means selecting representatives by lot, but the following section will clarify important variations of this general concept. Concerns about sortition abound, as evidenced by many of the other chapters in this volume. Here, I focus on one particular drawback—the hazard that a sortition body would produce incompetent officials. Jacques Rancière noted a first defense against this charge: "the drawing of lots has never favoured the incompetent over the competent."[12] Sortition is not a competence filter, but the other selection modes all share this problem. Only certification can pretend to ensure competence, on the condition that its test criteria are "sound"—though in whose judgment?[13]

Moreover, the majority of deliberative-democracy experiments, such as deliberative polls and citizens' juries, demonstrate that citizens learn fast and become more competent than elected officials on complex issues.[14] Finally, due to the "cognitive diversity" it provides, random selection can be an "epistemically superior mode of selection of representatives." Hélène Landemore explains that "decisions taken by the many are more likely to be right than decisions taken by the few." Indeed, sortition produces an assembly with a greater diversity of experiences and social profiles, which creates a stronger collective intelligence capable of tackling issues elected legislatures fail to address adequately.[15]

Selection and Deliberation Frameworks in Sortition

Which kind of officials do we want? If we want representatives who look like the represented, we shall choose sortition, for the democratic ideal of "government by the people." If we prefer socially distinct elites (an aristocratic view), we shall choose election. If we think that leaders should choose the representatives (an oligarchic perspective), we shall adopt nomination. If we want qualified representatives (leaning toward technocracy), we shall select through certification. Even if one chooses sortition over the alternative methods of selection, there remain many choices about how to create and organize a sortition body.[16] Gastil and Wright's sortition chamber presents one set of choices, but other sortition designs will reflect different decisions about mandates, target populations, and voluntary versus compulsory service.

Mandate and Duration

Regardless of the mode of selection, the deliberative rules and institutional architecture in which an assembly is embedded are crucial. This is especially the case for a sortition assembly, with the shifts from consultative minipublics to a powerful body granted legislative authority.[17] Most sortition theorists and advocates envision assemblies that are *deliberative* but not executive. These main missions, none of which are mutually exclusive, include the following:

1. *Consultation* of the population, as in a deliberative poll.[18]
2. *Providing information* to officials and citizens, through writing a statement.[19]
3. *Control* and *evaluation* of officials and policies.[20]
4. *Making a policy or budgetary decision*, as in some citizens' juries or participatory budgeting.[21]
5. *Legislation*, with an additional chamber of the parliament, as in Gastil and Wright's proposal.
6. *Constitution*, both for revising one or writing a new one.[22]
7. *Long-term issues*, such as climate change or techno-scientific risks.[23]

Regardless of its mandate, so far, every political system based on sortition has had short mandates and regular rotation of members.[24] By contrast, election favors reelection, certification is easily sustained once met, and nomination maintains small circles of initiates. Unlike consultative minipublics, a more enduring sortition chamber would constitute a bold deviation from precedent, which might be necessary for a full-functioning legislature.

Population

Regardless of the mode of selection, there is always a delimitation of the "relevant political body" and criteria to be part of the selection process. As in the case of elections, the lottery for sortition draws from the citizens of a given political unit, but the pool can sometimes be more inclusive. Some processes have drawn names from a phone book, which includes individuals not registered to vote—or not even eligible to do so. The Belgian G1000 reserved 10 percent of its seats for homeless people and undocumented immigrants. The pool is usually related to the level where the decision is implemented (such as workplace, local neighborhood, state).

Mixed Selection

The different modes of selection are not opposed, but instead complementary and combinable. In the French military, for example, members of the High Council of Military Function (Conseil Supérieur de la Fonction Militaire, CSFM) pass certification for their rank, then are sorted and elected by the other randomly designated soldiers.[25] The pairing of certification and sortition is also used in the California Citizens Redistricting Commission.[26]

To show the flexibility of the selection mix and stimulate democratic imagination, I propose that political parties could present manifestos and a long unranked list of candidates. Citizens could then vote on the manifestos, and the result would determine the proportion of representatives *randomly* selected from each party. This would avoid discussing candidates' charisma or personal life to focus on manifestos and concrete policy propositions.

Voluntary, Consensual, or Compulsory Service

When it comes to serving on a sortition body, there are different degrees to which doing so might be obligatory. Here, I distinguish three levels: voluntary, consensual, and compulsory.[27]

At the first level, sortition representatives are selected from a pool of *volunteers*, which means they actively desired to be selected. This method has the advantage of bringing motivated people, but the disadvantage of letting power in the hands of those who wanted it—"the worst of all evils," according to Plato or Rancière.[28] However, volunteering to take part in sortition was the functioning mode in Athens, Venice, Florence, and Aragon.[29]

An alternative carries out the lottery among the whole relevant political body, without any call for volunteers. In this case, the persons selected have a right to refuse the public office a posteriori. The vast majority of deliberative-democracy experiments function on this *consensual* model. To encourage acceptance of the invitation, organizers typically provide incentives for service, as do Gastil and Wright in their proposed sortition chamber. This approach fares better in terms of equality and of representativeness. By letting invitees decide whether to serve, even with strong incentives to do so, the resulting body differs from the larger population it aims to represent. Some demographic groups might be missing (or at least underrepresented) because their randomly selected members did not consider themselves as equal with the other selectees—not worthy of a seat in the sortition body. The same pattern appears for elections, in which underprivileged social classes vote less frequently than others.[30] The underrepresentation of disadvantaged social groups goes against principles of moral justice and inclusion, but it also poses a legitimacy problem: those second-class citizens who felt excluded might stop respecting laws they had no hand in creating.

One solution to this problem would be moving away from voluntary and consensual levels by making public service *compulsory* for those chosen through sortition. It might seem strange to regard participation as a *duty*; however, it is the secular practice of popular jury in France, the United States, British Commonwealth countries, and many others. Many countries, notably including Australia, make voting compulsory, and no country excuses its citizens from paying taxes. There are other advantages to this third approach. Obligatory sortition improves the impartiality of those chosen. It would be suspicious to elect a jury from volunteer candidates; one would wonder what interests they serve. A compulsory system also protects against the "free rider" phenomenon. Taking part in a deliberative assembly or jury is a heavy load in time and energy; a compulsory system spreads that burden as widely as possible.[31] Finally, obligation would push into service those who might otherwise perceive themselves as unworthy—thereby empowering the most disenfranchised segment of society.

How Sortition Meets Democratic Principles

Having distinguished sortition from other modes of selection, and with an appreciation for the different ways one can implement it, I turn now to how sortition expresses democratic values. Historical analysis reveals three successive principles for sortition: the random selection of citizens for public offices in ancient Athens, based on the principle of *equality*; the lottery to pick out members of popular jury, aiming for *impartiality*; and opinion polls giving a *representativeness* of the population through representative sample. Some authors in this volume address the issue of democratic values, but they overlook some of the novel ways sortition relates to equality, impartiality, representativeness—and the legitimacy this relationship produces.[32] Depending on its institutional architecture, sortition's democratic principles can be enhanced or diminished, but here I stress its greatest democratic potential compared to other modes of selection.

Equality

Without volunteering or quotas, sortition gives excellent *statistical equality* between individuals. Each citizen has the same chance to be randomly selected. For Cornelius Castoriadis, this principle is the same as universal suffrage and majority rule. Each citizen is considered equally politically competent; therefore, each voice is considered equal to others.[33] "The scandal of democracy, and of the drawing of lots that is its essence, is to reveal that [the title to govern] can be nothing but the absence of title." As Jacques Rancière says, the power of the people is "the equality of capabilities to occupy the positions of governors and of the governed."[34]

An answer to skeptics of this equality of capabilities is the evidence showing that citizens come to good decisions, if given the chance, as has been shown in so many deliberative-democracy experiments. Compared with the average voter, addled by political infotainment, a participant in a random assembly is demonstrably more competent.[35]

The second type of equality produced by sortition is the *deliberative equality* among the representatives. Once selected, all the representatives in a sortition body become equals. Lottery suppresses the affirmation of superiority, which in other selection modes might be expressed as, "I've won the election with a bigger majority"; "I was the first nominated by the authorities"; or "I've passed the test with better grades." All representatives drawn by lots have the exact same position, instead of being in the majority or the opposition. Each voice should be heard with the same attention, leading to a more equal footing for deliberation.

Finally, sortition can create an *inclusive equality* between representatives and represented. Indeed, the represented can say to their representatives, "Only chance distinguishes us, so we remain equals." As Gil Delannoi puts it, this "inclusion effect is not just coming from the fact that people elected by lots have an equal chance, but also from the fact that everyone knows that he or she can or could be selected."[36]

I expect that this affirmation of the equal political competence of all citizens could lead to another kind of inclusive equality—through greater mass participation in politics. Under sortition, it is no longer possible to say to citizens, "Your participation is your vote; give your power to the elected and be quiet while they work." Historical and recent cases show that with sortition the necessary moment of mass participation is not suppressed but moved from election toward the debates and votes on laws through referendum. Deliberative experiments are often linked with participatory and direct-democracy procedures, such as public debates, e-participation, or referenda, as was the case with every citizens' assembly, whether in Canada, Iceland, Belgium, or Ireland. These tools allow citizens to use their power directly instead of delegating it.[37] Moreover, as sortition would give a representative sample, possibly adjusted with quotas, excluded minorities would have a fair share in seats, creating a feeling of *inclusion* that further emboldens their participation.

Impartiality

Impartiality appears as the most obvious quality of sortition, as expressed in the *neutrality* principle. This is probably why the oldest use of random selection still exists through the popular jury, which judges admonish to remain impartial in their deliberations.

Neutrality is also the main principle justifying sortition for consensus conferences, particularly on techno-scientific issues in cases like the Danish Board of Technology.[38] There is a tension between interests such as public health or economic benefits, and it is necessary to ask the impartial opinion of lay citizens who have heard opposing experts. To consult only experts, activists, or industrialists would raise doubts about process neutrality. Suspicion can arise from the simple fact that an individual steps forward as a candidate (or receives a nomination) to participate. By contrast, a lottery increases the likelihood that people engaging in the deliberation have no hidden agenda and may, instead, seek the common good. Sortition also prevents cronyism and backdoor negotiations between small powerful groups, as there is no party line or campaign funding to negotiate.[39]

A lottery makes manipulation through media and advertising to win elections pointless. Nonetheless, parties and media still play an important role on how an issue is debated in the public sphere, especially in situations where a referendum follows the assembly deliberation. Random selection also increases neutrality by limiting bribery and the legal "buying" of representation through campaign contributions. The process of sortition is transparent, whether it is conducted physically or digitally by source code that anyone can check,[40] contrary to some elections with "forgotten" ballots or vote miscalculation. Chance suppresses favoritism and discriminations, though the risk of corruption may exist for bodies that have broad agendas and long-term offices, as in Gastil and Wright's proposal. Even so, sortition should mitigate the tendency toward corruption evidenced in the elected, nominated, and certified bodies that exist today.

A second kind of impartiality I call *unity*—or the discouragement of destructive forms of conflict. Sortition may make competition or partisan strategy pointless. For this "peace producing virtue of exteriority," as Bernard Manin calls it, lots were used in Italian republics to avoid "the violent tearing created by the open electoral competition."[41] Sortition avoids electoral campaigns, demagoguery, and factions, though it cannot guarantee that those do not form after the fact—especially if paired with an elected body, as Gastil and Wright envision.

Political parties are criticized for the division they create, as they are "combat organizations specially built to carry out a sublimated form of civil war [political campaign]," according to Pierre Bourdieu.[42] This fear of faction and division is a main reason why the French Parliament chose sortition for the CSFM in 1968. There is a need for a concertation process within the army to gather the views and approvals of the soldiers regarding reforms affecting their wages, work conditions, pensions, and so on. Nevertheless, the permanent imperative of ensuring the defense of the nation cannot allow electoral competition within the army. If all the voices—especially from lower ranks—must be heard in the concertation process, the selection of the representatives should provide diversity in the assembly but could not endanger the army's unity.[43] This unity is also desirable for broad public constituencies, as sortition prevents candidates from targeting a big part of the electorate while leaving behind or stigmatizing another part.

Among representatives and the larger publics they represent, debates are important. *Unity* here is not the absence of divisions, but the absence of longstanding—sometimes artificial—preestablished partisan cleavages that impede honest debate. New divisions and debates should rise from concrete issues, but they should do so based on empirical and normative disagreements that relate to laws, budgets, and other legislative tasks, rather than the public-relations imperatives of parties. The absence of party discipline allows randomly selected representatives to seek a common good, instead of pursuing factional interests.

Finally, sortition creates a special kind of impartiality, which I refer to as *unpredictability*. The professionalization of politics leads to a trend of politicians who all look alike, sometimes even across parties as well as within them. As Pierre Bourdieu argues, elected officials follow the rules and codes of their closed circles and become predictable:

> The sense of the political game that allows politicians to predict other politicians' positions is also what makes them predictable. Predictable, which means responsible, competent, serious, reliable; ready to play the game with constancy without surprise or treasons of the role imposed to them by the game's structure.[44]

According to the historian Alexandros Kontos, the ancient Athenian economic policy was predictable because the magistrates were not. By contrast, contemporary elections make politicians' strategies predictable, which allows the economic sphere to be volatile and uncertain. Kontos's point is that since sortition made it impossible for a specific class to stay in power, it allowed an unpredictable, frequently renewed assembly of poor people (the majority) to rule. The "free market" was tamed and speculation banned.[45] Unpredictability operates here in the same way people might operate behind philosopher John Rawls's "veil of ignorance." Selection by lottery prevents participants from knowing the positions of the others on the issue, their relative rhetorical skills, or their openness to changing their minds. Indeed, some minipublics have produced surprising results, as with Texas residents championing renewable energy or Irish citizens calling for marriage equality.[46]

Representativeness

The recent hegemony of elections gives the illusion of representation through authorization as the only legitimate method of democratic selection, but sortition provides an alternative. Through the law of large numbers, sortition enacts the old ideal of mirror representation since a *representative sample* provides a fair cross section of the population, in terms of social classes, ages, gender, and more.[47] Lottery also gives seats to ordinary citizens. Therefore, sorted representatives would have similar background to the population they represent. Gastil and Wright, along with other authors in this volume, have noted this, but they have overlooked subtle ways that sortition satisfies the principle of representativeness, by way of diversity and proximity.

"Parliament should be as a map for a territory, a miniature portrait of the People," said (in substance) John Adams, Mirabeau, and American anti-Federalists. Apart from mere geographical diversity, however, modern elections produce assemblies that do not capture the population's diversity. In France in 2013, for example, blue- and white-collar laborers were half of the workforce but were only 3 percent of MPs (with the majority of MPs being lawyers or senior officials). This lack of *diversity* goes against the ancient *quod omnes tangit* principles, meaning that everyone should discuss an issue concerning everyone. As rephrased by Dewey, "The man who wears the shoe knows best that it pinches and where it pinches."[48] As in the epistemic argument, the diversity of a representative assembly is also a question of efficacy.[49]

By including the full diversity of a public, sortition better represents it in a collective sense. Even when the size of a sortition body is too small to have a statistically representative sample of individuals, such as in a jury, the lottery aims to get the greatest diversity possible. Some deliberative experiments even make extra efforts to include marginalized people or minorities, like indigenous peoples in Canada.[50]

The so-called party diversity in modern democracies is actually weak, especially in two-party systems. Many people's concerns are not represented, and parties seem to be in decline. Moreover, through sortition, representativeness is necessarily *collective*: the whole assembly should represent the population as a coherent whole, not each member individually (and not just society's separate factions). Whereas an elected official may feel "personally representative" of a constituency because a majority of voters granted authorization through an election, sortition members have more latitude to represent the collective because they were chosen from the full population.[51]

Officials chosen through sortition also represent the population better by virtue of their enduring *proximity* to the public. Distance between sortition representatives and represented might grow ex post, but officials chosen by lot serve short terms, with regular rotation.[52] Sortition is consistent with the view that politics is an amateur job that should not be professionalized.[53] To look again at the example of representation within the French military, that system values *experiential proximity*. As one soldier holding office by lot explained in an interview I conducted, "We live the same conditions as the colleagues we represent."[54]

Elected and appointed officials split away easily from constituents with whom they do not share everyday life experiences, but they also do so due to the "iron law of oligarchy." Politicians and unionists who work together become colleagues, creating a connivance climate that leads to citizens' defiance. Proudhon gives testimony: "One needs to have lived in this ballot booth that we call National Assembly to realize to what extent men completely ignoring the state of the country are almost always the ones representing it."[55] Democratic proximity should be sharing the same life as the represented, not the false "proximity" displayed by politicians during their hand shaking. A single four-year term in the sortition chamber seems brief enough to maintain proximity, unlike a political career.

Legitimacy

A process that meets the principles of equality, impartiality, and representativeness should gain some measure of democratic legitimacy. Legitimacy is crucial because it underwrites consent—the willingness of the demos to accept decisions without the use of force. There are three elements composing this specific type of legitimacy: impersonality, independence, and humility (or nonsuperiority), which are connected to the three democratic principles—equality, impartiality, and representativeness—previously analyzed.[56]

First, *impersonality* comes from the character of representativeness within a sortition assembly. The assembly is "impersonal" because it can be representative only as a whole; no single member can claim to be "representative" on their own. Representatives selected by lot should gain public legitimacy because they have similarity and proximity to the people they represent. Sortition can generate a diverse and representative sample, without using quotas if the sample is big enough. Sortition was (and still is) linked to proximity, thanks to brief terms and rotation, contrary to communist officials that started their lives as factory workers but then never returned to their roots. There are also cases of proximity without similarity, like the young educated Maoist students going to farms and factories, sharing the living conditions of the working class, without coming from poor peasant backgrounds. The combination of both similarity and proximity produced by sortition, creating representativeness, enhances support and the quality of citizens' lives. Anyone represented by a sortition body can say, "Some members of that body look like me and share my living conditions." This also prevents the risk of charismatic leaders. Moreover, members resembling the represented come to office as unknowns, rather than as a candidate who built a personal brand. In this sense, members gain legitimacy by virtue of being (formerly) anonymous members of the demos.

Second, sortition's legitimacy differs from other selection modes because of the "direction" from which it comes. Contrary to a nomination, it comes not from the top, and unlike elections, it does not require climbing up from the bottom. Instead, members of a sortition body gain power and legitimacy *horizontally*: citizens remain lay citizens, even as sortition confers a temporary title on them.[57] In this way, sortition gains legitimacy by producing *independent* representatives who do not owe their title to anyone. This is a good solution for the concertation process in the French military, as neither the minister nor the soldiers would accept the authority of an assembly selected by the other.[58] Sortition is the only selection procedure that is impartial, neutral, and horizontal. Sortition representatives do not have to flatter an electorate, special interests, or a party hierarchy to get reelected. They are not submissive to those who nominated them. They do not have to follow rules set up by experts designing the test for certification. Independence from such constraints makes them, potentially, more legitimate in the public's eye.

Finally, the sortition body's members might retain a kind of *humility* that distinguishes them from officials selected through other means. A conventional representative has a feeling of personal superiority over all those who failed—or did not even try—to pass the selection contest in which he or she prevailed. That sense might come from having won an election, being a nominee chosen by elites, or being certified as a technocrat after passing prestigious tests. This is a reason why elected representatives so often fail to keep their promises or listen to popular protest; they believe themselves superior to "the people." By contrast, sortition is insulated from the aristocratic "distinction principle" linked to election,[59] nomination, or certification. Delannoi explains this crucial psychological dimension in these terms:

> "Sortition offends no one," noted Montesquieu. It doesn't create vanity for the winner nor rancour for the loser. It diminishes arrogance and bitterness … This soothing effect is individual, collective and systemic. There are almost no exceptions to it. Maybe a lottery winner can consider himself as "loved by the Gods" but such a favor is at least special and never owned with certitude. One cannot compare it to the feeling of one's own merit.[60]

Sortition produces a legitimacy based on *humility*. The randomly selected representatives do not consider themselves better or worse than other candidates or the majority of people that did not even try to be selected, because there is no credit to being designated by chance. One is not selected because one would be superior to the group, but because one is an equal part of the group. Thus the sortition representative can claim, "I have the right to speak for you, because nothing distinguishes me from you." Constituents accept this representative claim because they can tell themselves, "It could have been me selected for that job." Or, "It might be me next." Even without parties, elections always create a distinction. Voters can think of an elected representative coming from the same background and displaying proximity. A voter might say, "My representative looks like me and shares the reality of my everyday life. But they are different because they won an election, which is something I cannot do, since I do not possess the qualities to be elected." The same logic applies to nomination and certification.

By contrast, the only difference between the mass public and the people selected by sortition is that the sortition representatives must get to work deliberating in citizens' assemblies or juries. Training and experience deliberating may come to set these representatives apart, in terms of their legislative expertise, but that same career lies within everybody's reach. If we have to select a deliberative assembly, it is not to create an elite, but because deliberation cannot be undertaken by millions of people simultaneously. This means that citizens would be more likely to participate as the system considers them all politically competent.

The message sent by sortition is that anyone is assumed to have the ability to directly take part in deliberation. This message is even stronger when sortition is coupled with direct democracy, as happens in an important share of minipublics. This might lead to a "Pygmalion effect"—a self-fulfilling prophecy in which people who are told they are competent become more competent.[61] By contrast, the logic of delegation and election might have the opposite effect, a "Golem effect"[62]—that is, when people are told they cannot directly take part in deliberation but must delegate their power to better actors, they might become less motivated to care about politics. Sortition could reverse that trend and make its legislators' humility even more warranted, as the public starts to hold itself to a higher civic standard.

A lottery can be used to distribute desired offices, like in Italian republics, but also to assign duties necessary to the group that no one wants to do. In this perspective, holding a public office is nothing one should be proud of. Also, citizens might accept the sortition assembly's decisions because they want to be accepted in return when they will be sorted and seated. The last part of the legitimacy based on humility is the "authority of the ordinary." This is revealed by trust in "real people's popular wisdom" or "common sense." In such cases, the ordinary person receives the confidence and the support of the group.[63]

Conclusion

To sharpen our appreciation of sortition, I have distinguished it from other modes of selection, clarified the variety of frameworks it could operate within, and revealed less obvious ways in which sortition can thereby fulfill democratic principles. Those democratic principles, revealing what I call the *new spirit of sortition*, are potentialities not always present but enhanced or suppressed by the framework. Sortition is no magical solution to the problems of modern democracies, but taking this idea seriously gives us the opportunity to imagine democracy beyond elections. Envisioning a sortition body helps us see the contradictions between what passes for democracy and real democratic principles.

Explorations of sortition can also shift the debate from direct versus representative democracy to the question of the representative's selection process. Gastil and Wright's proposal for a sortition chamber and, more broadly, the "real utopian" notion of random selection could reopen the democratic imagination and spark experiments that yield more inclusive forms of representation, deliberation, and participation.

12

In Defense of Imperfection: An Election-Sortition Compromise

Arash Abizadeh

Representative democracies as we know them have many familiar deficiencies. Electoral campaigns and elected representatives are subject to the corrupting influence of money and special-interest groups. Elected representatives are disproportionately drawn from society's privileged elements. Politicians face strong strategic incentives for manipulation, deception, and viciousness in the campaign process and beyond, which damages the quality of public deliberation and feeds the public's cynicism, alienation, and sense of disempowerment. Under market capitalism, elected representatives face systemic obstacles to pursuing policies counter to private business interests.

Several potential remedies operate within the existing confines of representative democracy. A few prominent examples include public financing of electoral campaigns and public-interest media, restrictions on private contributions, mandatory participation in elections, and quotas for legislatures. Another remedy recently advocated by a number of writers—namely, sortition, or the selection of representatives by lottery—pushes beyond these confines.[1] This would represent a radical departure because, as Bernard Manin rightly observes, the selection of officers by elections has been one of the basic principles of modern representative government since its inception.[2]

The proposal to select legislators by lot comes in two varieties. The first is to combine elected with sorted legislative representatives, whether within a mixed chamber or—as Gastil and Wright propose—in separate chambers.[3] The second approach would eliminate elections entirely and rely exclusively on sortition for selecting legislators.[4] My purpose here is to defend proposals like Gastil and Wright's, not against those who reject sortition outright but against those who would use sortition to replace elections entirely. In particular, I defend combining an elected and a sortition chamber in a bicameral legislature, as Gastil and Wright propose.

The Inherent Limitations of Democratic Elections

I proceed on the normative assumption that representative democracy is justified to the extent that it (1) promotes civil *peace* by disincentivizing political violence and (2) renders policy *satisfactorily responsive* to people's legitimate interests, values, and norms, in part by (3) facilitating people's political *agency* in a way that (4) helps resolve conflicting interests and disagreements *impartially* and (5) treats people as *political equals*. An exclusively *electoral* representative democracy fails with respect to three of these criteria. It does not secure an adequate level of responsiveness, nor does it resolve conflicts impartially or treat people as political equals.

Elections are supposed to promote responsiveness via two mechanisms: people can use elections to *select* representatives they believe are disposed to serve their interests, or they can use elections to *sanction* representatives they believe have not served their interests (thereby providing forward-looking representatives an incentive to do so).[5]

Both mechanisms face serious obstacles. The electoral selection mechanism cannot work effectively on the basis of candidates' promises, for example, because representatives are not bound by those promises. By design, public officials have wide discretion to respond to new information and circumstances.[6] Alternatively, voters might judge candidates' dispositions on the basis of descriptive characteristics or partisan identity—on the assumption that representatives similar to themselves, or from a particular party, are disposed to serve their interests.[7] Are elections an effective means for securing descriptive representation? The record suggests not. The overwhelming majority of legislators in representative democracies come from privileged socioeconomic backgrounds. Do people identify with and hence vote for parties that promote their interests? The problem is people often do not form their partisan identity on the basis of informed judgments about parties' policies.[8] This is hardly surprising given the voters' well-documented ignorance about basic policy questions.[9]

Widespread voter ignorance also compromises the sanctioning or accountability mechanism. If people are disposed to vote out representatives for having failed to serve their interests, then representatives who anticipate this retrospective sanction have an incentive to serve constituents' interests. But the mechanism depends on voters discerning the extent to which outcomes causally depend on representatives' actions or policies. If voters punish or reward representatives because of outcomes for which the latter bear little responsibility, then representatives have little incentive to tailor policies to avoid sanction (because sanctioning will not depend on which policies they adopt). As a result, numerous social scientists have argued that retrospective voting is at best a crude mechanism for securing responsiveness.[10]

This problem is compounded by the well-known vulnerability of elections to domination and manipulation by the powerful. Winning competitive elections requires resources for political organization, disseminating public opinion, and mobilizing voters. Those who have greater financial resources or social standing consequently enjoy an inherent advantage over those who do not. Hence, in a conflict between haves and have-nots, elections favor the haves. Ignorant voters are especially vulnerable to manipulation because they easily fall prey to incomplete but misleading information, misinformation, and framing effects.[11]

If representative institutions are responsive to public opinion and societal interests, their responsiveness will be not only crude, but also partial. Elections systematically favor those with the resources to exert greater influence on electoral outcomes.[12] The problem is inherent in competitive elections: By incentivizing political agency, competitive elections incentivize powerful interests to shape and influence public opinion and to mobilize voters.[13]

Competitive elections not only fail to resolve conflicting interests and disagreements in an *impartial* way, but they also fail to treat people as *political equals*. Elections can treat people as equals in their status as *voters*, but elections do not treat them as equals *qua candidates*. Candidates typically receive votes not on the basis of a status everyone has in common—not as political equals—but on the basis of something for which they are deemed eminent or superior to others. Furthermore, competitive elections inherently favor the wealthy thanks to the costs required to disseminate information and to overcome rivals' prior eminence or salience. And because voters are free to vote for candidates in a discriminatory fashion (for example, on the basis of descriptive characteristics such as race, class, gender, and so on), not only do different individuals have unequal prospects, but they also do not even have equal opportunity of being elected.[14]

Pairing Sortition with an Elected Chamber

Sortition, by contrast, can enhance satisfactory responsiveness, help resolve conflicts impartially, and treat people as political equals. It can enhance responsiveness through the selection mechanism: random selection tends to yield an assembly that "mirrors" the population at large. We can expect a descriptively representative assembly to be inclined to make decisions reflecting what the population itself might have decided if it had, like the assembly, informed itself and deliberated about the matter.[15] One of the reasons why the membership of a sortition chamber will mirror the population—rather than comprise elites, as in elected assemblies—is precisely because random selection is not susceptible to influence, domination, or manipulation by the powerful. It therefore helps resolve conflicts impartially.[16] It treats people as political equals because every candidate has an equal prospect of being selected to office—regardless of social status, resources, and the like.[17]

A purely sorted legislature, however, would be a recipe for civil war. One of the great merits of selecting representatives via regular elections is that it disincentivizes violence in the face of social conflict. First, elections provide the losing side the prospect of winning power the next time around. Given the tremendous costs of civil war, sociopolitical groups with a reasonable prospect of future electoral success have an incentive to gain power peacefully rather than risk the consequences of resorting to violence.

Second, the losing side's prospects for future success in a political conflict partly depend on their own agency. Whether they win or lose future elections depends, in part, on what they *do* between those elections. This provides them with incentives to expend resources to organize politically, build coalitions, influence public opinion, and win over the electorate.

Finally, elections help reveal the balance of power in society. They provide the losing side good evidence that they cannot count on widespread public support should they resort to violence.[18]

It is true that sortition provides the prospect of future change as well, but it compares less favorably on other counts. Under sortition, the selection of representatives is not tied to any particular political program. Future changes in assembly membership are not sensitive to any exercise of agency on the part of groups, and sortition does not reveal the balance of power in situations of social conflict. With no prospect of seizing power by mobilizing and contesting future elections, social forces opposed to the current legislative agenda would have stronger incentives to choose violence.

Sortition is also not a mechanism for holding representatives accountable to the public. Therefore, it has no inherent link to people's political agency, as the argument about civil war has already emphasized. The mechanism of accountability provided by elections, unlike sortition, promotes responsiveness— however coarse—through people's exercise of agency. Facilitating agency has intrinsic as well as instrumental significance,[19] and instrumental significance is not confined to preventing civil war. Elected representatives depend on their constituents for reelection; as such, they are compelled to canvass support by responding to constituents' demands, opinions, and criticisms.[20] That the threat of electoral sanction is nonnegligible in securing representatives' responsiveness is indicated, for example, by higher levels of responsiveness among representatives in competitive districts.[21]

Given that the threat of sanction is a real possibility, groups in civil society have an incentive to mobilize support via public argumentation, interest articulation, and coalition formation. As Urbinati has argued, the electoral accountability mechanism in representative democracies incentivizes a two-way circulation of public justification, argumentation, and interest articulation between representatives and the public.[22] Elections foster a culture of mobilization and contestation—arguably indispensable for the ongoing health of democratic institutions—and help to articulate a range of arguments, policy proposals, and demands from multiple sites in the public sphere.[23]

By contrast, a pure sortition legislature fails not only as a mechanism of facilitating political agency, but it also fails to properly incentivize public discourses crucial to the epistemic quality of representatives' deliberations.[24] It is one thing for a representative assembly to be open to petitions or to being persuaded at its pleasure, as a sorted chamber—indeed, an enlightened monarch—might be. It is quite another for representatives to be forced on pain of sanction to respond to demands stemming from civil society.

Representative democracy therefore faces a contradictory set of imperatives. On the one hand, the very mechanism that is supposed to disincentivize violence, secure responsiveness, and promote political agency is also responsible for failure with respect to impartiality and political equality. On the other hand, sortition, which furnishes a potential remedy to elections' shortcomings with respect to responsiveness, impartiality, and equality, fails adequately to promote political agency and to disincentivize civil war. My view is that a bicameral legislature, with one chamber elected and another randomly selected, strikes the right institutional compromise between the values and norms that underlie representative democracy.

IV. ALTERNATIVE PATHS TOWARD SORTITION

13

A Gradualist Path Toward Sortition

Deven Burks and Raphaël Kies

Building democracy takes time, and deliberative democracy will prove no exception. To that end, we will explore one possible path toward more deliberative institutions via Gastil and Wright's proposal for a sortition chamber. We argue that deliberative innovations require a gradualist approach to implementation. Whereas other authors in this volume may take for granted that some form of sortition chamber will be institutionalized and focus instead on design questions, we consider the necessary conditions preceding institutionalization.

We undertake this effort because we believe Gastil and Wright's proposal has merit as a deliberative democratic reform. A sortition chamber's "hybrid legitimacy" may allow it to overcome critiques addressed to one-shot, single-issue consultative or empowered minipublics, which may lack institutional footing.[1] Conventional minipublics face multiple challenges, which include significant social or political uptake, electoral accountability, capture by interests, political redundancy, representativeness, and framing biases.[2] If a sortition chamber, prima facie, meets or precludes these different critiques, it represents a striking contribution to democratic innovation.

Whatever their merits, sortition reforms warrant a gradualist approach for three reasons, as we argue in the body of this chapter. First, a strong but unaccountable deliberative device like sortition may delegitimize both existing and prospective forms of citizen deliberation, including sortition bodies themselves. Second, a weaker deliberative device like citizens' consultation can be effective, though unstable institutional footing often causes such efforts to fail. Third, once it is proven to be effective and normalized, citizens' consultation will open a clearer path toward enhanced deliberative innovations like the sortition chamber. To prove these points, we draw on examples principally from the European Union, but we believe our argument applies equally well at local, regional, national, and transnational levels. If institutionalizing consultative minipublics is desirable and feasible at the EU level, it will be all the more so at all others.

Dangers of Delegitimization

Introducing a sortition chamber without considerable public trust and institutional redesign is likely to undermine sortition's wider implementation and delegitimize deliberative innovation more generally. These problems would arise, in part, because citizens and policy makers are ill prepared to implement a sortition chamber outright.

To understand why, we must consider the institutional mechanisms for implementation. Most likely, institutional redesign would be decided either through public referendum or via legislation authorized by public officials. Previous research suggests that three problems would arise from implementation via these two channels: resistance from citizens, resistance from decision-makers, and a lack of empirical evidence demonstrating the viability of continuous empowered embedded minipublics, let alone sortition chambers.

Resistance from Citizens

Because a sortition chamber reduces or limits the scope of powerful legislative institutions (elected or otherwise), it represents an especially daunting electoral reform. Though we lack clear cases for direct comparison, systemic changes such as this would face obstacles even higher than those confronted by more modest electoral reforms.[3]

Regarding potential opposition from lay citizens, research shows that when voters have no structured preferences on an issue, risk aversion leads many of them to favor the status quo.[4] Status quo bias may be compounded when the vote bears on issues or institutions embedded in constitutions, for which change requires a qualified majority.

Writing on referendums, Alan Renwick contrasts this "anxiety-based voting model" with "issue-based" and "cue-based" voting models, which suppose a well-informed voter or one reliant on heuristic shortcuts.[5] Although all three models help explain voter behavior, Renwick notes that "the prevalence of each of these forms of voting varies . . . in response to the saliency of the issue."[6] Moreover, the validity of the issue and cue models depend on the quality of public information, which may vary depending on cue-givers, misinformation campaigns, media coverage, and campaign spending.[7]

To this, we add Renwick's cautious assertion that "opinion during referendum campaigns tends to shift towards the status quo" and away from change.[8] The safest conclusion is that a sortition chamber referendum is unlikely to win majority support, especially when less ambitious changes (such as legislative term limits, campaign funding and voting reform, or public consultation) could accomplish similar objectives with higher chances of success.

Voter skepticism will come not only from a status quo bias, but also from the difficulty of grasping the sortition concept. If a sortition chamber meets criteria for democratic justification, it does so via complex tools and concepts. To appreciate sortition's virtues, one must simultaneously appreciate stratified random sampling, equal opportunity for selection, open agendas, cognitive diversity, deliberative public input, and the possibility of democratic legitimacy without electoral accountability.[9]

It is an open question whether voters (or decision-makers for that matter) would accept the premises behind this battery of complex concepts when deciding whether to implement a sortition chamber. Certainly, the ideas underlying sortition have appeal in the current climate of political disillusionment and institutional dysfunction, but the concepts themselves—and the uses to which they are put—remain unfamiliar, even unsettling. A sortition chamber is not a question of implementing more minipublics with limited service-time or decision-making power; it would fundamentally alter the lawmaking process. In short, citizens may be unsure whether a sortition chamber merits their support and whether they would later recognize the chamber as a legitimate source of laws.[10]

Resistance from Decision-Makers

We have asserted that citizens and voters are unlikely to support a sortition chamber if less ambitious reforms are possible and the concepts underpinning sortition remain unfamiliar. These difficulties seem even more pronounced with decision-makers within public institutions. Implementing a sortition chamber would, referendum or no, require policy makers' assent, as altering legislative institutions would involve tremendous legislative and administrative detail. In most polities, the move to sortition would require a constitutional amendment approved by the legislature itself.[11] Faced with entrenched constitutions and uncertain public opinion, public officials are likely to resist sortition absent sufficient political will and self-interest, social learning, and attitudinal change.

A standard story of rules emerges from the literature on public administration: rules are stable because of institutional rigidity, procedural hurdles (such as qualified majorities), and decision-makers' strategic motivations. Hence, systemic change, such as electoral reform, seldom occurs. Reform attempts are quite common, particularly at subnational or local levels,[12] but major reform remains rare.[13]

Two reasons for the rarity of structural reform apply to the case of sortition. First, from a rational-choice perspective, decision-makers will support an electoral reform if they believe it serves their own interests.[14] If a reform cannot appeal directly to such self-interest, it may require external pressure, such as social movements, voter initiatives, or judicial intervention.[15] When popular support is the primary driver, decision-makers must sign on for reforms and may even co-opt them to further their self-interest. Indeed, major electoral reforms often take the form of "elite majority imposition" or "elite-mass interaction," wherein policy makers either retain control of the reform process (and pursue strictly strategic goals) or lose control of the reform process to the public (but retain an essential role in defining its final form).[16]

Sortition advocates will have difficulty convincing legislators that eliminating or limiting their role in the decision-making process is conducive to their interests. Even so, a sortition chamber might appeal to politicians' long-term interests, if conditions such as "systemic threat" or "idealism" exist.[17] Decision-makers may be motivated to avoid future electoral instability, reestablish their own legitimacy, make electoral changes better to meet democratic ideals, or unload no-win decisions onto another party. However, background stability, normal politics, and uncertainty over the fallout from sortition may leave legislators unmoved.[18]

Returning to our central thesis, less ambitious approaches may face lower obstacles, while eventually reaching similar goals. Pursuing more ambitious reforms, such as a sudden switch to a sortition chamber, could set back the underlying goal of making lawmaking more deliberative by provoking voter backlash or legislative stonewalling.

The second challenge for structural reform is cultural. Whether decision-makers support an electoral reform follows from social learning, attitudinal change, innovation diffusion, regional contagion, and electoral fashion. Whether decision-makers back reform partially depends on whether innovations are *culturally available* to them, such that policy makers converge on a specific reform "through voluntary emulation or borrowing from other political systems, through interaction, through external actors imposing innovation, and through the entrepreneurship of expert networks."[19]

When deciding whether to initiate or back a reform, such as sortition, public officials may look to the reforms that organizations, states, and policy actors are undertaking. Decision-makers are more likely to consider and adopt reforms being considered or implemented by other actors, but a sortition chamber does not yet figure among such deliberative innovations. Thus, it is unlikely that decision-makers will consider the sortition chamber a viable reform path. They cannot arrive at sortition either through borrowing from another political system or through developing the idea in interaction with other systems. Similarly, there are at present no significant actors, internal or external, imposing such changes on decision-makers, nor sufficiently prominent and cohesive sortition expert networks acting as middlemen between sortition reform entrepreneurs and public officials.[20] Until these circumstances change, a sortition chamber will meet resistance from decision-makers, who will remain doubtful of its appropriateness as a legislative and electoral alternative.[21]

Lack of Empirical Evidence on Sortition Chambers

A final problem underlies resistance from citizens and decision-makers alike: there exists too little empirical evidence on the degree to which sortition would succeed as a legislative innovation. Many authors in this volume make plausible arguments for how a sortition chamber might overcome institutional challenges and internal hazards, but we can also imagine it falling short on those counts. Until more evidence is available on the effects of a sortition chamber (or a body sufficiently like it, such as an ongoing, empowered, and embedded minipublic), we cannot rule out different outcomes in terms of intrabody

accountability, interbody accountability, citizen professionalization, and citizen visibility.

Intrabody accountability designates the possibility of a sortition chamber member's being held to account by the chamber,
whether through informal sanctions by members or formal
sanctions by the oversight committee. Although this possibility
may follow simply from the fact of face-to-face interaction and
could constrain discourse and deliberation in important ways, it
is unclear how well this would function as an accountability
mechanism. Whereas a member's being held to account for her
remarks and reasons depends on members' willingness to hold
her to account, her being held to account for individual votes
would hinge on her voting record being made public, which
Gastil and Wright preclude by use of secret ballot. In a word,
more evidence is needed on how participants in such bodies
behave toward one another before we consider intrabody
accountability secure.

Interbody accountability concerns a sortition chamber's being
held to account by its counterpart within the bicameral legislature envisioned by Gastil and Wright. Insofar as direct relations
exist between the elected and the sortition chambers (such as a
reconciliation process, joint hearings, and intralegislative checks
and balances), the electoral counterpart may formally or informally demand reasons for the sortition chamber's decisions. It
may exercise an important check on the chamber's legislative
output if its joint approval is required for a bill's passage.[22]

This might also allow for transitive authorization and
accountability through the democratically elected counterpart's
direct authorization from—and being held to account by—the
electorate. In this way, the public might exercise indirect control
over the sortition assembly. The sortition chamber will be tran-
sitively accountable, however, only if the democratically elected
chamber is itself accountable (that is, it gives accounts to the
public and is held to account by voters). For some elected bodies,
one may reasonably conclude that this is not the case, given
falling turnout (as in the European Parliament), high incum-
bency rates (as in the US Congress), and so forth. Thus, whether

the elected chamber would exercise such accountability remains an open question—and a difficult one to answer given the absence of modern cases available to study.

We also know too little about the capacity of a sortition body. A significant level of professionalization and institutional know-how would be required from a chamber's members if they are to work effectively alongside more experienced political actors. Such professionalization might well increase assembly members' influence and avoid partisan contagion, but it could, by the same token, transform sortition members into yet another set of out-of-touch professional politicians.[23]

In the European Parliament, for example, an EU-level sortition chamber would need to learn the ins and outs of a decision-making process largely opaque to most citizens, given a lack of EU civic education. EU sortition chamber members could well become or be perceived as part of the "Brussels bubble." To decide the question one way or another, it is vital that we obtain evidence by observing participant behavior in ongoing minipublics that are both empowered and institutionally embedded.

We also do not know the degree to which sortition chamber members' deliberation would benefit from social uptake—and thereby play a role in formation of public will. Such a chamber may be guaranteed visibility through its share of the decision-making power and institutional linkage with well-known decision-makers. The chamber's novelty also may lead to increased attention from traditional and new media.

On the other hand, visibility comes in degrees, and it is equally conceivable that members could enjoy either too much or too little attention. The former could expose lay citizens serving in the chamber to uncharitable treatment or confrontation with politicians or experts in the media, which may prove detrimental to members' performance. Conversely, the chamber may lack the strong personalities vital for generating social uptake, as members are selected without regard for the personality traits or rhetorical gifts privileged in elections. Likewise, opaque institutional arrangements may hide what the chamber, in fact, does. In both cases, the media might choose to focus on members themselves or the institution's novelty rather than on disseminating arguments, reasons, and conclusions from deliberation.[24]

Taking the example of the EU, one proposal to increase visibility of European Parliament members involves democratic contestation and politicizing the EU agenda.[25] Yet, directly, an EU-level sortition chamber might not increase contestation and politicization in its own body, nor is it obvious that it would indirectly help its counterpart (the elected parliament) to emphasize partisan lines and amplify interests.

Given all these uncertainties, it is more reasonable to advocate more gradual deliberative innovations, such as the institutionalization of consultative minipublics at the national or transnational level. Should these minipublics prove successful, there will likely emerge greater public and political will for further deliberative innovations, such as sortition chambers. If studied carefully, these interventions could also make clear the likely benefits and liabilities of a more ambitious move toward sortition.

Effective Consultation

In this section, we lay out the reasons why continuous embedded consultative minipublics further citizen deliberation and how they can avoid the problems plaguing earlier consultative experiments. We begin by examining reasons for preferring such minipublics before taking up the example of a project that we have recently submitted at the EU level to institutionalize consultative minipublics. We then advance a design proposal for combining existing consultation procedures with decentralized minipublics as effective tools for deliberation, legitimacy seeking, and capacity building when properly integrated in the deliberative system.[26]

Reasons for Preferring Consultative Minipublics

Our argument for continuous embedded consultative minipublics has two parts. First, we contend that consultative minipublics are preferable to empowered ones. Second, we argue that consultative minipublics consistently fail to achieve social uptake owing to poor or critical media coverage.

Minipublics can be granted decision-making or agenda-setting power. Regarding decision-making power, no minipublic has been given ultimate decision-making power, to date, as such bodies lack familiar forms of public accountability, in the sense of being held to account by the public on whose behalf they would decide. Some minipublics have experimented with intermediate forms of decision-making power, as with the citizens' assemblies on electoral reform in British Columbia and Ontario and those on constitutional reform in Ireland, Iceland, and Luxembourg.[27] The Canadian citizens' assemblies were granted the power to choose a new voting system that would then be put to public referendum. In part, this owed to organizers' recognition that the assembly group "did not have the requisite authority to speak exclusively for the people."[28] After the British Columbia referenda narrowly missed a 60 percent threshold in a special provincial election (and a majority of voters rejected the Ontario referendum), no similar experiments in intermediate decision-making power were attempted.

In the case of Iceland and Luxembourg, citizens were granted the power to elaborate proposals on preselected areas of constitutional reform, which would then be discussed and voted on by the parliament. In Iceland, constitutional reform was still more ambitious, as it granted citizens the power to draft a new constitution combining electoral and participative procedures, subject to advisory referendum and parliamentary approval. Whereas a majority of Iceland's citizens backed the 2012 referendum on the draft constitution, the decision on the bill for a new constitution was delegated to the following parliament and remains in limbo. The constitutional process in Luxembourg finds itself in a similar position after rejection of the 2015 referendum's three questions concerning specific constitutional reforms.[29]

In contrast, Ireland's government seems to have taken the Constitutional Convention seriously, as they answered the latter's initial reports in a timely fashion, and two referenda took place in spring 2015 on questions raised by the convention, of which one (marriage equality) passed. Of the examples cited here, it qualifies as the most successful experience at the level of policy output.[30]

Yet the lessons from these experiments show that intermediate decision-making power alone is no guarantee of efficacy, nor are organizers and policy makers ready to entrust a minipublic with ultimate authority. Moreover, in none of these cases did the minipublic have the power to set the agenda. Instead, they were free to decide within a predefined set of parameters. Even intermediate decision-making power is deemed too much to pair with agenda-setting authority.

In these same cases, social uptake was weak, partly due to poor or critical media coverage. In the British Columbia case, surveys found that the public felt uninformed on the subject.[31] British Columbians were unsure what the ballot question meant, and many were surprised that a referendum was taking place at all. Though the referendum was nearly successful, with 55 percent turnout, many voters relied on preconceived notions when marking their ballots. They lacked even a distilled version of the electoral system education that assembly members had received. Likewise, in the Ontario case, "the Assembly's recommendations were also not widely discussed nor well understood by the public at large."[32] The Iceland case saw similar uptake problems due to the complexity of the process and to failures in organizing the elections to vote for members of the citizens' constituent assembly.[33]

All in all, this analysis shows the difficulty of implementing, let alone *institutionalizing*, empowered minipublics, due to political resistance, public skepticism, limited social uptake, poor or critical media coverage, and organizational failures. The relative success of the Irish case suggests—in our historical phase of sortition ignorance—that minipublics can be effective only if they meet four conditions: include politicians in the process; give citizens intermediate decision-making power on a predefined agenda; leave the final decision to political representatives or sovereign citizens through referendum; and organize them regularly on a broader range of topics, other than as one-off attempts at constitutional or electoral reform.

This last condition would institutionalize (or embed) minipublics and help to overcome pitfalls that noninstitutionalized (or dissociated) versions invariably face, in particular social and political uptake.[34] Put differently, no amount of empowerment can overcome the lack of institutionalization. If these experiments remain sporadic affairs, we will be unable to build the trust in minipublics required to introduce successfully something as ambitious as a sortition chamber. In the next section, we take the EU as an example to show how institutionalizing citizens' minipublics is feasible and desirable even in such a complex multilingual setting.

EU Citizens' Consultation

The example in question is a project that we have recently submitted at the EU level to institutionalize consultative minipublics when the European Commission organizes public hearings on its initiatives. Over the past decade, the EU has organized several projects to expand citizens' participation in policy making, from voting to engaging with EU-level institutions and holding them to account.[35] These projects have taken different forms including deliberative consultation (European Citizens' Consultation), deliberative polling (Europolis), and petition systems (European Citizens' Initiative). They have taken place with different kinds of communication (virtual or face-to-face) at different geographical levels (national, cross-border, or pan-European).

A recent analysis of such experiments suggested that, although valuable from a civic perspective, they did not fulfill their democratic ambition of informing and empowering a significant number of lay citizens on complex EU issues.[36] Having reached similar conclusions at the national level, we recommended a new strategy in a recent presentation taken up by the European Economic and Social Committee. One can break this experimental deadlock without transforming EU institutional settings by introducing minipublics within the context of the European Commission's public consultation website, previously known as "Your Voice in Europe."[37] Originally designed to allow stakeholders to contribute to commission initiatives, it has since evolved to become a broadly used consultation tool for stakeholders and citizens.[38] This tool serves three purposes: allow the commission to make use of external expertise and thus create better policies; ensure that EU actions are coherent and transparent; and increase the EU's democratic legitimacy by giving citizens greater voice in the decision-making process.[39]

Unlike other EU deliberative experiments, this consultation comes with minimal standards aiming to ensure that consultation is clear, inclusive, transparent, and sufficiently long (at least twelve weeks). More importantly, it also requires that the commission provides feedback, which involves acknowledging receipt of contributions and publishing them; publishing and displaying consultation results; and giving adequate feedback on how results were taken into consideration in the policy-making process.[40]

Currently, the commission struggles to provide feedback to individual contributions within a reasonable time. A May 2017 report shows that the commission failed to give participants feedback in roughly one-third of public consultations processed in 2016.[41] This delay owes to the high number of consultations to process (around one hundred per year) and the chronic lack of human resources facing the EU.

Likewise, lay citizens are almost absent from the consultative process, which is dominated by civil-society organizations, public authorities, and research centers.[42] Significant citizen participation occurred in the form of either petitions or consultations conducted as online surveys in an essentially multiple-choice format.[43] In other words, significant citizen participation most often proved superficial and had little social uptake. Although the reasons for this are well known (that is, topic complexity, lack of interest in EU affairs, and the procedure's low visibility), we see a way to reverse this trend.

Combining EU Consultation with Decentralized Minipublics

We contend that the strong imbalance in favor of organized groups can be tackled by introducing decentralized minipublics (in the different member states) to deliberate on select commission initiatives. If correctly designed and implemented, this process would enable diverse voices to be heard (through sociodemographic and geographical representativeness) when new EU initiatives are elaborated. It would, therefore, contribute to meeting the three objectives of EU public consultations—namely, better policy, coherence and transparency, and democratic legitimacy.

As we will argue in the last section of this chapter, if such consultative practices are regularly repeated and adapted at the national level (such as for select parliamentary and governmental initiatives), it would familiarize citizens with minipublics as an efficient consultative method and with the features and concepts that minipublics share with a sortition chamber. Before returning to possible transitions toward a sortition chamber, we should first sketch how these minipublics should be organized for efficient inclusion in the EU decision-making process and for increased information and participation among lay citizens. Specifically, we lay out initial proposals concerning issue selection, citizen selection, minipublic setup, and consultation outcomes.

Regarding issue selection, since it would make little sense to foresee consultation on all possible topics, we suggest that consultation be organized on a selection of topics concerning major initiatives (such as initiatives involving high costs, new legislation, or a large number of citizens). Similar to participative procedures like the Oregon Citizens' Initiative Review, a mixed commission—comprising political officials from the relevant decision-making bodies, organizers, and a sample of citizens—would select the topics to be discussed by the national minipublics.[44] The example of the Irish Constitutional Convention—comprising one-third political representatives and two-thirds citizens—suggests that involving politicians in the consultative process may be necessary to guarantee success, while benefiting both lay participants and consultation outcomes.[45]

Concerning citizen selection and minipublic setup, we favor decentralized consultation involving a limited number of citizens, of which one good example is the European Citizens' Consultations.[46] In each territorial unit, minipublics of thirty to sixty participants would be selected on the basis of representative sociodemographic criteria. To rationalize organizational and budgetary costs, the national commission representation could host these minipublics in the EU. In other cases, one could appeal to decision-makers, foundations, or wealthy individuals for funding.

To prepare for deliberation, the minipublic would receive a briefing from the initiative's opponents and proponents, as well as neutral experts. Using these sources, their own values and third-party research, minipublic members would weigh the propositions' pros and cons by means of facilitation techniques enabling all viewpoints to be heard and points of consensus to be uncovered. Depending on the topic discussed, the session could run from one to several full days. Once deliberations concluded, participants would summarize the different viewpoints (pro and con), remaining questions, and recommendations for courses of action in a national synthesis report. This would be made public and submitted to the commission or legislature with the request to take an official, justified position.

Important efforts should be made throughout the process to make the consultation accessible and visible. This might include promoting public events and deepening collaboration with national institutions, civil-society organizations, schools, national public media, and social media. Following the example of the Oregon Citizens' Initiative Review, minipublic participants could be invited on traditional media to debate the topic and inform the public about this innovative consultation method. This would likely have a positive impact on a population that increasingly identifies with opinions expressed by other "ordinary" citizens over and against "professional politicians" or "bureaucrats."

If such consultations can be implemented at the European level—that is, characterized by the usage of different languages, high levels of complexity, and strong resilience to reform—it should be that much easier to implement them at the national levels both from a legal and practical perspective. Indeed, a similar initiative has already been experimented in the New South Wales Parliament in Australia.[47] In the last concluding section, we will argue that a broad, decentralized institutionalization of minipublics is a necessary (but not sufficient) condition to lay the social and psychological foundations for implementing a sortition chamber.

Toward a Sortition Chamber

In this section, we contend that the institutionalization of consultative minipublics is the logical, necessary next step before we can seriously consider introducing a sortition chamber. As an intermediary step to a sortition chamber, institutionalized consultative minipublics will prove useful in at least four ways: testing potential behavioral changes in randomly selected participants within a future sortition chamber; gaining citizens' trust and support; gaining decision-makers' trust and support; and reinforcing citizens' links to a future sortition chamber and their ability to hold the chamber to account indirectly.

Behavioral Changes

As we argued earlier, introducing a sortition chamber presents two opposed dangers, the severity of which are difficult to gauge without empirical evidence. On one hand, a sortition chamber risks becoming a chamber of professionalized citizens, therefore losing its genuine link with the public. On the other, a longer stay in power, combined with a lack of political experience, could increase the risk of interest group influence and partisan contagion. In both cases, sortition chamber members would be assimilated among other politicians, with no net increase in democratic legitimacy and trust. This threat must be seriously weighed before introducing a sortition chamber.

Institutionalizing consultative minipublics would allow us to test the extent to which time spent in such minipublics affects lay citizens' behavior and autonomy. For instance, it would be particularly relevant to compare, over a limited time frame (such as one year), a continuous minipublic participating in all consultations with newly selected citizens for each consultation. This experimental approach would offer important lessons not just on whether lay citizens' behavior and autonomy are affected by long-term participation, but also on how a sortition chamber should be designed to avoid these dangers.

Citizens' Support

As far as citizens are concerned, institutionalized consultative minipublics should increase their awareness of sortition's functioning and benefits. Supposing that such minipublics were implemented regularly and successfully, the sortition process would increasingly be perceived as a valid method. Public acceptance of the idea would increase to the extent that the minipublics demonstrated the process's transparency and accessibility, incorporated citizens' input, and decreased the net influence of organized political and economic interests.

To evaluate the public's readiness to support a sortition chamber, national and international surveys should start tracking key attitudes. Standard questions related to perception and trust in democracy should be augmented with items measuring knowledge of—and attitudes toward—institutionalized consultative minipublics and related concepts, such as sortition.

Decision-Makers' Support

If these minipublics are efficient and the public calls for increased sortition in political institutions, public officials may come to view a sortition chamber as a necessary, inevitable reform. As renewed populism shows, with increasing appeal of authoritarian regimes and distrust in "classical representative institutions," the survival of the democratic system conceived at the end of the eighteenth century is at risk.

The political class, which largely backs the institutional permanence of democratic values and practices, would have no option but to reform the existing system by including sortition-based political practices as one part of broader reforms. They might do this first through institutionalized consultative minipublics, then via a sortition chamber. From a self-interested perspective, their participation in the design of this reform would allow them to retain strong influence over the process and to ensure their survival, in one capacity or another.

Citizens' Links and Holding to Account

Finally, from an institutional perspective, we maintain that institutionalized consultative minipublics would inherently strengthen the raison d'être behind a sortition chamber by building lay citizens' feedback into the agenda and main legislative initiatives. Moreover, the presence of such minipublics could also heighten the sortition chamber's interbody accountability. If one and the same minipublic were maintained from a legislative proposal's beginnings until its implementation, it could act as an agent verifying whether the decision reached is correctly executed—and whether sortition chamber members deliberate free of influence or threats, political or economic. This would arguably be the most efficient protective procedure, as both owe their existence and legitimacy to sortition.

Conclusion

In sum, if institutionalized consultative minipublics were successfully implemented, it would not only lay the foundation for a sortition chamber but also serve to gather citizens' opinions and maintain government's indirect accountability to citizens. From an interinstitutional perspective, a sortition chamber might become the privileged link with lay citizens who are not involved in interest or partisan groups. Meanwhile, the elected chamber would continue representing organized interests and broader ideologies through political parties. Thus, interest groups would find two distinct entry points for their demands.

This incremental reform could create a new institutional equilibrium wherein citizens feel better represented (through institutionalized consultative minipublics and a sortition chamber) and organized groups continue playing an important role in gathering different interests (through the elected chamber). Though a striking solution in theory, we have yet to see whether it would hold up in practice. Only time will tell, for deliberative democracy as for all else.

14

Sortition, Rotation, and Mandate: Conditions for Political Equality and Deliberative Reasoning

David Owen and Graham Smith

The sortition chamber proposal laid out by John Gastil and Erik Olin Wright defends extending sortition into the legislative branch of government and specifies how such a body would work. We sympathize with the motivation for this enterprise: sortition ought to be more widely institutionalized within contemporary democratic polities. Nevertheless, reflection on the practice of antecedents of the sortition chamber—in particular its historical use in ancient Greece and more recent application in contemporary minipublics—raises questions about its feasibility and desirability. Our critical analysis considers primarily the democratic value of the proposal to replace one-half of a bicameral elected system with a sortition chamber. We also offer general considerations for situating a sortition chamber within a democratic ecology more favorable to its operation.

Our central concern is that selection to the legislature by sortition in the form proposed by Gastil and Wright will fail to realize sufficiently two fundamental democratic goods, namely political equality and deliberative reasoning. As the proposal is currently conceived, there is a failure to recognize that, in both historical and contemporary practice, sortition is combined with other institutional devices to achieve these goods. First, the use of sortition for selection of members has typically been paired with sortition in allocation of offices within the institution, along with regular rotation of membership and offices after short periods of service. Second, such institutions have had a limited mandate rather than broad agenda-setting powers. We contend that there are good reasons to believe that, without the application of regular rotation and a limited mandate, the sortition chamber is unlikely to be able to defend its members against asymmetries in social and economic power to the extent necessary for such a body to be democratically effective and realize the goods of political equality and deliberative reasoning. If cogent, this objection undermines the feasibility and desirability of the proposed sortition chamber, both as a democratic institution and as a means of advancing the longer-term cause of participatory or deliberative democracy.

We conclude with an alternative proposal, which envisions a responsive sortition legislature that makes more extensive use of internal sortition and rotation and recognizes the importance of establishing limited mandates. We also argue for a steep increase in the number of members. As a first step toward infusing sortition into the legislative branch, we argue that our alternative is both more realistic (from a democratic standpoint) and more utopian (from a strategic standpoint).

Sortition and Institutional Design: Historical and Contemporary Lessons

Prior to the rise of mass political parties in the late nineteenth and early twentieth centuries, sortition was recognized as a more democratic mechanism of selection of representatives than election. It was seen as being less susceptible to the influence of economic and social power than electoral processes and as enacting a stronger commitment to political equality. In this section, we offer a brief reconstruction of the circumstances of sortition in two contexts—Athenian democracy[1] and the contemporary practice of deliberative minipublics—to explain the democratic reputation of sortition and the conditions of its effective use.

Athenian Democracy

For Aristotle, democracy as a specific type of regime is defined by citizens ruling and being ruled in turn. Establishing this principle involved citizens being eligible for all nonspecialist offices and selected by lot to fill them, where offices had short terms. These mechanisms and offices enabled and constrained the sovereign assembly as the open participatory space within which each citizen could speak. As exemplified in Athens, following Cleisthenes's reforms in 507 BC, the *ekklesia* (assembly) was surrounded by an ecology of institutions that used random selection: the *boule* (the Council of Five Hundred), magistracies, the *dikasteria* (people's courts), and, following the reinstatement of democracy after the Peloponnesian War in the fourth century BC, the *nomothetai* (legislative boards). The council had a variety of functions that cut across our modern understanding of legislative, executive, and judicial functions, most notably preparing the work of the assembly, implementing many of its decisions, and overseeing public administration. The people's court played a critical political function by overseeing all the other organs of the political system. The legislative boards reviewed proposals from the assembly; only where there was a majority would a proposal become law or an existing law be repealed.

The introduction of selection by sortition is best understood as a response to the experience—and continuing threats—of tyranny, oligarchy, and civic strife posed by aristocratic pursuit of power. But it would be a mistake to focus on sortition alone, because its introduction was complemented by other institutional reforms.

First, Cleisthenes took the rural villages and city neighborhoods (both called *demes*) as the basic units of political organization. These were then rearranged into ten tribes, or *phylai*. This re-articulation of the tribes—and their use with respect to selection for the council (fifty from each tribe), people's court's and legislative boards, and for election to the office of *strategoi* (one from each tribe)—was designed to break up both existing aristocratic alliances and established patron/client relationships based on aristocratic kinship networks.

Second, rapid rotation of membership and rotation of offices within sortition bodies reduced the risks of concentrations of power. An annual lot chose the five hundred members of the council, with fifty citizens aged thirty or over from each of the ten *phylai*, where the number from each *deme* within each *phylai* was proportional to its population.

The use of sortition extended further into the operation of the council, with fifty *bouletai* selected at a time to take on its main tasks for one-tenth of the year, with one randomly selected each day to act as chair. No one could serve more than twice on the council, which ensured widespread citizen participation in this key institution. Roughly one-third of all citizens are estimated to have served as a council member.

There was also widespread participation in the courts. For this purpose, six thousand citizens were selected by lot annually. Though there were occasional plenary sessions, most of the work of the popular courts took place in smaller courts, which varied in size from 501 for lesser cases up to 1,501 for the most serious. Not only were the jurors selected by lot from those willing to serve, but those selected were divided by lot into the number of groups required for each operating courtroom. Finally, each group was assigned by lot to a particular courtroom with checks to make sure that only assigned jurors entered the designated court. Courts sat for one day only.

When the legislative boards were introduced, they operated in a similar fashion—also drawing from the pool of six thousand.

Neither the courts nor the boards were deliberative in the modern sense. Members heard arguments from both sides, but they did not deliberate with each other before making a decision.

This widespread use of sortition in ancient Athens was designed to block threats to the democratic principles of *isonomia* (equality before the law) and *isegoria* (equality in the right to speak or participate). Sortition enacted and protected political equality in a society characterized by high levels of social and economic inequality. Cleisthenes's use of territorial units fractured existing clientelist relationships and the use of territorial representation (in both electoral and sortition contexts) into entrenched relationships based on *deme* and *phylai* against aristocratic kinship-based networks. The use of sortition in all roles not requiring specialist knowledge acted as a bulwark against concentrations of power and the effectiveness of bribery, especially in court judgments.

Two further features are salient for our purposes. First, the length of service was limited to a maximum of one year before rotation of membership. In many cases, active service was considerably less (for example, as little as one day in each court and board). Second, the institutions that used sortition were primarily *responsive* rather than *initiating* institutions. Put a little too simply, the *ekklesia* set the agenda and the *boule*, the magistracies, and the *dikasteria* (and later the *nomothetai*) exercised enabling, scrutiny, accountability, and implementation functions.

What can we draw from Athenian practice to inform the design of a sortition legislature? First, there is no direct historical equivalent to such a body. The people's courts or the later legislative boards bear the closest family resemblance, but these are a long way from the type of sortition chamber Gastil and Wright propose because of the Athenian bodies' more limited functions, larger size, rapid rotation, and nondeliberative character. Second, although the application of sortition can be a bulwark against the power of economic and social factions and realize particular forms of political equality, in Athenian institutions this was achieved by combining sortition with rapid rotation.

Deliberative Minipublics

Sortition has been used extensively in legal juries in countries such as the United States, the United Kingdom, and France, but rarely has it been considered for selection in modern political institutions. Recent years, though, have witnessed increasing interest in sortition within deliberative minipublics. Such bodies are typically sponsored by a political authority, but organized by an independent agency that facilitates group discussions among a (near) random sample of citizens, who take evidence from experts and interested parties.[2]

The recent wave of minipublics traces back to the pioneering work of Peter Dienel in Germany and Ned Crosby in the US who, respectively, created and organized planning cells and citizens' juries.[3] The intervening decades have seen the emergence of other designs that incorporate forms of sortition, including deliberative polls, consensus conferences, citizens' assemblies, reference panels, and G1000s. Notable experiments include the incorporation of elected politicians as members in the Irish Constitutional Convention and broader sets of social and political actors in G1000s in the Netherlands alongside randomly selected citizens. Very few minipublics, with the exception of cases such as the Citizens' Initiative Review, are an institutionalized element of political systems. Most are sponsored in an ad-hoc fashion, and the adoption of their recommendations is far from systematic.

There are differences in the ways that these institutions apply sortition. Most use stratification techniques to ensure a demographically representative cross section of particular social characteristics (such as gender, ethnicity, and age). To a certain extent, this resonates with selection from the *demes* in ancient Athens. Larger minipublics, such as deliberative polls, rely on simple random selection. Again, there are differences in the length of time that such bodies sit. G1000s are one-day events; most of the others run from two to four days. The outlier here are citizens' assemblies, which have run over a number of weekends. For example, the British Columbia Citizens' Assembly brought together 160 citizens and ran over a dozen weekends during a period of eleven months.

Why is sortition used in these institutions? First, organizers value sortition as a selection mechanism for its capacity to realize a particular form of political equality (that is, equal probability of being invited). Whether or not claims of descriptive representation can be sustained (given the impact of self-selection or stratification), sortition generates a more diverse sample of participants than established engagement mechanisms, which tend to replicate differential participation rates and thus differentials of power across social groups. Second, the combination of sortition with facilitation and balanced information creates the conditions for deliberative reasoning and considered judgment.

For advocates such as James Fishkin, minipublics are important because they combine random selection with deliberation to generate a counterfactual will formation—"what the public would think, had it a better opportunity to consider the question at issue."[4] In our view, more important is the connection with Athenian practice: Minipublics represent a safe haven[5] in which citizens are politically equal and protected from economic and social power. Unlike their Athenian forebears, however, minipublics are sites of collective deliberation and not just public judgment.

How can the practice of deliberative minipublics inform the design of the proposed sortition chamber? There has been an explosion of social scientific research, much of which provides evidence for the promise of minipublics: citizens who participate appear willing and able to reach sound judgments and recommendations on highly complex technical issues;[6] in turn, minipublics are viewed as trusted institutions by the wider public.[7]

Selection through sortition helps enable a deliberative politics by ensuring that a diversity of social perspectives is brought to bear, but it is only one among many design characteristics, not all of which transfer so easily to a permanent legislative body. Minipublics rely extensively on trained facilitation to ensure that interactions between the diverse participants, with very different capacities and experience, are free and fair. How suitable is such interventionist facilitation for a legislative body? Also, deliberative minipublics generally have been one-off affairs, which ensure a de facto rotation of membership between minipublics (as well as changes in sponsors, organizers, and facilitators). The longest period of participation has been around a dozen weekends for citizens' assemblies held in Canada, the Netherlands, and Ireland. The Irish Assembly (and its mixed Constitutional Convention cousin) is a rare example where a single minipublic has dealt with more than one issue. Finally, previous minipublics have been carefully crafted spaces in which citizens are protected from partisan interests. In this sense, there is a shared trajectory with the historical precedent of Athens. Interest groups, political parties, and the media are kept at arm's length. In sum, the one-off nature of minipublics, the variety of different sponsors, and the independence of organizers and facilitators all help to protect these spaces.

Ironically, protection from outside pressures and interference may also derive significantly from the fact that, to date, minipublics have been relatively marginal political institutions. Were minipublics to be used more extensively and to have more significant political import, this would almost certainly generate "powerful incentives for interest groups and partisan elites to try to manipulate [these] deliberative forums."[8] Here, we can draw parallels between minipublics and legal juries. The history of legal juries, as expressed in the evolution of laws against jury tampering and of options such as sequestration, points to the risks posed by external manipulation. Such devices may be used rarely today precisely because their availability serves as a general deterrent against external manipulations, while their presence serves to register both the gravity of the threat when such manipulation does occur and the seriousness with which it is regarded. The sortition chamber proposal in its current form does not avail itself of these kinds of protections.

Though the functioning of deliberative minipublics offers some grounds for optimism for the practice of a sortition legislature, differences in structural function and design make them a poor analogy for the proposed sortition chamber. Gastil and Wright's proposal requires much more significant time contributions from participants, requires engagement across a range of issues, and has significant political power—factors that enable and motivate the exercise of systematic pressure by interested external agents.

Evaluating the Sortition Legislature Proposal

Our exploration of the circumstances of sortition in both historical Athens and its contemporary application in deliberative minipublics suggests that the sortition chamber has qualitatively different characteristics from previous sortition institutions. First, there is no precedent for a political institution exercising significant public power that uses sortition as a selection mechanism but does not combine this with regular rotation and, where relevant, the use of sortition in the distribution of offices within the institution. Second, there appears to be no precedent for a sortition body that has such an expansive mandate ranging from agenda setting to scrutiny. Specifically, we cannot find any examples of the effective use of sortition bodies to undertake agenda-setting functions.

These historical and contemporary examples provide support for our contention that the proposed sortition chamber is wanting from a democratic perspective. The failure of the chamber either to combine sortition with rotation or to limit its mandate leaves the membership exposed to negative expressions of social and economic power.[9] We explore each of these design weaknesses in turn. Without incorporating these institutional devices, we claim, it is unrealistic to expect the chamber to be a body in which equals engage in a process of public reasoning orientated toward shared practical judgments.

The Case for Rotation

The use of sortition to select members to the proposed sortition chamber exemplifies a *formal* commitment to enacting political equality in the way that it brings a diversity of citizens into the center of formal and official political power. In so doing, it has the potential to alter citizens' self-understanding of the meaning of citizenship, being a vivid example of Aristotle's conception of democratic citizenship as ruling and being ruled in turn. Given the relatively small number of members, even if such chambers were implemented at other levels of governance, the chance of any particular citizen being selected for any such body during their lifetime remains slim. Nevertheless, one should not under-estimate how transformative the political effects of such a change could be with citizens seeing their peers in decision-making positions.

However, the realization of political equality is potentially only formal rather than substantive. This is because the proposal's sole focus on sortition in terms of selection unhelpfully abstracts from its historical pairing with other mechanisms and processes, such as regular rotation of membership and the use of sortition and rotation for offices *within* the sortition body. The application of these mechanisms is absent, leaving the functioning of the assembly, in particular its capacity to promote delib-erative rather than strategic action, vulnerable to those who would aim to subvert it for their own ends.

Two aspects of the proposal are particularly concerning for how power is exercised in the legislative body: the length of service and the distribution of offices within the assembly. Two options are envisaged for terms of office: either a five-year term or a two-year term with an option for renewal. In both instances, membership would rotate, with a portion of the body being refreshed each year.[10] Once selected, members would be allo-cated committee membership based on length of service and their preferences: "Current committee members who remain in the assembly could retain their most preferred committee assign-ments, then enter into a lottery with the rest of the selectees, each of whom would have ranked their preferences like students signing up for courses."[11]

To our knowledge, such long terms of continual service and the freedom of members to choose areas of work according to preference and length of service are unprecedented for a sortition body. In ancient Athens, where the council, courts, and boards selected members randomly by lot, there was relatively rapid rotation of tasks and offices. In the council, which had the longest term of service of one year, members held the most significant posts for only one-tenth of the year before rotation, and in the courts and boards citizens were randomly selected and rotated between cases.

The longest time commitment in a single contemporary minipublic has been the twelve weekends of the British Columbia Citizens' Assembly, which met over ten months. The Irish Citizens' Assembly met over a longer period of time (sixteen months) but demanded one fewer weekend of service from participants. In some deliberative minipublics, there are times when participants break into self-selected working groups. Even then, those subgroups are designed to avoid concentrating power in the hands of a small cadre of members, and facilitators ensure free and fair deliberation between participants.

This combination of length of service and choice of work areas based on that service has potentially serious negative effects on the capacity of the sortition chamber to realize political equality and deliberative reasoning in its day-to-day workings. We can see this in two ways. Internally, concentration of power—and with it the capacity to strongly influence proceedings of the assembly—is likely to rest with a small number of members who hold significant committee offices. There is brief mention in the sortition chamber proposal of possible experimentation with trained facilitators (or, more worryingly, current or former sortition legislators who would not necessarily have the relevant capacities), but it is not clear how this would be combined with the work of self-selected committees over long periods. If trained facilitators are not present or their role is reduced substantially compared to deliberative minipublics, then the domination by more powerful and socially privileged members is likely to appear and, with it, group dynamics that are antithetical to democratic functioning. In the current formulation of the sortition chamber, the relationship between facilitation and emergent modes of leadership is underspecified, although it is difficult to conceive how the style of facilitation common in minipublics could map onto this type of sortition body. It is then a reasonable concern that substantive equality and deliberative reasoning between members will be diminished.

Second, the relatively small number of members and their relatively long period of service expose the institution to the dangers of subversion by powerful interests beyond the chamber, including targeting by media outlets, yet members have relatively little protection unless significant changes are made to the wider institutional ecology. This is likely to be exacerbated where particular individuals within the sortition legislature are able to concentrate power by holding on to positions on committees (including the position of chair). These individuals will inevitably become particular targets for external groups looking to influence the deliberation and decisions of those committees, not least since they are also likely to become power brokers within the assembly.

Sortition is intended to guard against the negative impact of expressions of economic power and social influence, but once members of the sortition chamber are selected, they are vulnerable to traditional lobbying activities that transmit the inequalities of civil society to the formal political domain. They are left exposed in the same way as elected legislators—but without the defenses that membership of a political party can offer. Being a representative who is part of an organized political party reduces the scope of individual discretion over agenda setting, party discipline reduces discretion over voting, and party competition provides incentives for monitoring the conduct of legislators. While parties may undermine the deliberative potential of legislatures, as collective organizations they can, at their best, exercise power over their legislative representatives in ways that counter incentives for external targeting of individual representatives and their susceptibility to such targeting, while the accountability of party leaders to the wider membership acts as an obstacle to successful external targeting of the leadership.

A sortition chamber embedded within a bicameral system, as envisioned by Gastil and Wright, will also be subject to pressures from the elected chamber, especially when there is disagreement between them. We are familiar with bicameral legislatures competing with—and employing strategies of delegitimation toward—one another. It would be naive not to expect politically experienced politicians from the elected chamber to employ such strategies to embolden their standing and influence vis-à-vis the sortition chamber. It is not at all clear what resources the sortition chamber will be able or willing to bring to bear to withstand such strategic action.[12]

The small number of members, length of term, and specialization of roles also invite more insidious forms of influence—namely, corruption and bribery. Some of the practices that Gastil and Wright suggest as defenses against this, such as periods of private discussion and the use of secret ballots,[13] can have the opposite effect by reducing mutual accountability within the assembly and the already limited degree of public accountability generated by public voting.

It is plausible that these vulnerabilities may be reduced if legislators in both chambers, as well as individuals and organizations seeking to influence them, are subject to disciplinary scrutiny by a body such as the people's court on the Athenian model. No doubt, other changes—such as strengthening laws governing lobbying—could also act to reduce these vulnerabilities.

These problems are liable to be worsened by factions, alliances, and party organization within the body. Gastil and Wright stress that "a place for traditional caucusing should remain," or "members could organize themselves into a larger number of more cohesive groups of like-minded legislators, who share common values and priorities."[14] Either of these—and especially their combination—threatens to move the legislature away from the deliberative ideal of autonomous agents swayed by the force of the better argument and toward a more structured partisan-ship that works across issue areas.

Historical precedent, particularly from Athens, suggests that the combination of larger numbers and sortition in both initial selection and the allocation of offices, alongside rapid rotation, offer a possible solution to the challenges that we have posed, while the experience of contemporary minipublics suggests that the combination of sortition with trained facilitation is critical for deliberative quality. However, addressing these problems through the complementary mechanisms that we propose constructs a deeper problem for the proposed sortition chamber. The factors that potentially undermine political equality and deliberative reasoning within the legislature and expose members to powerful economic and social interests (its small size, long service, and specialization) are arguably necessary conditions for a key aspect of the sortition chamber proposal—its agen-da-setting function.

The Case for Limited Mandate

As far as we are aware, there is no historical or contemporary precedent for a single body, selected by sortition, that combines agenda setting and scrutiny in a deliberative fashion in the way that the sortition chamber intends. In Athenian democracy, a number of sortition bodies with very different and distinct polit-ical functions were employed around the central assembly. We can draw similar lessons from another contemporary field of participatory practice where the designers of participatory budgeting in Porto Alegre crafted different institutions for different aspects of agenda setting, rulemaking, and deci-sion-making. They recognized that combining functions in the same body is likely to have perverse democratic results.[15] Later participatory budgeting systems have been less effective in real-izing political equality, deliberative reasoning, and popular control precisely because of their failure to separate these functions.[16]

Gastil and Wright are enthusiastic about the capacity of

deliberative minipublics in making their argument for a sortition chamber. "Randomly selected bodies have shown an inclination," they argue, "to find common ground and recommend workable solutions to the policy problems placed on their agendas."[17] The final part of that sentence is indicative of the challenge the sortition chamber faces: deliberative minipublics work on problems *placed* on the agenda by others. They do not select, or even usually *frame*, these problems. Ensuring a safe space within which common ground and workable solutions emerge may be undermined if minipublics were to be a site for competition over agenda setting. We have the same concern for the sortition chamber—that agenda setting and scrutiny may pull the institution in different directions. The former function may well be detrimental to its democratic capacity.

Agenda setting can be broken down into at least three separate functions: collation of ideas, filtering of ideas, and management of the agenda once it has been agreed. Within traditional elected legislatures, these functions are undertaken (or at least overseen) principally by political parties. It is not at all clear how these functions would be realized in the proposed sortition chamber. As for collation of ideas, sortition legislators will not have knowledge of the full range of ideas. Though a demographically diverse group is epistemically important for collective judgment, it does not equate to full knowledge of the range and dimensions of issues facing the legislature. Therefore, there will need to be processes through which members are exposed to different possibilities.

How is this to be done? We can see a range of options, all potentially undesirable from a democratic perspective. One option draws on the practice of deliberative minipublics, where facilitation and provision of balanced information and witnesses are overseen by an independent body supported by a stakeholder advisory group. In their proposal, Gastil and Wright focus only on the provision of independent facilitation: helping "citizens work through their agenda, manage speaking time, and ensure respectful discourse."[18] How balanced information is to be provided to the sortition legislature is not clear, especially in relation to problem definition and agenda setting. Gastil and Wright are too relaxed, we fear, in their evaluation of the dangers of technocratic capture. The autonomy of members is in real danger of being compromised as more responsibilities are passed to independent or administrative agencies.

A second option is that certain members of the legislature—those who have served more years, are committee chairs, or who enter with the requisite political skills—would take on leadership roles and drive the agenda-setting process. But this immediately jeopardizes political equality and undermines deliberative equality as some members are privileged over others, while exacerbating incentives for external influence on key figures and roles within the assembly.

A third option implicit in the sortition chamber proposal relies on party caucuses or some other forms of faction to collate and filter ideas and manage the agenda-setting process. As we have already argued, this reduces political equality and replicates the very practices of elected legislatures that sortition is meant to ameliorate. The relative autonomy of the sortition legislature is lost, as is the deliberative difference that sortition bodies bring as countervailing powers. Without parties or organized factions, however, the different aspects of agenda setting will be vulnerable targets of lobbying and other more nefarious activities by organized interests.

Returning to the examples of the Athenian system and participatory budgeting, the deliberative qualities of the sortition chamber are under threat if it is takes on agenda setting and scrutiny functions. Deliberating over agendas is a very different activity from deliberating over options for a particular policy or legislative decision. Thus, for example, in agenda setting there is always the danger that members' favored ideas or issues are not taken forward or given low priority. This, in turn, generates incentives to engage in coalition building and tactical alliances (that is, mimicry of party formations) or else to confront a situation in which (except by luck) one loses out—at which stage the motivation to participate in the scrutiny of options on an issue one does not see as a priority is likely to be much reduced.

We recognize the need within contemporary democratic societies for what we might term *counterhegemonic agenda setting*. Elites get their issues placed on the agenda too easily and too often; this is, after all, one source of their power. But we are not convinced that the sortition chamber can realize this counterhegemonic potential. It will be subject to pressures from powerful organized interests that it will be unable to manage democratically. Those who wish to retain an agenda-setting role for a sortition legislature must provide a stronger account of how this role is to be facilitated and how leadership is to be enacted to drive agendas in a way that does not undermine political equality or deliberative quality.

Consequently, we hold that there are good reasons to remove agenda setting from the sortition chamber, making it a more responsive body that engages primarily in scrutiny. It may be possible to conceive of a separate sortition agenda-setting assembly—perhaps one that is embedded in a wider order of sortition bodies that generate ideas for collation and ranking, although there is little successful historical or contemporary practice to draw on, and our considerations of how it might function leave us with good reasons as to why it may be difficult to achieve. Certainly, it would be prudent to experiment with such a structure in lower-risk environments to discern the relevant design issues that it would confront before inserting such a body at the apex of the formal democratic system.

Conclusion: A Realistic and Utopian Alternative

Historical and contemporary precedents suggest that for an assembly to inhibit the unjustified exercise of power by economic and social groups, selection by sortition is not enough. To counter such activities and realize political equality and deliberative reasoning, one must combine sortition in selection with rapid rotation of membership and the use of sortition and rotation for office within the assembly. Even with those features in place, a single sortition body cannot fulfill agenda-setting and scrutiny functions simultaneously.

As it stands, the proposed sortition chamber is neither realistic nor utopian. It is too ambitious for the former, not ambitious enough for the latter. A more realistic approach to democratic design separates the functions of agenda setting and scrutiny. A more utopian outcome, in which the sortition chamber plays an agenda-setting role, requires a wholesale restructuring of the broader institutional ecology, which in the current formulation remains relatively untouched.

For those interested in the use of sortition in contemporary politics, there is a strong tendency to focus attention on legislative bodies. Such bodies are clearly important sites for democratic reform, but we need to consider the wider political canvas and reflect on the variety of roles that sortition can play to enhance the system's democratic qualities.

To stay within the scope of this book, however, we conclude by suggesting an alternative design for a sortition legislature. In doing so, we draw most directly on the practice of the people's courts and legislative boards in ancient Athens and more recent experience of deliberative minipublics. Our proposed sortition process would play a responsive role, draw on a much wider pool of members, and use sortition and more rapid rotation to assign members to work on particular legislative issues as they emerge.

By focusing on a responsive function for the assembly, we are not arguing that it is an elected chamber that must set the agenda, just that the agenda would be set outside the sortition legislature. In the first instance, it is likely that the body would be responsive to the agenda of the elected chamber and would thus play a role in overseeing and scrutinizing legislative and policy proposals from that chamber. There are other more or less participatory ways that the agenda might be set (for example, through an initiative process), but that is not our primary concern here. Neither will we be concerned with how a separate sortition body might play an agenda-setting role within the legislative system, though our earlier analysis augurs against such a body.

Second, we envision a much wider pool of members of the sortition assembly. The six thousand citizens from which the people's courts and legislative boards were selected in Athens may be a good starting point, although the number could be higher. Our preference is that service is compulsory, with exemptions for pressing personal or professional needs, as for the summons to jury service. As in the sortition chamber proposal, legislators would be compensated generously in recognition of the significance of their role. If compulsory service were deemed unacceptable, then the selection of the six thousand would be demographically stratified.

The full membership of six thousand citizens would meet as a body only for training purposes—to be educated about their legislative role. Following Athenian practice, a smaller pool of members would be summoned randomly from this larger body (applying stratification) to be divided by lot for smaller issue-based assemblies of between, say, 150 and 300 according to the number of tasks. And then finally, the members would be assigned by lot to the particular issue. A formula would be needed to ascertain how long each separate assembly would need to meet, but the longest citizens' assemblies that have worked on complex constitutional issues have required no more than twenty-five-day sessions. Those who serve in any given session would be ineligible for the next one. The six thousand body would itself be rotated on a regular basis, every one to two years.[19]

Unlike the Athenian courts and boards, the smaller issue-based assemblies would be deliberative in character and last longer than one day. To this end, they would work in similar ways to existing deliberative minipublics. A central administrative organization would need to be established, with independence from government. This would be a specialist body whose role would be to select trained facilitators by lot from a general pool for each session and to select an advisory board. The board, in turn, would oversee the development of balanced learning materials and the appointment of expert witnesses, who reflect the range of viewpoints and interests on the issue before an assembly.

In designing such an administrative body, we can draw on the experience of the autonomous public bodies charged with organizing public participation such as the Tuscany Regional Participation Authority (Italy), the National Commission for Public Debate (France), and the Quebec Environmental Public Hearings Board (Canada).[20] A danger of capture by technocratic or social and economic interests would remain, but that risk would be diluted by the random allocation of sortition legislators—and facilitators—to particular sessions.

As to the powers of the sortition legislature, there are a number of options. Let us assume initially that the sortition body is scrutinizing proposed legislation from the elected legislature. The weakest option would be delay—a mechanism for sending a piece of legislation back to the elected chamber for further consideration if it was not supported by a majority of the sortition legislature. This would leave the balance of power very much with the elected body.

An alternative would require a particular level of support from the sortition legislature for a bill to become law. It is possible to imagine a range of stipulations for how decision-making might progress. A simple majority might be all that is needed for passage of legislation, or a supermajority might be required. For example, 60 percent support in the sortition body might be required for legislation to pass, whereas below 40 percent would kill a bill. Anything in between would send the legislation back to the elected body for reconsideration.

An ingenious alternative that would bring the wider public into the process might follow the practice at Leeds University students' union in the UK, where passage requires 75 percent support from within a minipublic, less than 25 percent means failure, but any result in between triggers a binding referendum. Moreover, the sortition legislature could link to a popular petition process that bypassed the elected chamber to give the broader citizenry the authority to propose new laws or suggest repeals.[21] Petitions meeting a signature threshold would come before the sortition legislature, which would treat them in the same way as a proposal from the elected chamber. In these ways, the sortition legislature would play the role of reviewing, repealing, and inspecting laws not too dissimilar from the functions played by Athenian legislative boards.

We believe our formulation would be protective and transformative. It is protective because the large number of members of the body and the random allocation to issue-based assemblies—combined with the limited duration of each session—make it considerably more difficult for powerful economic and social forces to affect its practice. The Athenian concern to obstruct the bribery of juries by the wealthy provides a good analogy for the concerns of contemporary democracies with lobbying (and related activities), and we think their approach to dealing with the problem merits serious attention. Like its Athenian forebear, our model also has greater transformative power, by increasing substantially the likelihood of citizens being called to serve. This transformative power would be further amplified if the proposal was adopted for the numerous subnational legislatures within a polity.

In closing, we believe our proposal is transformative in another sense. Counterintuitively perhaps, it is utopian in its strategic ambition of being simply a *first step* toward more radical change in the democratic ecology. Our more prudent approach, grounded in historical and contemporary democratic experience, lessens the risk of damage to the reputation of sortition and citizen participation in the legislative process. As a result, we hope this would provide a stronger basis on which to develop the civic consciousness and political practices necessary for more radical future reshaping of democratic institutions through sortition.

15

Who Needs Elections? Accountability, Equality, and Legitimacy Under Sortition

Brett Hennig

Gastil and Wright envision a sortition chamber within a bicameral system, and in this chapter, I challenge their proposed retention of an elected chamber. I contend that in a democracy, elections are neither a fundamental nor an effective way to achieve accountability and political equality, and hence legitimacy.

This view strikes most people as absurd, or at least counter to the received wisdom that elections are the cornerstone of—or synonymous with—democracy. From a historical perspective, this response is unfounded. Since the so-called birth of democracy in ancient Athens until the publication of Alexis de Tocqueville's influential *Democracy in America* (1835–40), elections were synonymous with aristocracy, meritocracy, or—at best—"republican" government, whereas "pure democracy" entailed more direct methods of self-government, including rotation and sortition (that is, using random selection to fill public offices).[1]

Historical meanings aside, choosing representatives by way of elections leaves much to be desired, when compared to the sortition alternative. Below it is argued that democratic accountability under sortition would be as (or even more) robust as it is with elections. It is then argued that the superior political equality and deliberative quality of a sortition legislature would help it secure greater public legitimacy. In the final section, I argue that a unicameral sortition assembly would better secure democratic values than would Gastil and Wright's proposed bicameral legislature as the latter retains of an elected chamber.[2]

Accountability

Perhaps the most obvious justification for elections is their purported ability to hold rulers to account. In this view, the prospective fear of sanction—or the retrospective act of being sanctioned—results in politicians that are responsive to the electorate. Before addressing this "folk theory of democracy," however, it is instructive to take a step back to consider the general concept of political accountability.[3]

Avoiding Horizontal and Vertical Hazards

Political theorist John Dunn holds that accountability is, at heart, an attempt to ensure that rulers (and ruling groups or factions) do not abuse their position of power. Dunn recognizes two principal, potentially avoidable hazards of living in societies: *vertical* hazards from rulers and *horizontal* hazards from other members and groups in society.[4] Both of these hazards are real—and all too familiar.

The first two ways societies have attempted to limit these hazards, according to Dunn, is by instituting legal and constitutional constraints on governments. The programs of ancient and modern liberty (such as legal equality; civil liberties; and freedom from torture, arbitrary violence, and imprisonment, as encapsulated by constitutions and the "rights of man [sic]") are realizations of this ideal. In theory, the state retains a monopoly on legitimate violence, tightly constrained by rights, obligations, constitutions, and laws. These constraints are independent of the system of rule. Proponents of classical liberalism were concerned with ensuring rights in monarchies and aristocratic regimes; few foresaw the coming democratic struggles of the nineteenth and twentieth centuries.

Even if rulers face legal constraints, however, the risk remains that governments will translate their society's horizontal hazards directly into vertical hazards as antagonistic social groups compete for control of these institutions. The winning group, or coalition of groups, can then use the resources of the state to oppress or exploit other groups, or to simply strengthen their own social and financial position through preferential treatment and laws.

Political accountability attempts to address this breach. Dunn posits that the risk of horizontal hazards being transformed into vertical hazards can be minimized by "holding the key agents and implementers of public choice effectively responsible for the manner in which they make and implement these choices ... The locus of democratic accountability is this second approach to limiting the inherent hazards of political subjection."[5]

It is here that elections are used as the crutch on which political theorists prop up theories of accountability in representative democracy. Dunn acknowledges that the idea "has had a very good run for its money in modern political thinking" but "is an astonishingly optimistic way of envisaging political relations."[6] Electoral accountability fails due to the informational asymmetry between ruled and rulers and the impossibility of assigning a clear causal link between intention and consequence in any complex societal system.[7] To meaningfully sanction politicians would require a clear thread, involving "highly determinate conceptions of action," joining political intention, action, and outcome. Such a thread cannot, under usual circumstances, and by ordinary uninformed, uninterested citizens, be untangled—if it exists at all.[8]

What Motivates Voting Behavior

Dunn's more theoretical objections are confirmed by a wealth of research highlighted in a new critique of American elections by political scientists Christopher Achen and Larry Bartels. In *Democracy for Realists: Why Elections Do Not Produce Responsive Government*, they show that people often draw fictitious links between political cause and effect when assigning political responsibility. Even when voters make choices based on real shifts in their own financial positions, they do so myopically—forgetting anything other than the most recent changes.[9] If this amounts to "the consent of the governed," it is an ill-informed, shortsighted consent at best. As Achen and Bartels put it, retrospective sanctioning "simply will not bear the normative weight that its proponents want to place on it."[10]

Achen and Bartels are equally skeptical of the myth that politicians outline a program of ideas and an informed, attentive electorate votes for the set of ideas they most admire, and punishes those who fail to deliver on their promises.[11] Here again, the evidence reviewed by Achen and Bartels does not support this view. The crux of their argument is that "group and partisan loyalties, not policy preferences or ideologies, are fundamental in democratic politics."[12]

Who Gets Represented

Notwithstanding the above, politicians do react to events and attempt to win elections by convincing voters that they are responsive—at least when they are not out wooing financial backers for their next campaign.[13] Bartels's earlier book, *Unequal Democracy*, along with Martin Gilens's *Affluence and Influence*, shows that elected representatives in the US respond overwhelmingly to one particular social group—the affluent.[14] Bartels demonstrates that elites listen predominately to their own, with US senators being "vastly more responsive to affluent constituents than to constituents of modest means ... [while] the views of constituents in the bottom third of the income distribution received no weight at all in the voting decisions of their senators."[15]

Gilens finds a similar correlation between expressed preferences and policy outcomes, which "suggest that the political system is tilted very strongly in favor of those at the top of the income distribution." Analyzing mountains of national survey data and federal policy choices, Gilens concludes that "when preferences between the well-off and the poor diverge, government policy bears absolutely no relationship to the degree of support or opposition among the poor."[16]

One benign explanation for this pattern could be that middle- and upper-income preferences are similar. Thus, disregard for the poor could indicate a responsive majoritarian democracy, albeit a clear case of horizontal hazards being translated into vertical ones. Closer inspection of the data, however, disproved this hypothesis.[17] Low- and middle-income citizens *do* get what they want sometimes: in those instances when their preferences align with the rich. This fact (that middle-income citizens sometimes get what they want) is what contributes to the illusion of direct responsiveness.[18]

Political Agency and Accountability
Beyond the Electoral System

However bleak this picture may seem, democratic governments are not free to do as they please. In *The Life and Death of Democracy*, political theorist John Keane locates the nexus of accountability in the myriad institutions of civil society, the media, the judiciary, and other institutions that can keep power in check—all part of a "monitory" democratic system.[19] The few minutes it takes to cross or number a ballot cannot be the primary mode of holding rulers accountable for their actions. A second-term US president, who will never face the electorate again, is still held accountable in many important ways.[20]

This systemic view of accountability foregrounds the institutions and social practices that encourage—or even *demand*— that rulers justify their decisions and actions. A diverse, independent, and free press plays a key role in questioning representatives. An independent judiciary constrains the kinds of laws enacted and should ensure that rulers who break laws are prosecuted. An active civil society can scrutinize legislation and mobilize political activity to promote or oppose specific laws. Civil liberties guarantee that if dissenters find official justifications unconvincing (or unethical), they have legal avenues to express their outrage and organize resistance; even beyond lawful protest, nonviolent civil disobedience has a proud history in democracy.

More broadly, rulers are held to account through well-established (if too often flouted) norms requiring that they give reasons for their decisions and actions. Obviously, elected politicians can and do dissemble, with equivocations, convoluted strategic rationales, and explanations that please partisans but contradict the factual record. That reasons are given at all, however, shows the persistence of this norm and underpins the abiding faith in the *possibility* of a more deliberative politics.[21]

For the argument here, the important point is that elections are *not* a necessary component of this systemic accountability process. Ironically, elections may undermine effective accountability by shifting the media and the public's focus from substance to spectacle.[22]

Even if elections are the key moment of political agency for most people in modern democracies, agency should also be understood in much broader terms. Political activity has many facets, such as writing to a representative, signing a petition, participating in a town-hall meeting, donating to a political party or cause, or attending a demonstration. Democracies must include a plethora of avenues for citizen participation beyond elections.

If instituted, sortition would require continued attention to maintaining these possibilities for mass political participation. Support for sortition and support for stronger forms of participatory democracy go hand in hand. For example, a sortition legislature might be complemented effectively by a periodic political event or series of citizens' assemblies, such as a modified version of the Deliberation Day proposal, where a list of legislative priorities is collectively developed and delivered to legislators.[23]

More generally, a sortition system could work well alongside participatory budgeting, open consultative meetings, and strong social movements. Eliminating the expense of elections could free up human and financial capital for such civic activities. Whereas an elected representative must prioritize the interests of economic elites because of fundraising imperatives, a representative selected by lot might choose to meet, learn from, and respond to a far more diverse array of individuals and social groups.[24]

Equality, Legitimacy, and the Simulation Claim

A legislature populated using sortition would be accountable if the liberal freedoms and democratic norms of public justification of decision-making were continued—or hopefully even enhanced. The loss of elections would represent neither a lethal nor a particularly serious blow to democratic accountability, and as argued elsewhere, sortition would result in a descriptively representative assembly—unlike the gender-, racial-, and age-imbalanced assemblies of today.[25]

What about political equality? In an electoral system, this democratic ideal is fulfilled by giving every adult one vote— although it is relatively easy to show that this does not lead to political equality in practice.[26] With a unicameral sortition legislature, political equality manifests most directly in the equal *probability* of being selected to political office.

In a more concrete sense, however, sortition should produce an equality (or equivalence) of *outcomes*: the randomly selected sample should make the same decision that the entire adult population would have made, if every citizen had an equal opportunity to deliberate together. In more practical terms, the sample of people who happen to be chosen for a sortition legislature should produce the same laws that *any* such random sample would enact. It is this equivalence that makes a sortition legislature normatively desirable and from which it derives the most significant aspect of its legitimacy.

We want the randomly selected microcosm to simulate how any (or all) of us would decide policy matters under circumstances as close to ideal as possible.[27] As political theorist John Dryzek explains, this "simulation claim" requires a minipublic to give "a simulation of what the population as a whole would decide if everyone were allowed to deliberate."[28] Since having every adult participate in a process of informed, respectful deliberation is, however, infeasible, the best alternative is to build institutions that simulate this ideal. Sortition does precisely this.

This simulation claim comes in two versions: strong and weak. The stronger version requires that a representative microcosm of society should, under deliberative conditions, replicate *exactly* the decisions of any comparable microcosm. This is probably impossible to achieve, although it is amenable to empirical test by running parallel sortition assemblies on the same topic.[29]

The weak—and more practical—version of the simulation claim holds that, within a given community, groups of descriptively representative, term-limited, and randomly selected people who deliberate (under conditions where good deliberation can occur) will *approximate* what the entire community would have decided under similar conditions, over time and across the broad array of issues. This weaker claim allows that on certain topics, at certain times, and under less than ideal conditions, a sortition assembly or minipublic's decisions might deviate from what a similar group (or all of society) would have decided. Over time, however, and as the participants in an assembly are replaced and issues are revisited, such bodies should fulfill this weaker simulation criterion.

This weak version of the simulation claim is, to me, persuasive, but those who remain skeptical might appreciate an even weaker version. In this minimalist view, a descriptively representative microcosm of people need only get closer to the normative deliberative ideal than an elected body of politicians (even under the best possible electoral system) to be more legitimate and therefore desirable. For the reasons outlined earlier, there would likely be a large gulf between many important legislative decisions of politicians and those of a sortition legislature. This weakest simulation claim merely posits that the gap between what is normatively desirable and what we have at the moment would be narrowed significantly through sortition.

The Sortition Alternative

If our democratic ideal is popular sovereignty, and we recognize the impracticality of continual deliberative democracy on a mass scale, then sortition should outperform elections as a means of securing this ideal. We should select a representative sample of people to establish laws, while maintaining the larger accountability system secured through civil liberties, judicial oversight, social movements, and civil society more generally. Giving a sortition body legislative power (with rotation, time-limited terms of office, and a tried and tested deliberative decision-making process) would provide a robust test of at least the weaker versions of the simulation claim and thereby achieve—and increase—democratic equality and public legitimacy.

Though Gastil and Wright's proposal for a sortition chamber heads admirably in this direction, it falls short by preserving a parallel elected chamber. Political parties are the dinosaurs of our times. Elected politicians are not trusted, and party membership has suffered a long-term collapse—whereas membership in civil-society organizations has flourished of late.[30] Social movements and the mobilization of social forces do and can happen outside of political parties.

Gastil and Wright also defend the elected chamber as an important site of political bargaining. While it is true that bargaining may, in some contexts, be necessary, and can be a source of strength when otherwise disenfranchised social groups become organized, it is difficult to defend bargaining as an ideal mode of *legislative* decision-making, where the normative ideal of informed deliberation should predominate.[31] Preserving an elected chamber preserves horse-trading, pork-barrel politics, and illusory zero-sum battles.

The capture and distortion of the political process by vested interests and the influence of money also undermines Gastil and Wright's assertion that political parties are necessary for the development of political leadership. Electoral imperatives taint all party leaders, who compare poorly to leaders who emerge from civil society. Moreover, if levels of trust in our political representatives are indicative of satisfaction with the electoral system, the broader public has stated plainly its dissatisfaction with the status quo.

Fortunately, there is an alternative to electoral democracy, and recent examples of sortition-based policy making abound. Minipublics, in various forms and sizes, have a strong track record, at least in the primarily advisory charge given to them most often.[32]

The larger and more significant step from occasional minipublics to institutionalized sortition could take many forms. Sortition assemblies could be used as a tool for constitutional reform (see Fishkin's and Arnold's chapters in this volume), or they could become the local democratic norm if the G1000 democratic experiments continue their spread from Belgium to the Netherlands, Spain, the UK, and beyond. Or local governments experimenting with sortition, such as Toronto's Planning Review Panel or some of Rotterdam's area commissions, may inspire cities to take this method even farther.[33] Sortition will probably continue to be used to inform contentious policy decisions, as in the Nuclear Fuel Cycle Engagement policy jury in South Australia, or the deliberations on same-sex marriage and the constitutional ban on abortion at the Irish Constitutional Convention and the Irish Citizens' Assembly (see Arnold et al. in this volume).[34]

Or, as proposed by Gastil and Wright and others, sortition may be used to populate a second chamber in parliament or congress. Strategically, the first place to promote this could be at the subnational level, where a unicameral legislature exists amid strong public demand for a people's chamber. One example is Scotland, where a group of organizations has recently proposed such an assembly to complement the Scottish Parliament.[35] This could also happen in Australia, where the newDemocracy Foundation has a well-established record of policy decision-making using sortition and a mission to institutionalize sortition in government.[36] In France a campaign has been launched to replace the French Senate with a sortition chamber, and French president Emmanuel Macron has proposed that presidents should be held to account by an annual sortition body.[37] These examples show that sortition is a political idea with a promising future. Its modern rediscovery and resurgence is impressive.

Though a standalone sortition body should be our aim, for the reasons outlined above, the bicameral proposal of Gastil and Wright could be an important stepping stone toward unicameral sortition. An empowered sortition chamber would enable a direct comparison of the decision-making (and antics) of an elected chamber to that of a sortition chamber. If current research into sortition assemblies generalizes to legislative chambers, then the broader populace will have a higher level of trust and confidence in the outcomes of the sortition chamber.[38] A move to then eliminate the elected chamber would initiate the demise of the electoral oligopoly experienced in many nations, the elimination of the aristocratic device of election, and the end of politicians as we now know them. Though the idea of ending elections may be controversial now, I am confident that after people witness a sortition chamber in action, few would be sad to see elected politicians go.

16

Why Hybrid Bicameralism Is Not Right for Sortition

Terrill Bouricius

Proposals for incorporating sortition into the lawmaking process frequently envision a hybrid bicameral legislature with the members of one of the chambers selected by lot.[1] This could be a transitional model on the path to a fully sortition-based legislature—sort of a trial run to see if such a body can behave in a competent manner. But for many theorists it is the final goal. In the lead chapter of this volume, Gastil and Wright argue that despite the host of problems with election-based representation, there are important beneficial aspects of an elected chamber that would be lost in an all-sortition system. I will argue that the purported benefits of maintaining elections are illusory. Also, the all-purpose legislative chamber design is a mismatch for sortition, which would sabotage sortition's hoped-for benefits and delegitimize a sortition chamber. I will conclude by arguing that there are better ways to evolve into a virtually all-sortition lawmaking system.

Purported Benefits of Maintaining an Elected Chamber

In this section, I will examine several commonly asserted benefits of maintaining an elected chamber alongside a sortition chamber. Citizens would be loath to forfeit an elected chamber for fear of losing at least four presumed benefits: the societal benefits of parties; the utility of having elected officials as authorized negotiators; the political leadership cultivated by electoral politics; and the political expertise provided by elected officials. In turn, I will cast doubt on the existence, or importance, of each.

Benefits of Parties

Without elections, it is suggested that parties would atrophy, yet parties ideally play an important role in formulating political programs, educating the public about policy alternatives, and mobilizing citizens. Others argue that US parties "have become little more than political labels behind which well-financed candidates organize their electoral bids."[2]

Parties would inevitably change in an all-sortition system, but they would not necessarily atrophy. Active political parties have organized across the globe under nonelectoral regimes, even when outlawed. Rather than contending in elections, parties would aim to influence the general public, who would form the minipublics. And of course, political parties are not the only avenue for important social mobilization, with Black Lives Matter, Occupy Wall Street, and the pro-life movements in the US being examples. With parties stripped of their unique electoral significance, such popular mobilizations might be more common and effective under a sortition system.

But let's focus in on the effects of eliminating the competitive electoral function of political parties in an all-sortition democracy. Anthoula Malkopoulou argues that voting in elections "offers a real and continuous relationship between government and citizens that, aided by the excitement of competition, produces a higher incentive to stay informed and form an opinion about general political issues."[3] She speculates that "sortition does away with the momentum of discursive interaction and contestation, which the experience of election provides."[4]

We need to scrutinize the nature of the "discursive interaction" of partisan politics, and not presume that it is inherently beneficial for society. As with most news coverage, the engagement focuses on the tactics of the partisan contest itself, rather than the ideas that are presumed to underlie that contest. Not all electoral democracies experience the level of partisan animosity present in American politics, but the divisions within society into warring factions of us versus them certainly have some negative consequences that would carry over into civil society and hence into a minipublic. We need to consider whether incompatible interests result in antagonisms that in turn get expressed through political parties, or if political parties fan, or even manufacture, differences to frighten and mobilize constituencies. Both occur, but as I discuss in the next section, elections are not the only—nor necessarily the best—way to manage incompatible interests.

Researchers have found that people who are deeply engaged in partisan political issues and follow the news are also likely to have an elevated yet false sense of their own level of understanding of the issues.[5] This leaves them ill prepared for the meaningful give-and-take of deliberation. Disturbingly, it turns out that voters informing themselves (reading newspapers, watching TV news, and so on) to keep up on public issues do not become more adept at evaluating candidates or policy choices. A study by Brendan Nyhan of Dartmouth found that those with a favorable opinion about a particular political figure and who also had more political knowledge (in that they followed the news, for example) were more immune to factual corrections that contradicted their bias than were people who also had a favorable view of the politician but were less informed. Indeed, the factual corrections tended to harden the erroneous beliefs of the "better informed" participants, presumably as a sort of psychological defense mechanism.[6]

Thus, even balanced presentations, in a partisan environment fueled by competitive elections, may not lead to a common understanding of reality by citizens, as each chooses which facts to accept and which to reject. Partisan loyalty trumps reality. This "discursive interaction and contestation" frequently consists of parroting talking points generated by partisan propagandists, and may have more in common with the insult-yelling of die-hard fans of sports teams than the republican virtues hoped for by some theorists. In sum, the vaunted "discursive interaction and contestation" in a party-based environment may make citizens *less* capable of learning and deliberating if selected to serve in a minipublic.

Authorized Negotiators

Some issues are not amenable to the common-ground-seeking process of deliberation. Deliberation is based on the idea of participants being open to revising their opinions and preferences as they deliberate. However, as pluralists note, some public policy choices pit incompatible interests against each other and will inevitably have winners and losers. Negotiated compromise between conflicting interests is widely seen as the better way of resolving such conflicts compared to simply counting heads. Parties and elected representatives are seen to have legitimacy as bargaining agents empowered to cut deals on behalf of conflicting interests, whereas randomly selected citizens, not being authorized agents for constituencies, do not.

Because negotiation is such a prevalent part of decision-making in elected chambers (and elsewhere), it is common to assume that negotiation is the appropriate way to resolve conflicting interests. However, negotiation is not the only, or necessarily the best, alternative to deliberation. Negotiation reflects relative power, and often involves threats as well as inducements. *Should* public decisions necessarily be a manifestation of relative power? Even when power is more equal, negotiation often devolves to horse-trading on completely unrelated policy matters. Negotiation and bargaining among elected legislators can mean,

You get that amendment, which benefits your group but hurts society as a whole, and I get this other amendment, which benefits my group but hurts society as a whole. Indeed, legislators are especially motivated to negotiate deals when their sought-after policies cannot be justified as beneficial to society.

One alternative to both deliberation *and* negotiation (when incompatible interests clash) is arbitration with an impartial entity serving as judge in pursuit of fairness or justice. This tool is "off the table" as an option in elected chambers, which evince relative power (rather than fairness). One can imagine a dispute-resolution process in which each interest group on a particular issue offered their optimal compromise and a mini-public chose from among the possible compromises offered, using fairness, rather than power, as their standard. This process might deliver poor outcomes from time to time, but there is no reason to think results would be as bad as negotiated settlements within elected chambers today.

Cultivating Political Leaders

Gastil and Wright also assert that "elections create the possibility for political careers and the development of skillful politicians as political leaders."[7] I question the assumption that this variety of political leaders is, on balance, a positive thing for a democracy.[8] Leadership derives from the human proclivity for followership, which prompts citizens to suspend independent judgment and defer to leaders to whom they may have some emotional attachment. Followership is grounded in fast, "automatic," nonrational thinking.[9] Research suggests opinion leaders may lead people astray more often than to the best answers.[10] A leader may lead well on one matter, but also be followed on many unrelated matters about which the leader has no clue. Elected leaders also exhibit the dilemma of the package deal; a candidate with desirable leadership skills or personality traits may champion bad policies and vice versa, but the voters can't recombine these to create their ideal candidate.

Even if we accept, for the sake of argument, that good

leaders are beneficial, elections are a poor mechanism for selecting and promoting desirable ones. The skills, motivations, and traits needed to win elections, including public relations skills and extreme self-confidence, are not necessarily the optimal attributes for socially beneficial leaders. Elections tend to advance ego-driven men (meaning males) who are ill suited for the give-and-take of deliberation. A candidate's projection of confidence—whether justified or not—can carry the day in elections. It is cliché to suggest that the accrual of power also has a tendency to corrupt, even if the candidate isn't sociopathic at the outset. Dr. David Owen, former British foreign secretary and member of parliament in the UK, has even proposed that the medical community recognize a diagnosis of "hubris syndrome"—a sort of intoxication that can be brought on by serving in high office.[11] In a hybrid bicameral system, the persistence and prominence of power-motivated elected political leaders would tend to sabotage the benefits of sortition, as these leaders' influence would extend beyond their elected chamber to influence its counterpart.

Political Expertise

Another argument for maintaining elections is the presumed political expertise of elected officials. I am not aware of any compelling evidence that elections are effective at selecting individuals with unique competence at governing. James Surowiecki, in *The Wisdom of Crowds*, points out that we shouldn't believe people are more expert simply because they assert as much.[12] A feeling of certainty that one is right just as often signals a lack of intellectual humility. Failure to recognize one's ignorance impedes deliberation and stunts the growth of actual expertise.[13]

Moreover, we should not conflate *political* expertise and *policy* expertise. Often legislators' policy expertise is superficial or narrowly confined to a handful of issues with which their particular committees deal. In fact, most expertise resides in the professional staff and lobbyists (who draft nearly all bills), rather than in the politicians themselves.[14] One problem with *electing* representatives is that they have a distorted interest in consulting fundraising and campaign experts more than genuine policy experts and shaping policies accordingly.

By contrast, a sortition minipublic would presumably recognize the need to employ and consult genuine policy experts. Just as legislators hand off the details of drafting and negotiating legislation to staff, the sortition body would do the same—but without giving special consideration for lobbyists who want to tailor those details to their own purposes.[15]

Even assuming allotted citizens start out with cognitive biases comparable to those of elected representatives, it is far more feasible for a minipublic to require a well-designed deliberative architecture to dampen "the known cognitive biases of human beings,"[16] rather than exacerbate them. Citizen deliberators can also more feasibly be required to have training that minimizes psychological traps. Carey Morewedge and colleagues found that training can successfully reduce cognitive bias in both the immediate and long term.[17] Overcoming biases, such as motivated reasoning and automatic judgments, will create a more competent decision-making body.

Benefits of Sortition Are Lost with Continued Elections

My concern is that the hoped-for beneficial effects of sortition in one chamber would be overwhelmed by negative influence from the elected chamber. In this next section, I will argue that if an elected chamber deals with the same bills as its sortition counterpart, this would sacrifice many of the potential benefits of sortition.

Agenda Setting

Politicians who are constantly preparing for the next election seek out and bring to the fore those issues that they believe will help them in the next election. Important long-term issues (but with less public salience) often fail to make it onto the agenda until they become a crisis that cannot be ignored.

In a hybrid system, the agenda-setting priorities of the elected chamber will still monopolize the news, public awareness, and—unless artfully shielded—the attention of members of the sortition chamber. A substantial portion of the sortition chamber's agenda will be established by what bills the elected chamber sends them. As Murray Edelman explained in *Constructing the Political Spectacle*, "Perhaps the most powerful influence of news, talk, and writing about problems is the immunity from notice and criticism they grant to damaging conditions that are not on the list."[18] A sortition chamber in a hybrid system may be able to raise some issues, but political gravity will constantly draw it back to an agenda favored by elected politicians.

Rational Ignorance and Active Aptitude

When compared to mass voting, whether in candidate elections or issue referendums, sortition is often touted for its ability to overcome *rational ignorance*. When a citizen has one vote out of millions, there are no rational grounds for investing significant effort into learning the ramifications of the various choices on a ballot.[19] Elections and opinion polls reflect inevitably ignorant, off-the-cuff public opinion. But if placed within representative minipublics, where it is reasonable to believe that one's vote could really matter, lay participants would have motivation for a conscientious performance of duty—what seventeenth- to eighteenth-century philosopher Jeremy Bentham called "active aptitude."[20]

The fruition of sortition's hoped-for benefits is dependent on the political environment and the institutional design of the minipublic (term of office, size, volunteer or quasi-mandatory service, and so forth). Jon Elster adopts the terminology of Jeremy Bentham to summarize the desiderata of any minipublic using the example of a constituent assembly tasked with writing a constitution:

Generally speaking … the assembly ought to be organized to promote the moral aptitude, intellectual aptitude, and active aptitude of the framers. By moral aptitude I shall understand impartiality (in the negative form of disinterested and dispassionate decision making). By intellectual aptitude, I shall understand absence of cognitive bias at the individual level and diversity at the collective level. By active aptitude, I shall understand the full attention and concentration of the constitution-makers to their task, by making it seem worthwhile and by eliminating other charges that might occupy them.[21]

When paired with an elected chamber, however, the members of the sortition chamber are less likely to attain active aptitude. When people face a daunting cognitive task and experience uncertainty, it is natural for them to defer to those with higher status who project a demeanor of certainty.[22] Within a partisan electoral environment, where a strong sense of team loyalty or tribalism is fomented, it seems likely that many members of an allotted chamber would adhere to their favored party leaders' platforms. The sortition chamber would have a cognitive "social loafing" or "free-rider" problem. When another chamber dealing with the same pieces of legislation, full of articulate and often charismatic people who insist they have figured out the right answer, are pushing members of an allotted chamber to follow their lead, the slow and rational thinking falls by the wayside.

Team loyalty regularly trumps independent rational analysis. In studies conducted by Geoffrey Cohen, partisan voters were asked to evaluate a policy proposal in a news story. Some participants read a version of the story that suggested a policy (for example, a stingy welfare proposal) was favored by prominent Democrats, whereas other participants read a version of the story that suggested it was favored by prominent Republicans. The participants' own evaluations of the policy closely mirrored the suggested preference of the party they generally agreed with, regardless of whether the policy would independently be deemed liberal or conservative.[23]

Partisan leaders have immense influence when it comes to framing public understanding of policies. As one example, look at popular impressions of the 2010 Affordable Care Act (or "Obamacare"). In hopes of gaining some bipartisan support, President Obama jettisoned his earlier support of single-payer health care reform (favored by many health care reformers, especially on the left) and instead advanced a private market-based approach that mandated that Americans purchase insurance or face a tax penalty. This approach was originally advanced by the conservative Heritage Foundation in 1989 and enacted in 2006 in Massachusetts and embraced by its Republican governor Mitt Romney. Indeed, this kind of reform was known as "Romneycare" before it was repackaged and came to be known as Obamacare on a national level. Like the participants in the Cohen study described above, relying on the heuristic of partisan leadership, most Democrats quickly embraced Romneycare/Obamacare, while Republicans attacked it and even made its repeal a centerpiece of subsequent election campaigns. The ideological underpinnings and operational details of the reform became irrelevant as the mental shortcut based on team loyalty trumped substance.

The sortition chamber in a hybrid bicameral system may not degenerate to a mere rubber stamp for the elected chamber's decisions, but the full potential of sortition will not be realized. This loss of active aptitude underlies a whole host of other losses of anticipated sortition benefits.

The descriptive representativeness and diversity of cognitive styles touted by sortition advocates would be significantly harmed by the continuation of an elected chamber.[24] A chamber selected by lot would still *look* diverse, but the loss of active aptitude will mean that the private knowledge and perspectives distributed across that diverse membership will be less likely to be expressed by those members. Status deferral and information cascades will short-circuit the wisdom of crowds.[25]

The anticorruption potential of sortition, integrated into carefully designed assembly rules that promote "securities against misrule," is one of its most appealing characteristics.[26]

Continued elections, however, risk corrupting the lawmaking process as a whole. It is possible that the sortition chamber could draw attention to that corruption, but contrary to the maxim that "sunlight is said to be the best of disinfectants," experience suggests this is not an effective deterrent. Shining a light on institutionalized corruption is not enough.[27]

Danger of Delegitimation

In this section, I will set aside the concerns raised above and assume that all of the negative consequences of maintaining an elected chamber could be dealt with through careful design. If the sortition chamber is not a rubber stamp, what happens when the two chambers disagree about an important bill? In cases where both chambers are elected, they tend to have a nearly equal power relationship. But what would happen when one chamber is made up of people identified as chosen leaders, and one is made up of a random assortment of ordinary people? We can get an inkling by looking at countries where one chamber is elected and the other is not, such as the House of Lords in the UK or the Senate in Canada. In these cases, the bodies are *not* equal. The elected chamber is preeminent, even though the lesser body has the ostensibly prestigious title of "upper house."

What are some likely consequences of the sortition chamber rejecting a bill passed by the elected chamber? The two chambers would have a fundamentally different and conflicting basis for claiming legitimacy, which might be summarized as the principle of distinction and the principle of equality and likeness.[28] When in conflict with an allotted chamber, the members of the elected chamber would have a compelling strategic incentive to undermine the legitimacy of the sortition chamber. In contrast, the allotted members would not be protecting personal careers in politics, since they would shortly be "out of power" regardless. Unlike the allotted citizens, the elected members would tend to be highly practiced, articulate public speakers with exceptional public relations skills. Portraying themselves as champions for their constituents, the elected leaders would likely play the "natural aristocracy" card. It is easy to predict the themes they might use. The sortition chamber could be dismissed as, say, a random gaggle of dishwashers and hairdressers unaccountable because they never have to face the public in an election.

Worse still, the natural hostility of elected representatives toward the sortition threat to their power in a hybrid system makes the evolution toward a sortition democracy unachievable. If sortition begins in a hybrid system, it may die there.

A Better Beginning for Sortition

To avoid these problems, I propose a system that allows elections to coexist with sortition, though not in a bicameral design. In time, this could give way to an all-sortition system. Below, I explain why sortition should eschew an all-purpose chamber, use multiple citizen bodies, steer clear of elections, and extend its reach to the executive branch.

Avoiding an All-Purpose Legislative Chamber

An all-purpose legislative chamber is a mismatch for sortition, whether in a unicameral or hybrid bicameral system. All-purpose elected bodies manage a huge variety of issues by dividing into smaller committees. The chamber as a whole does not meaningfully deliberate, or even understand the nuances of most of the bills they nominally debate and vote on. Instead, members rely on one of a few heuristics. Commonly, they simply defer to the judgment of the members of their own party who serve on the committee of reference.

This approach has shortcomings for elected chambers, but it is even less appropriate for a sortition chamber. Even if members of the allotted body organized into partisan caucuses (undercutting one of the benefits of sortition), small committees would have a greater likelihood of being unrepresentative of the population, simply owing to smaller sample sizes. Deferring to even a conscientious committee could result in very unrepresentative decisions. The sheer number of bills under consideration by a bicameral chamber precludes dealing with them all in a committee of the whole. Hypothetically, this problem might be resolved with a vast chamber with hundreds of members on each committee, but this has not generally been advocated by advocates of hybrid bicameralism.[29]

Anthoula Malkopoulou notes that "lotteries may offer valuable improvement to current practices of democratic selection, but only if special measures are taken to compensate for the limitations they entail."[30] The special measures she intimates (such as limiting the role and power of minipublics) are nearly the opposite of those I favor, but we agree that one must fit the design to the unique character of minipublics.

Elected legislators constitute a full-charge governing body. They create the public agenda, propose policies, nominally draft bills, advocate for and against bills, amend and perfect those bills, and finally sit in judgment of the bills they have developed to decide whether they should pass into law. This violates a widely recognized principle that the bias caused by pride of authorship requires that the author should not also be the judge of the final product. Bicameralism allows a separate group of representatives to duplicate these vertically integrated tasks, but Gastil and Wright's proposal makes no attempt to divide responsibilities between the two chambers based on the relative strengths of each one's design. A better solution requires more sortition bodies, with distinct purposes for each one.

Multibody Sortition

I envision an interconnected network of minipublics, each with a specific legislative function and a specific topic or issue. In addition to being a more desirable end state, unlike a full-charge chamber, the means of transition are built into the model itself. The only substantial experience we have with modern-day sortition is with minipublics that have a single function and topic. It is questionable how well they inform us about how well a full-charge sortition chamber might function.

Peeling away issue areas one at a time not only allows communities to learn from the experience of recent experiments in terms of process, but it also avoids the danger of an elected chamber and a sortition chamber opposing each other head to head on a given bill, which could trigger the aforementioned delegitimation. I will first describe how a transition to a sortition-based democracy could occur, and then describe a possible model for a mature version.

The division of legislative tasks among distinct bodies, mostly selected by lot, overcomes many design dilemmas: mandatory service improves representativeness but would create bodies with members unwilling to perform their duties; a long term of office increases expertise but also concentrates power and invites corruption; and a smaller group facilitates deliberation but would compromise statistical sampling accuracy. The impulse is to seek out the "sweet spot" between merits and liabilities such as these. The better solution uses multiple bodies, each designed to maximize the benefits of certain attributes and counter the negative effects of that design decision with a check and balance from a separate body using countervailing design features.[31]

This single-issue and single-function minipublic design is pragmatic and also provides a path for evolution to an all-sortition democracy. By peeling away one issue area at a time from the traditional elected legislature and entrusting it to a compound sortition process, it might be possible to transfer power to a sortition wing of government step by step. There are certain inviting issue areas where this might begin, such as issues in which elected legislators either have a conflict of interest (election laws, as in the case of the British Columbia Citizens' Assembly,[32] ethics oversight, and the like), or "hot potato" issue areas that elected officials are happy to be rid of because they are no-win topics (such as the nuclear waste issue tackled by a minipublic in South Australia). Initially, bills with no substantial budget impacts are most appropriate, as coordinating conflicting budget requests is a higher-order challenge for a system based on separate minipublics.[33]

The goal is to institutionalize the transfer of an issue area on an ongoing basis. The authority of the sortition process must be decisive, rather than merely advisory. This must also be combined with verifiable independence, such that a minipublic is not subject to manipulation by the elected government through control of their staff or information flows. In the short term, this might be accomplished through facilitation by an impartial nongovernmental organization, such as Australia's newDemocracy Foundation or a university. Ultimately, however, there must be a budget and staff not beholden to the elected representatives. The staff and functioning of the sortition process should be overseen by a minipublic devoted to these tasks.

If the public appreciates the fruits of these minipublics, governments could feel a growing pressure to try this model for other issues, especially following scandals that crop up among elected representatives. This approach allows for baby steps, with a gradual popular assessment that might grow more favorable with each process refinement along the way. Creating an all-purpose sortition chamber dealing with all bills would require a greater leap of faith.

Key for the advance of a sortition-based democracy is the use of sortition in forming constitutional conventions or review bodies. A randomly selected constituent assembly seems far more likely than an elected chamber to transfer powers from elected bodies to other sortition bodies. There have already been precedents that suggest this strategy has potential. When the legislature of British Columbia established the Citizens' Assembly, it set up a process that allowed the assembly's recommendations to go directly to referendum without further involvement of the elected legislators. Ireland and Iceland have incorporated random selection in recent constitutional review bodies, although in an advisory role, explicitly interposing the elected legislature between the minipublic and the opportunity for referendum on the minipublic's proposals. Neither of these are the precise model needed, but they hint at the possibility.

Some sort of oversight minipublic (or commission, as Gastil and Wright propose) could adopt rules and procedures to improve the functioning of the sortition legislative process over time. Unlike an elected chamber, a minipublic can readily accept procedures and rules developed in advance by a separate minipublic devoted specifically to the challenge of assuring future minipublics will be well informed and as free of cognitive biases as possible. When designing procedures for others to use, especially when not knowing what issues will be tackled, there is a strong incentive to devise methods that minimize cognitive bias and misinformation.[34]

Sortition Without Elections

To see how this would work, consider this design for a sortition-based legislature with no electoral element. In this example, I distinguish among an agenda council, interest panels, review panels, policy juries, and rules and oversight councils.

An agenda council selected by lot (with stratified sampling) would do risk analysis, hear suggestions, employ researchers to investigate societal problems, and decide which issues needed legislative attention in the next period. Unlike in electoral systems, the incentives for spectacle, ill-informed voter salience, and vilification of opposing parties would no longer dominate. This council would probably serve multiyear terms with staggered rotation. Due to the length of service and workload, it is likely that many citizens would decline to serve, so its descriptive representativeness would be poorer than a short-duration jury (though superior to any existing elected legislature). Because this council would not be adopting any policies, it would not be prone to bribes. For example, a special interest seeking a tax break that bribes the item onto the agenda might end up with a tax *increase* at the end of the process, after entirely distinct bodies work through the issue. To complement this body, it might be desirable to also have a petition route to place topics on the agenda.[35]

The agenda council would issue a call for the creation of interest panels to prepare proposals to address the selected issues. The members of interest panels would be self-selected, with a new discussion group forming for every twelve citizens who volunteer. This allows any citizen who wants to participate in the democracy to do so without waiting for a lottery call, and it mirrors the ancient Greek principle of *ho boulomenos*. Interest panels might be face-to-face or virtual, using sophisticated online crowdsourcing platforms. It doesn't matter if interest panels favoring a given policy far outnumber those opposing it, since their sheer number has no significance. Diversity of input is the goal. Because participants would know their draft proposals would have to pass muster of subsequent sortition bodies, participants would be motivated to develop proposals that could pass muster with well-informed minipublics.

Ongoing sortition review panels would exist for each major issue area. To gain more knowledge about the topics covered, the review panels would serve for multiple years, with perhaps one-third of their members rotating off each year. Because citizens would not be compelled to serve, stratified sampling and strong incentives would be required to keep these bodies as descriptively representative as possible. Each of these panels would take expert testimony and work through—amend, recombine, and so forth—the raw material coming from the interest panels to develop a single legislative proposal.

These review panels bear a passing resemblance to traditional legislative committees. Unlike elected legislators on committees, the review panels would prioritize deliberation among diverse perspectives. Without the distractions of campaign public relations and fundraising, these professionally staffed panels would have the potential to be better versed than typical committees made up of elected politicians. The fact that these review panels do not have final authority to pass laws reduces their value to would-be bribers.

For each bill, the final decision would come from a policy jury. These would convene for a duration of a few days or weeks (depending on the complexity of the bill), be large, and have quasi-compulsory service to maximize descriptive representativeness. The members of the policy jury would hear pro and con presentations and could ask questions of experts. In line with the independence requirement for the Condorcet theorem and wisdom of crowds,[36] they would not engage in debate and would vote by secret ballot to protect against intimidation and bribery. Because of the possibility for passage of incompatible bills by separate policy juries, there would also need to be a coordinating minipublic for prioritizing and harmonizing conflicting bills.

Finally, there should also exist some meta-legislative bodies drawn by lot. A rules council, perhaps drawn from willing members of previous minipublics, would refine the procedures to improve the system over time. An oversight council, also drawn by lot, would oversee staff performance and impartiality to protect against bureaucratic capture and Michels's "iron law of oligarchy."

The nature of the check and balance in this design is very different than a bicameral legislature, which often results in gridlock rather than "balance." Each unit would have full authority within its narrowly circumscribed domain but have an incentive to consider the views of those who might disagree with them. By dividing up the legislative functions, we can protect against concentration of power and corruption. It also enshrines the principle that the authors of a proposal are not competent to also be the judges of their own handiwork.

Executive Selection

Looking beyond the issue of hybrid bicameralism, versus an all-sortition legislature, a diminution of sortition's benefits could also occur if elections were maintained for the executive branch. There would be a severe risk of charismatic elected executives dominating a sortition legislature even more than they might an elected one. Elected politicians in a legislative chamber, with typically elevated egos and concerns about preserving their own power, may jealously seek to defend the prerogatives of the legislative branch and resist a would-be authoritarian executive. Even elected legislatures frequently give up powers to a chief executive (for example, the unconstitutional war-making powers of US presidents).

This risk would be even more pronounced with an allotted legislature. A popularly elected charismatic chief executive with a penchant for self-aggrandizement would have the opportunity to use the "principle of distinction" to claim a popular mandate resulting from the election, while belittling the unelected and unimposing members of the randomly selected legislative branch. A group of randomly selected ordinary citizens lacks the personal investment and political capital necessary to defend the limited prerogatives of a body they will soon leave anyway.

I concur with the witticism of Douglas Adams that "those people who must *want* to rule people are, ipso facto, those least suited to do it."[37] Thus, an optimal sortition democracy should establish minipublics charged with recruiting and hiring a chief executive, who would have an administrative rather than policy-making role (akin to the city manager function advanced by the early twentieth-century Progressive movement). Rather than evaluating self-selected or party-nominated candidates, I would suggest a full-spectrum recruitment process to find a person fully willing to serve but who did not proactively seek the position. On a regular basis, a new minipublic would be called to evaluate the executive's performance and have the power to remove them. To avoid the motivation to remove a good executive just to choose a particular person as a replacement, the minipublic with removal authority would not be the same one charged with hiring a replacement.

Conclusion: An Evolution to Sortition

In summary, the model of the all-purpose legislative chamber is not a good fit for sortition lawmaking. A hybrid bicameral system would maintain the harmful aspects of competitive elections while sabotaging the potential benefits of sortition. The supposed benefits of elections prove illusory, but their harmful effects on a complementary sortition body would be all too real.

Most of all, when the two chambers disagreed on policy, the elected representatives would have the motive and skills to delegitimize the sortition chamber.

Instead, I contend that sortition works best when a system separates different legislative functions and assigns them to bodies optimally designed for each task, with new bodies formed for each new issue. Though generally relying on sortition, this design would also broaden participation through self-selected interest panels, open to all citizens, for the purpose of drafting proposals as raw material for minipublics to consider.[38]

Peeling away issue areas and transferring them one at a time from elected to sortition bodies provides a plausible path toward institutional change. Election campaigns and politicians would simply no longer deal with those issue areas that had been removed from their purview. Since they would not be going head to head on the same issue, this would reduce the motivation for elected legislators to challenge the legitimacy of the sortition model.

In this evolutionary vision, elected chambers may never fully disappear—but they could recede to the periphery, just as the powerful Council of Areopagus of predemocratic Athens endured but ended up with severely restricted responsibilities. In a similar way, ceremonial monarchs persist in many modern electoral democracies, but with few remaining legal powers. Path dependence may preclude the total abolition of electoral representation, but as a fundamentally oligarchic tool, elections should not be championed as necessary or beneficial for democracy.[39]

V. CONCLUSION

17

Sortition's Scope, Contextual Variations, and Transitions

John Gastil and Erik Olin Wright

The preceding chapters have introduced different conceptions of sortition, but even if the concept now feels familiar, it remains a radical departure from the status quo. Our opening essay championed the idea of establishing sortition as a powerful complement to an elected chamber, but even that bicameral arrangement would break from centuries of tradition. We laid out this proposal, and invited critiques, to glimpse future possibilities. The gravest doubt offered by our critics is the fear that a sortition body with a broad array of powers would become so overwhelmed that its members would welcome an administrative takeover by professional staff, follow the lead of the same political parties running the elected chamber, or fall prey to the enticements of special interests. Freed of any electoral accountability, the randomly selected citizen legislators might become corrupt power brokers, no better than the worst electoral counterparts.

Broadly speaking, the critics see two ways out of this problem: either drastically reduce the remit and powers of sortition bodies, making them serve very specific functions to improve existing centralized democratic institutions, or dissolve the

centralized power of the state itself and shift power to an assortment of more fragmented sortition bodies. We remain committed to the view that modern democratic societies require a strong
state capable of coherent action and thus reject the second, more
anarchist option of dismantling the state.[1] But we also believe it
is possible to have a strong state in which sortition plays not
simply a subsidiary role but is instead fully empowered and
integrated into the heart of the machinery of the state.

Still, the comments in this book have raised serious concerns
about incompetence, capture, and corruption. We don't deny
the risk of such outcomes—all of which occur already in legislative systems the world over. If a society rushes into empowered
sortition, it could unleash unintended consequences on a grand
scale. In this concluding chapter, we hope to show that one can
embrace radical possibilities and still be attentive to such risks.
We do this by revisiting three central issues—the scope of a
sortition body's responsibilities, its context dependency, and the
political transitions that could lead to it.

The Scope of a Sortition Body's Authority

We began this book by imagining a body with broad authority
analogous to existing legislative chambers. This worries critics
who saw too wide a gap between this expansive vision and the
realities of existing minipublics, which typically convene to give
nothing more than advice on a narrow range of issues over the
course of a few days or weekends. Now, there may be special
historical circumstances in which it is possible to move directly
from a system in which sortition assemblies play such a limited
role to a full-bore sortition chamber. One could imagine, for
example, a deep political crisis of legitimacy in the British bicameral system in which the House of Lords was directly converted
to a sortition assembly, and then its powers augmented fairly
rapidly to match those of the elected parliament. But in most
situations, the only plausible scenario for moving from limited
minipublics to wide-scope empowered sortition would take

place over an extended period of time with many intermediary stages. Such sensible caution about moving too fast, however, needn't induce a *fear* of going too far. We can think about sortition's scope incrementally and test its efficacy at each step.

The Transition Toward a Sortition Legislature

Most of the critics in this book recognize the need for state power but fear its abuse by a body of untested amateur legislators. Incremental implementation can test the gravity of that concern, and each step along the way should come with careful research into the behavior of sortition legislators and its consequences for democratic governance. Such a gradual transition is already under way, if one thinks about the stages of development over time among the randomly selected bodies and minipublics that already exist.

The first stage consisted of juries and grand juries, which showed the capacity of the public to render judgments on legal questions of limited scope. Diversification of these bodies in the twentieth century showed that juries could continue to function effectively even when encompassing a plurality of perspectives.[2] Starting in the 1970s, a variety of public forums borrowed on this tradition to create citizens' juries and policy juries, which sprung up alongside planning cells, consensus conferences, and other small bodies of randomly selected citizens.[3] These proved that small bodies of citizens can tackle the broader public-policy questions put before them—replacing legal verdicts or judgments with practical political recommendations. This broadened the reach of "juries" but at the cost of their authority.

A similar transition occurred with the "town meeting," which morphed from a legally authorized government into a metaphor for public deliberation generally. Drawing on romantic visions from Swiss cantons to New England town meetings, public deliberation processes such as Twenty-First Century Town Meetings tried to show that citizens could gather on larger scales and replicate the magic of the face-to-face meeting.[4] The deliberative poll took the idea farther by insisting on a rigorous random selection of participants to glean the "considered judgment" of a representative microcosm of the public.[5] Once more, these experiments sacrificed scope and authority for scale. In doing so, they showed that big bodies of citizens could render sound judgments on specific questions, at least when freed from the responsibilities of making final decisions.

Recent experiments have gone farther by giving citizens real authority. The Canadian provinces of British Columbia and Ontario both convened more than a hundred citizens to write new election laws, which were put to a public vote. Several times, the state of Oregon has authorized the selection of two dozen citizens to scrutinize ballot measures, then place their one-page analysis in the official voter pamphlet. In both cases, stratified random sampling was employed to ensure demographic representation, but true random selection was not achieved. Nonetheless, these small- and modest-sized bodies proved capable of taking on important public questions under a modicum of political pressure.[6]

The Irish Constitutional Convention described in this volume represents another step forward, in that the randomly selected citizens tackled more contentious questions, such as same-sex marriage. That said, they did so within a body that included elected politicians, though the elected made up a minority. They remained an advisory body, though with a standing that made their recommendations more politically potent. The fact that Ireland is now moving forward with a citizen-only body shows a willingness to move incrementally forward—to see how the citizens fare without the company of political veterans.[7]

From there, the next step is *not* a full sortition body, even in a bicameral legislature. Many other intermediate paths remain, including variations that appear in this volume. David Owen and Graham Smith propose a system that farms out specific questions to bodies drawn from an even larger pool of randomly selected citizens, who remain available for such service for a limited period of time.[8] James Fishkin describes convening single-use bodies that can operate legislative levers, such as providing a check on proposed constitutional amendments. All such proposals feature limited public service on the narrow-est-possible policy question.[9]

The next stage of innovation might go one of two ways. First, a citizen policy body serving for a year or more, akin to a grand jury, might function as an empowered oversight board on a public-policy domain that involves large institutions and complex legislation, such as criminal justice, health care, or the environment. Such a body might have veto power over proposed laws, or it might be authorized to convene investigations.

Second, a body convened for a more limited duration might have the authority to prioritize an issue for legislative action from a large menu of options. This body's agenda-setting author-ity would require considering the trade-offs tackling one versus another public concern, but it would not have to act on specific legislation. A set of existing bills, or citizen initiatives, might be placed on its agenda, and its endorsement of one or more of these potential laws might force a legislative up/down vote—perhaps with substantial amendments being subject to review by this same citizen body before passage.

The final stage could combine longer service duration with a broadened remit. That could come about in nonobvious forms, such as through a mixed-member body that seats citizens along-side legislators. In such a system, one could phase out elected seats gradually through each successive election cycle. The scope of this citizen chamber's authority could likewise grow gradu-ally, beginning with narrower regulatory questions or other issues that conventional legislatures fail to address effectively. In a bicameral system, the elected body can always handle issues outside the sortition body's remit.

Perhaps the ideal starting point for this last stage of develop-ment is to give a sortition body authority over the issues that pose the most serious conflicts of interest for elected bodies. Within constraints that vary by political system, legislators frequently have the authority to amend election laws, set legis-lative pay and benefits, and police themselves for ethical viola-tions. A sortition body could take on one or more of these roles, and it could also hear complaints from minority parties (or dissenting legislators within a majority party) about the application or unfairness of existing procedural rules for debate. Again, the point of such a transitional body is to expand gradually both its length of service and the breadth of its remit.

At every step in this transition, researchers can evaluate the capacity of citizen legislators to deliberate and render sound judgments. Remembering that there exists no independent standard by which to judge such a body's recommendations and decisions, one can still investigate whether such bodies absorb key policy facts, demonstrate empathy toward disadvantaged social groups, recognize the trade-offs of difficult policy choices, and formulate logical and well-evidenced rationales for their findings.[10] All the while, their behavior should compare favorably against *status quo alternatives*—as opposed to an idealized standard for governance.

A Sizable but Shared Service Load

Some might agree to the transitional approach to sortition, yet stop short of a sortition body with the service duration and load of responsibilities that we envision. Most of the authors in this volume remain skeptical of a strong central sortition body, but eschewing such an institution limits the capacity for empowered citizen deliberation to extend across the full breadth of public issues. Leaving those questions to an elected body means that a sortition chamber cannot consider the largest questions, which set the public's priorities *across* issues.

At least as a transitional stage, one compromise is to empower sortition to address the largest questions before the legislature— but in a different way. One scheme would retain a central sortition body that has the ability to shape the agenda and convene fresh minipublics; those more provisional bodies, in turn, have the authority to render final decisions on specific legislation.[11] Alternatively, the sortition body could be more reactive than generative. For instance, instead of creating new legislation, it could pick and choose among bills introduced in the elected chamber, then have the power to amend and force votes on those pieces of legislation. This would take advantage of the elected body's ability to draft complete laws but address the same body's inability to move forward legislation that party leadership suppresses—sometimes to protect narrow interests. Even just forcing public debate on such legislation might give them the exposure they need to win passage.[12]

The sortition body also could share its responsibilities with the wider public. We pointed toward this in our opening chapter's section on "Direct Public Engagement," but after reading the critiques of our proposal, it's clear that this idea requires elaboration. Most of all, we envision the sortition chamber not as a replacement but as a *complement* to other democratic institutions—from protests, petitions, and elections to minipublics, participatory budgeting, and other democratic innovations. Each provides a different path for expressing a public voice, and their additive virtue outweighs the downsides of tension between elected and sortition bodies. As Jane Mansbridge argues in her chapter, citizens could gain a different form of accountability from sortition without ceding the one they already have through elections.[13]

More than this, we see the plausibility of Dimitri Courant's hypothesis that sortition could embolden the wider public to find and use its voice.[14] In the past, the public has been responsive to other opportunities for *empowered* engagement, and a sortition body might provide an indirect civic spark to citizens who can identify with the members of that body.[15] Toward this end, a sortition chamber could elicit direct public input through multiple channels. It might create a new path for input by broadcasting and livestreaming sortition chamber debates, then posing specific questions to online forums for further debate and input. Online engagement tools are still in their infancy, and it's likely that more deliberative modes of debate will continue to develop. These various inputs would inform, rather than replace, the judgment of the sortition body.

The Context Dependency Problem

If the preceding discussion sounds too abstract, it is because we wish to stress the context dependency of attempts to institutionalize sortition. Any civic innovator must respect that a given reform's efficacy will depend on the social setting in which it appears. For example, sortition's success may depend on its acceptance by major social movements and nongovernmental organizations in some societies, whereas in others the key variable might be how the major political parties respond.[16] Or in a more fractured society, broader but shallow popular support might prove sufficient.

We envision sortition as a useful means of improving democratic governments both young and old, more capitalist and more socialist, and at both local and national levels. Thus, we more often describe sortition through design principles rather than procedural details. Sortition designs should adhere to democratic values but remain flexible enough to recognize and respond to the particular challenges in any given social setting.

With this in mind, we take a second look at two of the most persistent concerns about creating a sortition chamber that has both a wide scope of authority and multiyear terms of office. In our opening chapter, we addressed a sortition chamber's potential for corruption and the challenge of representing all sectors of society, but we now revisit those issues to underscore how social circumstances shape both their gravity and their remedy.

The Specter of Corruption

One reason we recommend an incremental approach to establishing sortition is the need to test such a body's resistance to external pressures. In conducting such tests, it will be important to take care when generalizing from a single case to all others. For instance, were a sortition chamber established in a high-functioning municipality rich in social capital, the corruption problem might prove modest. That finding would not necessarily foretell the fortunes of a sortition body instituted in a society known for endemic corruption.

More fundamentally, the political context shapes what counts as the most serious form of corruption. Though every political system has egregious cases of corrupt public officials, they vary tremendously in their overall level of corruption, with public perceptions of electoral systems being the most favorable in New Zealand and lowest in countries such as Venezuela, as recorded by Transparency International.[17] In high-functioning democracies, the gravest concern is whether officials serve in the public interest, broadly construed, whereas the most corrupt countries have persistent problems with the outright buying and selling of public offices and votes.[18]

In the context of sortition critiques, the more serious issue isn't bribery, per se, or other illegal activities. Those might happen in marginal cases, but the more serious danger is that lay citizens end up catering to—or being captured by—special interests. This can involve legal but unethical behavior, such as expecting long-term "payouts" via future employment or contracts after leaving office. More commonly, it means becoming responsive to elite economic interests or concentrated interests to the exclusion of broader public views, or the concerns of disenfranchised social groups.

Sortition legislators could become dependent on lobbyists owing to the direct influence of such persons, or owing to a dearth of influential input from independent media, political parties, public-interest groups, social-movement organizations, and the broader citizenry. Thus, guarding against that problem depends partly on ensuring the vitality of the public voices and public-interested expertise that reach sortition legislators. The prevalence of this form of corruption, then, is not an inevitable expression of flawed human nature so much as a failure to surround legislators with the resources and incentives to remain responsive to the public interest.[19] Once again, this comes down to the context in which sortition becomes institutionalized, rather than a flaw in the design of sortition.

That said, we do believe that procedural safeguards could help a sortition chamber perform better—or at least no worse—than its elected counterpart in a bicameral system. Even after hearing arguments to the contrary, we remain convinced that secret ballots are appropriate for a sortition chamber. These are a hallmark of many large-scale minipublics, most notably deliberative polls. They make quid-pro-quo voting impossible to verify, which makes it irrational to attempt buying a citizen legislator's vote. The secret individual ballots also stress the judgment of the whole body over the individual legislator, which protects individual dissenters within the legislature from rebuke by the majority. Anonymous ballots also shield individual members from public attack for expressing unpopular views. To require public sortition ballots confuses the body with its electoral counterpart, which has a different form of accountability.[20]

As for those cases where individual members commit egregious ethical lapses that fall short of criminal corruption, we suggested in our opening chapter that the sortition chamber should be capable of policing itself. An oversight board made up of current and former sortition members won't have the same partisan entanglements as equivalent committees in elected chambers. With no loyalties to parties or entrenched leaders, such a body should serve as an effective deterrent to corruption, or as a means of removing members who repeatedly violate the sortition chamber's ethical norms.

Failure to Represent the Full Society

Just as broader political context shapes the threat of corruption, so the structure of a society determines how difficult it is to achieve representation through random selection. Because our sortition chamber requires two or more years of public service, critics fear that there will be demographic groups for which even a carefully drawn sample with expert recruiters will fall short. Even if quotas for geography, income, gender, and ethnicity show the sortition body to represent the wider public, those statistics could obscure special subpopulations unable (or unwilling) to make the commitment to serve.

The magnitude of this problem depends on the nature of the larger society. The general public's readiness to serve in sortition will depend on preexisting levels of civic education and engagement. People also may be least equipped to serve in societies that have state-run media, a dearth of institutions that provide neutral information, and extreme partisan schisms prone to sparking political violence. In the worst cases, sortition recruiters would be asking alienated citizens to serve in a system they view as illegitimate, which would amount to putting themselves at risk for no foreseeable purpose. Recruitment would fail in such a setting just as surely as would sortition itself.

In a more favorable political setting, sortition recruitment might still need assistance in the form of incentives and legal protections. We noted in our opening chapter the importance of compensating citizen legislators, but there are also ways of ensuring that their service doesn't diminish the prospects for long-term income earnings. Experience in a sortition body would provide experience in networking, leadership, and deliberation, which has value across a wide variety of professions. Those in more specialized career arcs might need rules that preserve their existing employment or progress toward a degree—akin to the protections given civil and criminal jurors but broader because of the long term of service.

One difficult segment to recruit might be those individuals for whom extended time away from work poses special hazards. Consider those who run small businesses or maintain a thriving freelance practice. In such cases, the individual recruited for sortition may be irreplaceable. Time away from work could force the business to shut down or force their clients to seek services elsewhere. Restarting a practice or business after two to four years of service might prove impossible. Meanwhile, athletes, surgeons, or others whose careers have a time clock might have their jobs protected yet find that their skills have deteriorated—or failed to keep up with the competition.

In such cases, however, the question is not whether a particular individual cannot serve but whether a substantive public perspective goes unrepresented. If sortition bodies failed to recruit a young athlete, successful commercial artist, or independent contractor, would the sortition have greater difficulty fulfilling its mission? Put another way, if nonparticipation comes principally from specialized segments of privileged social categories, the interests of those groups will likely find full expression through other means.

More serious is the risk that incentives and safeguards prove insufficient to bring into the sortition body the voice of disadvantaged groups. The toughest cases are individuals who have dependents for whom no one else can care adequately. A single parent with young children, or an only child with an elderly parent, might feel that no other relative or professional caregiver could serve as a substitute, and a need for round-the-clock attention makes it useless to move the family to the city where the sortition body convenes.

These cases are more serious because the individuals whom sortition might fail to include have something in common—an appreciation for the value of personal care. Political theorist Joan Tronto has argued for reconfiguring our politics to become a "caring democracy," and excluding these voices might undermine such a project.[21] Still, even if it is impossible to completely eliminate the underrepresentation of people with significant care responsibilities, there are policies that could mitigate the problem. The sortition assembly could provide extensive, appropriate caregiving services and support. Provisions for delay, even for a significant number of years, could allow people to adjust the timing of their participation in an assembly. One might even imagine ways in which some sortition chamber participants could mix attending sessions in person with various forms of remote, cyber participation.

The Transition to Sortition

Experimentation with sortition's transitional forms may help address problems such as those we have revisited, including the integrity of sortition legislators and the effectiveness of their recruitment. One must recognize, however, that the transition problem and the end-state institutional form of sortition are not entirely distinct. That is, an experimentalist approach to creating democratic institutions means building the new institution over time and in ways that may not be foreseeable at the outset. The challenge for reformers is to figure out initial forms of sortition that can evolve into a fuller implementation through experimentation, rather than becoming a permanent obstacle to fuller implementation. We have shown that social context can affect how sortition works, but it can also create path dependencies for how sortition *evolves*.

This form of context dependency means that there probably exists no single optimal path for transitioning to a full sortition chamber. At the broadest level, the transition to sortition has different implications in societies with fundamentally different approaches to elections and the structure of government. For example, it matters whether the public elects a president or the legislature chooses its prime minister. In the latter case, it's unclear which chamber in a bicameral model such as ours would make that all-important choice. Even the very idea of random selection has a different meaning in countries with the jury system, for which the transitional phase of convening "policy juries" has more resonance.

More fundamentally, sortition-based reforms could involve delicate institutional redesign for the wider system, rather than just grafting it directly into that system. If sortition has the capacity to inspire more public engagement on issues, what channels might need to widen to accommodate public input? Or sortition might spur the creation of a more robust public media in societies that lack such a system. Even routine practices, such as the statistical services provided by government agencies, might change if the sortition body has informational needs that require collecting and reporting basic data in new ways. Whatever path sortition takes, it will be important to track the changing nature of related public institutions and social practices.

At this time, we might not be able to see past the first step on the path to sortition. Even so, we see at least three promising starting points. One path would begin with consultative mini-publics on special issues (such as election reforms), which would then expand gradually to address a greater variety of issues with greater authority or influence.[22] A second approach would infuse sortition into otherwise elected or appointed bodies to build confidence in the role of lay citizens. In proportional representation systems, that could happen via permitting voters to choose sortition rather than candidates on their ballots.[23] A third option launches wholesale sortition in low-stakes polities, such as student government, nongovernmental organizations, or even within government bodies.[24] Lessons learned there could be critical to the more high-stakes transitions to sortition in political institutions.

The bottom line is that conjecture can only get one so far. To move from the concept of a legislature elected by lot to an actual institution will require experimentation, attention to contextual circumstances, and recalibration of the institutional setting in which sortition develops. In time, we expect sortition may fare well among its democratic alternatives and prove that even with all the complexities of the present century, the public can, indeed, govern itself.

Notes

1. Legislature by Lot: Envisioning Sortition Within a Bicameral System, *Gastil and Wright*

1. For more on these three solutions, see the following: Bruce Ackerman and Ian Ayers, *Voting with Dollars: A New Paradigm for Campaign Finance* (London: Yale University Press, 2004); a special issue of *Representation* (50:1, 2014) provides insight into how less conventional voting systems influence the strategic behavior of parties, candidates, and public officials; Bruce Ackerman and James S. Fishkin, *Deliberation Day* (London: Yale University Press, 2005).

2. Josiah Ober, "What the Ancient Greeks Can Tell Us About Democracy," *Annual Review of Political Science* 11 (2008): 67–91.

3. Speech given in September at the 2017 *New York Times* Athens Democracy Forum.

4. Current reports are available at the Electoral Integrity Project website, www.electoralintegrityproject.com. Also see Terrill Bouricius, David Schecter, Campbell Wallace, and John Gastil, "Imagine a Democracy Built on Lotteries, Not Elections—Nexus," *Zócalo Public Square* (April 5, 2016).

5. See, for example, Lawrence Lessig, *Republic, Lost: How Money Corrupts Congress—and a Plan to Stop It* (New York: Grand Central Publishing, 2011).

6. For a deliberative critique of legislative elections in particular, see John Gastil, *By Popular Demand: Revitalizing Representative Democracy Through Deliberative Elections* (Berkeley: University of California Press, 2000).

7. Direct evidence of candidate personality traits is hard to come by, but research suggests that they have a meaningful link to ideological orientation and behavior. See Bryce J. Dietrich, Scott Lasley,

Jeffery J. Mondak, Megan L. Remmel, and Joel Turner, "Personality and Legislative Politics: The Big Five Trait Dimensions Among U.S. State Legislators," *Political Psychology* 33 (2012): 195–210.

8. This problem is exacerbated for women: see Jennifer L. Lawless and Richard L. Fox, *It Takes a Candidate: Why Women Don't Run for Office* (New York: Cambridge University Press, 2005).

9. Mark Smith, *American Business and Political Power: Public Opinion, Elections, and Democracy* (Chicago: University of Chicago Press, 2000).

10. Murray Edelman, *Constructing the Political Spectacle* (Chicago: University of Chicago Press, 1988).

11. Even in a political party with a working majority, a minority faction within the party might work with opposition members to thwart a victory for its own party leadership.

12. Current data are available at Gallup and Pew Research Center online.

13. See the 2017 online OECD report, *Government at a Glance*, available at www.oecd.org/gov/govataglance.htm. The figures for trust in parties refers to 2005–13, as reported in the 2013 edition of the OECD report.

14. For an accessible introduction to participatory budgeting, see Josh Lerner, *Everyone Counts: Could "Participatory Budgeting" Change Democracy?* (Ithaca, NY: Cornell University Press, 2014). On town meetings and how they could become more powerful, see Frank Bryan and John McClaughry, *The Vermont Papers: Recreating Democracy on a Human Scale* (Port Mills, VT: Chelsea Green, 1989).

15. This has been observed in a wide range of deliberative bodies using lay citizens. See, for instance, Kimmo Grönlund, André Bächtiger, and Maija Setälä, eds., *Deliberative Mini-Publics: Involving Citizens in the Democratic Process* (Colchester, UK: ECPR Press, 2014).

16. See, for example, the emergence of a concern about aboriginal political rights in a national deliberation on political reform held in Canberra; Lyn Carson, John Gastil, Janette Hartz-Karp, and Ron Lubensky, eds., *The Australian Citizens' Parliament and the Future of Deliberative Democracy* (University Park, PA: The Pennsylvania State University Press, 2013).

17. Robert A. Dahl, *Democracy and Its Critics* (New Haven: Yale University Press, 1989).

18. Dahl, *Democracy and Its Critics*, goes farther with this requirement when a demos does more than make rules for its own members. When states make laws enforceable on noncitizens, for example, the inclusion principle requires a demos to "include all adults subject to the binding collective decisions of the

association" (120). This goes beyond the scope of our proposal, but it's interesting to conceive the ways such populations could be mixed into a sortition assembly, perhaps on a provisional basis in relation to specific legislative questions.

19. The Deliberative Poll is a trademark of the Stanford Center for Deliberative Democracy; however, the term is not capitalized in this volume. This method of polling, along with many deliberative processes such as citizens juries, have become so widely adopted and diverse in their designs that their names have become vernacular. Capitalization is reserved for specific instances of processes, such as the 2012–14 Irish Constitutional Convention, and legally designated institutions, such as the Oregon Citizens' Initiative Review.

20. For a review of recent evidence, see Heather Pincock, "Does Deliberation Make Better Citizens?," in *Democracy in Motion: Evaluating the Practice and Impact of Deliberative Civic Engagement*, ed. Tina Nabatchi, John Gastil, Michael Weiksner, and Matt Leighninger (Oxford: Oxford University Press, 2012), 135–62.

21. Dahl, *Democracy and Its Critics*, 112 (italics added for emphasis). The omitted text offers the qualifier, "within the time permitted by the need for a decision." The time required for a small sortition legislature would be considerably less than for a mass public.

22. Figures provided by the CBO online, www.cbo.gov.

23. John Gastil and Peter Levine, eds., *The Deliberative Democracy Handbook: Strategies for Effective Civic Engagement in the Twenty-First Century* (San Francisco: Jossey-Bass, 2005).

24. John Gastil and Robert Richards, "Embracing Digital Democracy: A Call for Building an Online Civic Commons," *PS: Political Science and Politics* 50 (2017): 758–63.

25. Michael A. Neblo, *Deliberative Democracy Between Theory and Practice* (Cambridge: Cambridge University Press, 2015).

26. There are straightforward solutions to these problems; see Daron Shaw, Stephen Ansolabehere, and Charles Stewart, "A Brief yet Practical Guide to Reforming U.S. Voter Registration Systems," *Election Law Journal: Rules, Politics, and Policy* 14 (2015): 26–31. The barrier to such reforms—and the impetus for counterproductive voting laws—is that broader participation would hurt the electoral fortunes of the Republican Party; see Wendy Weiser, "In 22 States, a Wave of New Voting Restrictions Threatens to Shift Outcomes in Tight Races," *The American Prospect* (October 1, 2014).

27. There are risks in using strata in a sample to seek proportionate representation of minorities. Depending on the number of actual people this involves, the result can be that a few individuals from an oppressed group are thrust into the position of "representing

the interests" of "their" group in the assembly. Since these individuals are themselves randomly chosen, there is no reason to believe that they will have the temperament or experience to fulfill this role. For this reason, if a sortition assembly is serious about genuinely representing the interests of marginalized groups, there need to be other mechanisms in place to bring the perspectives of those communities into their deliberation in a meaningful way.

28. On the performance of juries, see Neil Vidmar and Valerie P. Hans, *American Juries: The Verdict* (Amherst, NY: Prometheus Books, 2007). On deliberative citizen bodies generally, see Grönlund et al., *Deliberative Mini-Publics*; Nabatchi et al., *Democracy in Motion*; and Gastil and Levine, *Deliberative Democracy Handbook*.

29. Evidence of the impact deliberation has on Australian and US participants appears in Katherine R. Knobloch and John Gastil, "Civic (Re)socialisation: The Educative Effects of Deliberative Participation," *Politics* 35 (2015): 183–200. On similar impacts on American jurors, see John Gastil, E. Pierre Deess, Philip J. Weiser, and Cindy Simmons, *The Jury and Democracy: How Jury Deliberation Promotes Civic Engagement and Political Participation* (Oxford: Oxford University Press, 2010).

30. UK government data accessed online July 2016.

31. Existing legislatures in most places are heavily biased toward people with wealth and high incomes. Whatever other problems in demographic representativeness a sortition assembly might have, it will certainly be a substantial improvement in terms of socioeconomic representativeness. See, for example, Martin Gilens and Benjamin I. Page, "Testing Theories of American Politics: Elites, Interest Groups, and Average Citizens," *Perspectives on Politics* 12 (2014): 564–81.

32. Alexander Guerrero, "Forget Voting—It's Time to Start Choosing Our Leaders by Lottery," *Aeon* (January 23, 2014).

33. Mark E. Warren and Hilary Pearse, eds., *Designing Deliberative Democracy: The British Columbia Citizens' Assembly* (Cambridge: Cambridge University Press, 2008).

34. Benjamin Snyder, "14% of Zappos' Staff Left After Being Offered Exit Pay," *Fortune* (May 8, 2015).

35. Aspen Institute program details accessed online July 2016 from its website, www.aspeninstitute.org.

36. Kennedy School program details accessed online July 2016 from its website, www.hks.harvard.edu.

37. State-by-state details on Next Generation workshops are available at the National Institute for Civil Discourse site, nicd.arizona.edu.

38. See for example, Carol S. Weissert and William G. Weissert, "State

Legislative Staff Influence in Health Policy Making," *Journal of Health Politics, Policy and Law* 25 (2000): 1121–48.

39. Alan Rosenthal, "The Good Legislature," *State Legislatures* (August 1999).

40. Andy Sullivan, "Insight: In Washington, Lawmakers' Routines Shaped by Fundraising," *Reuters* (June 12, 2013).

41. Claudio Maria Radaelli, *Technocracy in the European Union* (London: Longman, 1999).

42. Hank Jenkins-Smith, *Democratic Politics and Policy Analysis* (Pacific Grove, CA: Brooks/Cole, 1990).

43. This idea is adapted from a May 18, 2018, correspondence with Nicholas Gruen of Lateral Economics, who suggested an even stronger role for random selection in the commission election. In his scheme, the first step would create a modest slate of legislators eligible for the commission. A ballot listing these names would then let sortition legislators indicate whether any of those individuals were unfit to serve in that capacity. Those who failed to meet a high threshold would be removed from consideration, with random selection choosing commissioners from those who remain. To avoid embarrassment, the process would operate by secret ballot, with no public record of which names were removed prior to the final random selection.

44. The founder of the citizens' jury process argues along these lines—both for facilitation and experimentation and research on any new citizen body; see Ned Crosby, *System Four: A New Form of Democracy* (Unpublished manuscript, 1976). The Australian nongovernmental organization newDemocracy, for example, is experimenting with exercises wherein citizens critique prospective policies, or expert testimony on them, in terms of preset criteria (logic and depth, for example) to sharpen citizens' skills at critical thinking and deliberation (personal correspondence with Lyn Carson, October 2016).

45. Joseph M. Bessette, *The Mild Voice of Reason: Deliberative Democracy and American National Government* (Chicago: University of Chicago Press, 1997).

46. Bessette, *The Mild Voice of Reason*. Also see Amy Gutmann and Dennis Frank Thompson, *The Spirit of Compromise: Why Governing Demands It and Campaigning Undermines It* (Princeton: Princeton University Press, 2014).

47. Warren and Pearse, *Designing Deliberative Democracy*.

48. Technically, such rooms are often not fully private, but only researchers are likely to venture into them. Some minipublics even have a decision-making phase closed from public scrutiny, such that the participants cannot be identified individually with the particular votes that were cast. Other processes, such as the

deliberative poll, do not vote at all but record attitudes via confidential pre- and postdeliberation surveys; see James S. Fishkin, *When the People Speak* (Oxford: Oxford University Press, 2009).

49. John Gastil, Katherine R. Knobloch, Dan Kahan, and Don Braman, "Participatory Policymaking Across Cultural Cognitive Divides: Two Tests of Cultural Biasing in Public Forum Design and Deliberation," *Public Administration* 94 (2016): 970–87. A broader conception of consensus suggests other kinds of agreements that can be reached, short of policy agreement, per se; see Simon Niemeyer and John S. Dryzek, "The Ends of Deliberation: Meta-Consensus and Inter-Subjective Rationality as Ideal Outcomes," *Swiss Political Science Review* 13 (2007): 497–526.

50. Christopher F. Karpowitz, Chad Raphael, and Allen S. Hammond IV, "Deliberative Democracy and Inequality: Two Cheers for Enclave Deliberation Among the Disempowered," *Politics & Society* 37 (2009): 576–615.

51. Linking pay to attendance might help keep legislators present, but it can't regulate their behavior.

52. A special issue of the *Journal of Public Deliberation* (8:2, 2012) provides a range of views on participatory budgeting.

53. Jessica McKenzie, "Small but Successful Participatory Democracy Experiment to Continue in Utah," *Civic Hall* (August 4, 2015). For background, see Jeffrey Swift, "The People's Lobby: A Model for Online Activist Deliberation," *Journal of Public Deliberation* 9:2 (2013).

54. Current information available at citizenassembly.co.uk.

55. John R. Hibbing and Elizabeth Theiss-Morse, "A Surprising Number of Americans Dislike How Messy Democracy Is. They Like Trump," *Washington Post* (May 2, 2016).

56. The basic argument appears in Jane J. Mansbridge, *Beyond Adversary Democracy* (Chicago: University of Chicago Press, 1983). Also, see the essay Mansbridge coauthored with numerous colleagues, "The Place of Self-Interest and the Role of Power in Deliberative Democracy," *Journal of Political Philosophy* 18 (2010): 64–100.

57. See the special issue of *Representation* (50:1, 2014).

58. Party primaries within each district would determine the candidates who vie for votes in the general election.

59. Recent examples are available online from the Sortition Foundation, www.sortitionfoundation.org.

60. See Patrick Heller, "Moving the State: The Politics of Democratic Decentralization in Kerala, South Africa, and Porto Alegre," *Politics and Society* 29 (2001): 131–63.

61. Benjamin R. Barber, *The Death of Communal Liberty: A History*

of *Freedom in a Swiss Mountain Canton* (Princeton: Princeton University Press, 2015). Also see Matthias Benz and Alois Stutzer, "Are Voters Better Informed When They Have a Larger Say in Politics? Evidence for the European Union and Switzerland," *Public Choice* 119 (2004): 31–59.

62. Personal communication from the Icelandic sociologist Kris Arsaelsson, 2016.

63. A basic description is available at Participedia.net.

64. See, for example, work by the Native Nations Institute online, nni.arizona.edu.

65. Chris Wells, *The Civic Organization and the Digital Citizen: Communicating Engagement in a Networked Age* (Oxford: Oxford University Press, 2015).

2. Postscript: The Anticapitalist Argument for Sortition, *Wright*

1. This was the crux of a famous debate between Ralph Miliband and Nicos Poulantzas in the 1970s over whether the state should be viewed as *a state within capitalist society* or as a *capitalist state*.

2. Thus Lenin described bourgeois democracy as the "best possible shell" for capitalism. Others, more modestly, see democratic institutions in the capitalist state as creating obstacles for anticapitalist policies rather than necessarily producing optimal policies for capitalism. This, for example, is Claus Offe's view in his arguments about the class biases of negative selectivity in the design of state institutions and, using slightly different terms, Göran Therborn's argument about the class character of the organizational properties of state apparatuses.

3. There is a vast Marxist-influenced literature that makes this argument. For an analytically rigorous version of the argument, see Adam Przeworski, *Capitalism and Social Democracy* (New York: Cambridge University Press, 1986). For an extended discussion of the specific ways in which capitalist democracy impedes anticapitalist possibilities, see Joshua Cohen and Joel Rogers, *On Democracy* (New York: Penguin, 1983).

4. For a discussion of socialism as a radically democratic and egalitarian economic structure, see Erik Olin Wright, "The Socialist Compass," in *Envisioning Real Utopias* (London and New York: Verso, 2010).

5. The expression was coined by André Gorz, *Strategy for Labor: A Radical Proposal* (Boston: Beacon Press, 1976).

3. From Deliberative to Radical Democracy: Sortition and Politics in the Twenty-First Century, *Sintomer*

1. Hubertus Buchstein, "Countering the 'Democracy Thesis'— Sortition in Ancient Greek Political Theory," *Redescriptions* 18:2 (Autumn 2015): 126–57.
2. Aristotle, *The Politics* (Harmondsworth: Penguin, 1962), 168; translation modified.
3. Jacques Rancière, *Hatred of Democracy* (London: Verso, 2009), 47.
4. Bernard Manin, *Principles of Representative Government* (Cambridge: Cambridge University Press, 1997).
5. Yves Sintomer, *From Radical to Deliberative Democracy? Random Selection in Politics from Athens to the Present* (Cambridge: Cambridge University Press, 2019, forthcoming); Liliane Lopez-Rabatel and Yves Sintomer, eds., *Sortition and Democracy: Practices, Tools, Theories* (Exeter: Imprint Academic, 2019, forthcoming).
6. Antoine Vergne, "Le Modèle *Planungszelle*-Citizen Jury," in *La Démocratie Participative Inachevée: Genèse, Adaptations et Diffusions*, eds. Marie-Hélène Bacqué and Yves Sintomer (Paris: Yves Michel, 2010), 83–100.
7. Simon Joss and James Durant, eds., *Public Participation in Science: The Role of Consensus Conference in Europe* (London: Science Museum, 1995).
8. James Fishkin and Cynthia Farrar, "Deliberative Polling: From Experiment to Community Resource," in *The Deliberative Democracy Handbook*, ed. John Gastil and Peter Levine (San Francisco: Jossey-Bass, 2005), 68–79.
9. Robert A. Dahl, *After the Revolution? Authority in a Good Society* (New Haven: Yale University Press, 1970).
10. Peter Dienel, *Die Planungszelle* (Wiesbaden: Westdeutscher Verlag, 1997); Ned Crosby, *In Search of the Competent Citizen* (Plymouth: Center for New Democratic Processes, 2005); Denis C. Mueller, Robert D. Tollison, and Thomas Willet, "Representative Democracy via Random Selection," *Public Choice* 12 (1972): 57–68.
11. Jürgen Habermas, *Between Facts and Norms: Contributions to a Discourse Theory of Law and Democracy*, trans. William Rehg (Cambridge: MIT Press, 1996); John Dryzek, *Discursive Democracy: Politics, Policy, and Political Science* (Cambridge: Cambridge University Press, 1990); Jon Elster, ed., *Deliberative Democracy* (Cambridge: Cambridge University Press, 1988).
12. Julien Talpin, "Deliberative Democracy and Sortition in Politics: A Critical Assessment," in *Sortition and Democracy*.

13. Richard Sclove, *Democracy and Technology* (New York: Guilford Press, 2015); Michel Callon, Pierre Lascoumes, and Yannick Barthe, *Acting in an Uncertain World: An Essay on Technical Democracy* (Cambridge: MIT Press, 2011).

14. Benjamin Barber, *Strong Democracy: Participatory Politics for a New Age* (Berkeley/London: University of California Press, 1984); John Burnheim, *Is Democracy Possible?* (Cambridge: Polity Press, 1985); Ernest Callenbach and Michael Philips, *A Citizen Legislature* (Berkeley: Banyan Tree/Clear Glass, 1985); Lyn Carson and Brian Martin, *Random Selection in Politics* (Westport: Praeger Publishers, 1999); Robert A. Dahl, "The Problem of Civic Competence," *Journal of Democracy* 3:4 (October 1992): 45–59; John Gastil, *By Popular Demand: Revitalizing Representative Democracy Through Deliberative Elections* (Berkeley: University of California Press, 2000); Barbara Goodwin, *Justice by Lottery* (New York: Harvester Wheatsheaf, 2012); Bernard Manin, *Principles of Representative Government*; Yves Sintomer, *Le Pouvoir au Peuple: Jurys Citoyens, Tirage au Sort et Démocratie Participative* (Paris: La Découverte, 2007); Hubertus Buchstein, *Demokratie und Lotterie: Das Los als Politisches Entscheidungsinstrument von der Antike bis zu EU* (Frankfurt/ Main: Campus, 2009); David van Reybrouck, *Against Elections* (New York: Seven Stories Press, 2016).

15. "The Jury Selection and Service Act," 28 U.S.C., secs 1861–9.

16. James S. Fishkin, *The Voice of the People: Public Opinion & Democracy* (New Haven/London: Yale University Press, 1997), 162.

17. Mogens Herman Hansen, *Athenian Democracy in the Age of Demosthenes* (Oxford: Basil Blackwell, 1991), 231–2.

18. Aristotle, *The Politics*, III: 2, 1275a; Aristotle, *The Athenian Constitution* (Harmondsworth: Penguin, 1984), 110–2.

19. Liliane Lopez-Rabatel, "Sortition in Athens: Instruments and Words," in *Sortition and Democracy*.

20. Bernard Manin, "Comment Promouvoir la Délibération Démocratique? Priorité du Débat Contradictoire sur la Discussion," *Raisons Politiques* 42 (2011): 83–113.

21. Moses I. Finley, *The Invention of Politics* (Cambridge: Cambridge University Press, 1991), 73f.

22. Anja Röcke, *Losverfahren und Demokratie: Historische und Demokratietheoretische Perspektiven* (Münster: LIT, 2005); Yves Sintomer, *Petite Histoire de L'expérimentation Démocratique: Tirage au Sort et Politique d'Athènes à nos Jours* (Paris: La Découverte, 2011).

23. Peter Stone, "The Logic of Random Selection," *Political Theory* 37 (2009): 390.

24. Jeffrey B. Abramson, *We the Jury. The Jury System and the Ideal of Democracy*, 3rd ed. (Cambridge/London: Harvard University Press, 2003).

25. Ian Hacking, *The Taming of Chance* (Cambridge: Cambridge University Press, 1990).

26. Mirabeau, "Discours Devant les États de Provence," in *Œuvres de Mirabeau* (1825), VII:7, quoted in Pierre Rosanvallon, *Le Peuple Introuvable: Histoire de la Représentation Démocratique en France* (Paris: Gallimard, 1998).

27. Bernard Manin, *Principles of Representative Government*.

28. Ibid.

29. Yves Sintomer, "Random Selection, Republican Self-Government, and Deliberative Democracy," *Constellations* 17:3 (2010): 472–87.

30. Hans-Liudger Dienel, "Les Jurys Citoyens: Pourquoi Sont-Ils Encore Si Rarement Utilisés?" in *La Démocratie Participative Inachevée*, 105.

31. Tarso Genro and Ubiratan de Souza, *Orçamento Participativo: A Experiência de Porto Alegre* (São Paulo: Fundação Perseu Abramo, 1997); Archon Fung and Erick Olin Wright, eds., *Deepening Democracy. Institutional Innovations in Empowered Participatory Governance* (London/New York: Verso, 2003); Boaventura de Sousa Santos, ed., *Democratizing Democracy: Beyond the Liberal Democratic Canon* (London/New York: Verso, 2005).

32. Jane Suiter, David Farrell, and Clodagh Harris, "The Irish Constitutional Convention: A Case of 'High Legitimacy'?" in *Constitutional Deliberative Democracy in Europe*, ed. Min Reuchamps and Jane Suiter (Colchester: ECPR Press, 2016), 33–52.

33. Didier Caluwaerts, *Confrontation and Communication: Deliberative Democracy in Divided Belgium* (Brussels: European Interuniversity Press, 2012); Inge Henneman et al., *G1000, Le Rapport Final: L'innovation Démocratique Mise en Pratique* (Brussels, 2012); Vincent Jacquet et al., "The Macro-Political Uptake of the G1000 in Belgium," in *Constitutional Deliberative Democracy in Europe*, 53–74.

34. John Gastil, *By Popular Demand*.

35. Katherine R. Knobloch et al., "Did They Deliberate? Applying an Evaluative Model of Democratic Deliberation to the Oregon Citizens' Initiative Review," *Journal of Applied Communication Research* 41:2 (2013): 105–25; Katherine R. Knobloch et al., *Evaluation Report on the 2012 Citizens' Initiative Reviews for the Oregon CIR Commission* (State College: Pennsylvania State University, 2013); Katherine R. Knobloch, John Gastil, and Tyrone Reitman, "Connecting Micro-Deliberation to Electoral

Decision-Making: Institutionalizing the Oregon Citizens' Initiative," in *Deliberation: Values, Processes, Institutions*, ed. Stephen Coleman, Anna Przybylska, and Yves Sintomer (Frankfurt/Main: Peter Lang, 2015), 21–40.

36. John Gastil, Katherine R. Knobloch, Justin Reedy, Mark Henkels, and Katherine Cramer, "Assessing the Electoral Impact of the 2010 Oregon Citizens' Initiative Review," *American Politics Research* 46:3 (2018): 534–63.

37. Anja Röcke and Yves Sintomer, "Les Jurys de Citoyens Berlinois et le Tirage au Sort," in *Gestion de Proximité et Démocratie Participative*, ed. Marie-Hélène Bacqué, Henry Rey, and Yves Sintomer (Paris: La Découverte, 2005), 139–60.

38. Yves Sintomer, Carsten Herzberg, and Anja Röcke, *Participatory Budgeting in Europe: Democracy and Public Governance* (London: Ashgate, 2016).

39. Baogang He, "Participatory Budgeting in China: An Overview," in *Participatory Budgeting in Asia and Europe: Key Challenges of Deliberative Democracy*, ed. Yves Sintomer, Rudolf Traub-Merz, and Junhua Zhang (Hong Kong: Palgrave, 2011); Joseph Cheng, Yu Sheh, and Fan Li, "Local Government's Consultative Budgetary Reforms in China: A Case Study of Wenling City," *China International Journal* 13:1 (April 2015): 115–8.

40. Munkhsaikhan Odonkhuu, "Mongolia's (Flawed) Experiment with Deliberative Polling in Constitutional Reform," *ConstitutionNet* (June 29, 2017).

41. Maxime Mellina, "Une expérience démocratique de tirage au sort à la Fédération des associations d'étudiants de l'Université de Lausanne? Représentativité, effets symboliques et délibération," *Participations* (forthcoming, 2019).

42. Dimitri Courant, "Délibération et tirage au sort au sein d'une institution permanente: Sociologie du Conseil Supérieur de la Fonction Militaire (1968–2016)," *Participations* (forthcoming, 2019).

43. Mauro Buonocore, "Un Weekend Deliberativo all'Ombra del Partenone," *Reset* 96 (July–August 2006): 6–8.

44. Yves Sintomer, *From Radical to Deliberative Democracy?*

45. José Antonio Aguilar Rivera, "Las Razones de la Tómbola," *Nexos* (April 1, 2015).

46. Robert E. Goodin and John Dryzeck, "Deliberative Impacts: The Macro-Political Uptake of Minipublics," *Politics and Society* 34 (2006): 219–44.

47. David Held, *Models of Democracy*, 3rd ed. (Cambridge: Polity Press, 2006).

48. Yves Sintomer, "Délibération et Participation: Affinité Élective ou Concepts en Tension?" *Participations. Revue de Sciences Sociales*

sur la Démocratie et la Citoyenneté 1 (2011): 239–76.

49. Simone Chambers, "Rhetoric and the Public Sphere: Has Deliberative Democracy Abandoned Mass Democracy?" *Political Theory* 37:3 (June 2009): 323–50.

50. Archon Fung, "Deliberation Before the Revolution: Toward an Ethics of Deliberative Democracy in an Unjust World," *Political Theory* 33 (2005): 397–419.

51. Yves Sintomer, *Le Pouvoir au Peuple*.

52. Shaoguang Wang, *Democracy, Republic and Sortition: From Athens to Venice* (in Chinese; Beijing: CITIC Press, 2018).

53. James S. Fishkin, "Reviving Deliberative Democracy: Reflections on Recent Experiments," in *Deliberation: Values, Processes, Institutions*, 99–108.

54. Gordon Gibson, "Deliberative Democracy and the B.C. Citizens' Assembly," speech delivered on February 23, 2007.

55. Pierre Rosanvallon, *La Contre-Démocratie*.

56. Dominique Bourg et al., *Pour une Sixième République Écologique* (Paris: Odile Jaco, 2011); Rupert Read, *Guardians of the Future: A Constitutional Case for Representing and Protecting Future People* (Weymouth: Green House, 2012); Michael K. MacKenzie, "A General-Purpose, Randomly Selected Chamber," in *Institutions for Future Generations*, ed. Iñigo González-Ricoy and Axel Gosseries (Oxford: Oxford University Press, 2016).

57. Lyn Carson and Brian Martin, *Random Selection in Politics*, 13–4.

58. Hélène Landemore, *Democratic Reason: Politics, Collective Intelligence, and the Rule of the Many* (Princeton: Princeton University Press, 2012); Jon Elster, *Securities Against Misrule: Juries, Assemblies, Elections* (Cambridge: Cambridge University Press, 2013).

4. Random Assemblies for Lawmaking: Prospects and Limits, *Fishkin*

1. In this essay, I draw on points developed in more depth in *Democracy When the People Are Thinking: Revitalizing Our Politics Through Public Deliberation* (Oxford: Oxford University Press, 2018).

2. For an overview of current challenges facing deliberative democracy, see James S. Fishkin and Jane Mansbridge, introduction to "The Prospects and Limits of Deliberative Democracy," *Daedalus* 146:3 (Summer 2017): 6–13.

3. I build here on the discussion in James S. Fishkin, "Competing Visions," in *When the People Speak: Deliberative Democracy*

and Public Consultation (Oxford: Oxford University Press, 2009), 65–94. Here I will use the scheme for different purposes.

4. For more on non-tyranny as a principle of democratic theory, see James S. Fishkin, *Tyranny and Legitimacy: A Critique of Political Theories* (Baltimore: Johns Hopkins University Press, 1979).

5. See Fishkin, "Appendix: Why We Only Need Four Democratic Theories," in *When the People Speak,* 197–200.

6. Joseph A. Schumpeter, *Capitalism, Socialism and Democracy* (New York: Harper and Row, 1942); Richard Posner, *Law, Pragmatism and Democracy* (Cambridge: Harvard University Press, 2003). See also Ian Shapiro, *The State of Democratic Theory* (Princeton: Princeton University Press, 2003).

7. Robert A. Dahl, *Democracy and Its Critics* (New Haven: Yale University Press, 1989), 121.

8. For a discussion of the problem of inclusion in modern democracies, see Fishkin, *Democracy When the People Are Thinking,* 14–7.

9. Schumpeter, *Capitalism, Socialism and Democracy,* 263.

10. Tyranny through omission, through failures to act to provide needed resources or protect against actions by third parties, is a particular vulnerability. See my *Tyranny and Legitimacy* for an attempt to systematically review the possibilities.

11. See, for example, Federalist 63. For the many uses of this event for antidemocratic argument, see Jennifer Tolman Roberts, *Athens on Trial* (Princeton: Princeton University Press, 1994).

12. Carole Pateman, *Participation and Democratic Theory* (Cambridge: Cambridge University Press, 1976).

13. See Project Vote Smart's website for the provision of a great deal of very user-friendly information to voters, votesmart.org.

14. For an overview, see David Magleby, *Direct Legislation: Voting on Ballot Propositions* (Baltimore: Johns Hopkins University Press, 1984). For the relative ineffectiveness of voter handbooks and other efforts to get voters more informed, see 137–9. For an account of the tensions between direct and deliberative democracy, as well as proposed remedies, see John Gastil and Robert Richards, "Making Direct Democracy Deliberative Through Random Assemblies," *Politics and Society* 41:2 (2013): 253–81.

15. Bruce Ackerman and James S. Fishkin, *Deliberation Day* (New Haven / London: Yale University Press, 2004).

16. Thad Kousser, *Term Limits and the Dismantling of State Legislative Professionalism* (Cambridge: Cambridge University Press, 2004).

17. See Mark E. Warren and Hilary Pearse, eds., *Designing Deliberative Democracy: The British Columbia Citizens' Assembly* (Cambridge: Cambridge University Press, 2008); Patrick Fournier, Henk van

der Kolk, R. Kenneth Carty, Andre Blais, and Jonathan Rose, *When Citizens Decide: Lessons from Citizens' Assemblies on Electoral Reform* (Oxford: Oxford University Press, 2011).

18. See Fishkin, *Democracy When the People Are Thinking*, part III and part IV, section 2.

19. In Texas the deliberative poll was the only method used for integrated resource planning by the Public Utility Commission for every (then) regulated utility. In Japan the Fukushima national deliberative poll was commissioned by the government to help it make a decision about nuclear power. In Macau, the government convened a deliberative poll to decide whether there would be government involvement in a press council. The citizen deliberations turned against government involvement, a conclusion that was accepted by the government. In Mongolia the "Law on Deliberative Polling" requires a national deliberative poll before the parliament can consider constitutional amendments. There are also requirements for local deliberative polls for certain urban planning issues. For more on these cases, see Stanford's website for its Center for Deliberative Democracy, cdd.stanford.edu.

20. Josiah Ober, *Democracy and Knowledge: Innovation and Learning in Classical Greece* (Princeton: Princeton University Press, 2010).

21. I take the term *first democracy* from Paul Woodruff, *First Democracy: The Challenge of an Ancient Idea* (Oxford: Oxford University Press, 2005).

22. Mogens Herman Hansen, *The Athenian Democracy in the Age of Demosthenes* (Oxford: Blackwell, 1991), 303.

23. Hansen, *The Athenian Democracy*, 307.

24. A. R. W. Harrison, "Law-Making at Athens at the End of the Fifth Century B.C," *Journal of Hellenic Studies* 75 (1955): 34.

25. Grote notes that the *graphe paranomon* did not always work as intended. It could degenerate into a forum for personal attacks, turning "deliberative into judicial eloquence, and interweaving the discussion of a law or decree along with a declamatory harangue against the character of its mover." George Grote, *A History of Greece* (Cambridge: Cambridge University Press, 2010), 401–2.

26. The *nomothetai* also now faced its own version of the *graphe paranomon* designed also to incentivize responsible debate. See Hansen, *The Athenian Democracy*, 166.

27. Grote, *A History of Greece*, 399.

28. R. K. Sinclair, *Democracy and Participation in Athens* (Cambridge: Cambridge University Press, 1988), 70–1.

29. When participation flagged, incentives were instituted, which led

to criticism that these institutions, especially the juries that were constituted in the same way, were dominated by the poor and the elderly. The propensity of the poor and the elderly to do jury service was satirized by Aristophanes in *The Wasps*. See Aristophanes, *Clouds, Wasps and Peace*, ed. and trans. Jeffrey Henderson (Cambridge: Harvard University Press, 1998).

30. Sinclair, *Democracy and Participation in Athens*, 18n666.
31. Aristotle's *Politics* 1317b2, cited in Hansen, *The Athenian Democracy*, 313.
32. Hansen, *The Athenian Democracy*, 314.
33. The end of the story is not clear as of this writing. It will be posted on the Stanford Center for Deliberative Democracy website, cdd.stanford.edu.
34. See, for example, Ernest Callenbach and Michael Phillips, *A Citizen Legislature* (Berkeley: Banyan Tree Books, 1985); Keith Sutherland, *A People's Parliament* (London: Academic Imprint, 2008).
35. For an experiment within a deliberative poll that shows the added effect of discussion as opposed to just the provision of information, see Cynthia Farrar, James Fishkin, Donald P. Green, Christian List, Robert C. Luskin, and Elizabeth Levy Paluck, "Disaggregating Deliberation's Effects: An Experiment Within a Deliberative Poll," *British Journal of Political Science* 40:2 (2010): 333–47.
36. James S. Fishkin, Thad Kousser, Robert C. Luskin, and Alice Siu, "Deliberative Agenda Setting: Piloting Reform of Direct Democracy in California," *Perspectives on Politics* 13:4 (2015): 1030–42.
37. Arthur Lupia, "Shortcuts Versus Encyclopedias: Information and Voting Behavior in California Insurance Reform Elections," *The American Political Science Review* 88:1 (1994): 63–76.
38. Michael Binder, Cheryl Boudreau, and Thad Kousser, "Shortcuts to Deliberation? How Cues Reshape the Role of Information in Direct Democracy Voting," *California Western Law Review* 48:1 (2011): 97–128.
39. Precautions such as an added comparison group for matching might also be advisable in case of any imperfections in the sample. Matching will show whether small imperfections make any difference to the overall results. Stratified random sampling should be based on demographics and, where appropriate, geography, to ensure inclusion of relevant subgroups. Comparisons of participants and nonparticipants can be used to analyze any distortions in the sample, either attitudinal or demographic.

5. Lessons from a Hybrid Sortition Chamber: The 2012–14 Irish Constitutional Convention, *Arnold, Farrell, and Suiter*

1. Tom Arnold was the chair of the convention. David Farrell and Jane Suiter were, respectively, the chair and deputy chair of the Academic and Legal Support Group (ALSG) that supported the work of the convention. The survey work referred to in this chapter was carried out by Farrell and Suiter in conjunction with Clodagh Harris and Eoin O'Malley (two other members of the ALSG).

2. On mixed sortition chambers, see the chapter in this volume by Pierre-Étienne Vandamme and colleagues.

3. Gil Delannoi and Oliver Dowlen, *Sortition: Theory and Practice* (Exeter: Imprint Academic, 2010).

4. William Roche, Philip O'Connell, and Andy Prothero, eds., *Austerity and Recovery in Ireland: Europe's Poster Child and the Great Recession* (Oxford: Oxford University Press, 2016).

5. David Farrell, "Political Reform in a Time of Crisis," in *Austerity and Recovery in Ireland*, 160–76.

6. Jane Suiter, David Farrell, and Clodagh Harris, "Ireland's Evolving Constitution," in *Constitutional Acceleration Within the European Union and Beyond*, ed. Paul Blokker (London: Routledge, 2018), 142–54.

7. For further discussion, see David Farrell, Eoin O'Malley, and Jane Suiter, "Deliberative Democracy in Action Irish-Style: The 2011 *We the Citizens* Pilot Citizens' Assembly," *Irish Political Studies* 28 (2013): 99–113.

8. For analysis, see Jane Suiter and David Farrell, "The Parties' Manifestos," in *How Ireland Voted 2011*, ed. Michael Gallagher and Michael Marsh (Houndmills, Basingstoke: Palgrave Macmillan, 2011), 277–93.

9. For more, see *Fine Gael: Let's Get Ireland Working* (Fine Gael Manifesto, 2011); *One Ireland: Jobs, Reform, Fairness* (Labour Manifesto, 2011).

10. Programme for Government, 2011–16, Department of the Taoiseach, 2011.

11. This refers to Article 41.2 of the constitution, which states that "mothers shall not be obliged by economic necessity to engage in labour to the neglect of their duties in the home."

12. Programme for Government, 2011–16.

13. This memorandum (which has not been published) was subsequently provided to Tom Arnold when he assumed the position of chair.

14. Patrick Fournier, Henk van der Kolk, Kenneth Carty, André Blais, and Jonathan Rose, *When Citizens Decide: Lessons from Citizen Assemblies on Electoral Reform* (Oxford: Oxford University Press, 2011).

15. Farrell, O'Malley, and Suiter, "Deliberative Democracy in Action Irish-Style."

16. Another significant point of difference was the broader range of topics the convention was tasked with considering.

17. Terms of Reference for the Irish Constitutional Convention, presented to the Irish parliament in July 2012.

18. The Good Friday agreement of 1998, and its later review in the 2006 Saint Andrews Agreement, are the cornerstones of the Northern Ireland peace process. For more, see Niall Ó Dochartaigh, Katy Hayward, and Elizabeth Meehan, eds., *Dynamics of Political Change in Ireland: Making and Breaking a Divided Island* (London: Routledge, 2017). We can only speculate as to why reference was made in the memorandum to the Good Friday process, but it is likely that one reason was to ensure buy-in from the Sinn Féin party, which has elected representatives on both sides of the border in Ireland. In its 2011 manifesto (*Towards a New Republic*, Sinn Féin, 2011) the party had proposed an "all-Ireland Constitutional Forum."

19. Speech by Taoiseach Enda Kenny to the Dáil, July 10, 2012.

20. This lack of willingness to engage on the part of the Unionist parties is the common position both parties hold to any initiative that has an all-Ireland dimension to it.

21. For a sample of criticisms, see "Fine Words Don't Do Collins Justice," *Irish Independent* (editorial, August 20, 2012); "The Way Politics Is Done," *Irish Times* (editorial, July 12, 2012); Noel Whelan, "Constitutional Convention Will Have Its Remit Severely Pruned," *Irish Times* (February 25, 2012); Fintan O'Toole, "Tammany Hall Lives on in Feeble Reforms," *Irish Times* (June 28, 2012).

22. Notably Fournier et al., *When Citizens Decide*.

23. This reporting process is common to many minipublics and was developed into an elaborate system of "theme teams" in the AmericaSpeaks large-meeting process, which it called Twenty-First Century Town Meetings. See Carolyn J. Lukensmeyer, Joe Goldman, and Steven Brigham, "A Town Meeting for the Twenty-First Century," in *The Deliberative Democracy Handbook: Strategies for Effective Civic Engagement in the Twenty-First Century*, ed. John Gastil and Peter Levine (San Francisco, CA: Jossey-Bass, 2005), 154–63.

24. These topics were selected following a consultation process involving nine public meetings around the country, attended by a

thousand people in all, during October/November 2013. Arising from this process and from the additional eight hundred submissions made to the convention on "Any Other Amendments," a list of possible topics for the two additional meetings was compiled. The convention voted on this list to decide the two additional topics.

25. Johan Elkink, David Farrell, Theresa Reidy, and Jane Suiter, "Understanding the 2015 Marriage Referendum in Ireland: Context, Campaign, and Conservative Ireland," *Irish Political Studies* 32 (2017): 361–81.

26. For analysis, see Elkink et al., "Understanding the 2015 Marriage Referendum."

27. Suiter et al., "Ireland's Evolving Constitution."

28. See Iris Marion Young, *Inclusion and Democracy* (New York: Oxford University Press, 2000); Arthur Lupia and Anne Norton, "Inequality Is Always in the Room: Language and Power in Deliberative Democracy," *Daedalus* 146 (2017): 64–76.

29. Christopher F. Karpowitz and Chad Raphael, "Ideals of Inclusion in Deliberation," *Journal of Public Deliberation* 12:2 (2016): 17.

30. Matthew Flinders, Katie Ghose, Will Jennings, Edward Molloy, Brendan Prosser, Alan Renwick, and Graham Smith, *Democracy Matters: Lessons from the 2015 Citizens' Assemblies on English Devolution* (London: Democracy Matters, 2016), 42.

31. The semistructured interviews of nine citizen-members took place in February 2014. They were carried out by David Farrell, Jane Suiter, and Clodagh Harris.

32. Dáil debate, July 18, 2013.

33. Dáil debate, October 10, 2013.

34. Dáil debate, July 18, 2013.

35. These unstructured (anonymous) interviews were carried out in the Irish parliament building, Leinster House, by David Farrell and Jane Suiter. The generally positive comments of convention members about their experiences in the process are also shown in the section on "Voices of the Convention" contained in its final report (Ninth Report of the Convention on the Constitution).

36. David Farrell and Jane Suiter, "The Election in Context," in *How Ireland Voted, 2016*, 277–92.

37. The phrase "ecology of democratic institutions" comes from Mark Warren, "Citizen Representatives," in *Designing Deliberative Democracy: The British Columbia Citizens' Assembly*, ed. Mark Warren and Hilary Pearse (Cambridge: Cambridge University Press 2008), 69.

6. Intercameral Relations in a Bicameral Elected and Sortition Legislature, *Vandamme, Jacquet, Niessen, Pitseys, and Reuchamps*

1. The analysis in terms of desirability, achievability, and viability is borrowed from Erik Olin Wright, *Envisioning Real Utopias* (London: Verso, 2010).

2. For a contemporary account of this debate in Belgium, see Min Reuchamps et al., "Le G1000: Une Expérience Citoyenne de Démocratie Délibérative," *Courrier Hebdomadaire du CRISP* no. 2344–5 (2017).

3. For example, debates continue on a 2016 proposal from Green MPs in the lower house, who advocate forming parliamentary commissions composed equally by elected and sortition citizens, with decisions requiring a majority in both groups.

4. See Tom Arnold's contribution to this volume; Min Reuchamps and Jane Suiter, eds., *Constitutional Deliberative Democracy in Europe* (Colchester, UK: ECPR Press, 2016), chapter 2.

5. In the Belgian context, the question was likely to be understood as a question about the possibility of introducing a sortition chamber *alongside* an elected one. However, we recognize a regrettable ambiguity in the formulation of the question. This results from our attempt to make the questions understandable for people who have no prior knowledge of sortition and little understanding of bicameralism.

6. Accountability in sortition is even lower when such bodies use secret ballots, as advocated by Gastil and Wright. On the limitations of sortition compared to elections, see Hervé Pourtois, "Les Élections Sont-Elles Essentielles à la Démocratie?" *Philosophiques* 43:2 (2016); Pierre-Étienne Vandamme and Antoine Verret-Hamelin, "A Randomly Selected Chamber: Promises and Challenges," *Journal of Public Deliberation* 13:1 (2017).

7. See the contributions by Terrill Bouricius and Brett Hennig.

8. See Dimitri Courant's contribution to this volume.

9. For a good defense of party democracy, see Nadia Urbinati, *Representative Democracy: Principles and Genealogy* (Chicago: University of Chicago Press, 2006), chapter 1.

10. In his chapter within this volume, Terrill Bouricius adds that sortition representatives would likely not be properly equipped to defend themselves.

11. This is analogous to why elected officials are reluctant to attack the initiative and referendum process in countries and states where it exists, given the general popularity of such direct democratic processes. We thank John Gastil for this suggestion.

12. Arend Lijphart, *Democracies: Patterns of Majoritarian and Consensus Government in Twenty-One Countries* (New Haven: Yale University Press, 1984).

13. Adam Przeworski, *Democracy and the Limits of Self-Government* (New York: Cambridge University Press, 2010); Melissa Schwartzberg, *Counting the Many: The Origins and Limits of Supermajority Rule* (New York: Cambridge University Press, 2014).

14. See George Tsebelis and Jeannette Money, *Bicameralism* (Cambridge: Cambridge University Press, 1997), chapter 1. In the particular case of a legislature by lot, the second (sortition) chamber would also have the function to provide an assessment of law proposals by an informed (yet nonexpert) and reduced public opinion, which might have the desirable effect to force the elected chamber to justify its disagreements with the sortition chamber to the wider public.

15. Tsebelis and Money, *Bicameralism*; George Tsebelis, *Veto Players: How Political Institutions Work* (Princeton: Princeton University Press, 2002).

16. See Axel Gosseries, "Constitutions and Future Generations," *The Good Society* 17:2 (2008): 32–7.

17. Tsebelis and Money, *Bicameralism*, 104.

18. An alternative possibility, if the sortition chamber enjoys a high legitimacy, is that public pressure would force the elected chamber to compromise, which would mitigate the deadlock.

19. Path dependency can be a reason to take strong bicameralism as a given, but if this is what grounds Gastil and Wright's choice, one should be careful not to generalize their claim beyond the US context.

20. In France, for example, the Senate has a subordinate role, as it is possible for the government to give the last word to the National Assembly. Nonetheless, the Senate exercises influence on decisions even when it has a distinct majority—that is, even when its intervention amounts to political compromise rather than a mere technical improvement of the bill. See Tsebelis and Money, *Bicameralism*, 173–5.

21. The exact influence of the subordinated chamber depends on the differences of composition between the chambers and on the institutional rules defining the so-called *navette* process—that is, the number of possible movements of a bill from one chamber to the other and on the kind of dispute settlement rule that is institutionalized. The influence of the second chamber is the lowest where the political orientations of the two chambers coincide necessarily, due to the designation process or the electoral calendar. See, for example, Bernard Manin, "En Guise de Conclusion: Les Secondes

Chambres et le Gouvernement Complexe," *Revue Internationale de Politique Comparée* 6:1 (1999), 195. Yet in these cases, second chambers tend to be dismantled or reformed.

22. Yannis Papadopoulos, *Democracy in Crisis? Politics, Governance and Policy* (Basingstoke: Palgrave Macmillan, 2013).

23. Ian Shapiro, *Politics Against Domination* (Cambridge: Harvard University Press, 2016), 75.

24. This option is defended in Vandamme and Verret-Hamelin, "A Randomly Selected Chamber: Promises and Challenges."

25. As an in-depth study of the reasons for (non)participation to juries and minipublics reveals, rates of acceptance are higher where citizens feel they will be able to exercise genuine power. Vincent Jacquet, "Explaining Non-Participation in Deliberative Mini-Publics," *European Journal of Political Research* 56:3 (2017): 640–59.

26. David van Reybrouck, *Against Elections. The Case for Democracy* (London: The Bodley Head, 2016), 150–62. This scenario looks less likely when considering that, historically, bicameralism has often served as a compromise between competing forms of representation (See Manin, "En Guise de Conclusion," 196).

27. Lynn M. Sanders, "Against Deliberation," *Political Theory* 25:3 (1997): 347–76.

28. See Tom Arnold, David M. Farrell, and Jane Suiter's chapter in this volume for an optimistic view on the interactions between elected politicians and lay citizens during the Irish Constitutional Convention. For findings reporting existing influence, see Matthew Flinders et al., *Democracy Matters: Lessons from the 2015 Citizens' Assemblies on English Devolution* (London: Democracy Matters, 2016), 39–40.

7. Joining Forces: The Sortition Chamber from a Social-Movement Perspective, *Felicetti and della Porta*

1. See Kimmo Gronlund, Andre Bachtiger, and Maija Setälä, eds., *Deliberative Minipublics: Involving Citizens in the Democratic Process* (Colchester, UK: ECPR Press, 2014); Donatella della Porta and Dieter Rucht, eds., *Meeting Democracy: Power and Deliberation in Global Justice Movements* (Cambridge/New York: Cambridge University Press, 2013).

2. We refer specifically to actors who see improvements on the liberal democratic system as an integral part of their activism. This definition leaves out, among others, a galaxy of far-right social movements inclined toward minimalistic democracy or authoritarian

positions. Though increasingly relevant, such movements are beyond the scope of an essay interested in convergence between pro-democratization forces.

3. For a comprehensive overview of relationship between democratic innovation and social movements, see Julien Talpin, "Democratic Innovations," in *The Oxford Handbook of Social Movements*, ed. Donatella della Porta and Mario Diani (Oxford: Oxford University Press, 2015), 781–92.

4. See Antonio Floridia, *From Participation to Deliberation. A Critical Genealogy of Deliberative Democracy* (Colchester, UK: ECPR Press, 2017); John Parkinson and Jane Mansbridge, eds., *Deliberative Systems* (New York: Cambridge University Press, 2012).

5. See Archon Fung, "Countervailing Power in Empowered Participatory Governance," in *Deepening Democracy: Institutional Innovations in Empowered Participatory Governance*, ed. Archon Fung and Erik Olin Wright (London: Verso, 2003), 259; Talpin, *Democratic Innovations*, 5–8.

6. See Jürg Steiner, *The Foundations of Deliberative Democracy: Empirical Research and Normative Implications* (Cambridge: Cambridge University Press, 2012).

7. Francesca Polletta, "Social Movements in an Age of Participation," *Mobilization: An International Quarterly* 21:4 (2016): 487–8.

8. Self-interested actors, such as NIMBY movements, might contribute to deliberative democracy. Occasionally, however, they might undermine public deliberation, and therefore their involvement in it might be opposed. For extensive discussions on this aspect, see John S. Dryzek, "The Forum, the System, and the Polity: Three Varieties of Democratic Theory," *Political Theory* 45.5 (2017): 610–36; Jane Mansbridge et al., "The Place of Self-Interest and the Role of Power in Deliberative Democracy," *Journal of Political Philosophy* 18:1 (2010): 64–100.

9. See Andrea Felicetti, *Deliberative Democracy and Social Movements. Transition Initiatives in the Public Sphere* (London, UK: Rowman & Littlefield International, 2016).

10. Jane Mansbridge, "Cracking Through Hegemonic Ideology: The Logic of Formal Justice," *Social Justice Research* 18:3 (2005): 335–47.

11. See Sidney G. Tarrow, *Power in Movement: Social Movements and Contentious Politics* (Cambridge: Cambridge University Press, 2011).

12. Loïc Blondiaux and Yves Sintomer, "L'impératif Délibératif," *Politix* 15:57 (2002): 17–35.

13. See Sara M. Evans and Harry C. Boyte, *Free Spaces: The Sources of Democratic Change in America* (Chicago: University of Chicago Press, 1992).

14. We thank Erik Olin Wright for remarking upon this latter aspect.

15. John Parkinson, *Deliberating in the Real World: Problems of Legitimacy in Deliberative Democracy* (Oxford: Oxford University Press, 2006).

16. Lyn Carson, "How Not to Introduce Deliberative Democracy: The 2010 Citizens' Assembly on Climate Change Proposal," in *The Australian Citizens' Parliament and the Future of Deliberative Democracy*, ed. Lyn Carson, John Gastil, Janette Hartz-Karp, and Ron Lubensky (University Park, PA: Pennsylvania State University Press, 2013), 284-8.

17. Quote taken from draft workshop paper presented by Lyn Carson, which became her chapter in this volume. See the author for a copy of that earlier paper.

18. James S. Fishkin and Robert C. Luskin, "Broadcasts of Deliberative Polls: Aspirations and Effects," *British Journal of Political Science* 36:1 (2006): 184-8. Also see Lyn Carson's chapter in this volume.

19. Parkinson, *Deliberating in the Real World*, 13-4, 37.

20. Ibid., 15-6.

21. John Boswell, Simon Niemeyer, and Carolyn M. Hendriks, "Julia Gillard's Citizens' Assembly Proposal for Australia: A Deliberative Democratic Analysis," *Australian Journal of Political Science* 48:2 (2013): 164-78.

22. See Christopher Rootes, "Denied, Deferred, Triumphant? Climate Change, Carbon Trading and the Greens in the Australian Federal Election of 21 August 2010," *Environmental Politics* 20:3 (2011): 410-7.

23. James S. Fishkin, Robert C. Luskin, and Roger Jowell, "Deliberative Polling and Public Consultation," *Parliamentary Affairs* 53:4 (2000): 657-66.

24. For parallels with broader historical trends, see Talpin, *Democratic Innovations*, especially 2-5.

25. See David Toke, "USA: Consolidation of a Renewables Industry?" in *Ecological Modernisation and Renewable Energy* (New York: Palgrave Macmillan, 2011), 98-128; David Hurlbut, "A Look Behind the Texas Renewable Portfolio Standard: A Case Study," *Natural Resources Journal* (2008): 142.

26. Fishkin and Luskin, "Broadcasts of Deliberative Polls," 186.

27. James S. Fishkin, *When the People Speak: Deliberative Democracy and Public Consultation* (Oxford: Oxford University Press, 2009), 123.

28. Jane Mansbridge, "Deliberative Polling as the Gold Standard," *The Good Society* 19:1 (2010): 55.

29. Fishkin, *When the People Speak*, 123-4.

30. See John Gastil and Katherine Knobloch, *Hope for Democracy: How Citizens Can Bring Reason Back into Politics* (unpublished manuscript).

31. Ibid., *Hope for Democracy,* chapters 3–4.
32. Jane Mansbridge, "Using Power/Fighting Power," in *Democracy and Difference,* ed. Seyla Benhabib (Chichester, UK: Princeton University Press, 1996), 46–66.
33. Gastil and Knobloch, *Hope for Democracy,* 130–7.
34. Ibid., *Hope for Democracy.*
35. Jan van Damme, Vincent Jacquet, Nathalie Schiffino, and Min Reuchamps, "Public Consultation and Participation in Belgium: Directly Engaging Citizens Beyond the Ballot Box?" *Policy Analysis in Belgium* (2017): 215.
36. Didier Caluwaerts and Min Reuchamps, "The G1000: Facts, Figures and Some Lessons from an Experience of Deliberative Democracy in Belgium," in *The Malaise of Electoral Democracy and What to Do About It,* ed. Didier Caluwaerts et al. (Brussels: Re-Bel, 2014), 10–33.
37. Caluwaerts and Reuchamps, "The G100," 11; Vincent Jacquet and Min Reuchamps, "Who Wants to Pay for Deliberative Democracy? The Crowdfunders of the G1000 in Belgium," *European Political Science Review* 10:1 (2016): 1–21.
38. Didier Caluwaerts and Min Reuchamps, "Deliberative Stress in Linguistically Divided Belgium," in *Democratic Deliberation in Deeply Divided Societies: From Conflict to Common Ground,* ed. Juan E. Ugarriza and Didier Caluwaerts (New York: Springer, 2014), 46–7.
39. See Caluwaerts and Reuchamps, "The G1000." For an analysis of the deliberative limits of the G1000, see Didier Caluwaerts and Min Reuchamps, "Strengthening Democracy Through Bottom-Up Deliberation: An Assessment of the Internal Legitimacy of the G1000 Project," *Acta Politica* 50:2 (2015): 151–70.
40. See Caluwaerts and Reuchamps, "The G1000," 22.
41. Didier Caluwaerts, Vincent Jacquet, and Min Reuchamps, "Deliberative Democracy and the So What Question: The Effects of Belgium's G1000" (presentation, APSA Annual Meeting, 2016, 20).
42. Van Damme et al., "Public Consultation and Participation in Belgium," 229.
43. Talpin, *Democratic Innovations,* 5–8.
44. See Archon Fung, "Putting the Public Back into Governance: The Challenges of Citizen Participation and Its Future," *Public Administration Review* 75:4 (2015): 513–22; Talpin, *Democratic Innovations.*
45. Gianpaolo Baiocchi and Ernesto Ganuza, *Popular Democracy: The Paradox of Participation* (Stanford: Stanford University Press, 2016), 151.

46. Andrea Felicetti, Simon Niemeyer, and Nicole Curato, "Improving Deliberative Participation: Connecting Minipublics to Deliberative Systems," *European Political Science Review* 8:3 (2015): 1–22.

47. See Polletta, "Social Movements in an Age of Participation."

48. John S. Dryzek, "Democratization as Deliberative Capacity Building," *Comparative Political Studies* 42:11 (2009): 1379–402.

49. Ricardo Fabrino Mendonça, "Mitigating Systemic Dangers: The Role of Connectivity Inducers in a Deliberative System," *Critical Policy Studies* 10:2 (2016): 178.

8. Should Democracy Work Through Elections or Sortition?, *Malleson*

1. In addition to the lead chapter of this volume, see Ernest Callenbach and Michael Phillips, *A Citizen Legislature* (Exeter: Imprint Academic, 2008); Alex Zakaras, "Lot and Democratic Representation: A Modest Proposal," *Constellations* 17:3 (2010): 455–71; Kevin O'Leary, *Saving Democracy* (Stanford: Stanford University Press, 2006).

2. Terry Bouricius, "Democracy Through Multi-Body Sortition: Athenian Lessons for the Modern Day," *Journal of Public Deliberation* 9:1 (2013); Alexander A. Guerrero, "Against Elections: The Lottocratic Alternative," *Philosophy & Public Affairs* 42:2 (2014): 135–78; Brett Hennig, *The End of Politicians* (London: Unbound, 2017); David van Reybrouck, *Against Elections* (London: The Bodley Head, 2016).

3. Bernard Manin, *The Principles of Representative Government* (Cambridge: Cambridge University Press, 1997).

4. Probably the works that come closest to this are Anthoula Malkopoulou, "The Paradox of Democratic Selection: Is Sortition Better Than Voting?" in *Parliamentarism and Democratic Theory*, ed. Kari Palonen and José María Rosales (Toronto: Budrich, 2015); Peter Stone, "Sortition, Voting, and Democratic Equality," *Critical Review of International Social and Political Philosophy* 19:3 (2016): 339–56. Also see Arash Abizadeh "Representation, Bicameralism, and Sortition: Reconstituting the Senate as Randomly Selected Citizen Assembly," workshop paper, McGill University, 2016. Even these are quite different from the systematic comparison attempted here.

5. See, for instance, Hennig, *The End of Politicians*; Callenbach and Phillips, *A Citizen Legislature*.

6. The analysis here cannot be fully comprehensive. A comprehensive account would need to consider all three of the main

mechanisms of democracy: elections, sortition, and referenda/ initiatives, as well as complicated combinations thereof.

7. This is not meant as a hard-and-fast distinction, rather as a useful heuristic.

8. Also of relevance here is the important issue of the political equality of minorities, which I must bracket for space constraints, but see endnote 33 in this chapter.

9. Peter Esaiasson and Soren Holmberg, *Representation from Above: Members of Parliament and Representative Democracy in Sweden*, trans. Janet Westerlund (Aldershot: Darmouth, 1996).

10. Manin, *The Principles of Representative Government*.

11. James S. Fishkin, *When the People Speak* (Oxford: Oxford University Press, 2009), 17.

12. Most of these statistics refer to the 115th Senate, except for the median wealth, which refers to the 114th. Tami Luhby, "America's Middle Class: Poorer Than You Think," CNN (August 5, 2014); Jennifer E. Manning, *Membership of the 115th Congress: A Profile*, CRS Report No. R44762, Congressional Research Service (April 12, 2018). Also see material available at OpenSecrets.org.

13. Thinking along these lines, Bouricius approvingly cites Marx's famous comment that "the working class cannot simply lay hold of the ready-made state machinery, and wield it for its own purposes." See his chapter in this volume.

14. David E. Broockman, "Black Politicians Are More Intrinsically Motivated to Advance Blacks' Interests: A Field Experiment Manipulating Political Incentives," *American Journal of Political Science* 57:3 (2013): 521–36; David T. Canon, *Race, Redistricting, and Representation: The Unintended Consequences of Black Majority Districts* (Chicago: University of Chicago Press, 1999); Kenny J. Whitby, *The Color of Representation: Congressional Behavior and Black Constituents* (Ann Arbor: University of Michigan Press, 1997).

15. Michael B. Berkman and Robert E. O'Connor, "Do Women Legislators Matter? Female Legislators and State Abortion Policy," *American Politics Quarterly* 21:1 (1993): 102–24; Kathleen A. Bratton and Leonard P. Ray, "Descriptive Representation, Policy Outcomes, and Municipal Day-Care Coverage in Norway," *American Journal of Political Science* 46:2 (2002): 428–37; Michele Swers, *The Difference Women Make: The Policy Impact of Women in Congress* (Chicago: University of Chicago Press, 2002).

16. Nicholas Carnes, "Does the Numerical Underrepresentation of the Working Class in Congress Matter?" *Legislative Studies Quarterly* 37:1 (2012): 5–34; Nicholas Carnes and Noam Lupu, "Rethinking the Comparative Perspective on Class and Representation:

Evidence from Latin America," *American Journal of Political Science* 59:1 (2015): 1–18; Nathalie Giger, Jan Rosset, and Julian Bernauer, "The Poor Political Representation of the Poor in a Comparative Perspective," *Representation* 48:1 (2012): 47–61.

17. Gil Delannoi, Oliver Dowlen, and Peter Stone, *The Lottery as a Democratic Institution* (Dublin: Policy Institute, 2013); Abizadeh, "Representation, Bicameralism, and Sortition."

18. Oliver Dowlen, *The Political Potential of Sortition* (Exeter: Imprint Academic, 2008).

19. See David Owen and Graham Smith's chapter in this volume.

20. Hennig, *The End of Politicians*, 71.

21. Guerrero, "Against Elections."

22. Adam Przeworski, Susan Stokes, and Bernard Manin, eds., *Democracy, Accountability, and Representation* (Cambridge: Cambridge University Press, 1999).

23. Philip Pettit, "Representation, Responsive and Indicative," *Constellations* 17:3 (2010): 426–34.

24. This knowledge by itself may be enough to alter behavior. Consider the famous psychological experiment where merely having an image of a pair of eyes near a donation box encouraged people to behave more responsibly in paying for the coffee and tea they were drinking. Daniel Kahneman, *Thinking, Fast and Slow* (Toronto: Doubleday, 2011), 57–8.

25. Ilya Somin, *Democracy and Political Ignorance* (Stanford: Stanford University Press, 2013).

26. Guerrero, "Against Elections."

27. See John Dryzek and Carolyn Hendriks, "Fostering Deliberation in the Forum and Beyond," in *The Argumentative Turn Revisited*, ed. Frank Fischer and Herbert Gottweis (Durham: Duke University Press, 2012); Fishkin, *When the People Speak*; David M. Ryfe, "Does Deliberative Democracy Work?" *Annual Review of Political Science* 8 (2005): 49–71; see also Lyn Carson's chapter in this volume.

28. This is difficult but not impossible. Consider, for example, the functioning of the Congressional Budget Office in the US Congress and other similar bodies that manage to perform an important technical service while staying quite ideologically neutral.

29. For an overview of this evidence, see Fishkin, *When the People Speak*.

30. By competency I mean, loosely, the possession of general political knowledge of how society works (how the basic institutions function and what the major conflicts and fault lines in society are), as well as the ability to arrive at rational judgments (by understanding new information, learning, and drawing conclusions that coherently reflect underlying values).

31. See, for example, Bouricius, "Democracy Through Multi-Body Sortition"; Guerrero, "Against Elections"; Ethan Leib, *Deliberative Democracy in America: A Proposal for a Popular Branch of Government* (University Park, PA: The Pennsylvania State University Press, 2004).

32. It would be useful to do the selection by lot so as to prevent members from going into the area in which they already have fixed views.

33. Another issue of political equality is that of protecting the rights of minorities. The problem with electoral systems in this regard is that they are aggregative systems and so enable majorities to continually outvote entrenched minorities. Moreover, the electoral system may at times provide perverse incentives for politicians to actively stigmatize minorities (such as black people, Muslims, or welfare recipients), when doing so can bring overall electoral benefits. A sortition legislature may well perform somewhat better at protecting minorities due to its deliberative nature, since members, even prejudiced ones, would have no structural incentive to stigmatize minorities, and on the contrary would be encouraged to talk to each other and hear each other's experiences. This will not guarantee mutual understanding or respect, of course, but it may well help.

34. Though we haven't discussed it here, there is also an interesting question as to whether sampling should be random or stratified. Stratification ensures proportional representation but raises uncertainties about which specific characteristics should be stratified for.

35. Barbara Ransby, *Ella Baker and the Black Freedom Movement* (Chapel Hill: University of North Carolina Press, 2003), 142.

9. Accountability in the Constituent-Representative Relationship, *Mansbridge*

1. For the full argument, see Jane Mansbridge, "What Is Political Science For?" *Perspectives on Politics* 12:1 (2014): 8–17.

2. Per contra, see many others, including Michael Walzer, *Obligations: Essays on Disobedience, War, and Citizenship* (Cambridge: Harvard University Press, 1970).

3. books.google.com/ngrams, accessed August 16, 2018.

4. For the full argument, see Jane Mansbridge, "A Contingency Theory of Accountability," in *The Oxford Handbook of Public Accountability*, ed. Mark Bowens, Robert E. Goodin, and Thomas Schillemans (Oxford: Oxford University Press, 2014), 55–68.

5. Frances E. Lee, *Insecure Majorities: Congress and the Perpetual Campaign* (Chicago: University of Chicago Press, 2017).

6. For a fuller account of the core/periphery metaphor, see Jane Mansbridge, "On the Relation of Altruism and Self-Interest," in Jane Mansbridge, ed., *Beyond Self-Interest* (Chicago: University of Chicago Press, 1990), 133–43. Also see Jane Mansbridge, "A 'Moral Core' Solution to the Prisoners' Dilemma," in Joan W. Scott and Debra Keates, eds., *Schools of Thought: Twenty-Five Years of Interpretive Social Science* (Princeton: Princeton University Press, 2001), 330–47. On peer accountability, see inter alia Robert E. Goodin, "Democratic Accountability: The Distinctiveness of the Third Sector," *European Journal of Sociology* 44 (2003): 359–96.

7. For a fuller account of the fears that lead citizens not to participate in the face-to-face democracy of a small New England town meeting, see Jane Mansbridge, *Beyond Adversary Democracy* (Chicago: University of Chicago Press, 1983).

8. See Mark E. Warren and Hilary Pearse, eds., *Designing Deliberative Democracy: The British Columbia Citizens' Assembly* (Cambridge: Cambridge University Press, 2008).

9. For more on these assemblies, see Warren and Pearce, *Designing Deliberative Democracy*; Dimitri Courant, "Tirage au Sort et Concertation dans l'Armée Française: Le Cas du Conseil Supérieur de la Fonction Militaire (1969–2015)" (master's thesis, EHESS, September 2014); John Gastil, "Beyond Endorsements and Partisan Cues: Giving Voters Viable Alternatives to Unreliable Cognitive Shortcuts," *The Good Society* 23 (2014): 145–59.

10. Geoffrey Brewer, "Snakes Top List of Americans' Fears," *Gallup News Service* (March 19, 2001). So too, in this study of 1,011 Americans, only 34 percent of nonwhites reported being afraid of public speaking, compared to 43 percent of whites.

11. Claudine Gay, "The Effect of Black Congressional Representation on Political Participation," *American Political Science Review* 95 (2001): 589–602.

12. See Carol M. Swain, *Black Faces, Black Interests: The Representation of African Americans in Congress* (Cambridge: Harvard University Press, 1993), 218. For more on surrogate representation, see Jane Mansbridge, "Should Blacks Represent Blacks and Women Represent Women? A Contingent 'Yes,'" *Journal of Politics* 61 (1999): 627–57.

13. For more on the paucity of either empirical or theoretical work on the constituent-representative relation and a proposed ideal of "recursive representation" aimed at thickening that relation, see Jane Mansbridge, "Recursive Representation," in *Making Present,*

eds. Dario Castiglione and Johannes Pollak (Chicago: University of Chicago Press, 2018).

14. For tenants' association government, see the Toronto Community Housing Corporation case in Genevieve Fuji Johnson, *Democratic Illusion: Deliberative Democracy in Canadian Public Policy* (Toronto: University of Toronto Press, 2015).

10. How to Ensure Deliberation Within a Sortition Chamber, *Carson*

1. Ernest Callenbach and Michael Phillips, *A Citizen Legislature* (Berkeley Springs, CA: Banyan Tree Books, 1985); Lyn Carson and Brian Martin, *Random Selection in Politics* (Westport, CT: Praeger, 1999); Ethan Leib, *Deliberative Democracy in America: A Proposal for a Popular Branch of Government* (University Park, PA: Pennsylvania State University Press, 2004); David van Reybrouck, *Against Elections: The Case for Democracy* (London: Bodley Head, 2016); Brett Hennig, *The End of Politicians: Time for a Real Democracy* (London: Unbound, 2017).

2. See the newDemocracy or Participedia.net websites for case studies.

3. Gil Delannoi and Oliver Dowlen, *Sortition: Theory and Practice* (Exeter: Imprint Academic, 2010); Mogens Herman Hansen, *Athenian Democracy in the Age of Demosthenes* (Norman: University of Oklahoma Press, 1999); Keith Sutherland, Ernest Callenbach, and Michael Phillips, *A People's Parliament: A (Revised) Blueprint for a Very English Revolution* (Exeter: Imprint Academic, 2008).

4. Stephen Elstub and Peter McLaverty, eds., *Deliberative Democracy: Issues and Cases* (Edinburgh: Edinburgh University Press, 2014), citing Barker 1978, 142.

5. Daniel Yankelovitch, *Coming to Public Judgment: Making Democracy Work in a Complex World* (Syracuse: Syracuse University Press, 1991).

6. Tony Fitzgerald, "Politicians with a 'Winning at All Costs' Mentality Are Damaging Australia," *Sydney Morning Herald*, April 12, 2017. Italics added for emphasis.

7. Ibid.

8. These are adapted from political theorist Robert Dahl. In this volume, see Gastil and Wright's lead chapter, "Legislature by Lot."

9. John Urh, *Deliberative Democracy in Australia. The Changing Place of Parliament* (Cambridge: Cambridge University Press, 1998); Carolyn Hendriks and Adrian Kay, "From 'Opening up' to Democratic Renewal: Deepening Public Engagement in Legislative

Committees," *Government and Opposition* (forthcoming, published online first, 2017).

10. Henry Martyn Robert, *Robert's Rules of Order: Classic Manual of Rules of Order for Deliberative Assemblies* (Minneapolis: Filiquarian Publishing, 1876).

11. Tom Atlee, *The Tao of Democracy: Using Co-Intelligence to Create a World That Works for All* (Winnipeg: Writers' Collective, 2003); Peggy Holman, Tom Devane, Steven Cady, and associates, *The Change Handbook. The Definitive Resources on Today's Best Methods for Engaging Whole Systems* (Oakland: Berrett-Koehler Publishers, 2006); Sandy Schuman, *Creating a Culture of Collaboration. The International Association of Facilitators Handbook* (San Francisco: Jossey-Bass, 2006); Vivien Twyford et al., eds., *The Power of "Co": The Smart Leaders' Guide to Collaborative Governance* (Woolongong: Twyfords Consulting, 2012).

12. Some of the content for this chapter has been extracted verbatim from various research and development notes that the author prepared for the newDemocracy Foundation's website.

13. The *Journal of Public Deliberation* or Participedia.net are both good starting points.

14. For a useful description of minipublics, see Oliver Escobar and Stephen Elstub, "Forms of Minipublics: An Introduction to Deliberative Innovations in Democratic Practice," newDemocracy (May 8 2017), available on the newDemocracy website. In writing this chapter, I have in mind an entire chamber that has been randomly selected, as in Gastil and Wright's formulation. This is quite different from a partial-sortition chamber, as advocated by a candidate in a recent French presidential election and by activists in Belgium and Switzerland. I also set aside any argument that power should be decentralized by abandoning parliamentary chambers altogether.

15. John Parkinson and Jane Mansbridge, eds., *Deliberative Systems: Deliberative Democracy at the Large Scale* (Cambridge: Cambridge University Press, 2012).

16. Tom Dusevic, "Rage Against the Political Machine," *The Weekend Australian* (December 24–5, 2016), 14.

17. Dusevic, "Rage Against the Political Machine."

18. Lyn Carson, "Ignorance and Inclusion, Mr Jefferson, Might Be Good for Democracy," working paper series, United States Studies Centre, Active Democracy website (November 2009).

19. In a similar way, jury deliberation can make citizens more likely to vote (where voting is not compulsory). See John Gastil, E. Pierre Deess, Philip J. Weiser, and Cindy Simmons, *The Jury and Democracy: How Jury Deliberation Promotes Civic Engagement*

and Political Participation (Oxford: Oxford University Press, 2010).

20. Hélène Landemore, "Why the Many Are Smarter Than the Few and Why It Matters," *Journal of Public Deliberation* 8:1 (2012).

21. Sandy Hodge, Zelma Bone, and Judith Crockett, "Using Community Deliberation Forums for Public Engagement: Examples from Missouri, USA and New South Wales, Australia," Queensland Government Publications (n.d.).

22. John Gastil and Peter Levine, eds., *The Deliberative Democracy Handbook: Strategies for Effective Civic Engagement in the Twenty-First Century* (San Francisco: Jossey-Bass, 2005).

23. Daniel Yankelovitch, *Coming to Public Judgment: Making Democracy Work in a Complex World* (Syracuse: Syracuse University Press, 1991).

24. Daniel Yankelovitch, *The Magic of Dialogue* (Crows Nest, Sydney, Australia: Allen & Unwin, 1999).

25. Examples of such feedback can be found in research reports at the newDemocracy website.

26. Tina Nabatchi, John Gastil, Michael G. Weiksner, and Matt Leighninger, eds., *Democracy in Motion: Evaluating the Practice and Impact of Deliberative Civic Engagement* (Oxford: Oxford University Press, 2012).

27. Chris Barker and Brian Martin, "Participation: The Happiness Connection," *Journal of Public Deliberation* 7:1 (2011).

28. Lyn Carson, "Investigation of (and Introspection on) Organizer Bias," in *The Australian Citizens' Parliament and the Future of Deliberative Democracy*, ed. Lyn Carson, John Gastil, Janette Hartz-Karp, and Ron Lubensky (University Park, PA: Pennsylvania State University Press, 2013).

29. The author was involved in both of these minipublics. Also see reports available online at GreenCross Australia and University of Technology Sydney.

30. Jennifer Roberts and Ruth Lightbody, "Experts and Evidence in Public Decision Making," *Climate Exchange* (February 2017), available online at Climate Exchange website.

31. Paolo Freire, *Education: The Practice of Freedom* (London: Writers and Readers Publishing Cooperative, 1976).

32. Freire, *Education*; Paolo Freire, *Pedagogy of the City* (London: Bloomsbury Publishing, 1993).

33. Landemore, "Why the Many."

34. John Gastil, *Democracy in Small Groups* (Gabriola Island, BC: New Society Publishers, 1993).

35. Max Hardy, Kath Fisher, and Janette Hartz-Karp, "The Unsung Heroes of a Deliberative Process: Reflections on the Role of Facilitators at the Citizens' Parliament," in *The Australian*

Citizens' Parliament, 177–89.

36. Dale Hunter, Anne Bailey, and Bill Taylor, *Art of Facilitation: How to Create Group Synergy* (Tucson: Fisher Books, 1995).

37. Usually, "a leader is best when people barely know he exists, when his work is done, his aim fulfilled, they will say: we did it ourselves."

38. Twyford et al., *The Power of "Co."*

39. See the de Borda Institute website: http://www.deborda.org/faq/what-is-a-preferendum/

40. Gavin Mooney, "A Handbook on Citizens Juries with Particular Reference to Health Care," newDemocracy (2010), available on the newDemocracy website.

41. See the G1000 website.

42. See the What Do We Think website, Turnometro, or Beta Baoqu.

43. See the newDemocracy website.

44. Plato, *The Republic*, 2nd ed., trans. Desmond Lee (London: Penguin Books, 1974), 260–80.

45. Naomi Klein, *No Is Not Enough: Defeating the New Shock Politics* (New York: Penguin, 2017).

46. Mark E. Warren, "When, Where and Why Do We Need Deliberation, Voting, and Other Means of Organizing Democracy? A Problem-Based Approach to Democratic Systems" (presentation, American Political Science Association, 2012).

47. Barry Hindess, "Deficit by Design," *Australian Journal of Public Administration* 61:1 (2002): 30–8.

48. Delannoi and Dowlen, *Sortition*.

11. Sortition and Democratic Principles: A Comparative Analysis, *Courant*

1. This chapter is a shortened and completely revised version of a paper published in an earlier and longer version in Spanish—see Dimitri Courant, "Pensar el Sorteo. Modos de Selección, Marcos Deliberativos y Principios Democráticos," *Daimon: Revista Internacional de Filosofía*, 72 (2017): 59–79; and in English, see Dimitri Courant, "Thinking Sortition. Modes of Selection, Deliberative Frameworks and Democratic Principles," *Les Cahiers de l'IEPHI*, Working Papers 68 (2017); and in French, see Dimitri Courant, "Penser le tirage au sort. Modes de sélection, cadres délibératifs et principes démocratiques," in *Expériences du tirage au sort en Suisse et en Europe : un état des lieux*, eds. Antoine Chollet and Alexandre Fontaine (Berne : Schriftenreihe der Bibliothek am Guisanplatz, 2018).

2. Yves Sintomer, *From Radical to Deliberative Democracy? Random*

Selection in Politics from Athens to the Present (Cambridge: Cambridge University Press, 2018, forthcoming).

3. In this volume, see Gastil and Wright's lead chapter, "Legislature by Lot."

4. For empirical developments of this theoretical framework, see Dimitri Courant, "Tirage au Sort et Concertation dans l'Armée Française: Le Cas du Conseil Supérieur de la Fonction Militaire (1969–2014)" (master's thesis, EHESS, September 2014).

5. I leave aside filiation (heredity) and acquisition (buying of offices), as those two modes have almost disappeared.

6. Montesquieu, *De l'Esprit des Lois* (Paris: Garnier Flammarion, 1979), 134.

7. For more detail on sortition in ancient Athens, see chapters in this book by Owen and Smith and by Fishkin.

8. Bernard Manin, *Principes du Gouvernement Représentatif* (Paris: Flammarion, 2012).

9. Francis Dupuis-Déri, *Démocratie: Histoire Politique d'un Mot* (Montréal: Lux, 2013); Dimitri Courant, "Délibération et tirage au sort au sein d'une institution permanente. Enquête sur le Conseil Supérieur de la Fonction Militaire (1968–2016)," *Participations* (forthcoming, 2019).

10. Karoun Demirjian, "Grassley: Two Controversial Federal Bench Nominees Won't Be Confirmed," *Washington Post* (December 13, 2017).

11. See the website of the California Citizens Redistricting Commission, wedrawthelines.ca.gov.

12. Jacques Rancière, *Hatred of Democracy* (New York: Verso, 2006), 42.

13. Candidates and agents in charge of selecting representatives could be completely wrong about the candidates' real competences.

14. Sintomer, *From Radical to Deliberative Democracy.*

15. Hélène Landemore, "Deliberation, Cognitive Diversity, and Democratic Inclusiveness," *Synthese* 190:7 (2013): 1209–31.

16. Oliver Dowlen, *The Political Potential of Sortition* (Exeter: Imprint Academic, 2008).

17. In this volume, see Gastil and Wright's lead chapter, "Legislature by Lot."

18. James S. Fishkin and Robert Luskin, "Experimenting with a Democratic Ideal," *Acta Politica* 40 (2005): 284–98.

19. John Gastil and Robert Richards, "Making Direct Democracy Deliberative Through Random Assemblies," *Politics & Society* 41:2 (2013): 253–81.

20. Dimitri Courant, "Les Militants du Tirage au Sort. Sociologie d'un Nouvel Activisme Démocratique" (paper presented at the CLAIMS workshop, Paris, 2018).

21. Though conventional participatory budgeting does not incorporate random samples, randomly selected panels linked to participatory budgeting exist in Germany, France, and China. See Yves Sintomer, Anja Röcke, and Carsten Herzberg, *Participatory Budgeting in Europe: Democracy and Public Governance* (London: Routledge, 2016); Dimitri Courant, "From *Klérotèrion* to Cryptology: The Act of Sortition in the XXIst Century, Instruments and Practices," in *Sortition and Democracy,* ed. Liliane Rabatel and Yves Sintomer (Exeter: Imprint Academic, 2018b).

22. See Arnold, Suiter, and Farrell in this book.

23. Dominique Bourg, ed., *Pour Une 6e République Écologique* (Paris: Odile Jacob, 2011).

24. Contrary to religious uses of sortition, see Courant, "From *Klérotèrion* to Cryptology."

25. Courant, "Tirage au Sort et Concertation."

26. One could argue for tests to be used to filter potential sortition legislators from a larger pool, but this aristocratic argument goes against the democratic equality of the principle "one person, one vote."

27. This typology goes beyond the distinction between auto-selection and hetero-selection.

28. Rancière, *Hatred of Democracy.*

29. Sintomer, *From Radical to Deliberative Democracy?*

30. Daniel Gaxie, *Le Cens Caché* (Paris: Seuil, 1993).

31. Mancur Olson, *Logique de l'Action Collective* (Bruxelles: Université de Bruxelles, 2011).

32. Courant, "Tirage au Sort et Concertation."

33. Cornelius Castoriadis, *La Montée de l'Insignifiance* (Paris: Seuil, 1996).

34. Rancière, *Hatred of Democracy,* 47, 49.

35. Sintomer, *From Radical to Deliberative Democracy?*

36. Gil Delannoi, *Le Retour du Tirage au Sort en Politique* (Paris: Fondapol, 2010), 19.

37. This connection between sortition and direct democracy can be explained by the concept of legitimacy based on *humility*, as we will see below. See also: Dimitri Courant, "'We Have Humility': Perceived Legitimacy and Representative Claims in the Irish Citizens' Assembly" (paper presented at the American Political Science Association Conference, Boston, 2018).

38. The Danish Board of Technology is an official institution aiming to provide reliable information to the Danish Parliament. Since 1987, it has organized debates on technological issues among randomly selected citizens.

39. However, control procedures are useful to prevent ex post corruption by lobbies.

40. Courant, "From *Klérotèrion* to Cryptology."
41. Manin, *Principes du Gouvernement Représentatif*, 74–93.
42. Pierre Bourdieu, "La Représentation Politique," *Actes de la Recherche en Sciences Sociales* 36–7 (1981): 3–24.
43. Courant, "Tirage au Sort et Concertation."
44. Bourdieu, "La Représentation Politique," 6–7.
45. Alexandros Kontos, "La Démocratie, un Régime Politique Inconnu" (PhD thesis, Paris, 2001): 42, 258.
46. On the Texas case, see Felicetti and della Porta's chapter in this volume. On Ireland, see the chapter by Arnold, Suiter, and Farrell.
47. Sintomer, *From Radical to Deliberative Democracy?*
48. John Dewey, *The Public and Its Problems* (New York: Holt, 1929), 207.
49. Landemore, "Deliberation, Cognitive Diversity, and Democratic Inclusiveness."
50. This was done for the British Columbia Citizens' Assembly, along with many other minipublics. Determination of relevant subpopulations is contextual and should be open to political debate.
51. A sortition system could make districts useless. Moreover, if people represent districts, they might be encouraged to represent a part of the whole—not the whole.
52. Owen and Smith make this point in their chapter, as a critique of the multiyear terms of service suggested by Gastil and Wright.
53. Plato, *Protagoras* (Oxford: Oxford University Press, 2009).
54. Courant, "Tirage au Sort et Concertation," 102.
55. Pierre-Joseph Proudhon, *Les Confessions d'un Révolutionnaire* (Paris: TOPS, 2013).
56. Courant, "Tirage au Sort et Concertation."
57. My perspective differs from that of Kelsen, who only compared nomination and election, the first one creating a dependence to the top, and the second a dependence to the electorate. See Hans Kelsen, *La Démocratie: Sa Nature, Sa Valeur* (Paris: Dalloz, 2004).
58. Courant, "Tirage au Sort et Concertation."
59. Manin, *Principes du Gouvernement Représentatif*.
60. Delannoi, "Le Retour du Tirage au Sort," 14.
61. Robert Rosenthal and Leonore Jacobson, "Teacher Expectation for the Disadvantaged," *Scientific American* 218:4 (1968): 19–23.
62. Elisha Y. Babad, Jacinto Inbar, and Robert Rosenthal, "Pygmalion, Galatea, and the Golem: Investigations of Biased and Unbiased Teachers," *Journal of Educational Psychology* 74:4 (1982): 459–74.
63. I discovered legitimacy-humility studying the military. I asked if the CSFM-sorted officials had a title, to which the secretariat answered, "No, no title! We don't want them to become arrogant!" Courant, "Tirage au Sort et Concertation," 113. The

concept was also mentioned by members of the Irish Citizens' Assembly in interviews I conducted: "We have humility, we don't care about the fame, we just want to help people." See also Courant, "'We Have Humility.'"

12. In Defense of Imperfection: An Election-Sortition Compromise, *Abizadeh*

1. See Dennis C. Mueller, Robert D. Tollison, and Thomas D. Willett, "Representative Democracy via Random Selection," *Public Choice* 12 (1972): 57–68; Richard G. Mulgan, "Lot as a Democratic Device of Selection," *Review of Politics* 46:4 (1984): 539–60; Fredrik Engelstad, "The Assignment of Political Office by Lot," *Social Science Information* 28:1 (1989): 23–50; Gil Delannoi, Oliver Dowlen, and Peter Stone, "The Lottery as a Democratic Institution," in *Studies in Public Policy* (Dublin: Policy Institute, 2013); Terrill G. Bouricius, "Democracy Through Multi-Body Sortition: Athenian Lessons for the Modern Day," *Journal of Public Deliberation* 9:1 (2013).
2. Bernard Manin, *The Principles of Representative Government* (Cambridge: Cambridge University Press, 1997).
3. See also Kevin O'Leary, *Saving Democracy: A Plan for Real Representation in America* (Stanford: Stanford University Press, 2006); John P. McCormick, "Contain the Wealthy and Patrol the Magistrates: Restoring Elite Accountability to Popular Government," *American Political Science Review* 100:2 (2006): 147–63; Ernest Callenbach and Michael Phillips, *A Citizen Legislature* (Exeter: Imprint Academic, 2008); Alex Zakaras, "Lot and Democratic Representation: A Modest Proposal," *Constellations* 17:3 (2010): 455–71; Michael K. MacKenzie, "A General-Purpose, Randomly Selected Chamber," in *Institutions for Future Generations*, ed. Iñigo González-Ricoy and Axel Gosseries (Oxford: Oxford University Press, 2016); Pierre-Étienne Vandamme and Antoine Verret-Hamelin, "A Randomly Selected Chamber: Promises and Challenges," *Journal of Public Deliberation* 13:1 (2017); Arash Abizadeh "Representation, Bicameralism, and Sortition: Reconstituting the Senate as Randomly Selected Citizen Assembly," workshop paper, McGill University, 2016.
4. David van Reybrouck, *Against Elections: The Case for Democracy* (London: Bodley Head, 2016); Keith Sutherland, *A People's Parliament* (Exeter: Imprint Academic, 2008); Terrill Bouricius's chapter in this volume. An exclusive sortition system is also

explored in Alexander A. Guerrero, "Against Elections: The Lottocratic Alternative," *Philosophy & Public Affairs* 42:2 (2014): 135–78.

5. Bernard Manin, Adam Przeworski, and Susan C. Stokes, "Elections and Representation," in *Democracy, Accountability, and Representation*, ed. Adam Przeworski, Susan C. Stokes, and Bernard Manin (Cambridge: Cambridge University Press, 1999), 29–54; James D. Fearon, "Electoral Accountability and the Control of Politicians: Selecting Good Types Versus Sanctioning Poor Performance," in *Democracy, Accountability, and Representation*, 55–97.

6. Manin, *Principles of Representative Government*; Manin, Przeworski, and Stokes, "Elections and Representation," 30; Adam Przeworski, "Minimalist Conception of Democracy: A Defense," in *Democracy's Value*, ed. Ian Shapiro and Casiano Hacker-Cordón (Cambridge: Cambridge University Press, 1999), 35.

7. Jane Mansbridge, "Rethinking Representation," *American Political Science Review* 97:4 (2003): 515–28.

8. Christopher H. Achen and Larry M. Bartels, *Democracy for Realists: Why Elections Do Not Produce Responsive Governments* (Princeton: Princeton University Press, 2016).

9. Ilya Somin, *Democracy and Political Ignorance: Why Smaller Government Is Smarter* (Stanford: Stanford University Press, 2013).

10. Przeworski, "Minimalist Conception," 36–8; Achen and Bartels, *Democracy for Realists*.

11. James S. Fishkin, *When the People Speak: Deliberative Democracy and Public Consultation* (Oxford: Oxford University Press, 2009), 3–4.

12. Martin Gilens and Benjamin I. Page, in "Testing Theories of American Politics: Elites, Interest Groups, and Average Citizens," *Perspectives on Politics* 12:3 (2014): 564–81, argue that policy in the USA correlates more strongly with elite preferences. For criticism, see J. Alexander Branham, Stuart N. Soroka, and Christopher Wlezien, "When Do the Rich Win?" *Political Science Quarterly* 132:1 (2017).

13. Ronald Dworkin, *Sovereign Virtue: The Theory and Practice of Equality* (Cambridge: Harvard University Press, 2000).

14. Manin, *Principles of Representative Government*.

15. Fishkin, *When the People Speak*; Hélène Landemore, *Democratic Reason: Politics, Collective Intelligence, and the Rule of the Many* (Princeton: Princeton University Press, 2012).

16. Oliver Dowlen, *The Political Potential of Sortition: A Study of the Random Selection of Citizens for Public Office* (Exeter: Imprint

Academic, 2008); Oliver Dowlen, "Sorting Out Sortition: A Perspective on the Random Selection of Political Officers," *Political Studies* 57:2 (2009): 298–315; Peter Stone, *The Luck of the Draw: The Role of Lotteries in Decision Making* (Oxford: Oxford University Press, 2011).

17. Manin, *Principles of Representative Government*.

18. Przeworski, "Minimalist Conception."

19. On the intrinsic significance of participation or involvement, see Dworkin, *Sovereign Virtue*; Patchen Markell, "The Insufficiency of Non-Domination," *Political Theory* 36:1 (2008): 9–36.

20. David R. Mayhew, *Congress: The Electoral Connection*, 2nd ed. (New Haven: Yale University Press, 2004).

21. John L. Sullivan and Eric M. Uslaner, "Congressional Behavior and Electoral Marginality," *American Journal of Political Science* 22:3 (1978): 536–53.

22. Nadia Urbinati, *Representative Democracy: Principles and Genealogy* (Chicago: University of Chicago Press, 2006).

23. Jürgen Habermas, *Between Facts and Norms: Contributions to a Discourse Theory of Law and Democracy*, trans. William Rehg (Cambridge: MIT Press, 1996), 201–5; Philip Pettit, *On the People's Terms: A Republican Theory and Model of Democracy* (Cambridge: Cambridge University Press, 2012).

24. Hervé Pourtois, "Les Élections Sont-Elles Essentielles à la Démocratie?" *Philosophiques* 43:2 (2016): 411–39.

13. A Gradualist Path Toward Sortition, *Burks and Kies*

1. We owe the expression "hybrid legitimacy" to Julien Talpin, "How Can Constitutional Reforms Be Deliberative? The Hybrid Legitimacies of Constitutional Deliberative Democracy," in *Constitutional Deliberative Democracy in Europe*, ed. Min Reuchamps and Jane Suiter (Colchester, UK: ECPR, 2016), 93–108. Whereas Talpin's hybrid concerns whether epistemic, commonsense, democratic, and representative legitimacy can accrue in one constitutional setting, we only mean that the sortition chamber's blend of empowerment, continuity, and embeddedness could secure several forms of legitimacy that other kinds of minipublics lack by dint of design.

2. For a synthetic account exploring these challenges, see John Parkinson, *Deliberating in the Real World: Problems of Legitimacy in Deliberative Democracy* (Oxford: Oxford University Press, 2006).

3. One imperfect comparison might be universal suffrage.

4. For a succinct version, see Matthew Mendelsohn and Andrew

Parkin, "Introduction: Referendum Democracy," in *Referendum Democracy: Citizens, Elites and Deliberation in Referendum Campaigns*, ed. Matthew Mendelsohn and Andrew Parkin (Basingstoke, UK: Palgrave), 1–22.

5. Alan Renwick, "Referendums," in *The SAGE Handbook of Electoral Behaviour*, vol. 1, ed. Kai Arzheimer, Jocelyn Evans, and Michael S. Lewis-Beck (London: SAGE Publications, 2017), 433–58, especially 444–5.

6. Renwick, "Referendums," 445.

7. Renwick, "Referendums," 445–8.

8. Renwick, "Referendums," 450. For the datasets and broader argument, see 448–53.

9. On how sortition bodies aim (or fail) to achieve accountability, see various chapters in this volume, particularly the one by Jane Mansbridge.

10. For an initial examination of this question, see Pierre-Étienne Vandamme, Vincent Jacquet, Christoph Niessen, John Pitseys, and Min Reuchamps in this volume. They find that citizens are more open or, at least, more neutral to the idea of a sortition or mixed chamber whereas decision-makers are strongly opposed. Concerning the referendum on electoral reform formulated by the Ontario Citizens' Assembly, opinion polls collecting voters' reasons for supporting or opposing the reform suggest that they held neutral opinions on a sortition-selected body's being the source of the proposal. See Lawrence Leduc, "How and Why Electoral Reform Fails: Evaluating the Canadian Experience" (presentation, ECPR Joint Sessions Workshops, Lisbon, 2009).

11. Exceptions include Colorado, where the state constitution is routinely amended by a majority vote of the electorate.

12. See Shaun Bowler and Todd Donovan, *The Limits of Electoral Reform* (Oxford: Oxford University Press, 2013), 6–8.

13. A conclusion shared by Alan Renwick, *The Politics of Electoral Reform: Changing the Rules of Democracy* (Cambridge: Cambridge University Press, 2010), 10.

14. Bowler and Donovan, *The Limits of Electoral Reform*, 19–23. For a more general overview of rational choice theory as applied to institutions, see Peter A. Hall and Rosemary C. R. Taylor, "Political Science and the Three New Institutionalisms," *Political Studies* XLIV (1996): 936–57, especially 942–6. Finally, see also Bouricius and Vandamme et al. in this volume for parallel considerations.

15. Bowler and Donovan, *The Limits of Electoral Reform*, 23–5. On the relation between social movements and sortition, see Andrea Felicetti and Donatella della Porta in this volume.

16. Renwick, *The Politics of Electoral Reform*, 11–6.

17. Ibid., 12–3.

18. Ibid., 50–2. Renwick later emphasizes that exogenous factors also constrain outcomes, such as cognitive constraints and limited information (239–42).

19. Anthony R. Zito and Adriaan Schout, "Learning Theory Reconsidered: EU Integration Theories and Learning," *Journal of European Public Policy* 16:8 (2009): 1108.

20. A well-designed, largely-agreed-upon sortition design backed by sortition "experts" may prove vital to sortition's political and legislative uptake. Moreover, the diversity of approaches in this volume—for example, bicameral, unicameral, multibody, pure sortition, mixed sortition, one-shot, continuous, aggregative, deliberative, participatory, radical—are suggestive of the difficulties in forming a cohesive sortition expert network.

21. For discussion of cognitive constraints, attitudinal change, and diffusion, see also Renwick, *The Politics of Electoral Reform*, 47–68, especially 59–60. We leave open whether this cultural approach to institutional reform owes more to historical or sociological approaches to institutions. See Hall and Taylor, "Political Science and the Three New Institutionalisms," 937–42, 946–50.

22. For worries that it would not, see Bouricius and Vandamme et al. in this volume.

23. For concerns over professionalization and partisan contagion, see Tom Malleson, David Schecter, Bouricius, and Vandamme et al. in this volume.

24. Parkinson, *Deliberating in the Real World*, 99–123. For broader questions of the sortition chamber's participatory shortcomings, see Sintomer; Felicetti and della Porta; Malleson in this volume.

25. Andreas Follesdal and Simon Hix, "Why There Is a Democratic Deficit in the EU: A Response to Majone and Moravcsik," *Journal of Common Market Studies* 44:3 (2006): 533–62.

26. Nicole Curator and Marit Böker, "Linking Minipublics to the Deliberative System: A Research Agenda," *Policy Sciences* 49:2 (2016): 173–90.

27. On the assemblies in Ireland, Iceland, and Luxembourg, see respectively: Jane Suiter, David M. Farrell, and Clodagh Harris, "The Irish Constitutional Convention: A Case of 'High Legitimacy'?" in *Constitutional Deliberative Democracy in Europe*, ed. Min Reuchamps and Jane Suiter (Colchester, UK: ECPR, 2016), 33–52; Eirikur Bergmann, "Participatory Constitutional Deliberation in the Wake of Crisis: The Case of Iceland," in *Constitutional Deliberative Democracy in Europe*, 15–32; Raphaël Kies, *Les Consultations Citoyennes et les Réformes Constitutionnelles*, report for the Chamber of Deputies, Luxembourg, 2015.

28. Lawrence Leduc, Heather Bastedo, and Catherine Baquero, "The

Quiet Referendum: Why Electoral Referendum Failed in Ontario" (presentation, Canadian Political Science Association annual meeting, Vancouver, 2008), 8.

29. Patrick Dumont and Raphaël Kies, "Luxembourg," *European Journal of Political Research Political Data Yearbook* 55:1 (2016): 175–82.

30. For more on the Irish Constitutional Convention, see Tom Arnold in this volume.

31. Archon Fung, "British Columbia Citizens' Assembly on Electoral Reform," Participedia.net.

32. Leduc et al., "The Quiet Referendum," 1.

33. Aleksi Eerola and Min Reuchamps, "Constitutional Modernisation and Deliberative Democracy: A Political Science Assessment of Four Cases," *Revue Interdisciplinaire d'Études Juridiques* 77:2 (2016): 18.

34. For an overview, see the discussion of insiders and outsiders, followers and challenges in Didier Caluwaerts and Min Reuchamps, "Generating Democratic Legitimacy Through Deliberative Innovations: The Role of Embeddedness and Disruptiveness," *Representation* 52:1 (2016): 13–27.

35. Mundo Yang, "Europe's New Communication Policy and the Introduction of Transnational Deliberative Citizens' Involvement Projects," in *Is Europe Listening to Us? Successes and Failures of EU Citizen Consultations*, ed. Raphaël Kies and Patrizia Nanz (London: Routledge, 2013), 17–34.

36. Kies and Nanz, eds., *Is Europe Listening to Us?*; Espen Olsen and Hans Jörg Trenz, "From Citizens' Deliberation to Popular Will Formation? Generating Democratic Legitimacy in Transnational Deliberative Polling," *Political Studies* 62:1 (2014): 117–33.

37. Raphaël Kies, "The Seven Golden Rules to Promote EU Citizens' Consultation" (presentation, Fourth International Conference on Legislation and Law Reform, Washington, November 17–18, 2016); Elisa Lironi and Daniela Peta, "European Economic and Social Committee EU Public Consultations in the Digital Age: Enhancing the Role of the EESC and Civil Society Organizations," report for the European Economic and Social Committee, 2017.

38. Christine Quittkatt, "The European Commission's Online Consultations: A Success Story?" *Journal of Common Market Studies* 49:3 (2011): 653–74; European Commission, "Better Regulation Guidelines," commission staff working document, 2016, 17.

39. Christian Marxsen, "Open Stakeholder Consultations at the European Level—Voice of the Citizens?" *European Law Journal* 21:2 (2015): 261.

40. European Commission, "Better Regulation Guidelines," 84.
41. Lironi and Peta, "European Economic and Social Committee EU Public Consultations in the Digital Age."
42. Romain Badouard, "Combining Inclusion with Impact on the Decision? The Commission's Online Consultation on the European Citizens' Initiative," in *Is Europe Listening to Us?*, 153–72.
43. Marxsen, "Open Stakeholder Consultations at the European Level," 275.
44. In the EU case, decision-makers would include the commission, parliament, and council. On the Oregon case, see John Gastil, Robert Richards, and Katherine Knobloch, "Vicarious Deliberation: How the Oregon Citizens' Review Initiative Influenced Deliberation in Mass Elections," *International Journal of Communication* 8:1 (2014): 62–89.
45. Suiter et al., "The Irish Constitutional Convention."
46. Raphaël Kies, Monique Leyenaar, and Kees Niemöller, "European Citizens' Consultation: A Large Consultation on a Vague Topic," in *Is Europe Listening to Us?*, 59–78.
47. Carolyn Hendriks, "Coupling Citizens and Elites in Deliberative Systems: The Role of Institutional Design," *European Journal of Political Research* 55:1 (2016): 43–60.

14. Sortition, Rotation, and Mandate: Conditions for Political Equality and Deliberative Reasoning, *Owen and Smith*

1. There are other significant historical periods of the use of sortition—in particular, the Renaissance republicanism of Italian cities such as Venice and Florence in the thirteenth and fourteenth centuries and under the Crown of Aragon. In these periods, sortition was utilized primarily to select major and minor offices rather than assemblies, but this has some resonance with Athenian practice because sortition was introduced as a defense against faction and unstable coalitions. See Morgens Herman Hansen, *The Athenian Democracy in the Age of Demosthenes* (Oxford: Blackwell, 1991); Oliver Dowlen, *The Political Potential of Sortition* (Exeter: Imprint Academic, 2008); Yves Sintomer, *From Radical to Deliberative Democracy? Random Selection in Politics from Athens to the Present* (Cambridge: Cambridge University Press, 2018, forthcoming), originally published as *Petite Histoire de l'Expérimentation Démocratique: Tirage au Sort et Politique d'Athènes à Nos Jours* (La Découverte,

Serie "Poches," Paris, 2011). Our reconstruction of the institutions of Athenian democracy that follows draws on these texts.

2. Graham Smith, *Democratic Innovations: Designing Institutions for Citizen Participation* (Cambridge: Cambridge University Press, 2009), 72–110; Kimmo Grönlund, André Bächtiger, and Maija Setälä, eds., *Deliberative Mini-Publics: Involving Citizens in the Democratic Process* (Colchester: ECPR Press, 2014); Maija Setälä and Graham Smith, "Mini-Publics and Deliberative Democracy," in *Oxford Handbook of Deliberative Democracy*, ed. André Bächtiger, John Dryzek, Jane Mansbridge, and Mark E. Warren (Oxford: Oxford University Press, 2018).

3. The characteristics of these and other minipublic designs discussed in this section are explained in Smith, *Democratic Innovations*; Grönlund, Bächtiger, and Setälä, eds., *Deliberative Mini-Publics*; and Setälä and Smith, "Mini-Publics and Deliberative Democracy."

4. James S. Fishkin, *The Voice of the People: Public Opinion and Democracy* (Durham: Duke University Press, 1997). In *From Radical to Deliberative Democracy?*, Yves Sintomer points out that the Greeks did not have access to ideas about probability sampling, and thus the generation of random samples and the idea of counterfactual judgments were not part of their understanding of sortition bodies.

5. Simone Chambers, "Behind Closed Doors: Publicity, Secrecy, and the Quality of Deliberation," *Journal of Political Philosophy* 12 (2004): 289–410.

6. Setälä and Smith, "Mini-Publics and Deliberative Democracy."

7. Mark E. Warren and John Gastil, "Can Deliberative Minipublics Address the Cognitive Challenges of Democratic Citizenship?" *Journal of Politics* 77:2 (2015): 562–74.

8. Michael A. Neblo, *Deliberative Democracy Between Theory and Practice* (Cambridge: Cambridge University Press, 2015), 181; see also Yanis Papadopoulos, "On the Embeddedness of Deliberative Systems: Why Elitist Innovations Matter More," in *Deliberative Systems*, ed. John Parkinson and Jane Mansbridge (Cambridge: Cambridge University Press, 2012), 125–50.

9. In the analysis that follows, we consider a simple legislative assembly and avoid discussion of the UK case in which government ministers are drawn from both legislative assemblies. This would add a further level of complexity to the design of a sortition chamber.

10. See Gastil and Wright's lead chapter in this volume, "Legislature by Lot."

11. Ibid., 22.

12. We thank Terrill Bouricius for stressing this important point

during the 2017 Real Utopias workshop.

13. See Gastil and Wright's opening chapter in this volume, "Legislature by Lot."

14. Ibid., 28.

15. Smith, *Democratic Innovations*, 30–71.

16. Ernesto Ganuza and Gianpaolo Baiocchi, "The Power of Ambiguity: How Participatory Budgeting Travels the Globe," *Journal of Public Deliberation* 8:2 (2012); Yves Sintomer, Carsten Herzberg, Anja Röcke, and Giovanni Allegretti, "Transnational Models of Citizen Participation: The Case of Participatory Budgeting," *Journal of Public Deliberation* 8:2 (2012).

17. Quote comes from a workshop draft of the opening chapter of this volume by Gastil and Wright. The paper is available from the authors on request.

18. Gastil and Wright, "Legislature by Lot."

19. Alexander Guerrero also takes an issue-based approach to his sortition proposal, but, similar to Gastil and Wright, argues for smaller bodies without rapid rotation. See Alexander A. Guerro, "Against Elections; The Lottocratic Alternative," *Philosophy & Public Affairs* 42:2 (2014): 135–78.

20. Laurence Bherer, Louis Simard, and Mario Gauthier, "Autonomy for What End? Comparing Four Autonomous Public Organizations Dedicated to Public Participation" (presentation, ECPR Joint Sessions, Salamanca, 2014).

21. The initiative process would need to be implemented in a different way than current practice, where organized interests tend to dominate.

15. Who Needs Elections? Accountability, Equality, and Legitimacy Under Sortition, *Hennig*

1. Alexis de Tocqueville, *De la Démocratie en Amérique*, vols. 1–3 (Paris: Librairie de Charles Gosselin, 1835); Brett Hennig, *The End of Politicians: Time for a Real Democracy* (London: Unbound, 2017), 27–37; also see James Fishkin's chapter in this volume. In the first US presidential election (of 1788–89) less than 2 percent of the US population voted. In the UK at the same time, 1 to 3 percent of the population could vote in parliamentary elections. Elections, historically, were never democratic devices and were never intended to become such devices. See "US President—National Vote, 1788–1789," available online at Our Campaigns website (www.ourcampaigns.com), compared to "1790 Fast Facts," US Census Bureau, available online on the Census Bureau's

website; Neil Johnston, "The History of the Parliamentary Franchise," House of Commons Library Research Paper, 2013, 9.

2. "Outperform" here refers to the normative democratic ideal of informed, deliberative, representative decision-making in our legislatures. Note that this "ultimate aim" does not deny the likelihood that as a first strategic step a bicameral system may be necessary. Indeed, I have recently authored a proposal for just such a bicameral system in the Scottish Parliament, where randomly selected citizens in a permanent "House of Review" would serve staggered two-year terms. See Brett Hennig, Lyn Carson, Iain Walker, and David Schecter, *A Citizens' Assembly for the Scottish Parliament* (Sortition Foundation, Common Weal and new-Democracy Foundation, 2017).

3. Christopher H. Achen and Larry M. Bartels, *Democracy for Realists: Why Elections Do Not Produce Responsive Government* (Princeton: Princeton University Press, 2016), 1.

4. John Dunn, "Situating Democratic Political Accountability," in *Democracy, Accountability, and Representation*, ed. Adam Przeworski, Susan C. Stokes, and Bernard Manin (Cambridge: Cambridge University Press, 1999), chap. 11.

5. Dunn, "Situating Democratic Political Accountability," 330.

6. Ibid., 335.

7. Ibid., 330.

8. Ibid., 330n1.

9. Achen and Bartels, *Democracy for Realists*, 15.

10. Ibid., 16.

11. Ibid., 15; Achen and Bartels (24–7 and chap. 4) are especially dismissive of the classic theory outlined by Anthony Downs, *An Economic Theory of Democracy* (New York: Harper, 1957), and applied in books such as Robert S. Erikson, Gerald C. Wright, and John P. McIver, *Statehouse Democracy: Public Opinion and Policy in the American States* (Cambridge: Cambridge University Press, 1993), which places parties on a one-dimensional spectrum progressing toward the "median voter." See also Przeworski, Stokes, and Manin, eds., introduction to *Democracy, Accountability, and Representation*.

12. Achen and Bartels, *Democracy for Realists*, 18.

13. Tim Roemer, "Why Do Congressmen Spend Only Half Their Time Serving Us?" *Newsweek* (July 9, 2015).

14. Larry M. Bartels, *Unequal Democracy: The Political Economy of the New Gilded Age* (Princeton: Princeton University Press, 2010); Martin Gilens, *Affluence and Influence: Economic Inequality and Political Power in America* (Princeton: Princeton University Press, 2014).

15. Bartels, *Unequal Democracy*, 253–4.

16. Gilens, *Affluence and Influence*, 70.

17. Ibid., 81–3.

18. Martin Gilens and Benjamin I. Page, "Testing Theories of American Politics: Elites, Interest Groups, and Average Citizens," *Perspectives on Politics* 12:3 (2014): 564–81.

19. John Keane, *The Life and Death of Democracy* (London: W. W. Norton, 2009), 688–93, 706, but see 708: "monitory democracy is [not] mainly or 'essentially' a method of taming the power of government." Also see Dunn, "Situating Democratic Political Accountability," 334–5.

20. In any accountable system there must be "some set of established and observed rules" for selecting and replacing the rulers that is not at the discretion of the rulers themselves—this "important, if minimal, sense of political accountability" is why we are not concerned by the second-term US president, and why a system using sortition (with strict term limits) would continue to satisfy this minimal condition of accountability. See Dunn, "Situating Democratic Political Accountability," 333.

21. Amy Gutmann and Dennis Thompson, *Why Deliberative Democracy?* (Princeton: Princeton University Press, 2004). For definitions of *deliberative democracy* see 3, 7, 101, 116.

22. Murray Edelman, *Constructing the Political Spectacle* (Chicago: University of Chicago Press, 2008).

23. Bruce Ackerman and James S. Fishkin, *Deliberation Day* (New Haven: Yale University Press, 2005). Or the many innovative online deliberative tools may be used to achieve a similar goal.

24. Conor Friedersdorf, "Constant Fundraising: The Other Campaign-Finance Problem," *Atlantic* (April 18, 2012).

25. Hennig, *The End of Politicians*, chap. 4; and elsewhere in this volume.

26. Ibid.

27. Fishkin makes a similar point in his chapter in this volume.

28. John S. Dryzek, *Foundations and Frontiers of Deliberative Governance* (Oxford: Oxford University Press, 2010), 27.

29. Lyn Carson describes such parallel processes in her chapter within this volume.

30. W. Lance Bennett and Alexandra Segerberg, "The Logic of Connective Action," *Information, Communication & Society* 15:5 (2012): 739–68; David Karpf, *The MoveOn Effect: The Unexpected Transformation of American Political Advocacy* (Oxford: Oxford University Press, 2012).

31. See Gutmann and Thompson, *Why Deliberative Democracy?*, 114. Other nondeliberative forms of political interaction, such as protest and direct action, are also important in a democratic society, but again we would not wish them to occur in an ideal

legislature.

32. Oliver Escobar and Stephen Elstub, *Forms of Minipublics* (Research and Development Note, newDemocracy Foundation, 2017); Fred Cutler, Richard Johnston, R. Kenneth Carty, André Blais, and Patrick Fournier, "Deliberation, Information, and Trust: The British Columbia Citizens' Assembly as Agenda-Setter," in *Designing Deliberative Democracy: The British Columbia Citizens' Assembly*, ed. Mark E. Warren and Hilary Pearse (Cambridge: Cambridge University Press, 2008). On the limits of the minipublic analogy, see Owens and Smith's chapter in this volume.

33. Elsje Jorritsma, "Rotterdam Gaat Wijkpolitici Niet Kiezen Maar Loten," *NRC* (February 23, 2017).

34. There are many other recent examples detailed on the new-Democracy and Sortition Foundation websites.

35. Hennig, Carson, Walker, and Schecter, *A Citizens' Assembly for the Scottish Parliament*. There is also recent and significant institutional support for the introduction of such a bicameral system to the Parliament of the German-Speaking Community of Belgium.

36. That organization might target the state of Queensland, which has a unicameral parliament. For more on newDemocracy, see Lyn Carson's chapter in this volume.

37. See the Sénat Citoyen campaign website, senatcitoyen.fr; Gil Delannoi and Lyn Carson, *French Presidential Election and Sortition* (newDemocracy Foundation Research Note, 2017).

38. Mark E. Warren and John Gastil, "Can Deliberative Minipublics Address the Cognitive Challenges of Democratic Citizenship?" *Journal of Politics* 77:2 (2015): 582–74. Vandamme et al. in this volume show that in Belgium a sortition chamber inspires more confidence in 34.4 percent of people (33.3 percent disagree and 32.3 percent are neutral).

16. Why Hybrid Bicameralism Is Not Right for Sortition, *Bouricius*

1. In this volume, see Gastil and Wright's lead chapter, "Legislature by Lot." Also see Arash Abizadeh, "Representation, Bicameralism, and Sortition: Reconstituting the Senate as a Randomly Selected Citizen Assembly" (presentation, bicameralism workshop at McGill University, 2016). Also see Anthony Barnett and Peter Carty, *The Athenian Option: Radical Reform for the House of Lords* (Exeter: Imprint Academic, 2008); Keith Sutherland, "The Two Sides of the Representative Coin," *Studies in Social Justice*

5:2 (2011): 197–211.

2. Frank Fischer, *Democracy and Expertise: Reorienting Policy Inquiry* (Oxford: Oxford University Press, 2009), 61.

3. Anthoula Malkopoulou, "The Paradox of Democratic Selection: Is Sortition Better Than Voting?" in *Parliamentarism and Democratic Theory*, ed. Kari Palonen and José María Rosales (Toronto: Budrich, 2015), 250.

4. Ibid., 247.

5. Brendan Nyhan and Jason Reifler, "When Corrections Fail: The Persistence of Political Misperceptions," *Political Behavior* 32:2 (2010), 303–30.

6. Ibid.

7. Gastil and Wright, "Legislature by Lot."

8. I subscribe to the social construct analysis of political leadership advanced by Murray Edelman that "belief in leadership is a catalyst of conformity and obedience." *Constructing the Political Spectacle* (Chicago: University of Chicago Press, 1988), 37. Narratives about the accomplishments of leaders should be treated with extreme skepticism, as explained by Philip M. Rosenzweig, *The Halo Effect: How Managers Let Themselves Be Deceived* (London: Pocket Books, 2008).

9. Daniel Kahneman, *Thinking, Fast and Slow* (New York: Farrar, Straus and Giroux, 2015).

10. Joshua Becker, Devon Brackbill, and Damon Centola, "Network Dynamics of Social Influence in the Wisdom of Crowds," *Proceedings of the National Academy of Sciences* 114:26 (2017): E5070–6.

11. David Owen, *The Hubris Syndrome: Bush, Blair and the Intoxication of Power* (York: Methuen & Co., 2012).

12. James Surowiecki, *The Wisdom of Crowds: Why the Many Are Smarter Than the Few and How Collective Wisdom Shapes Business* (London: Economics, Societies, and Nations, 2004).

13. Studies have found no significant difference between liberals and conservatives in this regard, but it seems likely that the subset of individuals from across the political spectrum who are willing to run for office tend toward harmful "intellectual arrogance" rather than beneficial humility. See Mark R. Leary et al., "Cognitive and Interpersonal Features of Intellectual Humility," *Personality and Social Psychology Bulletin* 43:6 (2017): 793–813.

14. Victoria F. Nourse and Jane S. Schacter, "The Politics of Legislative Drafting: A Congressional Case Study," *New York University Law Review* 77:3 (2002): 575–624.

15. In his 2009 memoir, Senator Ted Kennedy estimated that 95 percent of the drafting and negotiating in Congress is done by staff rather than legislators. Edward M. Kennedy, *True Compass:*

A Memoir (New York: Twelve, 2011), 486.

16. Hélène Landemore, *Democratic Reason: Politics, Collective Intelligence, and the Rule of the Majority* (Princeton: Princeton University Press, 2013), 122.

17. Carey K. Morewedge et al., "Debiasing Decisions Improved Decision Making with a Single Training Intervention," *Policy Insights from the Behavioral and Brain Sciences* 2:1 (2015): 129–40.

18. Edelman, *Constructing the Political Spectacle*, 14.

19. Anthony Downs coined the term in *An Economic Theory of Democracy* (New York: Harper & Bros., 1957), while Bryan Caplan takes it one step farther, arguing that voters gain psychological utility from irrational loyalty in his book *The Myth of the Rational Voter: Why Democracies Choose Bad Policies* (Princeton: Princeton University Press, 2007).

20. By "aptitude," he does not refer to an inherent character trait but the effect of procedures. Jeremy Bentham and Philip Schofield, *Securities Against Misrule and Other Constitutional Writings for Tripoli and Greece* (Oxford: Clarendon Press, 2009).

21. Jon Elster, *Securities Against Misrule: Juries, Assemblies, Elections* (Cambridge: Cambridge University Press, 2013), 202.

22. Margaret T. Lee and Richard Ofshe, "The Impact of Behavioral Style and Status Characteristics on Social Influence: A Test of Two Competing Theories," *Social Psychology Quarterly* 44:2 (1981): 73–82.

23. Geoffrey L. Cohen, "Party over Policy: The Dominating Impact of Group Influence on Political Beliefs," *Journal of Personality and Social Psychology* 85:5 (2003): 808–22.

24. Ernest Callenbach and Michael Phillips, *A Citizen Legislature* (Berkeley, CA: Banyan Tree Books, 1985).

25. Cass R. Sunstein, *Why Societies Need Dissent* (Cambridge: Harvard University Press, 2003).

26. Jon Elster (echoing Jeremy Bentham) has stressed this "defensive" potential of sortition in *Securities Against Misrule*. Also see Oliver Dowlen, *The Political Potential of Sortition: A Study of the Random Selection of Citizens for Public Office* (Exeter: Imprint Academic, 2009).

27. Politicians such as Representative Charles Rangel and Representative Michael Grimm were re-elected despite standing under dark clouds of corruption. These and other examples can be found on the OpenSecrets website, www.opensecrets.org.

28. On distinction, see Bernard Manin, *The Principles of Representative Government* (Cambridge: Cambridge University Press, 1997).

29. In their chapter in this volume ("Sortition, Rotation, and Mandate"), David Owen and Graham Smith call for a large pool of randomly selected citizens, and they divide up tasks among

subgroups in a way that bears some resemblance to this idea—but without an all-purpose chamber.

30. Anthoula Malkopoulou, "The Paradox of Democratic Selection: Is Sortition Better Than Voting?" in *Parliamentarism and Democracy Theory Historical and Contemporary Perspectives*, ed. Kari Palonen and José María Rosales (Leverkusen: Budrich, Barbara, 2015), 230. Gastil and Wright do specify a number of reasonable, though modest, modifications to standard legislative chamber practices for a sortition body, but these do not seem sufficient to me. In his "Paris Commune" essay (1871), Karl Marx noted that "the working class cannot simply lay hold of the ready-made state machinery, and wield it for its own purposes." An all-sortition legislature would constitute a fundamental change of class control (whether one thinks of elected legislators as a "political class" or servants of a "capitalist class"), though expressly not in a Leninist "vanguard party" sort of way.

31. The ability of multiple minipublics to address various dilemmas of sortition design is described in Terrill G. Bouricius, "Democracy Through Multi-Body Sortition: Athenian Lessons for the Modern Day," *Journal of Public Deliberation* 9:1 (2013).

32. Mark E. Warren and Hilary Pearse, eds., *Designing Deliberative Democracy: The British Columbia Citizens' Assembly* (Cambridge: Cambridge University Press, 2012).

33. Although it has huge budgetary impacts, the 2017 impasse on "repeal and replacement" of Obamacare could have been an opportunity, especially with a nontraditional disrupter like Donald Trump. If there had been far more on-the-ground experience with sortition experiments in the US, it is possible to imagine how major chunks of public policy on health care could have been handed off to a sortition process. Conservatives don't trust government bureaucrats making decisions about their health care, and liberals don't trust insurance executives. But it might be that both sides could agree to let a large representative sample of ordinary citizens hear from a range of experts on the issue and make decisions on their behalf.

34. This is similar to John Rawls's "original position" thought experiment. By separating people choosing the procedures from the concrete policy matters by a virtual "veil of ignorance," they have an incentive to propose a fair and epistemically solid process for other minipublics to use. If the same body is both deciding on rules and dealing with policy, the incentive is to create rules that will favor the current majority in adopting their preferred policy.

35. Careful examination by the agenda council may suggest a particular issue doesn't warrant the calling of interest panels, but even

an objectively unworthy topic that can muster a significant petition interest might be important to have a review panel examine, even if no policy change gets advanced, so that the public is assured it was adequately looked at.

36. David Estlund, "Opinion Leaders, Independence and Condorcet's Jury Theorem," *Theory & Decision* 36:2 (1994): 131–62.
37. Douglas Adams, *Restaurant at the End of the Universe* (New York: Del Rey, 1997), 201.
38. Bouricius, "Democracy Through Multi-Body Sortition."
39. From the time of Aristotle up to the European Enlightenment, elections, through their "principle of distinction," were seen as the appropriate tool for aristocracy or oligarchy, while sortition was viewed as natural to democracy. See Manin, *The Principles of Representative Government.*

17. Sortition's Scope, Contextual Variations, and Transitions, *Gastil and Wright*

1. Robert A. Dahl, *Democracy and Its Critics* (New Haven: Yale University Press, 1989).
2. Dennis Hale, *The Jury in America: Triumph and Decline* (Lawrence, KS: University Press of Kansas, 2016).
3. The origins of these and related processes appear in John Gastil and Peter Levine, eds., *The Deliberative Democracy Handbook: Strategies for Effective Civic Engagement in the Twenty-First Century* (San Francisco: Jossey-Bass, 2005).
4. Carolyn J. Lukensmeyer, Joe Goldman, and Steven Brigham, "A Town Meeting for the Twenty-First Century," in *The Deliberative Democracy Handbook*, 154–63.
5. James S. Fishkin, *When the People Speak: Deliberative Democracy and Public Consultation* (New York: Oxford University Press, 2009).
6. Mark E. Warren and Hillary Pearse, eds., *Designing Deliberative Democracy: The British Columbia Citizens' Assembly* (Cambridge: Cambridge University Press, 2008). Also see Mark Warren and John Gastil, "Can Deliberative Minipublics Address the Cognitive Challenges of Democratic Citizenship?" *Journal of Politics* 77 (2015): 562–74.
7. See the chapter in this volume by Tom Arnold, David M. Farrell, and Jane Suiter.
8. See the chapter in this volume by David Owen and Graham Smith.
9. See the chapter in this volume by James Fishkin.
10. See the formulation of this problem in Sean Ingham, "Disagreement

and Epistemic Arguments for Democracy," *Politics, Philosophy & Economics* 12 (2013): 136–55. Also see the response, Robert Richards and John Gastil, "Symbolic-Cognitive Proceduralism: A Model of Deliberative Legitimacy," *Journal of Public Deliberation* 11 (2015).

11. We view this as drawing on two chapters in this volume: Owen and Smith's and Bouricius's.

12. The problem is often sparking legislative deliberation in the first place. See Joseph M. Bessette, *The Mild Voice of Reason: Deliberative Democracy and American National Government* (Chicago: University of Chicago Press, 1997).

13. See Mansbridge's chapter in this volume.

14. See Courant's chapter in this volume.

15. Carolina Johnson and John Gastil, "Variations of Institutional Design for Empowered Deliberation," *Journal of Public Deliberation* 11 (2015).

16. On social-movement organizations, see Felicetti and della Porta's chapter in this volume. On the response of political parties, see Bouricius's chapter.

17. Transparency International provides annual ratings at its online portal.

18. See Michael Johnston's overview (7–8) in his edited volume, *Political Corruption: Concepts and Contexts*, 3rd ed. (New York: Taylor & Francis, 2001).

19. Political critique isn't immune to the "fundamental attribution error" prevalent in social cognition: it is a common mistake to attribute actors' behavioral transgressions to character flaws, rather than to the circumstances in which they act. See, for example, Philip E. Tetlock, "Accountability: A Social Check on the Fundamental Attribution Error," *Social Psychology Quarterly* 48 (1985): 227–36.

20. See Mansbridge's chapter in this volume.

21. Joan Tronto, *Who Cares? How to Reshape a Democratic Politics* (Ithaca, NY: Cornell University Press, 2015).

22. See Deven Burks and Raphaël Kies's and Bouricius's chapters in this volume.

23. See the chapters in this volume by Pierre-Étienne Vandamme et al. and Tom Arnold et al.

24. Promising initiatives include those pursued by the Sortition Foundation and other cases documented at the Participedia.net compendium, including "Democracy in Practice: Democratic Student Government Program in Cochabamba, Bolivia."

Bibliography

Abizadeh, Arash. "Representation, Bicameralism, and Sortition: Reconstituting the Senate as Randomly Selected Citizen Assembly." Workshop paper, McGill University, 2016.

Abramson, Jeffrey B. *We, the Jury: The Jury System and the Ideal of Democracy*. 3rd ed. Cambridge: Harvard University Press, 2003.

Achen, Christopher H., and Larry M. Bartels. *Democracy for Realists: Why Elections Do Not Produce Responsive Governments*. Princeton: Princeton University Press, 2016.

Ackerman, Bruce, and Ian Ayers. *Voting with Dollars: A New Paradigm for Campaign Finance*. New Haven: Yale University Press, 2004.

Ackerman, Bruce, and James Fishkin. *Deliberation Day*. New Haven: Yale University Press, 2004.

Adams, Douglas. *The Restaurant at the End of the Universe*. New York: Del Rey, 1997.

Aguilar Rivera, José Antonio. "Las Razones de la Tómbola." *Nexos*, April 1, 2015.

Aristophanes. *Clouds. Wasps. Peace*. Edited and translated by Jeffrey Henderson. Cambridge: Harvard University Press, 1998.

Aristotle. *The Politics*. Harmondsworth: Penguin Classics, 1962.

———. *The Athenian Constitution*. Harmondsworth: Penguin Classics, 1984.

Atlee, Tom. *The Tao of Democracy: Using Co-Intelligence to Create a World That Works for All*. Winnipeg: Writers' Collective, 2003.

Babad, Elisha Y., Jacinto Inbar, and Robert Rosenthal. "Pygmalion, Galatea, and the Golem: Investigations of Biased and Unbiased Teachers." *Journal of Educational Psychology* 74, no. 4 (1982): 459–74.

Badouard, Romain. "Combining Inclusion with Impact on the Decision? The Commission's Online Consultation on the European Citizens' Initiative." In *Is Europe Listening to Us? Successes and Failures of EU Citizen Consultations*, edited by Raphaël Kies and Patrizia Nanz, 153–72. London: Routledge, 2013.

Baiocchi, Gianpaolo, and Ernesto Ganuza. *Popular Democracy: The Paradox of Participation*. Stanford: Stanford University Press, 2016.

Barber, Benjamin R. *Strong Democracy: Participatory Politics for a New Age*. Berkeley: University of California Press, 1984.

———. *The Death of Communal Liberty: A History of Freedom in a Swiss Mountain Canton*. Princeton: Princeton University Press, 2015.

Barker, Chris, and Brian Martin. "Participation: The Happiness Connection." *Journal of Public Deliberation* 7, no. 1 (2011).

Barnett, Anthony, and Peter Carty. *The Athenian Option: Radical Reform for the House of Lords*. Exeter: Imprint Academic, 2008.

Bartels, Larry M. *Unequal Democracy: The Political Economy of the New Gilded Age*. Princeton: Princeton University Press, 2010.

Becker, Joshua, Devon Brackbill, and Damon Centola. "Network Dynamics of Social Influence in the Wisdom of Crowds." *Proceedings of the National Academy of Sciences* 114, no. 26 (2017): E5070–6.

Bennett, W. Lance, and Alexandra Segerberg, "The Logic of Connective Action." *Information, Communication & Society* 15, no. 5 (2012): 739–68.

Bentham, Jeremy, and Philip Schofield. *Securities Against Misrule and Other Constitutional Writings for Tripoli and Greece*, edited by Philip Schofield. Oxford: Clarendon Press, 2009.

Benz, Matthias, and Alois Stutzer, "Are Voters Better Informed When They Have a Larger Say in Politics? Evidence for the European Union and Switzerland." *Public Choice* 119, no. 1/2 (2004): 31–59.

Bergmann, Eirikur. "Participatory Constitutional Deliberation in the Wake of Crisis: The Case of Iceland." In *Constitutional Deliberative Democracy in Europe*, edited by Min Reuchamps and Jane Suiter, 15–32. Colchester, UK: ECPR Press, 2016.

Berkman, Michael B., and Robert E. O'Connor. "Do Women Legislators Matter? Female Legislators and State Abortion Policy." *American Politics Quarterly* 21, no. 1 (1993): 102–24.

Bessette, Joseph M. *The Mild Voice of Reason: Deliberative Democracy and American National Government*. Chicago: University of Chicago Press, 1997.

Binder, Michael, Cheryl Boudreau, and Thad Kousser. "Shortcuts to Deliberation? How Cues Reshape the Role of Information in Direct Democracy Voting." *California Western Law Review* 48, no. 1 (2011): 97–128.

Blondiaux, Loïc, and Yves Sintomer. "L'Impératif Délibératif." *Politix* 15, no. 57 (2002): 17–35.

Boswell, John, Simon Niemeyer, and Carolyn M. Hendriks. "Julia Gillard's Citizens' Assembly Proposal for Australia: A Deliberative Democratic Analysis." *Australian Journal of Political Science* 48, no. 2 (2013): 164–78.

Bourdieu, Pierre. "La Représentation Politique." *Actes de la Recherche en Sciences Sociales* 36–37 (1981): 3–24.

Bourg, Dominique, ed. *Pour Une 6e République Écologique*. Paris: Odile Jacob, 2011.

Bouricius, Terrill G. "Democracy Through Multi-Body Sortition: Athenian Lessons for the Modern Day." *Journal of Public Deliberation* 9, no. 1 (2013): 1–19.

Bouricius, Terrill G., David Schecter, Campbell Wallace, and John Gastil. "Imagine a Democracy Built on Lotteries, Not Elections." *Zócalo Public Square*, April 5, 2016.

Bowler, Shaun, and Todd Donovan. *The Limits of Electoral Reform*. Oxford: Oxford University Press, 2013.

Branham, J. Alexander, Stuart N. Soroka, and Christopher Wlezien. "When Do the Rich Win?" *Political Science Quarterly* 132, no. 1 (2017): 43–62.

Bratton, Kathleen A., and Leonard P. Ray. "Descriptive Representation, Policy Outcomes, and Municipal Day-Care Coverage in Norway." *American Journal of Political Science* 46, no. 2 (2002): 428–37.

Broockman, David E. "Black Politicians Are More Intrinsically Motivated to Advance Blacks' Interests: A Field Experiment Manipulating Political Incentives." *American Journal of Political Science* 57, no. 3 (2013): 521–36.

Bryan, Frank, and John McClaughry, *The Vermont Papers: Recreating Democracy on a Human Scale*. Port Mills: Chelsea Green Publishing, 1989.

Buchstein, Hubertus. *Demokratie und Lotterie: Das Los als politisches Entscheidungsinstrument von der Antike bis zur EU*. Frankfurt: Campus Verlag, 2009.

Buchstein, Hubertus. "Countering the 'Democracy Thesis'—Sortition in Ancient Greek Political Theory." *Redescriptions* 18, no. 2 (2015): 126–57.

Buonocore, Mauro. "Un Weekend Deliberativo all'Ombra del Partenone." *Reset* 96 (July–August 2006): 6–8.

Burnheim, John. *Is Democracy Possible?* Cambridge: Polity Press, 1985.

Callenbach, Ernest, and Michael Phillips. *A Citizen Legislature*. Berkeley: Banyan Tree Books, 1985.

Callon, Michel, Pierre Lascoumes, and Yannick Barthe. *Acting in an Uncertain World: An Essay on Technical Democracy (Inside Technology)*. Cambridge: MIT Press, 2011.

Caluwaerts, Didier. *Confrontation and Communication: Deliberative Democracy in Divided Belgium*. Brussels: European Interuniversity Press, 2012.

Caluwaerts, Didier, and Min Reuchamps. "Deliberative Stress in Linguistically Divided Belgium." In *Democratic Deliberation in*

Deeply Divided Societies: From Conflict to Common Ground, edited by Juan E. Ugarriza and Didier Caluwaerts, 35–52. London: Palgrave Macmillan, 2014.

———. *The G1000: Facts, Figures and Some Lessons from an Experience of Deliberative Democracy in Belgium.* Unpublished manuscript, 2014.

———. "Strengthening Democracy Through Bottom-up Deliberation: An Assessment of the Internal Legitimacy of the G1000 Project." *Acta Politica* 50, no. 2 (2015): 151–70.

———. "Generating Democratic Legitimacy Through Deliberative Innovations: The Role of Embeddedness and Disruptiveness." *Representation* 52, no. 1 (2016): 13–27.

Caluwaerts, Didier, Vincent Jacquet, and Min Reuchamps. "Deliberative Democracy and the So What Question: The Effects of Belgium's G1000." Paper presented at the American Political Science Association annual meeting, Philadelphia, September 2016.

Canon, David T. *Race, Redistricting, and Representation.* Chicago: University of Chicago Press, 1999.

Caplan, Bryan. *The Myth of the Rational Voter: Why Democracies Choose Bad Policies.* Princeton: Princeton University Press, 2007.

Carnes, Nicholas, and Noam Lupu. "Rethinking the Comparative Perspective on Class and Representation: Evidence from Latin America." *American Journal of Political Science* 59, no. 1 (2015): 1–18.

Carnes, Nicholas. "Does the Numerical Underrepresentation of the Working Class in Congress Matter?" *Legislative Studies Quarterly* 37, no. 1 (2012): 5–34.

Carson, Lyn. "Ignorance and Inclusion, Mr. Jefferson, Might Be Good for Democracy." United States Studies Centre Working Paper Series, University of Sydney, Sydney, November 2009.

———. "Investigation of (and Introspection on) Organizer Bias." In *The Australian Citizens' Parliament and the Future of Deliberative Democracy,* edited by Lyn Carson, John Gastil, Janette Hartz-Karp, and Ron Lubensky. University Park, PA: Pennsylvania State University Press, 2013.

———. "How Not to Introduce Deliberative Democracy: The 2010 Citizens' Assembly on Climate Change Proposal." In *The Australian Citizens' Parliament and the Future of Deliberative Democracy,* edited by Lyn Carson, John Gastil, Janette Hartz-Karp, and Ron Lubensky. University Park, PA: Pennsylvania State University Press, 2013.

Carson, Lyn, and Brian Martin. *Random Selection in Politics.* Westport: Praeger Publishers, 1999.

Carson, Lyn, John Gastil, Janette Hartz-Karp, and Ron Lubensky, eds. *The Australian Citizens' Parliament and the Future of Deliberative*

Democracy. University Park, PA: Pennsylvania State University Press, 2013.

Castoriadis, Cornelius. *La Montée de l'Insignifiance*. Paris: Seuil, 1996.

Chambers, Simone. "Behind Closed Doors: Publicity, Secrecy, and the Quality of Deliberation." *Journal of Political Philosophy* 12, no. 4 (2004): 389–410.

———. "Rhetoric and the Public Sphere: Has Deliberative Democracy Abandoned Mass Democracy?" *Political Theory* 37, no. 3 (2009): 323–50.

Cheng Joseph, Sheh Yu, and Li Fan. "Local Government's Consultative Budgetary Reforms in China: A Case Study of Wenling City." *China International Journal* 13, no. 1 (2015): 115–18.

Cohen, Geoffrey L. "Party Over Policy: The Dominating Impact of Group Influence on Political Beliefs." *Journal of Personality and Social Psychology* 85, no. 5 (2003): 808–22.

Cohen, Joshua, and Joel Rogers. *On Democracy*. New York: Penguin, 1983.

Courant, Dimitri. "Tirage au Sort et Concertation dans l'Armée Française. Le Cas du Conseil Supérieur de la Fonction Militaire (1969–2014)." Master's thesis, EHESS, 2014.

———. "Du Klérotèrion à la Cryptologie: L'Acte de Tirage au Sort au XXIe Siècle, Pratiques et Équipements." In *Tirage au Sort et Démocratie*, edited by Liliane Rabatel and Yves Sintomer. Paris: La Découverte, 2018.

———. "Thinking Sortition: Modes of Selection, Deliberative Frameworks and Democratic Principles." Les Cahiers de l'IEPHI, Working Papers, no. 68 (2017).

———. "Les Militants du Tirage au Sort: Sociologie d'un Nouvel Activisme Démocratique." *Participations* (forthcoming, 2018).

———. "'We Have Humility': Perceived Legitimacy and Representative Claims in the Irish Citizens' Assembly" (paper presented at the American Political Science Association Conference, Boston, 2018).

Crosby, Ned. *In Search of the Competent Citizen*. Plymouth: Center for New Democratic Processes, 1975.

———. "System Four: A New Form of Democracy." Unpublished manuscript, 1976.

Curato, Nicole, and Marit Böker. "Linking Mini-Publics to the Deliberative System: A Research Agenda." *Policy Sciences* 49, no. 2 (2016): 173–90.

Cutler, Fred, Richard Johnston, R. Kenneth Carty, André Blais, and Patrick Fournier. "Deliberation, Information and Trust: The British Columbia Citizens' Assembly as Agenda Setter." In *Designing Deliberative Democracy: The British Columbia Citizens' Assembly*, edited by Mark E. Warren and Hilary Pearse, 166–91. Cambridge: Cambridge University Press, 2008.

Dahl, Robert A. *After the Revolution? Authority in a Good Society.* New Haven: Yale University Press, 1970.

———. *Democracy and Its Critics.* New Haven: Yale University Press, 1989.

———. "The Problem of Civic Competence." *Journal of Democracy* 3, no. 4 (1992): 45–59.

de Tocqueville, Alexis. *De la Démocratie en Amérique*, vols. 1–3. Paris: Librairie de Charles Gosselin, 1835.

Delannoi, Gil, and Lyn Carson. *French Presidential Election and Sortition.* Research Note. Sydney: newDemocracy Foundation, 2017.

Delannoi, Gil, and Oliver Dowlen, eds. *Sortition: Theory and Practice.* Exeter: Imprint Academic, 2010.

Delannoi, Gil, Oliver Dowlen, and Peter Stone. *The Lottery as a Democratic Institution.* Dublin: Policy Institute, 2013.

Delannoi, Gil. *Le Retour du Tirage au Sort en Politique.* Paris: Fondapol, 2010.

della Porta, Donatella, and Dieter Rucht, eds. *Meeting Democracy. Power and Deliberation in Global Justice Movements.* Cambridge: Cambridge University Press, 2013.

Dewey, John. *The Public and Its Problems.* New York: Holt, 1929.

Dienel, Peter. *Die Planungszelle: Der Bürger als Chance.* Wiesbaden: VS Verlag fur Sozialwissenschaften, 1997.

Dietrich, Bryce J., Scott Lasley, Jeffery J. Mondak, Megan L. Remmel, and Joel Turner. "Personality and Legislative Politics: The Big Five Trait Dimensions Among U.S. State Legislators." *Political Psychology* 33, no. 2 (2012): 195–210.

Dowlen, Oliver. *The Political Potential of Sortition.* Exeter: Imprint Academic, 2008.

———. "Sorting Out Sortition: A Perspective on the Random Selection of Political Officers." *Political Studies* 57, no. 2 (2009): 298–315.

Downs, Anthony. *An Economic Theory of Democracy.* New York: Harper, 1957.

Dryzek, John S. *Foundations and Frontiers of Deliberative Governance.* Oxford: Oxford University Press, 2010.

———. *Discursive Democracy. Politics, Policy and Political Science.* Cambridge: Cambridge University Press, 1990.

———. "Democratization as Deliberative Capacity Building." *Comparative Political Studies* 42, no. 11 (2009): 1379–402.

———. "The Forum, the System, and the Polity: Three Varieties of Democratic Theory." *Political Theory* 45, no. 5 (2017): 610–36.

Dryzek, John S., and Carolyn Hendriks. "Fostering Deliberation in the Forum and Beyond." In *The Argumentative Turn Revisited*, edited by Frank Fischer and Herbert Gottweis, 31–57. Durham: Duke University Press, 2012.

Dumont, Patrick, and Raphaël Kies, "Luxembourg." *European Journal of Political Research Political Data Yearbook* 55, no. 1 (2016): 175–82.

Dunn, John. "Situating Democratic Political Accountability." In *Democracy, Accountability, and Representation*, edited by Adam Przeworski, Susan C. Stokes, and Bernard Manin, 329–44. Cambridge: Cambridge University Press, 1999.

Dupuis-Déri, Francis. *Démocratie: Histoire Politique d'un Mot.* Montreal: Lux, 2013.

Dusevic, Tom. "Voters Rage Against the Political Machine." *The Australian*, December 24, 2016.

Dworkin, Ronald. *Sovereign Virtue: The Theory and Practice of Equality.* Cambridge: Harvard University Press, 2000.

Edelman, Murray. *Constructing the Political Spectacle.* Chicago: University of Chicago Press, 1988.

Eerola, Aleksi, and Min Reuchamps. "Constitutional Modernisation and Deliberative Democracy: A Political Science Assessment of Four Cases." *Revue Interdisciplinaire d'Etudes Juridiques* 77, no. 2 (2016): 319–36.

Elkink, Johan, David Farrell, Theresa Reidy, and Jane Suiter. "Understanding the 2015 Marriage Referendum in Ireland: Context, Campaign, and Conservative Ireland." *Irish Political Studies* 32, no. 3 (2017): 361–81.

Elster, Jon, ed. *Deliberative Democracy.* Cambridge: Cambridge University Press, 1998.

———. *Securities Against Misrule: Juries, Assemblies, Elections.* Cambridge: Cambridge University Press, 2013.

Elstub, Stephen, and Peter McLaverty, eds. *Deliberative Democracy: Issues and Cases.* Edinburgh: Edinburgh University Press, 2014.

Engelstad, Fredrik. "The Assignment of Political Office by Lot." *Social Science Information* 28, no. 1 (1989): 23–50.

Erikson, Robert S., Gerald C. Wright, and John P. McIver. *Statehouse Democracy: Public Opinion and Policy in the American States.* Cambridge: Cambridge University Press, 1993.

Esaiasson, Peter, and Sören Holmberg. *Representation from Above: Members of Parliament and Representative Democracy in Sweden.* Translated by Janet Westerlund. Aldershot: Darmouth, 1996.

Escobar, Oliver, and Stephen Elstub. *Forms of Mini-Publics.* Research and Development Note. Sydney: newDemocracy Foundation, 2017.

Estlund, David M. "Opinion Leaders, Independence, and Condorcet's Jury Theorem." *Theory and Decision* 36, no. 2 (1994): 131–62.

Evans, Sara M., and Harry C. Boyte. *Free Spaces: The Sources of Democratic Change in America.* Chicago: University of Chicago Press, 1992.

Farrar, Cynthia, James S. Fishkin, Donald P. Green, Christian List,

Robert C. Luskin, and Elizabeth Levy Paluck. "Disaggregating Deliberation's Effects: An Experiment with a Deliberative Poll." *British Journal of Political Science* 40, no. 2 (2010): 333–47.

Farrell, David and Jane Suiter. "The Election in Context." In *How Ireland Voted, 2016*, edited by Michael Gallagher and Michael Marsh, 277–92. Houndmills: Palgrave Macmillan, 2016.

Farrell, David, Eoin O'Malley, and Jane Suiter. "Deliberative Democracy in Action Irish-Style: The 2011 *We the Citizens* Pilot Citizens' Assembly." *Irish Political Studies* 28, no. 1 (2013): 99–113.

Farrell, David, Jane Suiter, and Clodagh Harris. "Bringing People into the Heart of Constitutional Design: The Irish Constitutional Convention." In *Participatory Constitutional Change: The People as Amenders of the Constitution*, edited by Xenophon Contiades and Alkmene Fotiadou, 120–36. London: Routledge, 2017.

Farrell, David M. "Political Reform." In *Austerity and Recovery in Ireland: Europe's Poster Child and the Great Recession*, edited by William K. Roche, Philip J. O'Connell, and Andrea Prothero, 160–76. Oxford: Oxford University Press, 2016.

Fearon, James D. "Electoral Accountability and the Control of Politicians: Selecting Good Types Versus Sanctioning Poor Performance." In *Democracy, Accountability, and Representation*, edited by Adam Przeworski, Susan C. Stokes, and Bernard Manin, 55–97. Cambridge: Cambridge University Press, 1999.

Felicetti, Andrea. *Deliberative Democracy and Social Movements. Transition Initiatives in the Public Sphere.* London: Rowman & Littlefield International, 2016.

Felicetti, Andrea, Simon Niemeyer, and Nicole Curato. "Improving Deliberative Participation: Connecting Minipublics to Deliberative Systems." *European Political Science Review* (2015): 1–22.

Finley, Moses I. *The Invention of Politics.* Cambridge: Cambridge University Press, 1991.

Fischer, Frank. *Democracy and Expertise: Reorienting Policy Inquiry.* Oxford: Oxford University Press, 2009.

Fishkin, James S. *Tyranny and Legitimacy: A Critique of Political Theories.* Baltimore: Johns Hopkins University Press, 1979.

———. *The Voice of the People: Public Opinion & Democracy.* New Haven: Yale University Press, 1997.

———. *When the People Speak: Deliberative Democracy and Public Consultation.* Oxford: Oxford University Press, 2009.

———. "Reviving Deliberative Democracy: Reflections on Recent Experiments." In *Deliberation and Democracy: Innovative Processes and Institutions*, edited by Stephen Coleman, Anna Przybylska and Yves Sintomer, 99–108. Frankfurt: Peter Lang, 2015.

———. *Democracy When the People Are Thinking: Revitalizing Our*

Politics Through Public Deliberation. Oxford: Oxford University Press, 2018.

Fishkin, James S., and Cynthia Farrar. "Deliberative Polling: From Experiment to Community Resource." In *The Deliberative Democracy Handbook: Strategies for Effective Civic Engagement in the 21st Century*, edited by John Gastil and Peter Levine, 68–79. San Francisco: Jossey-Bass, 2005.

Fishkin, James S., Thad Kousser, Robert C. Luskin, and Alice Siu. "Deliberative Agenda Setting: Piloting Reform of Direct Democracy in California." *Perspectives on Politics* 13, no. 4 (2015): 1030–42.

Fishkin, James S., and Robert Luskin. "Experimenting with a Democratic Ideal." *Acta Politica* 40, no. 3 (2005): 284–98.

———. "Broadcasts of Deliberative Polls: Aspirations and Effects." *British Journal of Political Science* 36, no. 1 (2006): 184–8.

Fishkin, James S., and Jane Mansbridge. "Introduction." *Daedalus* 146, no. 3 (2017): 6–13.

Fishkin, James S., Robert C. Luskin, and Roger Jowell. "Deliberative Polling and Public Consultation." *Parliamentary Affairs* 53, no. 4 (2000): 657–66.

Fitzgerald, Tony. "Politicians with a 'Winning at All Costs' Mentality Are Damaging Australia." *Sydney Morning Herald*, April 12, 2017.

Flinders, Matthew, Katie Ghose, Will Jennings, Edward Molloy, Brendan Prosser, Alan Renwick, and Graham Smith. *Democracy Matters: Lessons from the 2015 Citizens' Assemblies on English Devolution*. London: Democracy Matters Project, 2016.

Floridia, Antonio. *From Participation to Deliberation: A Critical Genealogy of Deliberative Democracy*. Colchester, UK: ECPR Press, 2017.

Follesdal, Andreas, and Simon Hix. "Why There Is a Democratic Deficit in the EU: A Response to Majone and Moravcsik." *Journal of Common Market Studies* 44, no. 3 (2006): 533–62.

Fournier, Patrick, Henk van der Kolk, Kenneth Carty, André Blais, and Jonathan Rose. *When Citizens Decide: Lessons from Citizen Assemblies on Electoral Reform*. Oxford: Oxford University Press, 2011.

Freire, Paolo. *Education: The Practice of Freedom*. London: Writers and Readers Publishing Cooperative, 1976.

———. *Pedagogy of the City*. London: Bloomsbury Publishing, 1993.

Friedersdorf, Conor. "Constant Fundraising: The Other Campaign-Finance Problem." *Atlantic*, April 18, 2012.

Fung, Archon. "Deliberation Before the Revolution: Toward an Ethics of Deliberative Democracy in an Unjust World." *Political Theory* 33, no. 3 (2005): 397–419.

———. "Putting the Public Back into Governance: The Challenges of Citizen Participation and its Future." *Public Administration Review* 75, no. 4 (2015): 513–22.

Fung, Archon, and Erik Olin Wright, eds. *Deepening Democracy: Institutional Innovations in Empowered Participatory Governance.* New York: Verso, 2003.

Ganuza, Ernesto, and Gianpaolo Baiocchi. "The Power of Ambiguity: How Participatory Budgeting Travels the Globe." *Journal of Public Deliberation* 8, no. 2 (2012).

Gastil, John. *Democracy in Small Groups: Participation, Decision Making, and Communication.* Gabriola Island: New Society Publishers, 1993.

———. *By Popular Demand: Revitalizing Representative Democracy Through Deliberative Elections.* Berkeley: University of California Press, 2000.

———. "Beyond Endorsements and Partisan Cues: Giving Voters Viable Alternatives to Unreliable Cognitive Shortcuts." *Good Society* 23, no. 2 (2014): 145–59.

Gastil, John, E. Pierre Deess, Philip J. Weiser, and Cindy Simmons. *The Jury and Democracy: How Jury Deliberation Promotes Civic Engagement and Political Participation.* Oxford: Oxford University Press, 2010.

Gastil, John, and Katherine R. Knobloch. *Hope for Democracy: How Citizens Can Bring Reason Back into Politics.* Unpublished manuscript, 2018.

Gastil, John, Katherine R. Knobloch, Dan Kahan, and Don Braman. "Participatory Policymaking Across Cultural Cognitive Divides: Two Tests of Cultural Biasing in Public Forum Design and Deliberation." *Public Administration* 94, no. 4 (2016): 970–87.

Gastil, John, and Peter Levine, eds. *The Deliberative Democracy Handbook: Strategies for Effective Civic Engagement in the 21st Century.* San Francisco: Jossey-Bass, 2005.

Gastil, John, and Robert C. Richards. "Making Direct Democracy Deliberative." *Politics and Society* 41, no. 2 (2013): 253–81.

———. "Embracing Digital Democracy: A Call for Building an Online Civic Commons." *PS: Political Science & Politics* 50, no. 3 (2017): 758–63.

Gastil, John, Robert C. Richards, and Katherine R. Knobloch. "Vicarious Deliberation: How the Oregon Citizens' Initiative Review Influenced Deliberation in Mass Elections." *International Journal of Communication* 8, no. 1 (2014): 62–89.

Gaxie, Daniel. *Le Cens Caché.* Paris: Seuil, 1993.

Gay, Claudine. "The Effect of Black Congressional Representation on Political Participation." *American Political Science Review* 95, no. 3 (2001): 589–602.

Genro, Tarso, and Ubiratan de Souza. *Orçamento Participativo. A Experiência de Porto Alegre*. São Paulo: Fundação Perseu Abramo, 1997.

Giger, Nathalie, Jan Rosset, and Julian Bernauer. "The Poor Political Representation of the Poor in a Comparative Perspective." *Representation* 48, no. 1 (2012): 47–61.

Gilens, Martin. *Affluence and Influence: Economic Inequality and Political Power in America*. Princeton: Princeton University Press, 2014.

Gilens, Martin, and Benjamin I. Page. "Testing Theories of American Politics: Elites, Interest Groups, and Average Citizens." *Perspectives on Politics* 12, no. 3 (2014): 564–81.

Goodin, Robert E. "Democratic Accountability: The Distinctiveness of the Third Sector." *European Journal of Sociology* 44, no. 3 (2003): 359–96.

Goodin, Robert E., and John Dryzek. "Deliberative Impacts: The Macro-Political Uptake of Mini-Publics." *Politics and Society* 34, no. 2 (2006): 219–44.

Goodwin, Barbara. *Justice by Lottery*. New York: Harvester Wheatsheaf, 2012.

Gorz, André. *Strategy for Labor: A Radical Proposal*. Boston: Beacon Press, 1976.

Gosseries, Axel P. "Constitutions and Future Generations." *Good Society* 17, no. 2 (2008): 32–7.

Gronlund, Kimmo, Andre Bachtiger, and Maija Setälä, eds. *Deliberative Mini-Publics: Involving Citizens in the Democratic Process*. Colchester, UK: ECPR Press, 2014.

Grote, George. *History of Greece: Rome the Time of Solon to 403 B.C.* London: Routledge, 2001.

Guerrero, Alexander A. "Against Elections: The Lottocratic Alternative." *Philosophy & Public Affairs* 42, no. 2 (2014): 135–78.

———. "Forget Voting—It's Time to Start Choosing Our Leaders by Lottery." *Aeon*, January 23, 2014.

Gutmann, Amy, and Dennis Frank Thompson. *The Spirit of Compromise: Why Governing Demands It and Campaigning Undermines It*. Princeton: Princeton University Press, 2014.

———. *Why Deliberative Democracy?* Princeton: Princeton University Press, 2004.

Habermas, Jürgen. *Between Facts and Norms: Contributions to a Discourse Theory of Law and Democracy*. Translated by William Rehg. Cambridge: MIT Press, 1996.

Hacking, Ian. *The Taming of Chance*. Cambridge: Cambridge University Press, 1990.

Hale, Dennis. *The Jury in America: Triumph and Decline*. Lawrence, KS: University Press of Kansas, 2016.

Hall, Peter A., and Rosemary C. R. Taylor. "Political Science and the

Three New Institutionalisms." *Political Studies* 44, no. 5 (1996): 936–57.

Hansen, Mogens Herman. *The Athenian Democracy in the Age of Demosthenes.* Oxford: Blackwell, 1991.

Hardy, Max, Kath Fisher, and Janette Hartz-Karp. "The Unsung Heroes of a Deliberative Process: Reflections on the Role of Facilitators at the Citizens' Parliament." In *The Australian Citizens' Parliament and the Future of Deliberative Democracy*, edited by Lyn Carson, John Gastil, Janette Hartz-Karp, and Ron Lubensky, 177–89. University Park, PA: Pennsylvania State University Press, 2013.

Harrison, Alick Robin Walsham. "Law-Making at Athens at the End of the Fifth Century B.C." *Journal of Hellenic Studies* 75 (1955): 26–35.

Hayward, Clarissa Rile. "Making Interest: On Representation and Democratic Legitimacy." *Political Representation* (2009): 111–35

He, Baogang. "Participatory Budgeting in China. An Overview." In *Participatory Budgeting in Asia and Europe: Key Challenges of Deliberative Democracy*, edited by Yves Sintomer, Rudolf Traub-Merz, and Junhua Zhang. Hong Kong: Palgrave, 2011.

Held, David. *Models of Democracy*, 3rd ed. Cambridge: Polity Press, 2006.

Heller, Patrick. "Moving the State: The Politics of Democratic Decentralization in Kerala, South Africa, and Porto Alegre." *Politics and Society* 29, no. 1 (2001): 131–63.

Hendriks, Carolyn M. "Coupling Citizens and Elites in Deliberative Systems: The Role of Institutional Design." *European Journal of Political Research* 55, no. 1 (2016): 43–60.

Hendriks, Carolyn M., and Adrian Kay. "From 'Opening Up' to Democratic Renewal: Deepening Public Engagement in Legislative Committees." *Government and Opposition* (2017): 1–24.

Henneman, Inge, et al. *G1000, le Rapport Final: L'Innovation Démocratique Mise en Pratique.* Brussels: G1000, 2012.

Hennig, Brett. *The End of Politicians: Time for a Real Democracy.* London: Unbound, 2017.

Hennig, Brett, Lyn Carson, Iain Walker, and David Schecter. *A Citizens' Assembly for the Scottish Parliament.* Glasgow: Common Weal Policy, 2017.

Herbst, Susan. *Numbered Voices: How Opinion Polling Has Shaped American Politics.* Chicago: University of Chicago Press, 1993.

Hibbing, John R., and Elizabeth Theiss-Morse. "A Surprising Number of Americans Dislike How Messy Democracy Is. They Like Trump." *Washington Post,* May 2, 2016.

Hindess, Barry. "Deficit by Design." *Australian Journal of Public Administration* 61, no. 1 (2002): 30–8.

Hodge, Sandy, Zelma Bone, and Judith Crockett. "Using Community

Deliberation Forums for Public Engagement: Examples from Missouri, USA and New South Wales, Australia." Queensland Government Publications, n.d.

Holman, Peggy, Tom Devane, Steven Cady, and associates. *The Change Handbook. The Definitive Resources on Today's Best Methods for Engaging Whole Systems*. Oakland: Berrett-Koehler Publishers, 2006.

Hunter, Dale, Anne Bailey, and Bill Taylor. *Art of Facilitation: How to Create Group Synergy*. Tucson: Fisher Books, 1995.

Hurlbut, David. "A Look Behind the Texas Renewable Portfolio Standard: A Case Study." *Natural Resources Journal* 48, no. 1 (2008): 129–61.

Ingham, Sean. "Disagreement and Epistemic Arguments for Democracy." *Politics, Philosophy & Economics* 12 (2013): 136–55.

Jacquet, Vincent. "Explaining Non-Participation in Deliberative Mini-Publics." *European Journal of Political Research* 56, no. 3 (2017): 640–59.

Jacquet, Vincent, et al., "The Macro Political Uptake of the G1000 in Belgium." In *Constitutional Deliberative Democracy in Europe*, edited by Min Reuchamps and Jane Suiter. Colchester, UK: ECPR Press, 2016.

Jacquet, Vincent, and Min Reuchamps. "Who Wants to Pay for Deliberative Democracy? The Crowdfunders of the G1000 in Belgium." *European Political Science Review* 10, no. 1 (2018): 29–49.

Jefferson, Thomas. Thomas Jefferson to James Madison, September 6, 1789. In *The Founders Constitution*, vol. 1, edited by Philip B. Kurland and Ralph Lerner, chap. 2, doc. 23. Chicago: University of Chicago Press, 2000.

Jenkins-Smith, Hank. *Democratic Politics and Policy Analysis*. Pacific Grove: Brooks/Cole, 1990.

Johnson, Carolina, and John Gastil. "Variations of Institutional Design for Empowered Deliberation." *Journal of Public Deliberation* 11 (2015).

Johnson, Genevieve Fuji. *Democratic Illusion: Deliberative Democracy in Canadian Public Policy*. Toronto: University of Toronto Press, 2015.

Johnson, Michael, ed. *Political Corruption: Concepts and Contexts*, 3rd ed. New York: Taylor & Francis, 2001.

Johnston, Neil. *The History of the Parliamentary Franchise*. Research Paper 13/14. London: House of Commons Library, 2013.

Jorritsma, Elsje. "Rotterdam Gaat Wijkpolitici Niet Kiezen maar Loten." *NRC News*, February 23, 2017.

Joss, Simon, and James Durant, eds. *Public Participation in Science:*

The Role of Consensus Conference in Europe. London: Science Museum, 1995.

Kahneman, Daniel. *Thinking, Fast and Slow.* New York: Farrar, Straus and Giroux, 2015.

Karpf, David. *The MoveOn Effect: The Unexpected Transformation of American Political Advocacy.* Oxford: Oxford University Press, 2012.

Karpowitz, Charles F., and Chad Raphael. "Ideals of Inclusion in Deliberation." *Journal of Public Deliberation* 12, no. 2 (2016).

Karpowitz, Christopher F., Chad Raphael, and Allen S. Hammond IV. "Deliberative Democracy and Inequality: Two Cheers for Enclave Deliberation Among the Disempowered." *Politics & Society* 37, no. 4 (2009): 576–615.

Keane, John. *The Life and Death of Democracy.* New York: W. W. Norton, 2009.

Kelsen, Hans. *La Démocratie: Sa Nature, Sa Valeur.* Paris: Dalloz, 2004.

Kennedy, Edward M. *True Compass: A Memoir.* New York: Twelve, 2011.

Kies, Raphaël. *Les Consultations Citoyennes et les Réformes Constitutionnelles.* Report. Luxembourg: Chamber of Deputies, 2015.

———. "The Seven Golden Rules to Promote EU Citizens Consultation." Paper presented at Fourth International Conference on Legislation and Law Reform, World Bank, Washington, November, 2016.

Kies, Raphaël, Monique Leyenaar, and Kees Niemöller, "European Citizens Consultation: A Large Consultation on a Vague Topic." In *Is Europe Listening to Us? Successes and Failures of EU Citizen Consultations,* edited by Raphaël Kies and Patrizia Nanz, 59–78. London: Routledge, 2013.

Kies, Raphaël, and Patrizia Nanz, eds. *Is Europe Listening to Us? Successes and Failures of EU Citizen Consultations.* London: Routledge, 2013.

Klein, Naomi. *No Is Not Enough: Defeating the New Shock Politics.* New York: Penguin, 2017.

Knobloch, Katherine R., John Gastil, Justin Reedy, and Katherine Cramer Walsh. "Did They Deliberate? Applying an Evaluative Model of Democratic Deliberation to the Oregon Citizens' Initiative Review." *Journal of Applied Communication Research* 41, no. 2 (2013): 105–25.

Knobloch, Katherine R., John Gastil, Robert C. Richards, and Traci Feller. *Evaluation Report on the 2012 Citizens' Initiative Reviews for the Oregon CIR Commission.* State College: Pennsylvania State University, 2013.

Knobloch, Katherine R., John Gastil, Tyrone Reitman. "Connecting Micro-Deliberation to Electoral Decision-Making Institutionalizing the Oregon Citizens' Initiative." In *Deliberation: Values, Processes, Institutions*, edited by Stephen Coleman, Anna Przybylska, and Yves Sintomer, 21–40. Frankfurt: Peter Lang, 2015.

Knobloch, Katherine R., and John Gastil. "Civic (Re)socialisation: The Educative Effects of Deliberative Participation." *Politics* 35, no. 2 (2015): 183–200.

Kontos, Alexandros. "La Démocratie, un Régime Politique Inconnu." PhD dissertation, Université Paris 8, 2001.

Kousser, Thad. *Term Limits and the Dismantling of State Legislative Professionalism*. Cambridge: Cambridge University Press, 2004.

Landemore, Hélène. "Why the Many Are Smarter Than the Few and Why It Matters." *Journal of Public Deliberation* 8, no. 1 (2012).

———. "Deliberation, Cognitive Diversity, and Democratic Inclusiveness." *Synthese* 190, no. 7 (2013): 1209–31.

———. *Democratic Reason: Politics, Collective Intelligence, and the Rule of the Many*. Princeton: Princeton University Press, 2013.

Lawless, Jennifer L., and Richard L. Fox. *It Takes a Candidate: Why Women Don't Run for Office*. Cambridge: Cambridge University Press, 2005.

Leary, Mark R., Kate J. Diebels, Erin K. Davisson, Katrina P. Jongman-Sereno, Jennifer C. Isherwood, Kaitlin T. Raimi, Samantha A. Deffler, and Rick H. Hoyle. "Cognitive and Interpersonal Features of Intellectual Humility." *Personality and Social Psychology Bulletin* 43, no. 6 (2017): 793–813.

Leduc, Lawrence. "How and Why Electoral Reform Fails: Evaluating the Canadian Experience." Paper presented at ECPR Joint Sessions Workshops, Lisbon, April 2009.

Leduc, Lawrence, Heather Bastedo, and Catherine Baquero. "The Quiet Referendum: Why Electoral Referendum Failed in Ontario." Paper presented at Canadian Political Science Association annual meeting, Vancouver, May 2008.

Lee, Frances E. *Insecure Majorities: Congress and the Perpetual Campaign*. Chicago: University of Chicago Press, 2017.

Lee, Margaret T., and Richard Ofshe. "The Impact of Behavioral Style and Status Characteristics on Social Influence: A Test of Two Competing Theories." *Social Psychology Quarterly* 44, no. 2 (1981): 73–82.

Leib, Ethan. *Deliberative Democracy in America: A Proposal for a Popular Branch of Government*. University Park, PA: Pennsylvania State University Press, 2004.

Lerner, Josh. *Everyone Counts: Could "Participatory Budgeting" Change Democracy?* Ithaca, NY: Cornell University Press, 2014.

Lessig, Lawrence. *Republic, Lost: How Money Corrupts Congress—and a Plan to Stop It*. New York: Grand Central Publishing, 2011.

Lijphart, Arend. *Democracies: Patterns of Majoritarian and Consensus Government in Twenty-One Countries.* New Haven: Yale University Press, 1984.

Lironi, Elisa, and Daniela Peta. *European Economic and Social Committee EU Public Consultations in the Digital Age: Enhancing the Role of the EESC and Civil Society Organizations.* Report. Brussels: European Economic and Social Committee, 2017.

Lopez-Rabatel, Liliane. "Sortition in Athens: Instruments and Words." In *Sortition and Democracy. Practices, Instruments, Theories,* edited by Liliane Rabatel and Yves Sintomer. Exeter: Imprint Academic, 2018.

Lopez-Rabatel, Liliane, and Yves Sintomer, eds. *Sortition and Democracy: Practices, Tools, Theories.* Exeter: Imprint Academic, 2018.

Lubensky, Ron, and Lyn Carson. "Choose Me: The Challenges of National Random Selection." In *The Australian Citizens' Parliament and the Future of Deliberative Democracy,* edited by Lyn Carson and John Gastil, Janette Hartz-Karp, and Ron Lubensky, 204–17. University Park, PA: Pennsylvania State University Press, 2013.

Lupia, Arthur. "Shortcuts Versus Encyclopedias: Information and Voting Behavior in California Insurance Reform Elections." *American Political Science Review* 88, no.1 (1994): 63–76.

Lupia, Arthur, and Anne Norton. "Inequality Is Always in the Room: Language and Power in Deliberative Democracy." *Daedalus* 146, no. 3 (2017): 64–76.

MacKenzie, Michael K. "A General-Purpose, Randomly Selected Chamber." In *Institutions for Future Generations,* edited by Iñigo González-Ricoy and Axel Gosseries, 282–98. Oxford: Oxford University Press, 2016.

Madison, James, Alexander Hamilton, and John Jay. *The Federalist Papers,* edited by Isaac Kramnick. London: Penguin Books, 1987.

Magleby, David. *Direct Legislation: Voting on Ballot Propositions.* Baltimore: Johns Hopkins University Press, 1984.

Malkopoulou, Anthoula. "The Paradox of Democratic Selection: Is Sortition Better Than Voting?" In *Parliamentarism and Democratic Theory: Historical and Contemporary Practice,* edited by Kari Palonen and José María Rosales, 229–54. Toronto: Verlag Barbara Budrich, 2015.

Manin, Bernard. *Principles of Representative Government.* Cambridge: Cambridge University Press, 1997.

———. "En Guise de Conclusion: Les Secondes Chambres et le Gouvernement Complexe." *Revue Internationale de Politique Comparée* 6, no. 1 (1999): 189–99.

———. "Comment Promouvoir la Délibération Démocratique? Priorité du Débat Contradictoire sur la Discussion." *Raisons Politiques* 42, no. 2 (2011): 83–113.

———. *Principes Du Gouvernement Représentatif.* Paris: Flammarion, 2012.

Manin, Bernard, Adam Przeworski, and Susan C. Stokes. "Elections and Representation." In *Democracy, Accountability, and Representation*, edited by Adam Przeworski, Susan C. Stokes, and Bernard Manin, 29–54. Cambridge: Cambridge University Press, 1999.

Mansbridge, Jane. *Beyond Adversary Democracy.* Chicago: University of Chicago Press, 1983.

———. "On the Relation of Altruism and Self Interest." In *Beyond Self Interest*, edited by Jane Mansbridge, 133–43. Chicago: University of Chicago Press, 1990.

———. "Using Power/Fighting Power*: The Polity." In *Democracy and Difference: Contesting the Boundaries of the Political*, edited by Seyla Benhabib, 46–66. Chichester: Princeton University Press, 1996.

———. "Should Blacks Represent Blacks and Women Represent Women? A Contingent 'Yes.'" *Journal of Politics* 61, no. 3 (1999): 627–57.

———. "A 'Moral Core' Solution to the Prisoners' Dilemma." In *Schools of Thought: Twenty-Five Years of Interpretive Social Science*, edited by Joan W. Scott and Debra Keates, 330–47. Princeton: Princeton University Press, 2001.

———. "Rethinking Representation." *American Political Science Review* 97, no. 4 (2003): 515–28.

———. "Cracking Through Hegemonic Ideology: The Logic of Formal Justice." *Social Justice Research* 18, no. 3 (2005): 335–47.

———. "Deliberative Polling as the Gold Standard." *Good Society* 19, no. 1 (2010): 55–62.

———. "A Contingency Theory of Accountability." In *The Oxford Handbook of Public Accountability*, edited by Mark Bowens, Robert E. Goodin, and Thomas Schillemans, 55–68. Oxford: Oxford University Press, 2014.

———. "What Is Political Science For? APSA Presidential Address." *Perspectives on Politics* 12, no. 1 (2014): 8–17.

———. "Recursive Representation." In *Making Present*, edited by Dario Castiglione and Johannes Pollak. Chicago: University of Chicago Press, forthcoming.

Mansbridge, Jane, James Bohman, Simone Chambers, David Estlund, Andreas Føllesdal, Archon Fung, Cristina, Lafont, Bernard Manin, and José Luis Martí. "The Place of Self-Interest and the Role of Power in Deliberative Democracy." *Journal of Political Philosophy*

18, no. 1 (2010): 64–100.

Markell, Patchen. "The Insufficiency of Non-Domination." *Political Theory* 36, no. 1 (2008): 9–36.

Marxsen, Christian, "Open Stakeholder Consultations at the European Level-Voice of the Citizens?" *European Law Journal* 21, no. 2 (2015): 257–80.

Mayhew, David R. *Congress: The Electoral Connection*. 2nd ed. New Haven: Yale University Press, 2004.

McCormick, John P. "Contain the Wealthy and Patrol the Magistrates: Restoring Elite Accountability to Popular Government." *American Political Science Review* 100, no. 2 (2006): 147–63.

McKenzie, Jessica. "Small but Successful Participatory Democracy Experiment to Continue in Utah." *Civic Hall,* August 4, 2015.

Mellina, Maxime. "Démocratiser la Démocratie? Le Tirage au Sort de l'Assemblée des Délégué.e.s de la Fédération des Associations d'Étudiant.e.s de l'UNIL." Master's thesis, Lausanne University, 2016.

Mendelsohn, Matthew, and Andrew Parkin. "Introduction: Referendum Democracy." In *Referendum Democracy: Citizens, Elites and Deliberation in Referendum Campaigns*, edited by Matthew Mendelsohn and Andrew Parkin, 1–22. Basingstoke: Palgrave, 2001.

Mendonça, Ricardo Fabrino. "Mitigating Systemic Dangers: The Role of Connectivity Inducers in a Deliberative System." *Critical Policy Studies* 10, no. 2 (2016): 171–90.

Montesquieu. *De l'Esprit des Lois*. Paris: Garnier Flammarion, 1979.

Mooney, Gavin. *A Handbook on Citizens Juries' with Particular Reference to Health Care*. Research paper. Sydney: newDemocracy, 2010.

Morewedge, Carey K., Haewon Yoon, Irene Scopelliti, Carl W. Symborski, James H. Korris, and Karim S. Kassam. "Debiasing Decisions: Improved Decision Making with a Single Training Intervention." *Policy Insights from the Behavioral and Brain Sciences* 2, no. 1 (2015): 129–40.

Mueller, Denis C., Robert D. Tollison, and Thomas Willet. "Representative Democracy via Random Selection." *Public Choice* 12, no. 1 (1972): 57–68.

Mulgan, Richard G. "Lot as a Democratic Device of Selection." *Review of Politics* 46, no. 4 (1984): 539–60.

Nabatchi, Tina, John Gastil, Michael G. Weiksner, and Matt Leighninger, eds. *Democracy in Motion: Evaluating the Practice and Impact of Deliberative Civic Engagement*. Oxford: Oxford University Press, 2012.

Neblo, Michael A. *Deliberative Democracy Between Theory and*

Practice. Cambridge: Cambridge University Press, 2015.

Niemeyer, Simon, and John S. Dryzek. "The Ends of Deliberation: Meta-Consensus and Inter-Subjective Rationality as Ideal Outcomes." *Swiss Political Science Review* 13, no. 4 (2007): 497–526.

Nourse, Victoria F., and Jane S. Schacter. "The Politics of Legislative Drafting: A Congressional Case Study." *New York University Law Review* 77, no. 3 (2002): 575–624.

Nyhan, Brendan, and Jason Reifler. "When Corrections Fail: The Persistence of Political Misperceptions." *Political Behavior* 32, no. 2 (2010): 303–30.

Ober, Josiah. "What the Ancient Greeks Can Tell Us About Democracy." *Annual Review of Political Science* 11 (2008): 67–91.

———. *Democracy and Knowledge: Innovation and Learning in Classical Greece.* Princeton: Princeton University Press, 2010.

Ó Dochartaigh, Niall, Katy Hayward, and Elizabeth Meehan, eds. *Dynamics of Political Change in Ireland: Making and Breaking a Divided Island.* London: Routledge, 2017.

Odonkhuu, Munkhsaikhan. "Mongolia's (Flawed) Experiment with Deliberative Polling in Constitutional Reform." *ConstitutionNet,* June 29, 2017.

O'Leary, Kevin. *Saving Democracy: A Plan for Real Representation in America.* Stanford: Stanford University Press, 2006.

Olsen, Espen, and Hans Jörg Trenz, "From Citizens' Deliberation to Popular Will Formation? Generating Democratic Legitimacy in Transnational Deliberative Polling." *Political Studies* 62, no. 1 (2014): 117–33.

Olson, Mancur. *Logique de l'Action Collective.* Bruxelles: Université de Bruxelles, 2011.

Owen, David. *The Hubris Syndrome: Bush, Blair and the Intoxication of Power.* York: Methuen, 2012.

Papadopoulos, Yannis. "On the Embeddedness of Deliberative Systems: Why Elitist Innovations Matter More." In *Deliberative Systems: Deliberative Democracy at the Large Scale*, edited by John Parkinson and Jane Mansbridge, 125–50. Cambridge: Cambridge University Press, 2012.

———. *Democracy in Crisis? Politics, Governance and Policy.* Basingstoke: Palgrave Macmillan, 2013.

Parkinson, John, and Jane Mansbridge, eds. *Deliberative Systems: Deliberative Democracy at the Large Scale.* Cambridge: Cambridge University Press, 2012.

Parkinson, John. *Deliberating in the Real World: Problems of Legitimacy in Deliberative Democracy.* Oxford: Oxford University Press, 2006.

Pateman, Carole. *Participation and Democratic Theory.* Cambridge:

Cambridge University Press, 1976.

Pettit, Philip. "Representation, Responsive and Indicative." *Constellations* 17, no. 3 (2010): 426–34.

———. *On the People's Terms: A Republican Theory and Model of Democracy*. Cambridge: Cambridge University Press, 2012.

Pincock, Heather. "Does Deliberation Make Better Citizens?" In *Democracy in Motion: Evaluating the Practice and Impact of Deliberative Civic Engagement*, edited by Tina Nabatchi, John Gastil, Michael Weiksner, and Matt Leighninger, 135–62. Oxford: Oxford University Press, 2012.

Plato. *The Republic*. 2nd ed. Translated by Desmond Lee. London: Penguin Books, 1974.

———. *Protagoras*. Oxford: Oxford University Press, 2009.

Polletta, Francesca. "Social Movements in an Age of Participation." *Mobilization: An International Quarterly* 21, no. 4 (2016): 485–97.

Posner, Richard. *Law, Pragmatism and Democracy*. Cambridge: Harvard University Press, 2003.

Pourtois, Hervé. "Les Élections Sont-Elles Essentielles à la Démocratie?" *Philosophiques* 43, no. 2 (2016): 411–39.

Proudhon, Pierre-Joseph. *Les Confessions d'un Révolutionnaire*. Paris: TOPS, 2013.

Przeworski, Adam. *Capitalism and Social Democracy*. Cambridge: Cambridge University Press, 1986.

———. "Minimalist Conception of Democracy: A Defense." In *Democracy's Value,* edited by Ian Shapiro and Casiano Hacker-Cordón, 23–55. Cambridge: Cambridge University Press, 1999.

———. *Democracy and the Limits of Self-Government*. Cambridge: Cambridge University Press, 2010.

Przeworski, Adam, Susan Stokes, and Bernard Manin, eds. *Democracy, Accountability, and Representation*. Cambridge: Cambridge University Press, 1999.

Quittkatt, Christine. "The European Commission's Online Consultations: A Success Story?" *Journal of Common Market Studies* 49, no. 3 (2011): 653–74.

Radaelli, Claudio Maria. *Technocracy in the European Union*. London: Longman, 1999.

Rancière, Jacques. *Hatred of Democracy*. London: Verso, 2009.

Ransby, Barbara. *Ella Baker and the Black Freedom Movement*. Chapel Hill: University of North Carolina Press, 2003.

Read, Rupert. *Guardians of the Future: A Constitutional Case for Representing and Protecting Future People*. Weymouth: Green House, 2012.

Renwick, Alan. *The Politics of Electoral Reform: Changing the Rules of Democracy*. Cambridge: Cambridge University Press, 2010.

———. "Referendums." In *The SAGE Handbook of Electoral Behaviour*, vol. 1, edited by Kai Arzheimer, Jocelyn Evans, and Michael S. Lewis-Beck, 433–58. London: SAGE Publications, 2017.

Reuchamps, Min, and Jane Suiter, eds. *Constitutional Deliberative Democracy in Europe*. Colchester, UK: ECPR Press, 2016.

Reuchamps, Min, Didier Caluwaerts, Jérémy Dodeigne, Vincent Jacquet, Jonathan Moskovic and Sophie Devillers. "Le G1000: Une Expérience Citoyenne de Démocratie Deliberative." *Courrier Hebdomadaire du CRISP*, no. 2344–5 (2017): 5–104.

Richards, Robert, and John Gastil. "Symbolic-Cognitive Proceduralism: A Model of Deliberative Legitimacy." *Journal of Public Deliberation* 11 (2015).

Robert, Henry Martyn. *Robert's Rules of Order: Classic Manual of Rules of Order for Deliberative Assemblies*. Minneapolis: Filiquarian Publishing, 1876.

Roberts, Jen, and Ruth Lightbody. *Experts and Evidence in Public Decision Making*. Report, ClimateXChange. Glasgow: University of Strathclyde, 2017.

Roberts, Jennifer Tolbert. *Athens on Trial: The Antidemocratic Tradition in Western Thought*. Princeton: Princeton University Press, 1994.

Röcke, Anja. *Losverfahren und Demokratie: Historische und Demokratietheoretische Perspektiven*. Münster: LIT, 2005.

Roemer, Tim. "Why Do Congressmen Spend Only Half Their Time Serving Us?" *Newsweek*, July 29, 2015.

Rootes, Christopher. "Denied, Deferred, Triumphant? Climate Change, Carbon Trading and the Greens in the Australian Federal Election of 21 August 2010." *Environmental Politics* 20, no. 3 (2011): 410–17.

Rosanvallon, Pierre. *Le Peuple Introuvable: Histoire de la Représentation Démocratique en France*. Paris: Gallimard, 1998.

———. *La Contre-Démocratie*. Paris: Seuil, 2006.

Rosenthal, Alan. "The Good Legislature." *State Legislatures,* August, 1999.

Rosenthal, Robert, and Leonore Jacobson. "Teacher Expectation for the Disadvantaged." *Scientific American* 218, no. 4 (1968): 19–23.

Rosenzweig, Philip M. *The Halo Effect: How Managers Let Themselves Be Deceived*. London: Pocket Books, 2008.

Ryfe, David M. "Does Deliberative Democracy Work?" *Annual Review of Political Science* 8 (2005): 49–71.

Sanders, Lynn M. "Against Deliberation." *Political Theory* 25, no. 3 (1997): 347–76.

Santos, Boaventura de Sousa, ed. *Democratizing Democracy: Beyond the Liberal Democratic Canon*. London: Verso, 2005.

Schuman, Sandy. *Creating a Culture of Collaboration. The International Association of Facilitators Handbook*. San Francisco: Jossey-Bass, 2006.

Schumpeter, Joseph A. *Capitalism, Socialism and Democracy*. New York: Harper and Row, 1942.

Schwartzberg, Melissa. *Counting the Many: The Origins and Limits of Supermajority Rule*. New York: Cambridge University Press, 2014.

Sclove, Richard. *Democracy and Technology*. New York: Guilford Press, 1995.

Setälä, Maija, and Graham Smith "Mini-Publics and Deliberative Democracy." In *The Oxford Handbook of Deliberative Democracy*, edited by André Bächtiger, John Dryzek, Jane Mansbridge, and Mark E. Warren. Oxford: Oxford University Press, 2018.

Shapiro, Ian. *Politics Against Domination*. Cambridge: Harvard University Press, 2016.

———. *The State of Democratic Theory*. Princeton: Princeton University Press, 2003.

Shaw, Daron, Stephen Ansolabehere, and Charles Stewart. "A Brief Yet Practical Guide to Reforming U.S. Voter Registration Systems." *Election Law Journal: Rules, Politics, and Policy* 14, no. 1 (2015): 26–31.

Sinclair, R. K. *Democracy and Participation in Athens*. Cambridge: Cambridge University Press, 1988.

Sintomer, Yves. *Le Pouvoir au Peuple: Jurys Citoyens, Tirage au Sort et Démocratie Participative*. Paris: La Découverte, 2007.

———. "Random Selection, Republican Self-Government, and Deliberative Democracy." *Constellations* 17, no. 3 (2010): 472–87.

———. *Petite Histoire de l'Expérimentation Démocratique: Tirage au Sort et Politique d'Athènes à nos Jours*. Paris: La Découverte, 2011.

———. "Délibération et Participation: Affinité Élective ou Concepts en Tension?" *Participations* 1, no. 1 (2011): 239–76.

———. *From Radical to Deliberative Democracy? Random Selection in Politics from Athens to the Present*. Cambridge: Cambridge University Press, 2019.

Sintomer, Yves, Carsten Herzberg, and Anja Röcke. *Participatory Budgeting in Europe: Democracy and Public Governance*. London: Ashgate, 2016.

Sintomer, Yves, Carsten Herzberg, Anja Röcke, and Giovanni Allegretti. "Transnational Models of Citizen Participation: The Case of Participatory Budgeting." *Journal of Public Deliberation* 8, no. 2 (2012).

Smith, Graham. *Democratic Innovations: Designing Institutions for Citizen Participation*. Cambridge: Cambridge University Press, 2009.

Smith, Mark. *American Business and Political Power: Public Opinion, Elections, and Democracy*. Chicago, University of Chicago Press, 2000.

Snyder, Benjamin. "14% of Zappos' Staff Left After Being Offered Exit Pay." *Fortune*, May 8, 2015.

Somin, Ilya. *Democracy and Political Ignorance: Why Smaller Government Is Smarter*. Stanford: Stanford University Press, 2013.

Steiner, Jürg. *The Foundations of Deliberative Democracy: Empirical Research and Normative Implications*. Cambridge: Cambridge University Press, 2012.

Stone, Peter. "The Logic of Random Selection." *Political Theory* 37, no. 3 (2009): 375–97.

———. "Sortition, Voting, and Democratic Equality." *Critical Review of International Social and Political Philosophy* 19, no. 3 (2016): 339–56.

———. *The Luck of the Draw: The Role of Lotteries in Decision Making*. Oxford: Oxford University Press, 2011.

Suiter, Jane, and David M. Farrell. "The Parties' Manifestos." In *How Ireland Voted 2011*, edited by Michael Gallagher and Michael Marsh, 29–46. Houndmills: Palgrave Macmillan, 2011.

Suiter, Jane, David M. Farrell, and Clodagh Harris. "Ireland's Constitutional Convention: An Experiment in Representation." In *Constitutional Acceleration Within the European Union and Beyond*, edited by Paul Blokker. London: Routledge, 2018.

———. "Ireland's Evolving Constitution." In *Constitutional Acceleration Within the European Union and Beyond*, edited by Paul Blokker, London: Routledge, 2018.

———. "The Irish Constitutional Convention: A Case of 'High Legitimacy'?" In *Constitutional Deliberative Democracy in Europe*, edited by Min Reuchamps and Jane Suiter, 33–52. Colchester, UK: ECPR Press, 2016.

Sullivan, Andy. "Insight: In Washington, Lawmakers' Routines Shaped by Fundraising." *Reuters*, June 12, 2013.

Sullivan, John L., and Eric M. Uslaner. "Congressional Behavior and Electoral Marginality." *American Journal of Political Science* 22, no. 3 (1978): 536–53.

Sunstein, Cass R. *Why Societies Need Dissent*. Cambridge: Harvard University Press, 2003.

Surowiecki, James. *The Wisdom of Crowds: Why the Many Are Smarter Than the Few and How Collective Wisdom Shapes Business, Economics, Society and Nations*. London: Little Brown, 2004.

Sutherland, Keith, Ernest Callenbach, and Michael Phillips. *A People's Parliament: A (Revised) Blueprint for a Very English Revolution*. Exeter: Imprint Academic, 2008.

———. "The Two Sides of the Representative Coin." *Studies in Social*

Justice 5, no. 2 (2011): 197–211.

Swain, Carol M. *Black Faces, Black Interests: The Representation of African Americans in Congress*. Cambridge: Harvard University Press, 1993.

Swers, Michele. *The Difference Women Make: The Policy Impact of Women in Congress*. Chicago: University of Chicago Press, 2002.

Swift, Jeffrey. "The People's Lobby: A Model for Online Activist Deliberation." *Journal of Public Deliberation* 9, no. 2 (2013).

Talpin, Julien. "How Can Constitutional Reforms Be Deliberative? The Hybrid Legitimacies of Constitutional Deliberative Democracy." In *Constitutional Deliberative Democracy in Europe.*, edited by Min Reuchamps and Jane Suiter, 93–108. Colchester, UK: ECPR Press, 2016.

———. "Deliberative Democracy and Sortition in Politics: A Critical Assessment." In *Sortition and Democracy. Practices, Instruments, Theories*, edited by Liliane Lopez-Rabatel and Yves Sintomer. Exeter: Imprint Academic, 2018.

———. "Democratic Innovations." In *The Oxford Handbook of Social Movements*, edited by Donatella della Porta and Mario Diani. Oxford: Oxford University Press, 2015.

Tarrow, Sidney G. *Power in Movement: Social Movements and Contentious Politics*. Cambridge: Cambridge University Press, 2011.

Tetlock, Philip. "Accountability: A Social Check on the Fundamental Attribution Error." *Social Psychology Quarterly* 48 (1985): 227–36.

Toke, David. "USA: Consolidation of a Renewables Industry?" In *Ecological Modernisation and Renewable Energy*, edited by David Toke, 98–128. London: Palgrave Macmillan, 2011.

Tronto, Joan. *Who Cares? How to Reshape a Democratic Politics*. Ithaca, NY: Cornell University Press, 2015.

Tsebelis, George. *Veto Players: How Political Institutions Work*. Princeton: Princeton University Press, 2002.

Tsebelis, George, and Jeannette Money. *Bicameralism*. Cambridge: Cambridge University Press, 1997.

Twyford, Vivien, Stuart Waters, Max Hardy, John Dengate, and Owen Thomson. *The Power of "Co": The Smart Leaders' Guide to Collaborative Governance*. Woolongong: Twyfords Consulting, 2012.

Urbinati, Nadia. *Representative Democracy: Principles and Genealogy*. Chicago: University of Chicago Press, 2006.

Urh, John. *Deliberative Democracy in Australia. The Changing Place of Parliament*. Cambridge: Cambridge University Press, 1998.

van Damme, Jan, Vincent Jacquet, Nathalie Schiffino, and Min Reuchamps. "Public Consultation and Participation in Belgium: Directly Engaging Citizens Beyond the Ballot Box?" In *Policy Analysis in Belgium*, edited by Marleen Brans and David Aubin,

215–34. Bristol: Policy Press, 2017.

van Reybrouck, David. *Against Elections. The Case for Democracy.* London: Bodley Head, 2016.

Vandamme, Pierre-Étienne, and Antoine Verret-Hamelin. "A Randomly Selected Chamber: Promises and Challenges." *Journal of Public Deliberation* 13, no. 1 (2017).

Vergne, Antoine. "Le Modèle *Planungszelle*—Citizen Juries: Quelles Logiques de Diffusion?" In *La Démocratie Participative Inachevée: Genèse, Adaptations et Diffusions*, edited by Marie-Hélène Bacqué and Yves Sintomer, 83–100. Paris: Yves Michel, 2010.

Vidmar, Neil, and Valerie P. Hans. *American Juries: The Verdict.* Amherst: Prometheus Books, 2007.

Walzer, Michael. *Obligations: Essays on Disobedience, War, and Citizenship.* Cambridge: Harvard University Press, 1970.

Wang, Shaoguang. *Democracy, Republic and Sortition: From Athens to Venice* (in Chinese), Beijing: CITIC Press, 2018.

Warren, Mark E., and John Gastil. "Can Deliberative Minipublics Address the Cognitive Challenges of Democratic Citizenship?" *Journal of Politics* 77, no. 2 (2015): 562–74.

Warren, Mark E. "When, Where and Why Do We Need Deliberation, Voting, and Other Means of Organizing Democracy? A Problem-Based Approach to Democratic Systems." Paper presented at the American Political Science Association Annual Meeting, New Orleans, August 2012.

———. "Citizen Representatives." In *Designing Deliberative Democracy: The British Columbia Citizens' Assembly*, edited by Mark E. Warren and Hilary Pearse, 50–69. Cambridge: Cambridge University Press, 2008.

Warren, Mark E., and Hilary Pearse, eds. *Designing Deliberative Democracy: The British Columbia Citizens' Assembly*. Cambridge: Cambridge University Press, 2008.

Weiser, Wendy. "In 22 States, a Wave of New Voting Restrictions Threatens to Shift Outcomes in Tight Races." *American Prospect,* October 1, 2014.

Weissert, Carol S., and William G. Weissert. "State Legislative Staff Influence in Health Policy Making." *Journal of Health Politics, Policy and Law* 25, no. 6 (2000): 1121–48.

Wells, Chris. *The Civic Organization and the Digital Citizen: Communicating Engagement in a Networked Age.* Oxford: Oxford University Press, 2015.

Whitby, Kenny J. *The Color of Representation: Congressional Behavior and Black Constituents.* Ann Arbor: University of Michigan Press, 1997.

Woodruff, Paul. *First Democracy: The Challenge of an Ancient Idea.* Oxford: Oxford University Press, 2005.

Wright, Erik Olin. *Envisioning Real Utopias*. New York: Verso, 2010.

Yang, Mundo. "Europe's New Communication Policy and the Introduction of Transnational Deliberative Citizens' Involvement Projects." In *Is Europe Listening to Us? Successes and Failures of EU Citizen Consultations*, edited by Raphaël Kies and Patrizia Nanz, 17–34. London: Routledge, 2013.

Yankelovitch, Daniel. *Coming to Public Judgment: Making Democracy Work in a Complex World*. Syracuse: Syracuse University Press, 1991.

———. *The Magic of Dialogue: Transforming Conflict into Cooperation*. Sydney: Crows Nest, 1999.

Young, Iris Marion. *Inclusion and Democracy*. New York: Oxford University Press, 2000.

Zakaras, Alex. "Lot and Democratic Representation: A Modest Proposal." *Constellations* 17, no. 3 (2010): 455–71.

Zito, Anthony R., and Adriaan Schout. "Learning Theory Reconsidered: EU Integration Theories and Learning." *Journal of European Public Policy* 16, no. 8 (2009): 1103–23.

About the Authors

Authors

John Gastil is a professor in the Department of Communication Arts and Sciences at the Pennsylvania State University, where he is a senior scholar at the McCourtney Institute for Democracy. Gastil's research focuses on the theory and practice of deliberative democracy, particularly as it relates to how people behave as voters or members of small decision-making groups. Recent books he has authored or coedited include *The Jury and Democracy* (2010), *Democracy in Motion: Evaluating the Practice and Impact of Deliberative Civic Engagement* (2012), and a second edition of *Democracy in Small Groups* (2014).

Erik Olin Wright is Vilas Distinguished Research Professor at the University of Wisconsin. His academic work has been centrally concerned with reconstructing the Marxist tradition in ways that attempt to make it more relevant to contemporary concerns and more cogent as a scientific framework of analysis. From 2011 to 2012, he served as president of the American Sociological Association. His most recent books include *Envisioning Real Utopias* (2010); *American Society: How It Really Works* (with Joel Rogers, 2011 and 2015); *Understanding Class* (2015); and *Alternatives to Capitalism* (with Robin Hahnel, 2016).

Contributors

Arash Abizadeh is associate professor of political theory at McGill University. His research focuses on democratic theory; questions of identity, nationalism, and cosmopolitanism; immigration and border control; and seventeenth- and eighteenth-century philosophy, particularly Hobbes and Rousseau. His forthcoming book is titled *Hobbes and the Two Faces of Ethics*.

Tom Arnold was chair of the Irish Constitutional Convention (2012–14), and he serves as chair of the All Ireland Civic Dialogue on Brexit. He has served as director general of the Institute of International and European Affairs, director of the Scaling Up Nutrition Movement, chief executive of Concern Worldwide, and assistant secretary general of the Irish Department of Agriculture and Food. He is a member of the Royal Irish Academy.

Terrill Bouricius is a democracy reformer and retired politician. From 1981 to 1991, he served on the city council of Burlington, Vermont (along with mayor Bernie Sanders). He then served a decade as a member of the Vermont House of Representatives. After leaving elective office, he worked on ranked-choice voting, but since 2004, he has focused on sortition reform internationally. Some of his publications on sortition include "Democracy Through Multi-Body Sortition: Athenian Lessons for the Modern Day" (*Journal of Public Deliberation*, 2013) and a chapter on sortition in *Methods for Sustainability Research* (2017).

Deven Burks is a PhD candidate in political philosophy at the University of Luxembourg and the Université Catholique de Louvain. His research interests lie in theories of public discourse and political epistemology but also take up democratic theory and varieties of deliberative democracy. His doctoral thesis bears on rival conceptions of justification, discourse, and institutions in the works of John Rawls and Jeffrey Stout.

Lyn Carson is the research director for the newDemocracy Foundation and one of its founding directors. She is a former professor in politics at the University of Sydney and a former elected representative in local government. She has published widely on deliberative democracy over the past twenty-five years and been involved with most of Australia's early experiments with public deliberation. Her primary interest is in sortition that is coupled with deliberation. Relevant books include *Random Selection in Politics* (with Brian Martin, 1999) and *The Australian Citizens' Parliament and the Future of Deliberative Democracy* (2013), for which she was lead editor.

Dimitri Courant is a PhD candidate in political science at the University of Lausanne and the University Paris-VIII. His research focuses on sortition, democracy, deliberation, and representation. His sociological analysis of political uses of random selection in the twentieth and twenty-first century covers various areas and countries: pro-sortition activism; evolution of lottery equipment both material and digital; and qualitative comparative studies of empirical cases of randomly selected deliberative assemblies in France, Ireland, and Switzerland. He recently published in the reviews *Daimon: Revista Internacional de Filosofía* (2017), *Participations* (2019), and in the collective book *Sortition and Democracy* (2019).

David Farrell, MRIA, is professor of politics and chair of the School of Politics and International Relations at University College Dublin. A specialist in the study of parties, electoral systems, and elections, he is currently researching deliberative minipublics in Ireland. He was the research director of the Irish Constitutional Convention (2012–14) and the research leader of the Irish Citizens' Assembly (2016–18). His most recent books include *The Post-Crisis Irish Voter: Voting Behaviour in the Irish 2016 General Election* (coedited; Manchester University Press, 2018) and *A Conservative Revolution: Electoral Change in Twenty-First Century Ireland* (coedited; Oxford University Press, 2017).

Andrea Felicetti is a postdoctoral researcher at the Centre for Political Research, KU Leuven. He previously held research positions at the Scuola Normale Superiore (Center on Social Movement Studies), European University Institute, University of Lille 3, University of Louvain (Hoover Chair of Economic and Social Ethics), and University of Canberra (Center for

Deliberative Democracy and Global Governance). He obtained his PhD in 2014 at the School of Politics and International Relations, Australian National University. His research interests include democracy, public sphere, and social movements. He is the author of *Deliberative Democracy and Social Movements* (2016), and his work has been published in several international journals.

Donatella della Porta is professor of political science dean of the Institute for Humanities and the Social Sciences, and director of the doctoral program in political science and sociology at the Scuola Normale Superiore in Florence, where she also leads the Center on Social Movement Studies. Her research addresses many topics, including social movements, political violence, terrorism, corruption, the police, and protest policing. She has directed the ERC project Mobilizing for Democracy. She received the Mattei Dogan Prize. She holds multiple honorary doctorates. Her most recent books include *Movement Parties in Times of Austerity* (2017), *Where Did the Revolution Go?* (2016), and *Social Movements in Times of Austerity* (2015).

James Fishkin holds the Janet M. Peck Chair in International Communication at Stanford University, where he is professor of communication, professor of political science (by courtesy), and director of the Center for Deliberative Democracy. He is the author of *Democracy When the People Are Thinking* (2018), *When the People Speak* (2009), *Deliberation Day* (2004, with Bruce Ackerman), and *Democracy and Deliberation* (1991). He is a Fellow of the American Academy of Arts and Sciences, a Guggenheim Fellow, a Fellow of the Center for Advanced Study in the Behavioral Sciences at Stanford, and a Visiting Fellow Commoner at Trinity College, Cambridge.

Brett Hennig is a director and cofounder of the Sortition Foundation, whose aim is to promote and institute the use of stratified, random selection in government. He is the author of *The End of Politicians: Time for a Real Democracy* (2017), which draws on a wealth of recent evidence to demonstrate that groups of randomly selected, everyday people can and do make balanced, informed, and trusted decisions. The book argues that citizens' assemblies are legitimate, accountable, competent, and above all, convincing demonstrations that we can govern ourselves.

Vincent Jacquet is a Fonds de la Recherche Scientifique post-doctoral researcher at Université Catholique de Louvain, Belgium. His main research interests include deliberative democracy, democratic innovations, sortition, and political participation. His doctoral thesis investigated randomly selected citizens' refusal to take part in deliberative minipublics, and key findings have been published in the *European Journal of Political Research* (2017).

Raphaël Kies is researcher in political science at the University of Luxembourg. He is coresponsible for national and European electoral studies and for the introduction and evaluation of innovative methods of political participation at the national and European level. His publications include articles as well as books on e-democracy, local democracy, and deliberative democracy. Two recent publications are *Promises and Limits of Web-Deliberation* (2010) and, with Patrizia Nanz (ed.), *Is Europe Listening to Us? Successes and Failures of EU Citizen Consultation* (2013).

Tom Malleson is assistant professor of social justice and peace studies at King's University College at Western University. His research focuses on radical democracy, theories of justice, egalitarianism, and feminist theory. Recent book publications include *Fired Up About Capitalism* (2016) and *After Occupy: Economic Democracy for the 21st Century* (2014). His latest project is *A Care Manifesto: Part-Time for All* (with Jennifer Nedelsky, forthcoming in 2019). He is also a longtime antiauthoritarian activist and organizer.

Jane Mansbridge is Charles F. Adams Professor of Political Leadership and Democratic Values at the Harvard Kennedy School. From 2012 to 2013, she served as president of the American Political Science Association. She is currently writing on representation, deliberation, everyday activism, and the need for legitimate coercion. Her authored and coedited books include *Beyond Adversary Democracy* (1980), *Why We Lost the*

ERA (1986), *Beyond Self-Interest* (1990), *Feminism* (with Susan Okin, 1994), *Oppositional Consciousness* (with Aldon Morris, 2001), and *Deliberative Systems* (with John Parkinson, 2012). A recent coedited book, *Political Negotiation* (with Cathie Jo Martin, 2015), introduces the study of legislative negotiation.

Christoph Niessen is a FRESH Research Fellow at the Fonds de la Recherche Scientifique and PhD student in political and social sciences at Université de Namur and Université Catholique de Louvain, Belgium. He has worked on deliberative minipublics and their relation with politicians and stakeholders. His current research deals with minority self-governance and autonomy dynamics in multinational western European states.

David Owen is professor of social and political philosophy in the department of Politics and International Relations at the University of Southampton. His research has ranged widely across issues in post-Kantian philosophy, citizenship and migration studies, and democratic theory. His authored or edited books include *Multiculturalism and Political Theory* (2007, coedited with Tony Laden), *Recognition and Power* (2007, coedited with Bert van den Brink), *Nietzsche's Genealogy of Morality* (2007), *Prospects of Citizenship* (coauthored with Gerry Stoker et al., 2011), and *Michel Foucault* (2014).

John Pitseys is a researcher at the Centre de Recherche et d'Information Socio-Politiques and lecturer in politics and political philosophy at the Université Catholique de Louvain, Belgium. His research interests include democratic theory, deliberation, transparency, and governance. He has published articles in *Global Environmental Politics*, *Revue Française de Science Politique* and *Droit et Société*. He recently authored *Démocratie et Citoyenneté* (CRISP, 2017).

Min Reuchamps is professor of political science at the Université Catholique de Louvain, Belgium. His teaching and research interests are federalism and multilevel governance, democracy and its different dimensions, relations between language and politics, in particular the role of metaphors, and participatory and deliberative methods. He recently edited *Minority Nations in Multinational Federations: A Comparative Study of Quebec and Wallonia*

(2015), coedited *Constitutional Deliberative Democracy in Europe* (with Jane Suiter, 2016), and coauthored *The Legitimacy of Citizen-Led Deliberative Democracy: The G1000 in Belgium* (with Didier Caluwaerts, 2018).

Yves Sintomer is honorary senior fellow at the Institut Universitaire de France and professor of political science at Paris 8 University. In addition, he is associate professor at Basque Country (Spain), Neuchâtel, and Lausanne (Switzerland) Universities. His most recent books include *Participatory Budgeting in Europe: Democracy and Public Governance* (with C. Herzberg and A. Röcke, 2016); *From Radical to Deliberative Democracy? Random Selection in Politics from Athens to the Present* (2019, forthcoming); and *Sortition and Democracy: Practices, Tools, Theories* (2019, forthcoming). His writings have been published in eighteen languages.

Graham Smith is professor of politics and director of the Centre for the Study of Democracy, University of Westminster, UK. His academic work focuses primarily on democratic theory and practice, and he has a particular interest in the role and function of participatory democratic institutions. He is author of *Democratic Innovations: Designing Institutions for Citizen Participation* (2009). He was one of the organizers of the Citizens' Assembly on Brexit, is an international collaborator with the Participedia project, and is chair of the Foundation for Democracy and Sustainable Development.

Jane Suiter is associate professor at Dublin City University, Ireland. Her research interests center on communication, deliberation, and participation. In particular, her expertise lies mainly in the areas of social media, referendums, and other modes of engaging the public in decision-making processes, such as citizens' assemblies. She is coprincipal investigator on the Irish Citizens' Assembly, having also worked on other real-world deliberative events such as the Constitutional Convention and We the Citizens. She is the author with Min Reuchamps of *Constitutional Deliberative Democracy in Europe* (2016).

Pierre-Étienne Vandamme is a postdoctoral researcher in political philosophy at the University of Louvain, Belgium. His research interests include democratic theory, theories of justice, and civic education. He is the author, with Antoine Verret-Hamelin, of "A Randomly Selected Chamber: Promises and Challenges" (*Journal of Public Deliberation*, 2017). Other publications have appeared in *Critical Review of International Social and Political Philosophy*; *Constellations*; and *Law, Ethics and Philosophy*.

Acknowledgments

For assistance with the preparation of this book and the September 2017 conference, we thank University of Wisconsin–Madison graduate student researcher Jake Carlson and Penn State undergraduate Ethan Paul. The conference attendees helped refine all of these essays: in addition to the authors in this volume, appreciation goes to Archon Fung from Harvard University's Kennedy School of Government, Ned Crosby from the Jefferson Center for New Democratic Processes, sortition advocate Campbell Wallace, and David Schecter, who serves as associate director of research and development for the newDemocracy Foundation. We also appreciated the insights offered by two doctoral students from the University of Wisconsin–Madison's sociology program, Kristinn Arsaelsson and Sara Gia Trongone. We are also grateful to the *Politics & Society* journal, which helped make the conference possible and published selections from this book in a special issue.

An earlier version of our sortition proposal benefited from comments by Sam Bowles, Lyn Carson, Hélène Landemore, Tom Malleson, and Pierre-Étienne Vandamme. Helpful comments also came from conferences Erik Olin Wright attended in 2016—the regular meeting of the Analytical Marxism Group and a special "Utopia for Our Times" event in Louvain, Belgium, celebrating the five hundredth anniversary of the publication of Thomas More's *Utopia*.

As ever, we thank family and friends who have offered support and feedback along the way. Our book has benefited from their kind—and frank—feedback every step of the journey.

John Gastil, State College, Pennsylvania
Erik Olin Wright, Madison, Wisconsin